RACIAL SITUATIONS

RACIAL SITUATIONS

CLASS PREDICAMENTS OF WHITENESS IN DETROIT

John Hartigan Jr.

PRINCETON UNIVERSITY PRESS   PRINCETON, NEW JERSEY

Library of Congress Cataloging-in-Publication Data

Hartigan, John, 1964–
Racial situations : class predicaments of whiteness
in Detroit / John Hartigan, Jr.
p.   cm.
Includes bibliographical references and index.
ISBN 0-691-02886-9 (cloth : alk. paper)
ISBN 0-691-02885-0 (pbk. : alk. paper)
1. Whites—Michigan—Detroit—Ethnic identity.
2. Detroit (Mich.)—Race relations.   I. Title.
F574.D49A1   1999
977.4'34004034—dc21   99-17477

This book has been composed in Sabon

http://pup.princeton.edu

Printed in the United States of America

10 9 8 7 6 5 4 3 2 1

10 9 8 7 6 5 4 3 2 1
(Pbk.)

Contents

Illustrations

Acknowledgments

THIS WORK was made possible by a great deal of generous support. I was able to undertake my fieldwork thanks to a fellowship from the Social Science Research Council; this research was drafted and revised while I was a predoctoral fellow at the National Museum of American History, Smithsonian Institution; a grant from the Harry Frank Guggenheim Foundation provided me with further support while I saw this project through to completion. I am very grateful to these fine institutions. This book would hardly be legible without the extremely kind efforts of many colleagues who trudged through the early drafts, offering a range of advice, insight, and encouragement: I am indebted to Lorraine Kenny, Anjie Rosga, Marvette Perez, Pete Daniel, Joe Dumit, Katherine Ott, Bruce Grant, David Issacson, Sylvia Sensiper, Laura Helper, Steven Gregory, Anthony Kaye, Carolyn Martin Shaw, Roger Rouse, Helen Rozwadowski, and Karen-Sue Taussig. Matt Wray and Kathleen Stewart, in particular, contributed great critical insights at moments when I was stymied and frustrated. In general, this work has benefited from the insights of the other scholars who have worked in Detroit. I want to especially thank Thomas Sugrue and members of the Southeastern Michigan Study Group, particularly Andrea Sankar, Deb Jackson, and again, Roger Rouse. My greatest debt in this regard, though, is to Charlie Bright, for his expert understanding of the political and historical dynamics that are centered in Detroit and for teaching me the fundamentals of scholarship when I was an undergraduate at the University of Michigan. I have also had the fortune and benefit of long, enduring relations with two of my mentors, Kathleen Stewart and Susan Harding. Katie and Susan taught me all that I know about ethnography, and they have painstakingly tried to teach me the craft of writing. I am not sure for which lessons I am more indebted, but I would not have attempted this undertaking if I had not had their wisdom and examples to draw upon: many, many thanks! I owe a great deal of thanks to Donna Haraway and Jim Clifford, who both taught me much of what I needed to know about making sense of this material. Their mentoring has been engaging, astute, humorous, and always incredibly generous. And, of course, there is Hayden "O.H." (Original Hillbilly) White, who, like a good "native," is lurking in the background of this project. I have also learned much from a host of fellow students. This project gelled through engaging discussions with Ron Eglash, Vicente Diaz, Marita Sturken, Ruth Frankenberg, Elena Creef,

Marcella Greening, Matt Meyers, and (again) Joe, Anjie, and Lorraine. And I especially want to thank Sheila Puese and Billie Harris for keeping me on-line and plugged in through all the numerous bureaucratic frenzies. I am also grateful to my colleagues in the department of sociology and anthropology at Knox College for all of their encouragement and support as I rethought and reworked this material. Additionally, I want to thank all the librarians who contributed generous efforts to this project, especially Jim Roan and Stephanie Thomas (at the National Museum of American History), Polly Lasker (Smithsonian Institution Central Reference and Loan), Sharon Clayton and Laurie Sauer (Knox College), and the Interlibrary Loan people at UCSC, who never cut me off. I am very grateful to Mary Murrell for her insights and patience during the arduous process of bringing this book to print; as well, I am grateful for Margaret Case's skillful work with this very unruly manuscript.

Detroit is my hometown, but I had not lived there for more than a decade when I returned to undertake this project. Much had changed, and the neighborhoods I chose to study were fairly unfamiliar to me. I am indebted to the people in these neighborhoods who invited me into their homes and made time for my clumsy and intrusive questions. The heart of this project is their stories. For their tolerance and reflections, I am very grateful; I hope I have fairly conveyed their versions of the world. I want to thank my parents for their enduring support, encouragement, and all their lessons, big and small, that helped me get it together. In the end, my biggest thanks go to Rebecca Lyle, who endured and shared the hardships and pleasures that this project entailed. Her expert statistical advice was also a huge help. Once again, thank you all!

Names and Transcriptions

I HAVE MAINTAINED the anonymity of participants in this project by changing peoples' names in this book, with two exceptions. First, there are several people in these pages who played roles in historical developments in Detroit. I have used their real names. And in Warrendale, people who were frequently quoted in local newspapers or on TV are represented here by their real names.

To assure the greatest degree of readability in the transcriptions of peoples' comments, I have relied upon minimal linguistic conventions for representing speech and conversation. In order to convey the pauses in statements and stories, I relied upon elipses (three dots) to represent a pause. Four dots are used to indicate any deleted portions of a statement.

Abbreviations

ALUA	Archives of Labor and Union Affairs, Wayne State University, Detroit
CCDC	Corktown Citizens District Council
CDBG	Community Development Block Grant
CDC	Citizens District Council
CHS	Corktown Historical Society
CPW	Concerned People of Warrendale
DFP	*Detroit Free Press*
DMIC	Detroit Mayor's Interracial Committee
DN	*Detroit News*
DPS	Detroit Public Schools
DSR	Detroit Street Railway
ICP	Inner City Parents
MHTNPHC	Most Holy Trinity Non-Profit Housing Cooperative
MSHDA	Michigan State Housing Development Authority
NA	National Archives, Washington, DC
POA	Property Owners' Association (Briggs)
UCS	United Community Services of Metropolitan Detroit
WCO	Warrendale Community Organization
WP&G	*Warrendale Press and Guide*

RACIAL SITUATIONS

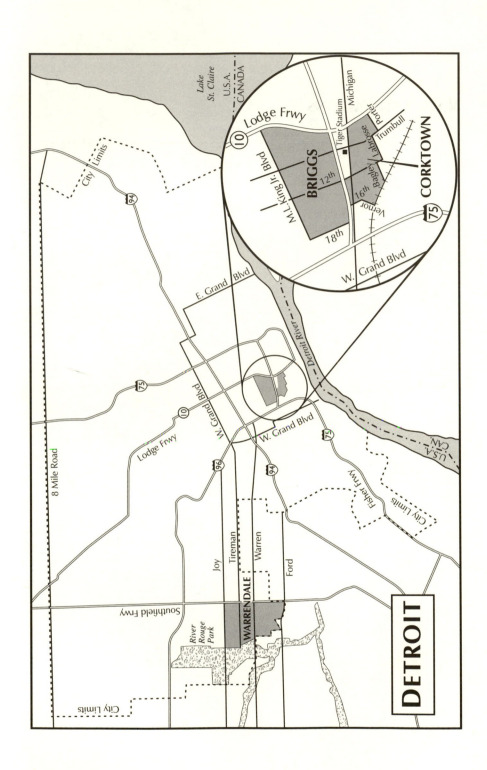

Introduction

White people find it extremely hard to live in an
environment that they don't control.
  —*Mayor Coleman A. Young*

PUBLIC DEBATE and scholarly discussions on the subject of race in the
United States are burdened by allegorical tendencies. Abstract racial figures dominate our thinking, each condensing the specificities of peoples'
lives into strictly delimited categories—"whites" and "blacks," to name
the most obvious. The media convey "racial" incidents as clashes between monolithic groups over irreconcilable views and irreducible interests. The series of spectacles that include the Clarence Thomas hearings
and the trials of O. J. Simpson seem to have taught us that "whites" see
things one way and "blacks" see them another way. Given the national
stage on which these dramas unfold, certain broad readings of racial
groups across this country are warranted.[1] But as such spectacles come to
represent the meaning of race relations, they obscure the many complex
encounters, exchanges, and avoidances that constitute the persistent significance of race in this country.

It is easy to criticize stereotyped thinking on the part of journalists, but
academic discourse on race demonstrates a similar tendency, depicting
whiteness and blackness as static, bounded cultural orders, one dominant
and the other subordinate. Social researchers grappling with the enduring
effects of racism rely upon the figures of "whites" and "blacks" to convey
the discrepant life chances and contrasting advantages and disadvantages
that distinguish racial populations in this country.[2] At the same time, we
argue—unconvincingly it seems—that races are mere social constructs,
that they do not really exist, and that racial stereotyping must stop. How
are we to effect a change in Americans' tendency to view social life
through a lens of "black and white" when we rely upon and reproduce
the same categories in our analyses and critiques of the way race matters
in this country?

The cultural figures of "whites" and "blacks" will not easily be de-
posed, but we can loosen their powerful hold by challenging the economy
of meaning they maintain.[3] That is, by grasping the instances and situations in which the significance of race spills out of the routinized confines
of these absolute figures, we can begin to rethink the institutionalization
of racial difference and similiarity in this country. James Clifford makes

a comparable observation about the "controlled fictions of difference and similitude that we call ethnographic accounts."[4] He asserts that the allegorical tendency in ethnography cannot be eradicated; yet the penchant for depicting cultures as seamless, homogeneous entities can be undermined through an attention to the specificity and the particular circumstances by which their representations are generated. I offer a similar suggestion about "racial attitudes," that odd product of social surveys and research. Instead of relying upon composite views of "race" in a national perspective, we need to dwell more attentively on the disparate and unstable interpretations of racial matters that people develop in the course of their daily lives. In order to think differently about race we need to pay attention to the local settings in which racial identities are actually articulated, reproduced, and contested, resisting the urge to draw abstract conclusions about whiteness and blackness. Rather, we need to take these situations as examples of a different sort—as insights into the daily processes by which people make sense of racial matters in particular locales. The assertion that race is culturally constructed will remain a stunted concept unless it is linked to a heightened attention to the ways people actually construct meaningful lives in relation to race. This book attempts such a shift in perspective by providing a glimpse into the daily lives of whites in Detroit, perhaps this country's "blackest" city.

For whites, everyday life in Detroit does not constitute a space removed from the allegorizing tendencies that characterize media coverage of race.[5] But it does form a ground where the distances and discrepancies between their experiences and those of whites generally are made manifest. I recognized this most sharply in relation to the death of Malice Green. Malice, another in the long line of black men to die in police custody, was beaten by a pair of white Detroit police officers; he died from massive head wounds during his arrest. The officers were quickly tried on murder charges. On August 23, 1993, when the guilty verdicts were announced, I tried to gauge the reaction of whites in Briggs, the inner-city neighborhood where I based my fieldwork. I started in O'Leary's, one of the few remaining corner bars, where I often found "hillbillies" spending quiet afternoons. George worked behind the bar; Floyd and Orin were resting on their elbows, sipping beers, eyeing alternately the TV and the open door. Outside, a hot breeze stirred the tall, dry grass in the empty fields across the street, once packed with houses that have long since burned. As usual on a summer day, crickets were the loudest sound.

I had become a "regular" at O'Leary's over the course of the year I spent living in Briggs, so it was an easy matter to spark the conversation. But the subject of Malice Green had lost its initial interest for these men, as it had for most of the residents, white and black, in this neighborhood. Polls across the metropolitan area showed a clear racial divide in perceptions of whether or not the officers were guilty. But opinions in Briggs, some twenty blocks from where Malice was killed, were not racially differentiated. The cops, Larry Nevers and Walter Budzyn, had patrolled these neighborhood streets, and many men—again, white and black—knew them, for a variety of reasons. The question of their guilt was hardly raised—it was assumed. Several men had seen the officers beat other kids on other blocks on other nights; no one seemed to doubt that the key difference was that a black man had died this time.

Although the "hillbillies" I had spoken with about the case over the previous eight months recognized the racial aspects of the trial and the charges, they felt that the killing itself was not racially motivated.[6] The opinion most often expressed on the topic was that the two white cops did not care about the color of the "punk" they were beating: they were playing rough cops and ended up killing somebody. George recalled seeing Nevers in action before; he told how Nevers "beat the shit out of a kid right out here on Ash, in front of the bar." Floyd remembered the time he watched Nevers use his gun to shatter the nerve of a young man he had smashed against a car: "The whole neighborhood was out there watching, and he didn't care. He just put it up against his head, cocked it and said he was going to shoot him right then and there." Floyd and George slipped into personal reflections, recounting the beatings they received from cops when they were young men on these streets, and it became apparent why they felt that race had not been a factor in the officers' violence. Floyd related, "Like with us, when we got busted for anything, they'd tell you, 'Do you want to go to jail, or do you want me to settle the matter right now?' Well, if they didn't take you in, they'd beat the shit out of you right then and there. . . . That was how they did it." George both laughed and grimaced at Floyd's account, then moved the conversation on to other stories of the "bad old days."

Floyd, George, and other whites in Briggs regarded the fact that the murder trial had been racialized with detachment. Although the local and national media focused on the whiteness of the police officers, whites in Briggs felt little sense of threat from the outcome of the verdict. They also did not fall prey to the anxiety, widely promoted in media coverage, that a race riot might ensue if the officers were found not guilty. Even though they felt certain that the verdict would be guilty, they did not fear being racially victimized, as whites, in an uprising on these streets.

I asked George if it was going to be a quiet night, and he asked, "Why wouldn't it be quiet?" On the TV news, reports came from the site of Green's death (transformed into a shrine) where large numbers of angry blacks from Detroit and around the country were rallying and awaiting the trial's outcome. Skittish whites were shown leaving early from their jobs downtown, concerned over the possible aftermath of the verdicts.

Figure 1. Shrine at site where Malice Green died

Esther, a white woman, came in, settled down at the corner of the bar, and told how offices downtown were being closed in anticipation of the verdicts. George scoffed and said, "It's not going to be like that." He pointed out how there had been a black man in here, a delivery driver for Budweiser, watching the news with them when the verdicts were announced. All were in accord that the guilty verdicts were just. George said, "There ain't gonna be no trouble no way. Maybe over there on 23rd, but that's out-of-town people anyway. They've had a whole mess of people up from Alabama and Mississippi. They'd be the only ones causing trouble. There ain't gonna be no trouble here." A fracas did occur at the site where Green died, between blacks and "radical" whites from out of state, but George's prediction held true. The calm that followed the verdicts continued the general peace that had held sway before the trial, and remained unremarkable.

This sense of detachment from the racial anxieties consuming many whites points to gaps within whiteness, that web of assumptions of normativity maintaining the social privileges and powers linked to white skin. The situation of these white "hillbillies," proximate to both the scene of the crime and the courthouse where whiteness was figuratively on trial, disrupted the complex process of racial identification that animated white audiences. But their position entailed more than residency in Detroit; it involved their personal histories in this "inner-city" neighborhood over the previous forty years. In Detroit, white racialness is constituted, evaluated, and revised in numerous disparate settings. Its structure and content are shaped by the centuries-long history of race in the United States, but its contours and quirks, which spring from the local versions and effects of that history, delineate a certain distance or remove from the shape of whiteness nationally. In the interstices of these various instances of whiteness, there are a number of lessons to be learned for those who want to understand the workings of race in the United States.

In response to the verdicts, "whites" and "blacks" were shown once again to see things in distinctly opposite ways. Opinion surveys in the following days, and again a few months later when final sentences were passed, loudly proclaimed: "Detroiters poles apart on verdict."[7] In the poll reported in the *News*, 85 percent of blacks saw the verdicts as fair; only 45 percent of whites concurred, and 35 percent of whites felt that lesser charges should have been brought.[8] Among whites, 23 percent also responded that they felt less safe or secure following the verdicts; only 8 percent of blacks expressed the same sentiment. As with reactions to the verdicts in the trials of the Los Angeles police officers charged with beating Rodney King, such polls stressed homogeneous social orders, depicting "whites and blacks" as opposing entities whose boundaries are well defined, with uniform contents.[9] An array of commentators grappled with the significance of race in these stories and found its meanings to be clear and redundant; exceptions passed as superfluous, though perhaps obligatory, aspects of accurate coverage. They rarely considered whites or blacks who disrupted received racial characterizations. Citizens whose training in reading the significance of race comes mainly through such media accounts learn to see race as a series of abstractions, whereby social forms are ready-made to contain whatever meanings arise. The whites featured in this book, however, have learned about race from an array of sources; their grapplings with the unruly meanings of racial difference and identity constitute a complex account of how race still matters.

This book offers a view into three predominantly white neighborhoods in Detroit. Two are located within a mile of the city's downtown, and the third forms a portion of Detroit's western boundary, abutting the affluent suburb of Dearborn. These different field sites allow me to examine a range of issues concerning the interplay of class and race. Briggs and Corktown are positioned within the "inner city"; Corktown is debatably gentrifying and Briggs constitutes an extreme poverty zone. Warrendale, like many of Detroit's outlying neighborhoods, is home to city workers and retirees from the area's auto plants, middle-class or working-class whites who for financial or sentimental reasons resisted the pull of "white flight" to the suburbs. The fundamental issue that I grappled with in the twenty months (July 1992 through February 1994) that I spent interviewing whites in Detroit was how their class background has influenced their experience and understanding of racial identity and difference. What I found is that class—a composite of occupation, residential location, and family history—profoundly shapes how whites identify racially. The way whites perceive the interests and intentions of people of color, as well, depends upon their class position.

Although I pursued this study as a comparative project, the first half of this book relates the history and daily life of whites in Briggs, a neighborhood in which more than 50 percent of the residents live below the poverty line.[10] The experiences of Briggs residents take center stage for a variety of reasons, largely connected with the role poor whites play in both social-scientific and popular understandings of race. A comfortable conviction holds sway among middle-class whites that racism is concentrated in the lower classes—that it is certainly present in working-class whites, but bubbles up most vigorously from the hearts of poor whites, as allegorized in the cultural figure of "white trash."[11] This book undertakes a thorough reexamination of this assumption. I have set out not merely to debunk stereotypes of poor whites, but to develop a comparative framework whereby the racial thinking characterizing one class can be considered in relation to sentiments in other class formations. Too often researchers pursue "class analysis" by confining their attention to one class, overlooking the relational basis of class identity and the cultural continuum along which class distinctions operate.[12] Although poor whites ground this book, I frame their racial engagements in sustained contrast with whites in the working and middle classes of Corktown and Warrendale in order to understand how whites in different classes engage with race.

Another reason for highlighting the condition of poor whites in Briggs is that they disrupt scholarly and lay assumptions about the content and character of "inner cities" and the "underclass" in the United States. Just as cultural critics and social activists tirelessly remind white Americans that the "typical" welfare recipient is not black but white, that the "face" of poverty in this country most certainly is white, so too I feel obliged to stress an overlooked point: the crumbling cores of urban areas in this country are not uniformly occupied by African Americans.[13] These zones have been colored black for two primary reasons: objectively, they are disproportionately inhabited by African Americans and, subjectively, this image resonates with the long-standing racial fears that animate many white Americans. Challenging this representation by dwelling on the lives of poor whites in Detroit's inner city raises the issue of scale in assessments of racial conditions.[14] A central concern of this book is to rethink what counts as "racial" by examining experiences and situations that run counter to depictions of racial conditions viewed on a national scale. The problems raised by dwelling on such "exceptions to the rule" are most obvious in the case of political and academic debates about the urban underclass. But the insight gained by this approach is also readily apparent.

William Julius Wilson established the urban underclass as a subject of academic study and political debate by detailing the emergence of extreme poverty areas (zones where the poverty rate stands at 40 percent or more) in the nation's largest cities. These neighborhoods, he argues, are prey to "concentration effects"; because of the intense poverty and "social isolation" of these zones "from mainstream patterns of behavior," residents are subjected to debilitating social conditions. Although he regards social isolation as "a product of the class transformation of the inner city," Wilson also stresses the racial texture of this phenomenon: "poor whites rarely live in such neighborhoods. . . . [W]hereas only 7 percent of all poor whites live in the extreme poverty areas, 32 percent of all poor Hispanics and 39 percent of all poor blacks live in such areas."[15] These statistics paint a bleak but convincing image of the racial aspects of inner-city life.

But what happens when we shift the scale of attention and ask about the 7 percent of whites who live in such neighborhoods? Are they simply an exception to the rule, or do they provoke a rethinking of how "race" matters? In Detroit, a city that for Wilson and others epitomizes the emergence of an underclass, poor whites are plentiful; the Briggs neighborhood contains only one of several concentrations on the city's southwest side.[16] In 1990, more than 52,000 white Detroiters lived in census tracts where the poverty rate exceeded 40 percent. Whites occupy "distressed" neighborhoods (tracts with high levels of poverty and joblessness, female-headed households, teenage school drop-outs, and people drawing public-assistance income) and "severely distressed" areas (which includes the above indicators plus "exceptionally high" rates of school drop-outs) in greater numbers than occur in New York City, Los Angeles, Chicago, or any of the other ten largest cities in the United States.[17] What makes Detroit unique among these major cities is that it so clearly provides evidence that the underclass is not uniformly black or Hispanic.

Detroit

At first glance, Detroit seems to present all the proof one needs to conclude that the racial order in this country is drastically bifurcated between dominant whites and subordinated blacks. The population of Detroit is approaching 80 percent black, whereas its surrounding suburbs are almost all more than 90 percent white.[18] In Detroit, as in other metropolitan areas, the spatial divide between white and black is accentuated by a division between those who are advantaged and disadvantaged in terms of access to health care, education, home mortgages, or protection from violent crime and other dangers of urban life.[19]

The role that race played in carving out this landscape is undeniable. In cities like Detroit, whites shifted en masse to the promising, sprawling green fields of the suburbs.[20] Between 1950 and 1990, Detroit lost 1.4 million white residents. The common term for this phenomenon, "white flight," is not a misnomer; it accurately conveys the racial character of this demographic movement. But it also entails a "remainder effect," easily neglected or overlooked in generalizations about what happened in Detroit and other major cities that suffered drastic population losses in this period. Marilyn Strathern uses remainder effects—a concept linked to the chaotic nature of information and the "not quite" replication of fractals—to focus on the gaps between social levels, which complicate generalizations about cultural phenomena. Racial absolutes that nationally seem to define this dynamic dissolve when you attend to the fine-grained processes evident in the thinking of whites in particular neighborhoods who are deciding whether to stay or move.

Whites left behind by "white flight" form another exception to the rule, since their circumstances contrast sharply with that of the vast majority of the white population. Only 22 percent of Detroiters are white, the smallest percentage of whites in the 150 most populous cities in the United States. But their situation as a local minority—a condition that whites will increasingly experience in the next century—is revealing in terms of how race can and will matter in this country. What does "race" mean to these people; when and how do they decide a situation is "racial"? These questions are best answered by viewing Detroit through multiple versions of the city, rather than as a single entity. Urban anthropology increasingly involves a detailed mapping of the disjunctive, discursive, and spatial orders a city maintains, in addition to depicting the social conditions that shape its general character. As Alejandro Portes and Alex Stepick stress in their study of Miami—another city composed, like Detroit, of numerous "reversals vis-à-vis traditional American urban life"—we have to hold in view racial and class "discourses that do not clash directly, but rather slide past each other as if moving on different planes."[21]

Although only 22 percent of Detroiters are white, it still boasts the largest concentration of whites of any city in Michigan. Even though Detroit looks and sounds "black" sociologically and culturally, it is home to hundreds of thousands of whites, variously identifying or at odds with this unwieldy civic entity. What does "race" mean to these people; when and how do they decide a situation is "racial"? These questions are the subject of this book.

Three Neighborhoods

The three neighborhoods where I worked variously reflect the effects and
extent of Detroit's crisis—from its depopulation to the steady deterioration of its economic base. Briggs and Corktown, taken together, constitute the oldest residential area in Detroit, with houses dating back to the
late 1800s. They originally formed one neighborhood, following the parish boundaries of Most Holy Trinity Church. The area was settled and
populated by varying waves of immigrants, first the Irish in the 1840s,
later the Maltese and Mexicans in the early 1900s. In the 1940s, southern
whites from Appalachia poured into Detroit, frequently settling in the
area now known as Briggs. Landlords turned once stately single-family
mansions into rooming houses that were quickly overcrowded by "hillbillies." The housing stock was already old by the time the southerners
arrived; it deteriorated rapidly as too many people were crammed into
too little space. Today, the remaining mansions-turned-boarding-houses
are largely empty, their occupants mostly dispersed as a result of the drastic welfare cuts initiated by Governor John Engler in 1990. Off the major
thoroughfares, a plain of grasslands encompasses the remaining scattered
houses. More than 24,000 people once lived in this area; now only 2,900
remain. Over half of Briggs residents are white, some 30 percent are
black, and 10 percent are Hispanic.[22]

A freeway project sundered this area in the late 1960s. Since that time
the portion now known as Corktown (so named for the original Irish
immigrants) has slowly attracted a small contingent of whites from outside the city. Their professional credentials distinguish them from the
whites and blacks in Briggs, who largely survive on underpaid work in
unstable jobs. The Irish influence remains in this neighborhood, represented by several bars and a restaurant. The Maltese and Mexican immigrants, however, maintain an enduring presence. Indeed, Corktown bor-
ders the area called "Mexican Town," a concentration of restaurants that
forms an economic base for the large Latino population on the city's
southwest side. The Victorian-era housing stock has fared much better
here than in Briggs, and is the subject of a vigorous wave of renovation
and restoration projects, which typically signal the process of gentrification. The boundaries of Corktown are a matter of some interest in this
part of Detroit, which includes remnants of light industry, new commercial developments, and a sizable, predominantly black, low-income residential complex. Corktown "proper," a zone delineated with the kind
of exacting attention to demographics and property values that charac-
terizes the efforts of politically astute neighborhoods across the country,
is 64 percent white, 21 percent Hispanic, 8 percent Maltese, and only

Figure 2. Walking to the liquor store in Briggs

4 percent African American—an interesting accomplishment in the inner city of Detroit.[23]

Warrendale began as a housing development in the 1920s, just one among many of the city's outlying areas converted from farmland into closely nestled single-family dwellings. The Depression brought a temporary halt to construction, but the postwar boom provided the momentum that carried white auto workers from cramped apartment dwellings near the downtown to these houses with driveways and lawns, and, in the process, from the working class to the middle class. However, signs of change in the economic character of Warrendale are obvious: rates of home ownership are dropping significantly, and the increased presence of rental homes unnerves many of the older residents; housing prices fell between 1980 and 1990 by 22 to 33 percent across the five census tracts that comprise the neighborhood; poverty rates have doubled in some of these tracts and tripled in others.[24] Warrendale is 80 percent white. Although some of the signs of pending downward mobility can be associated with the recent influx of blacks into the neighborhood's northwest corner, they also seem to involve an interesting "return" of whites to the city. Residents I spoke with pointed to whites who were unable to afford starter homes in the neighborhoods where they were born and raised moving in from the suburbs.

Initially, I planned to compare only Corktown and Briggs, since they so neatly framed contrasting directions of inner-city neighborhoods. I decided to include Warrendale because of a conflict that broke out there in the summer of 1992. The Detroit Board of Education unexpectedly re-opened a previously closed community school in Warrendale, calling it the Malcolm X Academy and instituting an Afrocentric curriculum. The fury of white protesters opposing the school was a riveting spectacle in Detroit and received fleeting attention from the national media. Although novel aspects of this conflict were sparingly acknowledged by the local press—whites accused the school board of attempting to "resegregate" black children—most of the coverage made it seem a hackneyed reaction by whites who were terrified of blacks.[25] I was intrigued by the dispute, however, and the following spring, after the turmoil had eased and the press had left, I started interviewing people there about the controversy. These interviews form the basis of the last chapter, "Between 'All Black' and 'All White.'"

The intense media scrutiny of white interests in Warrendale makes this field site distinct from the other two, but the racial objectification of these whites brings into relief a dynamic that links these locations and a theme animating this book. These sites offer contrasting examples of the process of racialization as it pertains to whites. Virginia Dominguez regards racialization as the process whereby "differences between human beings are simplified and transformed into Difference. . . . Racialization is produced and reproduced through ideological, institutional, interactive, and lin-guistic practices that support a particular construction of Difference."[26] This process, associated with objectifications of people of color, reduces individuality to the point that only racialness matters. This book exam-ines the way that whites, too, are subjected to racialization, a process most sharply apparent in the way the significance of white racialness is framed in relation to political debates and public controversies. There are copious distinctions between the ways, in general, whites and blacks are racialized—the social and political ramifications are hugely different. But by examining how whites are racialized—always unevenly, always fol-lowing the contours of class distinctions—we can think more clearly about the way racial identity varies by social and geographical location. Indeed, the way whites respond to racial objectification is a reflection of their situatedness, spatially and in terms of class privilege.

The Localness of Race

This book highlights the ways race functions as a local matter. Academic studies consistently bifurcate racial subjects into distinct registers, and treat them as a function of either individuals or social collectives. Racism, for instance, is alternately analyzed as a characteristic of individuals, a product of social institutions, or some complicated commingling of the two.[27] The following pages present a view that draws out, in contrast, the distinctive role of *places* in informing and molding the meaning of race. This approach derives from a developing tendency among anthropologists to regard race as they do culture—as a relentlessly local matter.[28] Dan Segal uses the concept of "racial idioms" to convey how these meanings are inflected by place-specific features, often involving contests over class and gender identity.[29] Stressing the localness of race still requires attending to all of its critical dimensions: economic, historical, social. And it neither negates nor denies analyses of race that operate at the national or global level. The fundamental assertion made here is that racial identities are produced and experienced distinctly in different locations, shaped by dynamics that are not yet fully comprehended.[30]

In Detroit, I found that the meaning of race not only varies from location to location, depending on the localized effects of economic orders, demographics, dominant political styles, and class compositions but, recursively, that racial identities are constitutive of place: that racial identities are projected onto social space as a means of identifying individuals and positing the significance of their connection to collective orders. This dynamic reflects what Michael Taussig refers to as "a poetics of place and race that is no less political and economic than it is aesthetic."[31] Neighborhoods are considered—by insiders and outsiders—to be "white" or "black" according to shifting criteria, but the designation almost always masks the inevitable degrees of racial heterogeneity in any location. The projection of such racial identities onto places is the focus of Chapter 1, "History of the 'Hood," which relates the collapse of Briggs as a "white neighborhood." The cultural poetics that inform these identifications—composed by the local repertoire of stories, concerns, topics of interest, and events, each uniquely shaped by the neighoborhood's class composition—appear most tangibly in the types of situations that were racialized in these locales.[32]

In each area, I analyze incidents or encounters that residents regarded as "racial situations." In these events, the designation "racial" often bore a provisional or unstable air, in contrast with the certainty that usually accompanies this term's deployment by scholars or political activists. In these situations I focused on the interpretive process whereby participants judged the interests, intentions, motivations, and actions that composed such encounters.[33] In the course of an unfolding racial situation, a threshold is crossed whereby competing interpretations ("it was a friendly argument" or "it was just kids acting up") are overwhelmed by the abrupt clarity of the setting's racial aspects. Race is seized upon in an absolute manner. Disputants may contest whether it was always there just below the surface, held in suspense, or if race was "interjected," as it is said to be in political races or other such contests.[34] But, surely, someone decides "to make something out of it." To understand racial situations, one must be attentive to the way local discourses or interpretive repertoires are brought to bear by participants.[35]

The primary frustration I suspect many readers will find in this approach is that ambiguities and ambivalences come to the fore, yet are largely left unresolved.[36] I have tried to maintain the gap I perceive between the certainty encompassed by experts' designations of "racial" and the uncertainty or instability of deployments of the term by "natives." Certainty established one day could dissolve the next. This instability in local readings of "racial" leads me to suspect that people are provisional in their racial assessments in a way that is missed, overlooked, or underestimated by most social scientists, because this is not something that is easily captured in a one-time survey or interview. Such "opinions" are complex products of competing interpretive repertoires that vary from neighborhood to neighborhood. Margaret Wetherell and Jonathan Potter describe interpretive repertoires as "discernible clusters of terms, descriptions and figures of speech often assembled around metaphors or vivid images. . . . They are some of the resources for making evaluations, constructing factual versions and performing particular actions."[37] In the United States, interpretive repertoires for articulating a sense of place fundamentally involve class. Whether neighborhoods are racially homogeneous or heterogeneous, class distinctions animate residents' discussions of their neighbors, family, and strangers. When I stress the role of class in this book, I am not asserting that race can be simply reduced to class, as some theorists argue.[38] Rather, I emphasize how racial categories and conflicts are consistently textured by class distinctions.[39] What appears to be fairly consistent according to class formation is the type of conflicts or situations involving race and the interpretive modes that are brought to bear in understanding racial identity. This is seen most concretely in the types of interracial encounters and conflicts that occur in these residential areas.

The Warrendale dispute, for example, presents another in a long line of racial conflicts that have exploded in working-class communities over schools and children.[40] The sense of "fairness" called into question by the Board of Education's actions in opening the Malcolm X Academy involves concerns that are specifically based in class identity, though expressed through a racial idiom.[41] Schools are simply not a "racial" issue in the other two neighborhoods. In the underclass area of Briggs, where many local schools are closed and abandoned, the remaining elementary school is not seen as a special resource vulnerable to incursions by racial outsiders.[42] Given the social heterogeneity of this zone, racialized versions of any such contests are not sustainable. Even in the 1970s, when the area had a far higher concentration of whites, issues related to the schools were not easily racialized (see the section "Franklin School" in Chapter 1). This speaks as much to the relation of poor people to community schools as it does to the positive effects of racial integration. In Corktown, on the other hand, white professionals tend to have "careers" rather than children; the few who do have children send them to private schools rather than to the Detroit public schools. Their class status maintains "community" as an intentionally constructed synthesis between their homes and the city, an investment in structures that do not directly involve the public schools. The class compositions of these three sites provide the backgrounds against which the significance of racialness emerges. And in these zones, class distinctions are arrayed along a divide between those whites who fulfill assumed decorums or etiquettes for "belonging" and those who, in failing to match conventionalized modes of behavior, find their racialness uncomfortably objectified.[43]

White People or Whiteness?

This book's origins lie in the developing critical attention to whiteness as a cultural construct. The work of Ruth Frankenberg, David Roediger, and bell hooks influenced the initial design of the research I set out to conduct in Detroit.[44] Whiteness has developed into a contentious but vigorous subject of study.[45] Whiteness stands as a concept that reveals and explains the racial interests of white people, linking them collectively to a position of social dominance. As a subject of academic and political scrutiny, whiteness has two primary characteristics: first, its operations are assumed to be fairly uniform, establishing the normativity of white mores and behaviors, along with the social homogeneity valued by this collective; whiteness manifests a certain logic in its political, aesthetic, and historical sensibilities—that blackness is its symbolic other. Second, in structural terms, whiteness is articulated and lived by whites as a residual category of social forms that elude the marks of color or race. Whiteness effectively names practices pursued by whites in the course of maintaining a position of social privilege and political dominance in this country.

This definition of whiteness establishes a powerful tool for critiquing the racial subtexts in American politics and popular culture, but it makes for a clumsy analytic object in explaining the way race operates in Detroit. Whatever its status nationally, whiteness is not hegemonic within this city. Blackness is locally dominant: "black power" shapes the politics; "black dollars" and "black fashion" define the landscape of consumption.[46] This is not to make the absurd assertion that whiteness is irrelevant in Detroit; rather, its operations do not possess a generically "unmarked" or "normative" character.[47] White racialness, here, is the subject of frequent marking and is often chastised as being out of place. White Detroiters are visibly engulfed in what Howard Winant refers to as "the crisis of white identity."[48] The evidence of this "crisis" is discrepant and varied within the city, just as it is across the country, with regions differently buffeted by demographic shifts that are undermining the majority status of whites.[49] But Winant stresses that whites have been distinctly *racialized* in the post-civil rights era, and this is clearly evident in Detroit.[50] Since whiteness assumes a static order of white dominance and black subordination, I find the racialness of whites to be a more relevant subject of inquiry in Detroit.

I raise this distinction as more than a matter of semantics. There is a keen anxiety among those who study whiteness, that it will be ensconced in academia as a separate subdiscipline—white studies—perhaps mirroring the privileged position this ideological order has historically maintained.[51] This is a valid concern. I suggest the means to short-circuit this development is to expand this intellectual endeavor beyond the effort to establish definitively what makes whiteness unique by, instead, trying to determine what is generically racial about whites.[52] A first step in this direction is to learn from the long struggle to establish that blackness is a heterogeneous rather than homogeneous social order.[53] Stressing the heterogeneity of whites, though, muddies the clarity with which whiteness can be analyzed as a cultural construct.[54] But by viewing whites as a racial minority, in different class positions, subjected to racial predicaments and racialized judgments, we can begin to recognize racial dynamics—those involving ambiguities and uncertainties—that will become increasingly common in this next century.

The racialness of whites as a local minority is often starkly apparent in neighborhood disputes or conflicts between white residents and black city officials. But class differences also inflect its significance. This constitutes a second problem I encountered in trying to analyze whiteness in Detroit. I did not find whites uniformly grappling with the meaning of race by treating blackness as an other—whether in a general symbolic sense or personified in the faces of neighbors or strangers. I found that when whites talk about race they consistently invoke or mobilize class distinctions between themselves and their white neighbors. They assess when or whether race matters by considering which whites are involved in a situation. Indeed, *intraracial* distinctions are a primary medium through which whites think about race.

Racial matters in each of these neighborhoods are articulated through local idioms, discourses that whites and blacks speak with varying degrees of commonality in positioning themselves, neighbors, and strangers in relation to marked and unmarked identities. In the most salient labels and categories "race" is rarely established in pure forms; rather, it is conflated with class distinctions in a series of terms that negotiate the significance of being white without drawing uniformly on either a historical notion of whiteness or a clear opposition to blackness.[55]

In each neighborhood there are marked identities that can be assigned to whites.[56] In Briggs certain whites are labeled "hillbilly." Southern whites arriving in Detroit between the 1940s and the 1960s were scorned by contemptuous native white Detroiters. "Hillbilly" inscribed a stigmatized intraracial distinction, articulating a sense of refinement and sophistication that these "rude," out-of-place whites could not attain.[57]

In Corktown the marked term is "gentrifier." Whites emphasize the conflicting evidence as to whether this neighborhood is undergoing gentrification in any "classical" definition of the term. Few original residents are being displaced; only a handful of recently arrived whites have moved into the area; the value of land seems hardly to have shifted over the past few decades; and yet whites in this area are obsessed and unnerved by the significance of their racial and class position. As white professionals in the "inner city," they often feel out of place. They express this anxiety by objectifying minute social differences between themselves and other whites in the neighborhood through the term "gentrifier." With great alacrity, these whites argue over who among them represents "true gentrification."

In Warrendale, the marked term is "racist."[58] When the opening of the Afrocentric Malcolm X Academy was announced, many whites in the area fervently protested the school board's decision. Residents contested the academy for a number of reasons, but in media accounts they were depicted as "racists" opposing a "black school." Flustered and enraged by this depiction, residents turned to arguing over who among them represented the "real racists." The basis for their designation of "racist" involves subtle distinctions of class—those who ruptured middle-class decorum were typically assumed to be the most racist. As whites argued over how positions in favor of or in opposition to the school could be equated with racism, they also attempted to articulate a means of addressing the racial interests they perceived as the basis for the Malcolm X Academy. School officials promoted the Afrocentric curriculum as a means of countering the devastating effects of the inner city on poor black youths, but white residents charged that the board was attempting to "resegregate" black children through the use of a "separatist," "black nationalist" ideology. These divergent views reflect clear class distinctions between black professionals and white working-class homeowners. In this muddled and polemicized zone, "racist" was applied to almost all of the participants, black or white. It was a designation that showed the paucity of public discourse in providing means of articulating racial stakes in such conflicts.[59]

With each of these labels—"hillbilly," "gentrifier," "racist"—white racialness is distinctly objectified. These names are part of local discourses that not only evaluate the racial content of the communities and their interests but also police boundaries of status and privilege. Whites are marked as much in relation to ongoing class dynamics as they are to any tangible set of beliefs or actions in relation to race or racism. As a rule, whites are differently positioned in relation to the privileges that whiteness is assumed to ensure. In Briggs, "hillbilly" denotes poorer whites who display no interest in attaining the respectable lifestyle that some local whites strive to maintain as they dream still of the bygone days when Briggs was a "respectable" neighborhood. In Warrendale "racist" is applied to whites who are less politically savvy and more economically unstable than the whites who most quickly use the term. Yet the class distinctions operating within these categories are not simply directed toward maintaining distance from the "lower" economic orders. In Corktown, "gentrifier" denotes class privilege, inscribing a heightened sense of being out of place for those whites who arrived in this inner-city zone with more money than their white neighbors. Whites resist being labeled as "gentrifiers" in order to elude being objectified as privileged. In avoiding or deploying these categories, these whites evince an interest in being unmarked in terms of class, as well as in relation to race. And in the deployment of these categories, in their application to certain whites, and in the strenuous efforts of others to avoid being so labeled, the significance of white racialness is subject to continual reappraisal. Not all whites are susceptible to being designated by these categories, and on this uneven ground more vague contests over whiteness are at work. These contests demonstrate that the significance of white racialness is also generated and manipulated in classed conflicts over the objectification of an individual's racial identity. To borrow an insight from historians of class formations, whiteness "does not come included as a standard accessory"; it is always constructed anew by white people, "using local material drawn from the larger context of social life" as it is experienced and expressed, in this case, in particular neighborhoods.[60]

Structure of the Book

This book is divided into two parts. The first half examines the history and current situations of poor whites in Briggs. The second half features detailed accounts of how whites in Corktown and Warrendale contend

with the significance of white racialness. The juxtaposition of these ethnographic field sites is designed to heighten a recognition of the crucial
role that class plays in the way that whites engage racial matters.

The first chapter, "History of the 'Hood," conveys in detail the collapse of a once-thriving inner-city neighborhood and how its deterioration forms a novel ground on which whites negotiate the significance of
race. This is a microanalysis of the lengthy economic and political processes that produce inner-city zones of concentrated poverty.[61] My analysis also works at complicating popular narratives of "white flight," which
influence and reinforce the homogeneously colored view most Americans hold of the inner city. This section attempts to reconstruct everyday
perceptions and experiences of white and black residents of this zone as
it was transformed by forces national in scope but tangibly local in their
effects.

Whiteness, as an ideological order, requires material supports. In Detroit's core, these supports—segregated residential areas, race-conscious
political and social institutions, racially selective employers—gradually
deteriorated over fifty years. The social practices, legal strictures, and economic policies that constitute racial discrimination were effectively challenged by political force and demographic pressure. The means for assuring white privilege and for maintaining the illusion of its supremacy were
undermined in Detroit. For whites who remained in the city, especially
those in the decimated inner-city areas, the significance of race has drastically altered.

Within the first chapter, the section entitled "Disgrace to the Race"
relates the ways that "hillbillies" disrupted the naturalized racial order
that northern whites quietly maintained before World War II. With the
marked term "hillbilly," native white Detroiters intraracially policed the
social status of whiteness, maintaining a sense of normative behavior that
"hillbillies" transgressed. The next section, "The Color Line," conveys
how the local structural supports for whiteness were undermined in the
1940s, shattering this area's identification as a "white neighborhood."
"Riots and Race" details the perceptions that whites and blacks hold of
the Detroit riots in 1943 and 1967. Residents of Briggs regard only the
former as racial; the basis for this distinction reveals the considerations
that come into play as whites and blacks develop criteria for determining
what counts as "racial." "Franklin School" draws this chapter to a close
by presenting contrasting white interpretations of the majority-black
Board of Education's decision to close this once predominantly white
school. Disparate white views reflect contrasting perceptions of the significance of race in relation to black political power.

The second chapter, "A Hundred Shades of White," provides a detailed ethnographic perspective on daily social interactions in Briggs con-

centrating on how a local, provisional sensibility about racial matters is developed by these "hillbillies."[62] As poor whites, they experience numerous reminders of the social distance between themselves and suburban whites, whose racialness largely goes unmarked. The meaning of this distance, and how it affects their encounters with black neighbors and strangers, is partly assessed with the term "hillbilly." The first section of this chapter, "Hillbillies," tracks the way this label is applied to particular whites, sketching the class contours of this rhetorical identity. "That White and Black Shit" then describes how "hillbillies" negotiate interracial situations, relying at times on varied uses of the term "nigger." This section contrasts their uses of "nigger" in relation to other whites and in reference to blacks; rather than a transparent indication of their racism, these instances of name-calling convey the range of charged, volatile ambiguities that pertain to racial identity in this zone. This point is borne out by the last section, "The Wicker Chair and the Baseball Game," which examines two instances in which the significance of white racialness was sharply challenged.

The second half of the book further develops my argument that class shapes the significance of white racialness in its subjective sensibilities and in its various forms of objectification. The depictions of Corktown and Warrendale serve to contextualize the dynamics related to the racialness of whites in Briggs. Since I lived only in Briggs during the course of my fieldwork, I was not able to compile an ethnographic view of daily life in these other two neighborhoods; nor was I able to observe much of the give-and-take of their informal modes of socializing. Rather, these two chapters are drawn almost entirely from formal interviews and a few scattered impromptu exchanges. Partially to compensate for the lack of ethnographic detail, I include lengthier extracts of the residents' comments and stories. On the whole, though, my primary focus in each of these sites is consistent with the shape of my inquiries in Briggs—how do labels that conflate racial and class identity for whites operate in local interpretive repertoires?

In this second half, I rely heavily on discourse analysis to draw out the contours of class identity, following the lead of ethnographers like Douglas Foley and Shirley Brice Heath.[63] Applying discourse analysis to questions of class identity does not dismiss its material, economic basis in hierarchized relations linked to occupation and other forms social stratification. Rather, the discursive approach asserts that the significance of these relations and material conditions are assessed and evaluated in the narratives and speech of people in particular locations.[64] However objective material conditions may appear to social analysts, their significance is usually a matter of local discussion and debate. This underscores the important recognition that class, like race, is culturally constructed; it is situational and relational rather than just an abstract variable. As John Frow asserts, "There is no class essence and there are no unified class actors, founded in the objectivity of a social interest; there are, however, processes of class formation, without absolute origin or telos, with definite discursive conditions, and played out through particular institutional forms and balances of power, through calculations and miscalculations, through desires and fears and fantasies."[65]

Additionally, I follow David Halle's ethnographic approach to grasping the dynamics of class identification. Rather than asking informants to select from a limited series of abstract categories—middle class, working class, and so on—he relied on terms that arose in the course of his fieldwork, thus "enabl[ing] people to accept and discuss a particular identity in the class structure. What validates the responses is that workers assent to such an identity and talk fluently about it."[66] Similarly, I asked questions about the terms residents in these sites used most frequently in discussing both their identity and the character of their neighborhoods. Like Halle, I used "follow-up questions exploring the image of the class structure" underlying their responses, but since my interest is in the way class position shapes the significance of white racialness, I attended primarily to terms that conflate racial and class identity, such as "gentrifier" and "racist."

Most important, though, my approach to class is fundamentally informed by one of Halle's central findings: that workers articulate a sense of their position in the class system through a series of three images, keyed respectively to their lives at work, at home, and as Americans. Since my interviews were concentrated in the second of these imagistic realms— which Halle considers to be the most ambiguous and fluid—the class distinctions mobilized by these whites do not articulate clearly bounded identities. Indeed, both Corktown and Warrendale are composed of heterogeneous class elements, although the contours of distinct class characters are present in each. Articulations of this character, however, are subject to dynamic interpretive engagements through place-specific discourses; that is, people judge the class identity of themselves and their neighborhood in a dense local idiom that attends to both demographics and gossip.

The third chapter, "Eluding the R-Word," opens up the comparative class perspective, featuring whites in the neighborhood adjacent to Briggs, Corktown. These whites also confront uncertainties about the significance of white racialness in the inner city, but their class position assures that the ambiguities they confront will not be as volatile as those facing whites in Briggs. The first section, "The Fact of Whiteness" features residents' descriptions of the racial character of this zone and how they account for the concentration of whites that has developed in Detroit's core. "Encounters" conveys the type of interracial situations that occur here, highlighting how the contrasts of class position imparts a different charge to racial matters than it does in Briggs. "Gentrifier" tracks the interplay of claim and counter-claim in relation to ascriptions of this label. Whites actively use this term to sort out the complicated question of who really belongs in this neighborhood. The final section of this chapter, "History," frames the discourse that whites here prefer to use in contrast to designations of "gentrification" in explaining the collective aspects of the interests and desires that brought them to reside at the core of Detroit.

The last chapter, "Between 'All Black' and 'All White,'" features the whites of Warrendale in their conflicts over the Malcolm X Academy. Although the concentration of whites is greater here, and this neighborhood is farther removed from the dangers of inner-city life, whites in Warrendale have a more perilous sense of their situation, both racially and in terms of class. The section, "Statements," reviews the way whites' comments in relation to the academy were objectified in the media and by their neighbors or school and city officials. "White Enclave" represents the prevailing depiction of Warrendale. Area whites tried to counter this representation by developing a contrasting attention to the relative degrees of whiteness in other Detroit neighborhoods and the city's suburbs. That is, they argued against this image by pointing to other places that were "whiter than we are." "Racist" details the way this label was applied to whites and the way some residents contested the limits the term set for how race could be generally discussed. "Curriculum" examines the way whites made an issue of the Afrocentric perspective developed at the academy. In particular, I emphasize the powerful effects that Afrocentric discourse had on the whites who engaged most intensely in this dispute.

1

History of the 'Hood

IN 1930 the area encompassing Briggs was populated by over 24,000 people, 99 percent of whom were white.[1] This zone was tabulated as five census tracts. In 1990, fewer than 3,000 people remained in approximately this same area; blacks made up 56 percent of the population and only one census tract was required.[2] The city has been gutted of people and wealth, but not to the same extent as Briggs. Today the lack of adequate housing, the rates of poverty, unemployment, and lack of education are all worse in Briggs than in Detroit at large. And yet Briggs is proportionally far whiter than Detroit as a whole. The whites who remain are an odd residual of the generic racial narrative, "white flight"; they stayed behind as friends and families poured out of the neighborhood and the city.

Whites with the longest memories of this part of Detroit emphasize three events when they explain what happened to their neighborhood: the arrival of the "hillbillies" beginning in the 1940s, the riots of 1943 and 1967, and the closing of Franklin Elementary School in 1978. These events stand out as markers of the shifting racial order in Detroit. They also varyingly overlap or meld with national narratives, particularly concerning "hillbillies" and "race riots." Local whites' interpretations of these events sometimes mimic nationally circulated versions, but at key points they stand in sharp contrast to the way whites across the country perceive similar or related situations. The points of correspondence and dissonance provide a means for recognizing how shifts in scale affect the significance of race; the local operation of racial categories also demonstrates how class-based distinctions animate the role of place in constituting racial identity and difference.

Residents' accounts of the neighborhood's demise convey a great deal about the mutable significance of race in its complicated relation to supporting institutional and residential structures. In their stories, race is distinctly objectified, conforming to "common-sense" notions in each period. Sifting through the layers of history in Briggs reveals a series of interpretive repertoires that residents have fashioned to make sense of race; their central categories and objects (such as "hillbillies" or riots) convey distinct coagulations of local and national frames of reference. Racial categories are a product and object of history; their textures and

Figure 3. Elm Street, Briggs

materiality depend on the steady accretion of cultural time, across which social stratification has been read and encoded through epidermal differences between growing and aging bodies. Racial formations are the result of historical movements of people and shifts in economic structures; they provide the basis for refashioning political orders and modes of representation. Yet, although racial categories compose understandings of the results of historical processes, narrative versions of who were the "winners" and the "losers" of decades-long developments and transformations determine what actually counts as historical for residents and participants in these temporal transformations. Race is not simply historically produced; it provides an interpretive basis for the recognition and manipulation of history itself.

The general progression conveyed in the following compilation of accounts is of a shift in the architectonics of whiteness, from a time when it was stabilized in the city through a host of social and political operations to a moment when it became construed as "out of place" in this inner-city core. This transformation also occurred in other urban areas over the postwar period. Although the drastic demographic scale of events in Detroit might seem unique, I suspect that these versions of how whiteness took flight for the green fields of the suburbs will have strong resonances with other locations. The purpose of this chapter is to examine the way the significance of white racialness is objectified and assessed after so many of the material and structural supports of whiteness have collapsed locally. Admittedly, the fragmentary and partial nature of the evidence mobilized in this account—drawn from scattered residents' recollections of this decimated neighborhood—forms a tenuous basis for generalizing about race.[3] But the partialness of this material also reflects an interesting dynamic of racial matters: people are not hesitant to moblize the broad explanatory power of "race" and "racial" in relation to their limited personal, idiosyncratic views of the social world. The following is not a definitive account of how race (as a general political relation of social aggregates) mattered in this part of Detroit. Rather, this chapter presents race as a shifting interpretive subject, mobilized by white and black residents to make sense of what happened to their neighborhood and as a means for explaining the differences and similarities that matter in their daily experiences.

"Disgrace to the Race"

The local whites' obsession with "hillbillies" struck me early in my inquiries about the neighborhood's history. One cold gray afternoon, I stopped in at the oldest business in Briggs, a corner dry cleaner established in the early 1920s. One of the two brothers who ran the place was working the front counter. He chatted with a long-time friend, Joe, a white man in his late sixties, propped up on a wooden bench against the shop's large front window. I asked the two men if they could tell me what the area was like in the 1940s. Henry, from behind the counter, answered first, amiably offering, "It was a good neighborhood . . ."

Joe interrupted quickly, "Yeah, until them Kentucky hillbillies came in. Shoot, cut, fight, shoot, cut, fight . . ."

Henry said, "Don't pay him any mind. He's from there too," gesturing with an amused wink.

This upset Joe, who bellowed, "No! I'm from Tennessee. But I don't want to be a hillbilly. I don't carry a knife. I don't try to kill nobody. I don't go shooting . . . ," his speech degenerated into a frustrated stammer that Henry amiably interrupted. "Well, I say there's good and bad in everybody."

But Joe would not settle for that, replying, "Yeah? Well it seems like bad is all I've ever run into from Kentucky."

As Henry moved on to list the businesses that once lined this now largely abandoned section of Trumbull Avenue—a restaurant across the street next to another dry cleaner, a grocery store, a bar, a confectionery, and a drug store, plus apartment buildings—Joe grumbled in the background and soon found a way to return to the subject that disturbed him most: "hillbillies." He broke in with an officious voice, declaring, "In

World War II, these hillbillies from Harlan, Kentucky, coal miners, come up here 'cause they automated the coal mines. Shoot, cut, and fight, shoot, cut, and fight . . . " Henry relented to his friend's interest in the rough side of life in Briggs, remarking that, "It used to be a jumping neighborhood around here. You could look into the bar over there. We lived upstairs, but it was just like watching TV, the way they carried on in there. Saturday night fights." Joe made sure I knew it was the "hill-billies" who were responsible for provoking these fights.

This was not just one old man's bitter recollection. I found that whites born in the area before World War II drew the same angry correspon-dence between the neighborhood's demise and the arrival of the "hill-billies." At first this surprised me. In the ten years since I had lived in Detroit, I found it quite common for whites to blame Detroit's dissolution on the rise of black self-rule. On talk shows, in editorial commentaries, and personal conversations, I often heard very racialized explanations of "what happened" from whites who blamed the "black administration" for corruption, and blacks in general for fermenting the social chaos in Detroit.[4] I expected white residents to express similar sentiments. Instead, these native Detroiters, who recalled an area that was self-sufficient, with stores catering to their needs, easy streetcar service to and from down-town, and many bars for an evening's socializing, traced a direct corre-spondence between the arrival of white "hillbillies" and the deterioration of both the physical and social conditions in the area. Given the drastic shift in the neighborhood's racial demographics I expected that whites would express a strictly racial explanation of events, blaming the neigh-borhood's decay on black inmovers. Instead, they emphasized the role of other whites—"hillbillies"—highlighting the shift in the neighborhood's class "character."

"Hillbillies" began arriving in Detroit in large numbers as early as the 1920s.[5] In the wake of this migration, along with the traumatic effect of the Depression and the increasing presence of southern black migrants in the city, white Detroiters found their stable, conventionalized notions of social difference starting to erode. The physical means by which that dif-ference was ordered and contained by the structure of residential areas in the city also began to crumble.[6] Until the 1940s, blacks were confined through the strictures of racial segregation to a clearly established, over-crowded, and decrepit ghetto. "Hillbillies," however, tended to settle in neighborhoods throughout the center of Detroit. These neighborhoods were all within the Grand Boulevard area, however, the zone that pro-vided the initial contours of the "inner city" in Detroit.[7] This reflects the fact that most white migrants were poor and generally unskilled for most jobs in Detroit. Since their arrival coincided with the rapid deterioration of aging housing stock and the increased problem of overcrowding in these neighborhoods, "hillbillies" were easily scapegoated for the decline of living conditions among working-class whites. And just as the implicit, yet physically emphatic, color line in Detroit was becoming problematic, "hillbillies" undermined an easy assertion of a conventionalized sense of racial solidarity among whites.

For native white Detroiters, the disturbing aspect of "hillbillies" was exactly their racialness. Ostensibly they were of the same racial order (whites) as those who dominated economic, political, and social power in local and national arenas. But "hillbillies" shared many regional characteristics—in speech, diet, and lifestyle—with the southern blacks arriving in Detroit, which destabilized the fixity of northern racial stereotypes.[8] In their narratives of what happened to the neighborhood, older whites used "hillbilly" as a marked term of boundary maintenance for a diffuse sense of racial identity.[9] "Hillbilly" was the name given to southern whites who either willfully or "ignorantly" failed to assimilate into northern norms of respectability (that is, whiteness). They were objects of contempt for transgressing a racial order that was rapidly losing its semblance of naturalness. "Hillbilly" labeled problematic white bodies and behaviors that disrupted the implicit color line in Detroit at a time when its informal, behavioral dictates were a primary means for maintaining racial segregation. They were somebody for white Detroiters to blame when the actions in defense of the color line exceeded the decorums of white society, as will be seen in the next section, "Riots and Race."[10]

The crux of the matter was a nebulous but enduring sense of cultural difference between northern and southern whites. Aside from the fact that they had waged a vicious war against each other, the two groups have long found numerous, contemptuous means of differentiating themselves.[11] In spite of their shared epidermal markings, the cultural differences between northern and southern whites have long been read via bodily registers. Elmer Aker, in the first sociological study of migrant whites in Detroit, described "the typical southern white [a]s tall, slender, withy; he moves with a somewhat listless, slouching gait; his face bears a wooden inscrutibleness, a slightly melancholy aspect; and his eyes meet you at a sidelong glance, with long, distrustful looks of inquiry. The smile of comfortable assurance and the frank eye of fellowship he does not have."[12] In this regard, ostensibly white bodies legibly rendered subtle means of assuming naturalized orders of cultural differences between whites, discursively manipulated by the category of "hillbilly."[13]

Delores, a white woman in her mid-sixties, was born and raised in the area now called Briggs. She left in 1950 to join a convent, then returned in the early 1970s as one of many Catholic missionaries and social workers who sought to revive the neighborhood and its people. She worked in Community on the Move, the first grass-roots organization in this area, arranging programs and meals for senior citizens. Community on the Move was established in 1966 and was composed of white and black residents who were attempting to combat the rising incidence of crime and the steady deterioration of the housing stock. Community on the Move successfully pushed through adoption by the city council of a renewal plan for the area, but the group began dissolving as residents recognized that the developer for this project was primarily interested in creating more expensive residential housing in place of their dilapidated homes. Delores watched the group finally collapse over allegations of financial mismanagement among its leaders. When Community on the Move disbanded, she moved on to work in another parish on the southwest side of Detroit.

Delores stressed the multiethnic character of the neighborhood in her childhood. By way of illustration she referred to the small building where she grew up; there were eight families living there—two German, one Scottish, and the others were Irish. Now that corner is a tangle of weeds and young saplings, with no dwellings. Delores allowed that "it was a well-used neighborhood even in those days. But it didn't have the . . . y'know . . . what do I want to say? It didn't look run down. They were hard-working people, most of them were factory workers, or maybe clerks in stores, that type of workers." Her description is worth quoting at length because it encompasses the chain of association older whites make between "hillbillies" and the neigborhood's decline.

DELORES: The people were poor, but they were hard working. A few owned their own homes, but it was mostly rental property. So as those older people died out, and it all became rental property, well it just started to go down. And one of the things that hit the neighborhood in a very negative way, during the war, and that would've been in the '40s, white Appalachians began coming into the neighborhood, and in droves, in order to work in the war plants. And property building during the war had ceased, and so they had . . . rent . . . what do they call that . . . rent ceilings, made by law, because people were raising their rent so high. You had whole families, like, all those big houses, well many of them are gone now. But there used to be lovely Victorian houses along Trumbull Avenue. But all along there, those houses, during the war, almost became like boarding houses. They . . . uh the landlords would take those places and divide them up into apartments, so you would have whole families living in maybe two or three rooms. So things were crowded. And that didn't help the housing situation. And then, another thing, many of these people had literally come from the back hills of country living, into a city that was overcrowded, and they didn't know how to live in it. And we'd hear stories . . .

about like when people would take their dish water and throw it right out the window like they used to do at home [laughs]. Uhm, one of the vulgar stories was about . . . some . . . some family that called up the landlord to come get the toilet now, it was full. And the people that literally did not know how to live a city life. So that helped to . . . to kinda tear down some of those buildings too.

JH: Were there conflicts between the Appalachians and the other residents?

DELORES: Yes, ohhh, yes. And they were looked down on. Uh . . . now in our particular area, there was a great influx of Negroes. And of course, then we had the race riots here in the '40s; and I was going to Western High School at the time of the race riots. And I remember some of our . . . we only had one or two black kids at the time at Western, because most of the black youngsters went over to Northwestern. And uh . . . but I remember coming out of school and hearing some kids say "well, let's go downtown and catch ourselves a nigger"; that was during the race riots. So there was a lot of feeling. But in our particular neighborhood, there were not many blacks. It was mostly all white Appalachians. But the feeling towards the white Appalachians was about the same as the black and white feeling was.

JH: Was that mainly because of their backwardness in the city?

DELORES: That, sure, and then some of their . . . the old neighborhood, I would say, was one that you could call . . . without exaggerating . . . it had a Christian tone to it. Then in came the white Appalachians and you had a lot of unfaithfulness among men, and treating their women . . . I remember this one woman, I used to help take care of her kids for a pittance, just because I felt so sorry for her. She was literally living in a garage down the street, off of Spruce. And the landlord had fixed up this garage in the back; it was full of cockroaches and all of those things. And she was one that . . . her husband would batter her. And he would take her out for an evening, and while she sat there, he would be flirting and dancing with other women. It was that kinda treatment. It was that kinda treatment, and uhh . . . things like that that gave a kind of, ah tone that the older folks in that neighborhood didn't appreciate.

JH: How long did the tension last?

DELORES: It wasn't a conflict of fighting, in the sense of the race riot, at least not to my knowledge. It was just this feeling that they were riffraff, y'know. And of course the landlords were profiting from these folks, because they needed a place to live, and they were dividing up their property and they were getting as much money out of their property as they could. But a lot of the damage was being done to their property too, by SOME people who didn't know how to live in it. And . . . not only that, but many of them were old houses, and when you fill an old house with a lot of people it's going to make for a lot more wear and tear, so no matter how much you try to take care of it . . . and also, that was during the war and you just couldn't get a lot of the materials you'd need to make repairs.

As Delores spoke, she seemed uncertain how to fix the blame for what happened to the neighborhood between competing groups or causes: white Appalachians, landlords, the war, loose morals, deteriorating and overused housing stock. Her narrative, though, turns on the assertion of an equivalence between the southern whites and blacks as objects of contempt for native white Detroiters: "the feeling towards the white Appalachians was about the same as the black and white feeling was." Other whites drew similar connections, noting, for instance, that local bars initially refused service to both "hillbillies" and blacks, and that both groups were unwelcome in the neighborhood after World War II.[14]

White resentment of "hillbillies" indicates a critical aspect of how racial identities are established and maintained; their boundaries are policed internally as well as externally. Intraracial distinctions are just as essential to constituting racial identities as are interracial oppositions.[15] And they are often quite volatile, given that racial formations are nonstatic and difficult to maintain. Racial differences are not developed and arranged solely according to a seamless logic of self and other, where abstract figures absolutely divide social terrains. Rather, racial matters of belonging and exclusion consistently involve class distinctions. This is a difficult social dynamic to recognize, but one that is fundamental and needs to be considered in making sense of how whites think about race in contemporary situations.

The intraracial differences among whites that "hillbillies" objectified were heightened during the 1950s and 1960s, when tensions over housing and jobs intensified.[16] The 1950s marked the beginning of the economic dispersion that would devastate the city—Detroit's financial order was showing signs of deterioration.[17] The anxiety generated by "hillbillies" was widespread among white Detroiters. In a survey conducted by Wayne State University, one of the questions asked was, "What people in Detroit are undesirable?" The responses are as follows:

Criminals, gangsters, etc.	26%
Poor southern whites; hillbillies, etc.	21%
Non-self supporting, transients, drifters, etc.	18%
Negroes	13%
Foreigners	6%
People who had come lately	4%
Others	12%

Clearly Delores and Joe were not the only white Detroiters who felt that the contempt for hillbillies was running as strong as or stronger than the disdain for blacks. Not only was "Negroes" given by only slightly more than in 10 respondents, but the amorphous category "Other" scored

about the same. The overall focus of negative feeling was on recent arrivals, both white and black, native-born and foreign. Combining "transients" with "people who have come lately," "hillbillies," "foreigners,"
and "others," over 60 percent of the negatively perceived groups fall in
this category. These were people who had yet to be regarded as belonging
in the city.

In relation to "hillbillies," the sense of contempt expressed by native
Detroiters was specific and virulent, as a sample of the responses convey:

> "Southerners or hillbillies—Detroit means nothing to them; they don't keep
> up their homes. They just come to Detroit, earn money, and go back home.
> They add nothing to the city."
>
> "The hillbilly is sure a great detriment. He is not thrifty or a help; just a big
> brawler who cares not how or where he lives; repairs nothing and does nothing
> to beautify the city."
>
> "The Southerns and the hillbillies who migrate here because of the higher
> wages. They are not permanent residents, have no pride. They do not keep up
> their homes so there are eyesores where they live."

The "anti-Negro" responses that were listed are interesting, particularly
because of a connection between "hillbillies" and "Negroes" drawn by
respondents:

> "The poor truck from the South—both white and Negro. They are not good
> citizens."
>
> "Sure! The nigger and the hillbilly."

As Arthur Kornhauser, the study's author, summed up these responses,
"the number of references to recent Southern migrants and hillbillies appears to reflect a significant negative feeling in the city."[18]

This "negative feeling" toward "hillbillies" can be contextualized in
two ways. First, during World War II, larger numbers of white southerners than blacks arrived in the city; in a direct sense, white Detroiters associated problems of overcrowding primarily with the arrival of southern
whites. Between 1940 and 1944, Detroit received 142,120 migrants.[19]
Over 110,000 of these (78 percent) were white. Fewer than 20,000 of
these migrants came from within the state of Michigan—most were from
the South. In this period the southern states from Texas to Virginia sent
64,735 white migrants to the Detroit area, compared with just 29,975
nonwhites.[20] Since blacks were largely confined to Detroit's east-side
ghetto and employers rarely considered hiring blacks for anything but the
most menial and dangerous occupations, whites did not directly compete
with them for the crucial resources—housing and jobs. Although there is
anecdotal evidence of landlords and employers rejecting southern white

migrants out of hand, surely these were a modest means of containment. Thus, "hillbillies" put pressure on labor and housing markets that were becoming more difficult for working-class whites to negotiate.

White resentment of "hillbillies" also mirrored the contempt native black Detroiters held for the southern black migrants pouring into the city. Native black Detroiters expressed an elaborate class-based loathing for the lifestyles and mores of the newly arriving southern blacks in the 1920s and 1930s.[21] Indeed, the Detroit Urban League was established as a moralizing means by which to force migrant southern blacks to conform to the decorums and conventions of black middle-class culture.[22] Historians have largely analyzed this intraracial class divide and conflict as a function of the color line in Detroit, and of the struggle of elite blacks to maintain the status positions they had long struggled to establish in the white-dominated city of Detroit.[23] The contemptuous response of northern whites to the growing presence of rural, southern white migrants in the city appears to follow a similar logic, with an attention to maintaining the color line. As Detroiters, white and black, negotiated rapid permutations of the implicit and explicit manifestations of the color line, intraracial prioritizing of class difference was a central dynamic in the social lives of both racial collectives.

Anti-"hillbilly" sentiment was not confined to Detroit; it was broadly expressed across the urban Midwest as white migration from Appalachia ebbed and flowed through the 1950s and 1960s.[24] Chicago received the largest influx of these white migrants, and it was here that the racial threat posed by "hillbillies" was most clearly articulated.[25] The image of the reckless, ill-bred "disgrace to the race" that surfaced in the industrial Midwest was broadcast through national publications such as *Harper's*, which in 1958 announced "The Hillbillies Invade Chicago," in an essay that opened with this highlighted quote: "The city's toughest integration problem has nothing to do with the Negroes. . . . It involves a small army of white, Protestant, Early American migrants from the South—who are usually proud, poor, primitive, and fast with a knife."[26]

"Hillbillies" were glaringly obvious to northern whites because their mores and behaviors confused what had once been fairly stable caricatures of the differences between whites and blacks. Uncomfortably, the "hillbilly," as with "white trash" in the South, bore the characteristics of laziness, poverty, and potential for violence that, for whites, had previously been exclusively associated with blacks.[27] Albert Votaw, in *Harper's*, summed up the disturbing aspects of these ostensibly white people:

> These farmers, miners, and mechanics from the mountains and meadows of the mid-South—with their fecund wives and numerous children—are, in a sense, the prototype of what the "superior" American should be, white, Protestant, of

early American, Anglo-Saxon stock; but on the streets of Chicago they seem to
be the American dream gone berserk. This may be the reason why their neighbors often find them more obnoxious than the Negroes or the earlier foreign
immigrants whose obvious differences from the American Stereotype made
them easy to despise. Clannish, proud, disorderly, untamed to urban ways,
these country cousins confound all notions of racial, religious, and cultural
purity.[28]

By confounding of "all notions of racial, religious, and cultural purity,"
the "hillbilly" disturbed whites throughout the urban Midwest. Votaw
continued by listing the oft-cited "traits" of these members of the "inferior rural classes": their "motionless relaxation that infuriates bustling
city people," their affinity for alcohol and violence, and a host of other
opposed and out-of-place "habits." As with "ethnic" immigrants, the
problem posed by the "hillbillies" was their resistance to "assimilation."[29] Southern whites arrived with a spectrum of abilities and inade-
quacies that either facilitated or undermined their assimilation into mainstream white culture.[30] Those that did not "assimilate," whether willfully
or "ignorantly," those who failed to incorporate the cultural decorums
maintained by northern whites, found themselves severely stigmatized.

   The final section of Votaw's essay posed the question of whether they
are "A Disgrace to the Race." He found a ray of hope "in the fact that the
southern whites are not a solidly homogeneous group. The few who have
come from cities are ripe for assimilation and critical of rural folk, particularly of the mountaineers." He suggested a class-based strategy by which
these "few" are encouraged to persuade their regional compatriots to develop the "attribute for success according to the American dream—even
in its narrowest form." Such a strategy recognized that the group policing
this line most emphatically was the one closest to it: white southerners. As
with Joe, they shared common southern roots and so were vulnerable to
being marked by this regional stigma. Those who made the choice to
assimilate to northern mores then relentlessly used "hillbilly" to accentu-
ate the distance they had achieved from their regional roots. In this regard, "hillbilly" operates as a rhetorical identity used to position individuals, to set them discursively apart from those with whom they share
ostensible features.[31] This rhetorical aspect of "hillbilly" remains active
in Detroit, marking an ever-changing line between proper and improper
behavior for whites, as will be examined in the next chapter.

   The image of the "hillbilly" was broadcast nationally in a number of
forms, from TV shows to cartoons.[32] Academics, journalists, and pro-
ducers of popular culture generated images of "hillbillies" that people
in their everyday lives came to rely on to negotiate shifting boundaries around white racial identity in the United States. Recursively,
this national attention directed toward "hillbillies" made them all the

more recognizable in Briggs. In referring to "hillbillies," I found native white Detroiters availing themselves of nationally produced images and stereotypes.

Margaret was born in 1927 in a neighborhood a few blocks to the north of Briggs. In 1958 she rented a place on 17th Street and has lived on that block ever since. We talked in her kitchen while she rolled cigarettes from a can of Bugler tobacco; she does this in the morning before her arthritis gets too bad. She keeps them in an "antique" metal Philip Morris box with a sliding top.

> JH: Do you remember when the people from Appalachia started moving in here?
>
> MARGARET: I don't know . . . I guess there was some of 'em in here already. You'd hear a lot of them say, we're going back to West Virginia. Most of 'em that come up, they already had relations here. They already had somebody here that they knew . . . There was Ma and Pa Kettle . . . [I laughed] That's what we used to call them. They were from West Virginia. But they moved up here a long time ago. We used to have a store on the corner, and they lived right next door. And finally the boys took the mother back south after the father died. But I think one of them came back up. Then there was the folks that owned that four-family flat, the one that was the first one to go [to be abandoned]. They were from the South. They sold and went back, and then it started deteriorating. Well most of them were up here, y'know, then their relations came. Y'know, little by little. And a lot of 'em let their houses go. I think what it is, a lot of people weren't paying their rent. And you can't pay the taxes without the rent . . . Then we got Tobacco Road on the corner here, but they finally got burnt out.

The family she was referring to lived at the end of the block. I had noticed the house because it was at the center of a sprawl of kids and toys, garbage and car parts, with tall grass growing up against the side of the house. I was hoping to develop ties with this family, but their house burned that winter and they never returned. Apparently the blaze started from a wood fire that they were using to heat the house. When I first met Margaret in Ruby's Bar, this family was a topic of conversation; she was describing what was wrong with the neighborhood. She referred to them at the time and ever after solely as "Tobacco Road."

Margaret's account relies on two nationally circulated images of poor southern whites; both are, in an objective sense, misapplied. She referred first to the comic figures from the popular Ma and Pa Kettle movies, which featured a family of "Okies" in their westward trek. The second image is drawn from Erskine Caldwell's novel, *Tobacco Road*, which is set in the lowlands of Georgia. Both figures are regionally quite distinct

Figure 4. The remains of "Tobacco Road"

from the whites who migrated from West Virginia. But the signifiers that became fused and mobile for Margaret were the transience of these whites, their large, sprawling families, and their poverty. Her key association for white southerners was with the house on her block "that was the first one to go." She noted that "a lot of 'em let their houses go," slipping into disrepair and gradual collapse.

A large house still stands between Margaret's and what is left of "Tobacco Road." It is the former home of Frank Navin, who owned the Detroit Tigers and the stadium where they played, which at the time (1912–1937) bore his name, Navin Field. Now the house is rented out to Shirley, a white woman who came up from Kentucky in the early 1960s. Each of her four daughters was born in a different northern industrial town. Two daughters still live with her, each with her black boyfriend and their interracial children. In the house that stood next door, toward Margaret's, the family was dealing drugs. They spray-painted the windows black after moving in and, until the house was raided by police, the kids who lived there regularly exchanged packets and money with the drivers of cars that pulled up in front. After the raid, the older kids returned and burned the house down. Margaret owns the house adjacent to this one and rents it out.

> MARGARET: In fact, I rented that place to one of the relations [in the Navin house] one time, but that didn't work out.

I asked if it was for rowdiness, and she shook her head no, rubbing her fingers together. "They couldn't get the cabbage . . . And in and out, in and out. They say they'll move in, they pay you for a little bit, then all of a sudden they're a few months' rent behind. Then they take their time moving out. But like I said, there was a lot of 'em from the South here already, and of course, they'd bring their relations up here, and move in, and they'd pile up."

There was a difference between native white Detroiters and "hillbillies," a difference that remains active and troublesome to some whites in this zone. But if "hillbillies" made the color line ambiguous, the increased presence of blacks provoked some native whites to make it emphatic again.

The Color Line

The work of boundary maintenance that the rhetorical identity "hillbilly" performed is modest in comparison with the organized, violent resistance that white homeowners put up against efforts by blacks to escape from containment in the ghetto.[33] Black Detroiters had long faced violent protests when they moved into white neighborhoods. The most famous of these incidents was the battle at the home of Ossian Sweet in 1925.[34] Racial conflicts over housing reached the riot stage with street fights over the Sojourner Truth housing project in 1942, a wartime housing development designated for blacks but viciously coveted by whites.[35] In these violent acts, an explicit, material interest in whiteness was articulated through assertions of a residential color line between blacks and whites. As historian Thomas Sugrue explains, "the sustained violence in Detroit's neighborhoods was the consummate act in a process of identity formation. White Detroiters invented communities of race in the city that they defined spatially. Race in the postwar city was not just a cultural construction. Instead, whiteness, and by implication blackness, assumed a material dimension, imposed onto the geography of the city. Through the drawing of racial boundaries, whites reinforced their own fragile racial identity. Ultimately, they were unsuccessful in preventing the movement of blacks into many Detroit neighborhoods, but their defensive measures succeeded in deepening the divide between two Detroits, one black and one white."[36] This color line was active in the area now called Briggs, but its obvious emergence and remission involved a period of five years, from 1945 to 1949. The disjointed fashion in which whiteness was locally articulated and asserted is evidenced in the stories of older African-American residents.

An interesting conundrum emerged as I interviewed black residents about the neighborhood's history. Two families identified themselves as the "first blacks" to move into Briggs, but both arrived in the late 1940s, some twenty years after blacks first began moving into the area. This confusion reflects more than a conflict between oral histories and archival records. The discrepancy involves a disjointed effort by whites to link articulations of racial interests to the material structures of this neighborhood as a bounded and defensible entity. What separates Jennie Overton and Howard King—two of the "first blacks" to move into this area— from those who preceded them between 1920 and 1945 is the emergence of a newly powerful political figure in Detroit: the white homeowner. The area that Briggs encompasses today was an early defensive battleground for this figure; the wake of its local defeat reveals an intriguing glimpse of how racial formations oscillate between static and unsteady orders.

Blacks started moving into this area during the 1920s, though not in large numbers. In 1935, according to a survey conducted by the Detroit Housing Commission, there were 84 blacks living in the approximately forty-block area in between National (now Cochrane) and 14th, Vernor Highway and Myrtle.[37] In this zone as a whole there were 278 black residents in 1930, and their numbers continued to increase until 1960 when, like whites, blacks began pouring out of this area.[38] Bill, a black man in his seventies, moved into the area when he was a child; his mother brought him from "Black Bottom," the east-side slum, in 1940. He told me there was a smattering of blacks living across 14th Street who fit in with the diverse ethnic residents.[39]

> BILL: Ever since the war, this neighborhood was mixed. Always has been mixed. It was all kinds of people living here—Polacks, Jews, colored, whites, hillbillies . . . there was some good hillbillies around here. We could go downtown . . . we didn't have to lock no doors. You could go downtown, you could go anywhere you want. You didn't lock your door. You didn't have to do nothing. Your neighbors would watch for you.

A few whites who grew up in the area in the 1940s remembered black children as neighbors and playmates. Patrick and John—two white brothers who run one of the Irish bars still operating on a stretch of Grand River that forms the northern boundary of Briggs—named a string of black playmates they recalled from their childhood on Wabash and Pine. West of 14th Street, Patrick told me, "was all Irish in there . . . We had a gang of 'em." He reeled off family names and stories of the other Irish families. John, holding his hand level with the table top, told me that the neighborhood had been "integrated" since he was that tall.

But these accounts are at odds with the stories of Jennie Overton and

Howard King.[40] Their stories center on the intense racial hostility that their arrival provoked, shortly after the end of World War II. During the postwar period in Detroit, popular and political understanding of racial orders changed, making the presence of "new" blacks in this zone suddenly problematic. Between 1940 and 1950, Detroit's black population doubled (from 149,119 to 300,506), and the strictly preserved segregation of residential areas was strained to the breaking point. Blacks escaping from Detroit's east-side ghetto entered into direct competition for housing with whites, flush with the benefits of high-wage jobs but extremely anxious over how long the good times would last.

As full prosperity came to characterize Detroit following World War II, home ownership surged. The number of white, owner-occupied households rose from 161,812 in 1940 to 254,707 in 1950. But for many of these whites, their grasp on affluence was tenuous, since it was linked to the cycles of the auto industry. The numerous anxieties to which they were prone were largely addressed through the formation of home-owners' associations, which articulated their concerns by championing the cause of whiteness with a vengeance.[41] This huge mass of middle- and working-class whites became the dominant political force in the city, and neighborhoods were turned into fiercely contested racial terrains. According to Sugrue, 192 homeowners' associations were formed between 1943 and 1965; their explicit goals were to maintain racial "purity" of these neighborhoods. At times in conjunction with, but often at odds with these groups, real estate agents profitably manipulated the anxiety-ridden connection drawn by whites between shifts in racial composition of a neighborhood and the subsequent decline in property values.[42] Realtors became the most powerful private defenders of racial barriers in the city and, from this position, they adroitly developed "blockbusting" tactics that reaped huge profits for those who could panic whites into selling low, turn these properties around quickly, and sell high to black inmovers.[43]

The local dynamics of this turbulent period in Detroit's history were narrated to me by Howard King and Jennie Overton. Howard, a tall black man in his mid-forties, told me how his family was received when they arrived from Alabama in 1949. I spoke with him one morning where he worked, in the woodshop of an organization established to help inner-city kids. The group operated out of an old, ornately designed bank, with huge stone pillars in front and a large vault that now served as a storage area. Howard was the only Briggs resident involved with their programs; the rest of the staff were suburban whites. We talked about his childhood in the neighborhood, the time he served in the state penitentiary at

Jackson for second-degree murder, and how he got involved with various community projects after he was released. He described his family's arrival from Alabama as "an experience."

> HOWARD: My mother told me how my uncle used to have to stay up on the roof at night because they were putting wreaths on the door, and throwing dead rats up on the porch and saying, "nigger go home" and all this here and what not, and sending a hearse here . . . But there was a family, by the name of Self, a gentleman by the name of Mr. Self, and his kids, we raised up together . . . He stood by my family's side, and supported them and helped crush a lot of the racism that they encountered around that time. He was a respected individual.
>
> JH: How long did the hostility last?
>
> HOWARD: Close to a year, before things got settled down, but it was still pretty bad.
>
> JH: Did other black families start moving in?
>
> HOWARD: My other relatives started moving in, and then it was Hispanics . . . Mexicans and stuff started moving in on the block where we were staying.

Four blocks away, Mrs. Jennie Overton and her husband bought their house on Harrison in 1948 and were aggressively met with organized protests by whites. She still lives in the same house, but her husband has since passed on. When I visited her, she had me find a seat on top of the papers, sewing patterns, clothes, and other stuff piled along the sofa. Although the first of the cool autumn days had just started, her large heater in the middle of the living room, surrounded by the half-chewed-up tile floor, kept the room overly warm. Much of the furniture seemed to be from the era when she and her husband first moved in.

She had come up from Georgia in 1947. Her husband had been in the navy, and after being discharged he "started traveling around." He liked Detroit well enough, so he got a job in one of the car plants and moved Jennie north. In Georgia, he had held a "civil service job with the government," so they were able to buy this house right away. Pulling out one of her many picture albums, she showed me photographs of the two of them in several clubs in Los Angeles, where he was based for most of his service. She also talked about attending balls here in Detroit, and noted, "my people were always high class."

Her voice was labored and slow, but her recollections were sharp, except with names.

> MRS. OVERTON: We got with a real estate man, and he was going to let us have a house. So, we picked from different houses, and so finally my husband said that we would take this one. And what we didn't know . . . what nobody bothered to tell us . . . blacks had never been in this neighborhood at all. There

weren't no black people here. There were French, and Maltese, and some Jews, but there weren't no blacks in here. There were all different nationalities living in this packed-up place. We didn't know that there'd be arguments, or confusion, that they didn't want certain people in here. The real estate man didn't tell us. He was surprised too, and he'd been in the real estate business for years.

The biggest problem was caused by a minister who had a church around the corner. She was not sure what country he was from, but he was foreign-born. He fueled the protests by offering to find people housing if they would picket out in front of her place, a powerful lure at a time when the scarcity of available housing in Detroit was severe.

MRS. OVERTON: They had so many people out there, they were in droves, and they were from the corner down here.
JH: Did they throw anything at the house?
MRS. OVERTON: Oh yeah, they had busted out the glass and such. So finally we just went out on the porch. We figured, well, if they want to do something to us, they'd do it to us out there. That's what we did. They didn't throw no more then.

The protest lasted for three months. Their lawyers helped them arrange for a police escort that stayed until the protest was discontinued. A young labor activist with the United Auto Workers, Coleman Young, also provided his personal assistance and protection.

MRS. OVERTON: Coleman came right here that night they started to picket. It was a Saturday, and Coleman was here Saturday and he was here Sunday night. The assistant mayor was here too—all of them were here. I don't care that they might say something about him. They all get into it, all politicians . . . It's still impressive to me. I don't care what they say about Coleman now [as the city's mayor]—Coleman was here! Coleman was here . . . The first night he came here, you couldn't see out there. You didn't know what was Coleman and what wasn't Coleman, it was so many people. And some of them had on their white KKK suits. They had on them white suits. I don't know whether they were or not, but my brother said, "that's KKK" [laughing]. But they dressed up that way whether they was or not. They tried to intimidate us. And we went out there and said, "You can be a Klu and you can be a Klan, I ain't moving, and I don't know what you're going to do. You can stay out there and dress all day and all night, we still staying here." We just went to work every day. I was working in a private home for some real rich people; they still are; they still are real rich people.

She counted this point as a reaffirmation of her people being high class. She also described how they went out to balls on a regular basis, even during the protest. They also managed to entertain a lot of company. She

and her husband would get escorted in and out by the police when they
went to the balls.

> MRS. OVERTON: We'd be all dressed up for the ball . . . wearing kinky curls.
> We kept some high-class company. Well, what we call high-class. It'd be funny,
> cause I'd get all dressed up, and we'd go out, and the police would sit here and
> watch the house [laughs]. And I had a good time doing it. I didn't have to worry
> about some people would tear the place up, because the police was sitting up
> there in front. We'd get back and they'd make a path for us, walking us up to
> the door, made sure we got in all right. I didn't have a thing to worry about.
> After I found that out, I tried to find a reason to go out all the time.

When I talked to Howard, he insisted that his family had been the first
blacks in the neighborhood and that they endured sporadic insults and
garbage thrown at their house *because* they were the first blacks in the
neighborhood. But Mrs. Overton was indignant at his version of events,
which she had apparently heard before. The King family had moved in
the *next* year, she stressed to me.

> MRS. OVERTON: I remember the King family when they moved in, because
> my husband and my brother went up there to visit them. I never associated with
> them, and they never associated with us. But we knew when they moved in, the
> same lawyers for us, when they moved in, come and told us about them moving
> in. So that's when we knew they were moving in.

She went on to point out that "my people wasn't like them people up
there, them people you were talking about [the Kings]. I ain't gonna say
nothing about those people who said that they were here first. I could say
plenty, but it would all be no-good stuff, so I won't. But I know them kids
ain't that great. Look where they stand today—those boys. The women
were pretty nice, but the men folk weren't. And you can see how the kids
turned out—they pretty rough kids, and they just grew up rowdy too.
Them boys is something else." The class distinctions she stressed between
herself and the Kings suggest that they shared no common ground of
social groups or activities—a situation that heightened their different perceptions of conditions in the neighborhood.

Howard's and Mrs. Overton's stories demonstrate both the contingency of racial formations and the instability of their perceptual basis.
They were part of a demographic shift that transformed the local significance of race; white perceptions of blacks shifted in scale, from viewing
them individually to seeing them as representatives of a collective that
threatened their white racial identity. Blacks lived in the area prior to the
arrival of Howard and Mrs. Overton without being subjected to racialized assaults. But these two were part of a surging movement of blacks
out of slum areas on the east side of the city and up from the southern

states. Their arrival was also framed by the rapid investment in what proved to be a collapsing color line in Detroit's emerging "inner city."[44] Their stories point to the extremely local range of attention of residents in this area. Howard and Mrs. Overton could each be the "first blacks" in the neighborhood because they lived four blocks apart. Although this spatial difference hardly seems great today, at the time—in a much more densely populated period—it presented a social distance that was accentuated by the class divisions between the two families. Even though Howard knew Bill, neither he nor Mrs. Overton knew he lived there before either of them. Where he lived—on 14th Street, a half-dozen blocks away—was an entirely different social world, and none of the other black families that lived in this zone during the 1930s was known to either Howard or Mrs. Overton.

In a sense, what separated them all was whiteness. Howard and Mrs. Overton arrived in Detroit just as white homeowners were forming a powerful political interest group. The white backlash struck them so severely that it seemed they must be the first black inmovers. They were apparently the first blacks to be attacked by whites in this area for being black, because they moved in after property owners had decided to insist upon this area being a "white neighborhood." But white property owners' attempts to organize a defense of whiteness failed, largely because the requisite structural, spatial supports were not in place in this zone, which had not been designed with either class or racial segregation in mind. Also property owners found that their economic interests were not shared by the majority of whites in this zone, quite simply because so few whites owned property here.

Houses in Briggs range in size from the small "cottages" or "shotgun shacks," built and owned by workers in the last century, to grand Victorians and brick homes from the 1920s. A residue of the "walking city," Briggs retains the structural heterogeneity that reflected the variety of classes that lived here, from the working poor to the upwardly climbing middle class, but the residents were predominantly working class.[45] By 1910—as cities throughout the United States expanded with streetcar systems, which led to suburbanization—restrictive covenants were invented, a novel structural device that distinctly reconfigured urban space, inscribing class and racial homogeneity in most new housing developments. These covenants established that buyers of properties had to match the racial identity of the seller—white. In Detroit, properties in the older neighborhoods within the Grand Boulevard were generally not covered by these covenants, since they predated this racist legal innovation. As blacks began moving in greater concentrations into neighborhoods that had previously been overwhelmingly white, whites forming homeowner organizations in Detroit's oldest neighborhoods found the "racial characteristics" of their neighborhoods—an increasingly critical factor in determining the value of a property—impossible to maintain.

Briggs is part of a larger area claimed by the Property Owners' Association (POA), an organization established in 1945 that "pledged themselves, Individually and Collectively to maintain Property Values, Economic Stability, Racial Characteristics from all Adverse Influence."[46] The area, bounded by Buchanan Street, Grand River Avenue, Brooklyn Avenue, Michigan Avenue, and Maybury Grand, drew the attention of the Detroit Mayor's Interracial Committee (DMIC) because of ten racial incidents that occurred there from September 1945 to the following September. Although such incidents were not uncommon in Detroit at the time, the ten cases "represent[ed] the greatest concentration of incidents" in Detroit.[47] Agents for the DMIC were at a loss to pinpoint the cause of the incidents. They noted that "Colored families have lived intermingled with white families in many of the blocks in this sector of town for a number of years and there has been a general absence of significant racial tension."[48]

The incidents—which involved street demonstrations at particular properties and at the offices of real estate brokers involved in the property transactions, threats (direct and implied) made to prospective black buyers and to real estate agents, and in one case an arson attack against a property—showed clear signs of being organized by the POA. As the "Summary" of these incidents reported by the DMIC states, "Resistance of the type offered by the west side community does not just develop spontaneously. It has been apparent that some formal organization exists for the prevention of the transfer of property to Negroes."[49] The POA circulated a letter to a number of Detroit firms involved in real estate transactions in this area, threatening to resist "by every means at our command" efforts to "Introduce into a White Neighborhood Colored People thereby causing strife, Discord, and inharmony."[50] But by the time the POA tried to assert that the area was composed of "white neighborhoods," it was already too late, since black families had been making inroads over the previous two decades.[51]

The racial incidents over housing in this zone present an interesting case of how places come to be racially identified and contested. What observers at the time could not explain was why the influx of blacks had suddenly provoked such a harsh reaction among whites; neither was it apparent why the period of organized intolerance lasted for only a few years.[52] Blacks moving into the Briggs area after 1950 seem to have encountered few problems. Many whites remained in this neighborhood as blacks became a majority in the area and the city at large. Although such perplexities cannot be reduced solely to issues of class, economic interests clearly played a fundamental role here.

At the time, as it continues to be today, this area was largely made up of renters (83 percent of all residents in this zone in 1940), an indication of why the earlier-arriving blacks drew no organized protests.[53] The vast majority of ostensibly white people in this zone did not have the kind of financial interests at stake that drove homeowners to insist that the area constituted a "white neighborhood." Whiteness, as experienced and expressed by these homeowners, was imbricated with economic interests; in this mode of articulation, it did not extend an interpretive basis for the majority of whites in this zone to recognize themselves. As the protests organized by white property owners dwindled, white renters continued to live in this zone, long after its identity as a "white neighborhood" collapsed.

Were the interests of the Property Owners' Association representative of those of other whites in this zone? As noted in the records of the DMIC, the protests in this area showed signs of a high degree of organization. Observers for the DMIC noted that the owners had means for motivating whites to participate in these protests, as evidenced by the minister who organized protests around Jennie Overton's house. Whatever the depth and breadth of support for the POA, there is one clear indication that the protests did not draw on a raw, broad core of racial animosity in the area. Over the peak period of protest, the years 1945 and 1946, the Detroit Street Railway tabulated the number of "racial incidents" on their various streetcar and coach lines. On the 14th Street line, which crossed the center of this zone, there were no such incidents on the coach and only one on the streetcar line.[54] Since riding on these lines involved the most intimate and—in the years preceding the riot of 1943—the most volatile forms of interracial contact, it is probably fair to assume that many whites in this zone were uninterested in the assertion of white identity that was being promoted by the POA.

The dynamics of the POA's protests are clearly more complicated than available materials adequately document. DMIC agents provided case studies of each of the ten incidents, offering a glimpse of the dense racial politics involved with the organization of protests to resist black in-movers. In an incident on Sycamore, a few blocks from where I lived during the course of my fieldwork, two apartments in a four-family unit were rented to three black men. Their attempts to move in were met by street protests; they eventually gave up and moved elsewhere. The DMIC agent involved with the case, Thomas Kleene, pointed to the landlord's ulterior economic motives in renting to these black men:

> It seems evident that the transaction by which the apartments were rented to Negroes was an attempt to force the white residents of the other two flats to vacate. KUNKLE [of the Olympia Realty Company] has reportedly stated that the white occupants are not desirable tenants, and that he is anxious to get rid

of them. The tenants, on the other hand, claim that the reason for KUNKLE'S attitude is their insistence that certain repairs and improvements be made on the property. It is claimed that after numerous unsuccessful attempts to force the owners to make the necessary changes, the matter was taken to the OPA [Office of Price Administration] which ordered a reduction in the rent.[55]

In this case, the presence of "undesirable" whites—perhaps "hillbillies," but certainly of a lower class than other white residents—constitutes the motive of a landlord to manipulate racial anxieties.[56] The landlord used potential black renters to police the "quality" of white residents.

Realtors dealing with property in the area were taken by surprise by the threats and acts of vandalism that accompanied protests of property exchanges. Pickets were formed not only at the properties in question, but also at the owners' homes and at the offices of the real estate companies. Anonymous threats were also made to the real estate agents, who in some instances received as many as one hundred threatening telephone calls. The confusion confronting realtors and members of the DMIC is related in another report by Kleene, concerning a black family that bought a house on Vermont but moved out and canceled the deal after their house was attacked and damaged by a mob:

> The fact that there was so much opposition to Negro occupancy of the house at 2722 Vermont Ave. came as a considerable surprise to GLADING [real estate agent]. This individual stated that he made inquiries in the neighborhood before the sale, and that he was informed that there were a number of Negro families already living in the vicinity. He was at a loss to explain this apparent inconsistency, although he agreed with the suggestion that perhaps the resistance was founded on the fear of present inhabitants that the addition of more colored residents would ultimately lead to the immigration of a large number of lower class negroes.[57]

These two incidents convey the interplay of class anxieties and racial confusions at work in the transformations of this neighborhood. The racial transition was accompanied by a change in the class "character" of the area, as is frequently the case. The visage of the class threat was difficult to fix, however, since it clearly blurred racial identities and boundaries. It manifests clearly in one particular form in the efforts of "respectable" homeowners to distance themselves from indecorous, overtly racist, acts being perpetrated in defense of propertied interests. Here, the figure of the "hillbilly" surfaces in relation to these battles.

As with the blame for the neighborhood's deterioration—and, as will be seen in the next section, with the reaction of whites to street violence committed during the riot of 1943—"hillbillies" were a reliable means of locating and limiting the extent of whites' engagement with racial violence. The vituperative figuring of "hillbillies" illustrates an enduring

connection between whiteness and forms of social decorum. The most
extreme instance of violence in the period 1945–1946 involved an arson
attack on a 17th Street house purchased by a black couple, Omega and
Rohabena Nelson, in September 1945. The fire only partially damaged
the house, and while repairs were under way the couple stayed at her
mother's home on 24th Street. While they were there, Irene Valentine, a
white woman who owned a house at 1362 Perry Street, offered to buy
their now vacant property for $2,500 or to trade title to a rooming house
on Charlotte Avenue owned by Mrs. Valentine. Kleene reported, based
on the information of Samuel Gibbons of the Watson Realty Company
who was present at this meeting, that "when the colored family indicated that they probably would not accept either of the Valentine offers,
Mrs. Valentine is supposed to have made a remark to the effect that,
'Your neighbors did not burn your house the first time, but if you try to
rebuild they will do a better job next time.' "[58]

Kleene took note of a strange decorum by which any demonstration of
obvious racism was elaborately avoided by Mrs. Valentine, in a mode
that seemed to be consistent with that of POA members concerned about
the legal implications of their actions. Kleene related that the offer and
threat were both made

> in a business-like fashion without display of prejudice or animosity. None of
> the colored people in attendance showed any enthusiasm for the proposed
> transfer, and it was then that Mrs. Valentine made the threatening remark as
> quoted. It is to be noted that she made no reference to any individuals or to
> anything she might do herself, but only to neighbors in general. When [Mr.]
> Valentine entered, he made a number of remarks, probably insincere, in the
> opinion of the informant, about the original burning of the 17th Street house,
> and *he attempted to lay the blame on several groups, first the "hillbillies" and
> second "the Jews."* The latter accusation reportedly provoked his wife, who is
> believed by the informant to be a Jew.[59]

This exchange indicates an early usage of "hillbilly" to distance *proper*
whites from direct connection with overt acts of racist violence, a form
of displacement that whites continue to follow today by believing that
racism is concentrated in the "lower classes."[60] "Hillbillies" were soon to
be widely regarded by native white Detroiters as responsible for the racial
violence in the 1943 riot. Foreshadowing this class-coded displacement,
in this incident of conflict over the residential color line "hillbillies" were
invoked as a scapegoat for the actions and interests of property-owning
whites.[61]

Again, it is important to recognize how the arrival of southern whites
and blacks in Detroit during the 1940s and 1950s disrupted naturalized
conventions of white racial identity. Not only were the decorums of race
ruptured, the surety of class divisions were also called into question as the

huge core of Detroit's inner city began to emerge as a sprawling, untenable zone of poverty. Poor whites were a disturbing problem for respectable white Detroiters. Additionally, the viable medium for expressing an interest in and the achievement of upward mobility—home ownership—proved to be an emotionally laden, tenuous option.[62] In this part of Detroit, the coherence of race and class differences was destabilized as the residential structures charged with organizing them proved insufficient; they failed to reinforce the privileged remove that, in the nation as a whole, corresponded with whiteness. In all of these drastic changes, it was easy for white Detroiters to respond to racial and class threats simultaneously, in one complicated expression of social contempt—"hillbilly." What this expression reflects is an interesting moment when regional identities achieved a certain salience in relation to reconfigurations of the color line. By way of illustration, I turn to stories from a native white Detroiter who recalls this muddled time.

Laura was born in 1923 on a ferry crossing the river from Canada. Since she was born across midstream, heading toward the United States, she was declared an American. Her American grandmother sold one of the last farms to be developed into blocks of houses along Grand River. I gradually got to know Laura at O'Leary's bar, where she is a regular. She agreed to talk to me about the history of the neighborhood in exchange for washing her dog.

After bathing the dog, I had to remind her I was interested in the history of the neighborhood. She proudly exclaimed, "Then you must want to know about Standard Beef! They were right over there, behind us. We were right behind the killing floor. That was when the Western Market was still here [it was demolished in the construction of Interstate 96]. They butchered the cattle right in back of us. My husband always had a lot of whiskey and beer in the house. The men doing the butchering would come over on their breaks and get a nip. They'd bring me all kinds of meat: hearts, tongue, liver, and I'd cook 'em up. They'd have some to eat, and the rest would be for us."

The trucks would come in and the cattle would file out into the yard, waiting to be butchered behind their house. She recalled the surge of activity, the large meals, scouring the vegetable stands once they closed for any decent produce that was left behind, and, of course, the great bouts of drinking. The local bars are the core of most of her stories; they dominated the social and physical landscape. Most of the bars were Irish in the early days. "There were so many of them, you could walk out of one and stumble into another." Her first job was vending ice and coal from her wood-wheeled truck. Her route included most of the bars and the inside of almost everybody's home. She marks "history" by the advent of the refrigerator and the mass marketing of gas heat, which combined to put her out of work for the first time. For Laura, "the refrigerator changed everything."

She supported her young daughter by working in the war plants in the 1940s. "Uncle Sam taught me how to weld. They wanted me to go to work in one of the east-coast shipyards, but my mother wouldn't let me go." After the war, she took up painting. "I got a couple of ladders, and hired a guy to help me. I set him to plastering and I did the painting. That worked good, I stayed busy. Then I got up on McGraw, where it's all colored. I couldn't ever get off McGraw either [laughing], they all had jobs for me. The homes over there were beautiful."

When she found work again as a welder it was when the freeways eviscerated the inner-city neighborhoods of Detroit. She worked at repairing tools the construction crews would break and hauling out the scrap they left in their wake. Sewer pipes were her main haul, old wooden pipes that she would drive down and dump into the river where the construction refuse was unloaded.

> LAURA: I didn't think I could do it, I really didn't. But my boss had faith in me; he kept telling me I could do it. He had seen me handle a boom truck before. So I had to back this big rig right up to the river, right up to the edge there. I was scared I was going to go backwards right into the river. I never did though.

On life in Detroit:

> It all changed in the '40s. That was when all the southerns started coming in here looking for work. They were everywhere. They started coming up from the South, and they kept coming. Then we had that rebellion, you know about that. It was the South and the North fighting. And they fought it out right here on 12th Street; they went at it for days. They brought in the militia, and the northerners won. The North settled down, and then the South began to come in here. Now it's more of the South in here than anything.

Her story confused me at first; I lost the cultural bearings that went with "southern." The term collapsed the distinction I relied upon in sorting out the different experiences of white and black migrants to the city. And what rebellion? When she mentioned 12th Street and the "militia," though, her version became clearer; 12th Street was the backbone of the 1967 riot. It dawned on me that she was invoking a regional perspective that intriguingly ignored a racial reading of the riot in 1967. The riot, for her, marked the culmination of two decades of white *and* black southern migration in the city, which forever transformed the neighborhood.

> JH: What happened after that?
> LAURA: Well, you had northern people acting like they [the southerners] were invading their territory; they were up in arms, and they fought each other.

But now they shake hands. Now they get along like brother and sister. But there are more southerners here now than there is anything else. That's because the northerners just went further north. That's where they are now, up north! In Houghton Lake, up by the Soo, and all them places.

The story I expected to hear was about "white flight," how whites had left the city after the fearsome three-day uprising. But from her perspective, four blocks from 12th Street, the conflict had more to do with regional orders and their changing balance than it had to do with race. Laura described going on vacation up north, to the places she named, and running into old neighbors who had left Detroit after 1967. One couple owned a restaurant and bar, and another ran some rental resort cabins. They reminisced about "old times," and she was sorry they had moved: "they were my friends you know." But their leaving was not abstracted by her as "white flight." Whites, after all, had been leaving the neighborhood since the 1930s, and by the 1960s blacks, too, were pouring out of this zone. She is part of a core of whites that did not leave this part of Detroit behind.

> JH: What about you? Did you ever think of leaving?
> LAURA: No! Never. I always tell everybody this is my home. When I finally leave this life, I won't go from here. I love this place. It's my home.

From her window I saw the looming green exit sign that offers drivers the choice of going north on I-96 to Lansing, or going south on I-75 to Toledo. She asked me to excuse the mess—she was trying to housebreak her new puppy. Papers were scattered on the pantry floor and in the kitchen, some were urine-soaked. The last year, she said, had been the hardest on her. "I used to be able to climb all over these walls. But now, with that damned arthritis I can't do nothing. I'm losing my wind too, can't breathe." She complained about her last trip to the doctor. "They always ask you, 'Do you smoke? Do you smoke?' They never ask you, 'Did you work in a factory? Were you ever a welder?' What do they know anyways?" The smell of the coke ovens wafting from downriver made me wonder if they ever ask, "Do you live in an industrial area?"

Riots and Race

Two riots fall within residents' memories, the first in 1943, the second in 1967. Both are nationally recognized as "race riots," and each was temporally framed by other violent urban disorders. Yet white and black residents in this zone consistently referred only to the riot of 1943 as a racial conflict. Although Laura's version of 1967 was the only strictly "regional" interpretation I heard, people stressed to me in their narratives that this particular battle waged during the internal war of the Great Society was not a racial conflict, at least not locally.[63] Since the riot of 1967 is a key event in the "white flight" narrative, it is surprising that whites in Briggs felt little sense of threat during the days of burning, looting, and the subsequent violent suppression of such activities by the police and National Guard. Whites have for long been terrified by images of armed black insurrection, and this was certainly the general response of whites to the riots of the late 1960s. What differentiated the local interpretations and perceptions of this event from those of the majority of whites in Detroit and across the nation?

As anthropologists Beth Roy and Ted Swedenberg demonstrate so well, accounts of riots are an intriguing (though never transparent) means for grasping the process of identity constitution across problematic shifts in scale from local to regional or national collectives.[64] The views of the 1967 riot held by whites in Briggs suggest that "whiteness" is not a simple attribute that they share with whites in other parts of the city and country. If a sense of whiteness-made-vulnerable impelled most whites to leave Detroit because of the riots, the following commonly shared interpretations of these events suggest that the cultural construction of whiteness unevenly and disjointedly incorporates "whites."[65]

Between the two riots, the contours and contents of whiteness in Detroit were drastically altered, as was the city and the material structures by which social stratification was spatially maintained. In 1943, the line between white and black, although gradually eroding, was still quite distinct and was ratified residentially, occupationally, and in terms of physical health. There was a "white slum" on the west side (the area including Briggs), a "black slum" on the east side, and by every measure the black slum was a more miserable place to live.[66] In 1967, however, the two slums had merged, forming an "inner city" that was then leaping across its boundaries, spreading "blight," crime, and racial integration through the rest of Detroit.[67] As collective entities, whiteness and blackness began to lose the strict residential reinforcements that made their earlier differentiation in Detroit emphatic. Whiteness was strategically repositioned or reconstituted in the city's outlying neighborhoods and (primarily) the suburbs, through the development of an economic infrastructure— FHA and VA mortgages, federal subsidies for freeway construction, water supplies and sewage facilities for racially exclusive communities, and so on; inner-city zones were debarred from these forms of investment by red-lining practices in neighborhoods that were racially mixed or economically heterogeneous.[68] As a mode of communal organization, privileging racial commonalties over all other modes of differentiation, by 1967 whiteness had become untenable in Detroit's core. White residents' narratives of the riots of 1943 and 1967 demonstrate the extent to which the contours and experience of whiteness were radically transformed in the intervening twenty-four years. This transformation derived from the intertwined mutation of urban spaces and cultural orders.[69]

Racial identity in Detroit, prior to World War II, was partly predicated upon a seamless equation between fairly homogeneous spatial zones and the projection of essentialized, collective orders ("whites" and "blacks"). As neighborhoods in the city's core became racially mixed, people were left to assess the significance of race without relying on the redundancy between their self-image and the homogeneity of the spatial areas in which they resided. The significance of race was increasingly considered in discontinuous encounters and through the disjointed circulation of rumors, conversations, and stories. The perceptual and interpretive basis of "racial" was reconstituted for whites who remained in the inner city of Detroit.[70]

The primary basis for this reconstitution in Briggs involved the rapid integration of the neighborhood. Between 1950 and 1960, the census tract where Margaret (see "Disgrace to the Race") and Laura (see "The Color Line") lived went from 6 percent to 33 percent black. By 1960, the tract directly north of them was the first in this zone to become more than 50 percent black. In the area as a whole, blacks were 30 percent of the population in 1960.[71] This degree of integration surely drove some whites away, but those who remained did not find themselves uniformly racialized by the conflagration that shook Detroit in July of 1967. Until the 1992 riot in Los Angeles, this riot stood as the nation's worst: 43 people killed, 7,231 arrested, and over 1,700 stores and businesses looted. A combined force of 17,000 men from the Detroit Police Department, the Michigan State Police, the National Guard, and troops from the United States Army were deployed to quell the looting and burning. The riot was sparked by a police raid of a blind pig (an after-hours drinking establishment) on 12th Street, in a neighborhood that, although more affluent than the Briggs area, was suffering from increased incidence of crime and greater concentrations of poverty following the influx of residents dislocated by urban renewal demolitions in Detroit's core black neighborhoods, Hastings Street and Paradise Valley.[72]

I asked Margaret about the riot one afternoon while she was showing me pictures from her photo album. The pictures were of friends now dead or gone, but she brought them out mainly to show me all the houses crowded in the backgrounds. She proudly pointed out that there was a house on every lot up and down the street, where now waist-high grass stretches. Then we talked about the riot. Margaret said, "There was looting and burning, but we were all right. We'd sit out in the yard and drink our beer. Shorty [a white friend] went over and raided the A&P up on

Myrtle [she laughs]. He wanted Laura and Dave and I to go along . . . We said no." Instead, they had a party in her yard with beer that Laura got from a relative who ran a tavern.

> MARGARET: We just sat out with our beer, nothing bothered us. See, this wasn't really a riot. The real riot was in '43. That was a race riot. That was over on Belle Isle . . . We had the troops in, the national guard. They patrolled all of the streets. My mother worked cleaning offices in a building downtown, and she had to stay there until it was over. She was there for two nights. They were turning over streetcars and everything. There was a lot of fighting in the street and everything.

At the time, they were living on Roosevelt Street, about twelve blocks northwest of the house she lives in now. She recalled the racial stakes in that riot and the tension in her neighborhood, where a couple of black families were living. "The woman who lived across the street, her children were colored, y'know. So we kept 'em inside the house, y'know, so they'd be safe. Until everything cooled down . . . We always had good neighborhoods . . . until now. God, I'm really surprised it's turned this way." There were no violent incidents in that neighborhood, nor were any recorded in this area, where a number of blacks were living at the time. Margaret was the first person I questioned about the riot in 1967 in a formal interview, and the distinction she made between it and the riot in 1943 caught me by surprise. But as I asked other residents, white and black, who lived through the earlier conflict, this contrast held.

Shotgun is a black Cherokee from North Carolina, living now on 18th Street. He came to Detroit in the late 1930s, "running from the law." His first home was in Delray, a village settled largely by Hungarians, which was annexed by Detroit in 1905, making it a mill town within a metropolis.

> SHOTGUN: I stayed there until they had the Mayor Jeffries race riot [1943]. And I went to school right there at the Canada bridge, to learn how to talk. When I come here I couldn't talk.
>
> JH: You couldn't talk English?
>
> SHOTGUN: Oh, I had one store, a man would sell to me, he was on Waterman and Jefferson. And he could understand me enough to let me have eggs, milk, butter, and Karo syrup. That's all I'd eat. When they had the race riot, they broke that school up.
>
> JH: Which riot was that?
>
> SHOTGUN: The Jeffries riot. Mayor Jeffries . . . I was in the receiving hospital when that riot broke out. And I come home, and I went back to Delray. And I walked all the way from downtown down Fort Street. And all the streetcars

had all the glass knocked out of 'em and all. I walked all the way to Delray. I just took my time and watched myself, but didn't nobody bother me. The fighting was back down here over on Woodward and Hastings. That's where the fighting was, that time. The fighting didn't reach to 12th Street that time.

JH: Was that white and black fighting?

SHOTGUN: Yeah. They's throwing rocks, and breaking windows in cars and Ben Turpin was in the police and he shot a couple of fellas, and they brought 'em in the hospital. I was standing up there, and I saw so much blood it give me the shakes. They moved me in the south ward, to make room for all the wounded coming in.

We were sitting out in front of his place, while he rested from cutting up the old logs and used tires he uses for heat in the winter. Both the electricity and the gas have been off in his place for about three years. His black cowboy hat rested high on his head, and a country music station played on the portable radio sitting up on his porch.

JH: What was the '67 riot like?

SHOTGUN: They wasn't doing nothing but burning up and started stealing. That's all the colored people were doing. Burning up and stealing. They were stealing first, then they burned it up when they got through.

He was bitter about the stores being burned, especially the A&P. "That was nice for us to have, but they broke in it and stole everything there was out of it but three jars of pickles. And then set it on fire. White people, too. White people burned up the pawn shop on Warren." Like all the other residents I spoke with about events of 1967, he stressed that both whites and blacks participated in looting and burning, thus sidestepping a "racial" reading.

Two local aspects of the riot in 1967 stand out in residents' narratives that undermine racial characterizations of this event: both whites and blacks participated in the rampage, and neither group violently racialized the other. As Margaret and Shotgun noted, whites and blacks both looted or "raided" stores and businesses. Televised accounts of the riots focused on the vast majority of the rioters, who were black. Whites across the city and the nation, riveted to their TV screens, were emotionally steeped in a sense of racial vulnerability, interpolating themselves as potential victims of a portended all-out race war. But white residents who watched the riot unfold on their streets instead of on their televisions recognized friends and neighbors of both races rampaging. Those old enough to recall what a "race riot" looked and felt like did not see the same event developing. Unlike in 1943, this time neither whites nor blacks in this zone were objects of communal racial animosity or violence. There is little evidence of white or black Detroiters targeting each other racially, and this zone was no exception; white residents I spoke with did not recall a sense of being threatened as whites.

The 1943 riot, by all informed accounts, was a race riot. Whites and blacks fought each other over challenges to, and reassertions of, the color line in Detroit. Opposed racial interests were expressed emphatically and violently in community-oriented attacks and counterattacks. As historians Dominic Capeci Jr. and Martha Wilkerson describe it, "the activities of rioters bore a decidedly racial and interracial character. Race more than any other factor underscores the most frequent, most intense physical violence in this and earlier riots. Living amidst wartime uncertainty, and competition over class, power, and the color line, they fought as racial entities for racial ends."[73] Whites and blacks responded to and participated in the violence of 1943 as distinct communities, insisting on blunt, visceral differences in a city where the spatial orders for maintaining hierarchies of social differentiation were proving obsolete. Although the Briggs area was distant from the fighting in 1943 (which was concentrated downtown and in the east-side, black community), both whites and blacks clearly recalled what was at stake in those clashes. Even though none of the residents that I spoke with was directly involved, they all recognized that racial identity was prioritized: victims were targeted by attackers responding to a host of recent and past racial affronts to their social collective. In 1967, this was not the case.

Wanita (white) and Bill (black) (see "The Color Line") are long-time residents. She moved here as a child in 1924 when her parents sold their farm in a nearby township after the barn burned. He came from "Black Bottom" with his mother in 1940 and settled over on 15th Street. They now share Wanita's house, a 125-year-old structure on Temple, a street that had a DSR streetcar line running down its center. She enjoyed describing how self-sufficient the area was, with its many businesses from a variety of stores to the foundry that operated day and night across the street; only the abandoned shell of the foundry remains, an ominous, empty hulk.

> WANITA: We had it beautiful until the riots. That's when they burned us out.
> JH: What were they like?
> WANITA: Well, I heard this baloney about everybody being afraid, and that it was colored and white. NO way, NO way! They just wanted to go ahead and get in the places and steal. They waited on the corners, and I mean white and colored. I watched them. I lost a complete friend from finding out she walked in and took stuff out of the market. I don't believe in stealing. And she went in

Figure 5. Bill and Wanita

there, and she come home with baskets and baskets [whispers] of groceries. And then they messed up the market. And the dime store, they burned that up. I mean, that's what really ruined the neighborhood to start with.[74]

Bill recalled hardware stores and pool halls on Myrtle that were burned in the riot. Wanita again described the looting and how a music store was cleaned out of all its instruments. She re-emphasized that the riot was not a racial conflict.

WANITA: There wasn't them riots, black and white. They just wanted to come in and loot. The people wasn't fighting with each other. To me, they were burning things so they could get things. And what they've done, and just like they're doing out in California [referring to the Los Angeles riot in 1992]. What they've done is they've only hurt themselves.

BILL: They tore up Ned's, he was a friend of mine, they tore up his store on Wood and Glencourt. That was big Ned's.

WANITA: YOU should've seen them. They were carrying drums down the street . . . If they could've carried the piano, I think they would've took it too. And, to me, the people all got along all right. It wasn't the people. It was just some of them wanted things. I get so tired when I hear that . . . that it was a riot on account of colored and white. It was not.

BILL: It wasn't nothing to do with colored and white. Hell, colored have always lived over here. This always been a mixed neighborhood, as long as I can remember.

Several whites I spoke with, all men, recalled looting or "raiding" area stores. They fearlessly participated in what seemed, at first, to be a carnivalesque event.[75] Their participation in the riot marked a keen divide between themselves and their more respectable white neighbors like Wanita. Not surprisingly, it seems "hillbillies" like Floyd (see the "Introduction") were a sizable proportion of the whites that "raided." He, too, emphasized the biracial aspect of the riot. "We were out here on Trumbull. We just went into the store, got some wine and some whiskey. Then I went to another store and got me some new shoes, and I got a coat out of another store. Just like that, just walked in and got 'em. It was both white and black getting stuff out of the stores. There was no difference at all. We were just all getting anything or whatever we wanted. Then I went home and got really drunk."

These days Floyd is quick to suspect blacks of "looking for trouble," especially when he is alone on the street late at night. He relates this suspicion to his experiences of being mugged by black men. But in the riot, he noted, "there was no difference at all." He made no mention of arming himself for protection, as he does now. Nor, for that matter, did I hear other whites tell of taking any precautions that involved weapons, though there was, and still remains, plenty of firepower in homes in this zone.

It was easier for me to find blacks who felt threatened in the riot, since they were targeted by the police and National Guard forces charged with restoring order. Mrs. Overton's recollections of the 1967 riot were succinct. "It was rough and quiet—just that, rough and quiet. We just stayed here at home. We didn't get out there where they were all stealing and breaking in. We didn't have no trouble here." When I asked Howard what the riot was like, he replied, "Dangerous! . . . It was an experience. I didn't really participate because I had real strict parents and an uncle that I really had a lot of fear of . . . that didn't play that . . . But a lot of the business owners, they're the ones who set their own property on fire."

JH: I've been hearing that from people.

HOWARD: It's the truth. That's right. Cutting their losses and getting out. And even though a lot of stupid people did burn down some of these stores, but uhh a lot of like big businesses . . . used to be a guitar and drum shop, a really big place over there. I hear they torched their own building. Really, I wouldn't say that the riot that was here, in '67, was people fighting each other. It wasn't like that. It was looting and tearing up.

JH: So were whites and blacks fighting each other?

HOWARD: No, not around here. 'Cause we had bonded. 'Cause when I was coming up, it was a real good friend of mine, he was a white, a young man by the name of Ron Ashley. He and his family was from Canada. We was like brothers—we fought together and we ate together. It was a bond between us. I really didn't know what racism was until I started gong to public school. You know, I encountered it as a young child, but I really learned what it was when I started going to public school.[76]

The interracial friendship patterns Howard relates are a primary basis for undercutting strictly "racial" readings of events in 1967, especially given the sharp contrast between social relations in this neighborhood and those Howard experienced in Detroit's public institutions in the 1960s. Whatever acts of racial conflict he encountered as a young child, Howard felt they dimmed in comparison with the systematic violence of diminished expectations inscribed upon him by his white teachers in the public school system.

The only white I spoke with who recalled a sense of unease about being white in this zone during the riot of 1967 was Pat, a woman who lived only three blocks from the worst of the fires in this zone.[77] She works as a volunteer in the huge Trinity Episcopal Church on the three-way corner of Grand River, Trumbull, and Martin Luther King Jr. When we talked, she was in the midst of preparations for the church's weekly soup kitchen. In 1967 she was living on Elm and Cochrane; "scary!" was all she first said when I asked her what the riots were like. She went on to elaborate:

Like I said, I lived on Elm and Cochrane. And . . . across the street, right across the street. That whole corner [pointing to Grand River and Trumbull] was a dime store, and a doctor's office, an ice cream parlor, a Chinese restaurant, and a little boutique. That's just right where the gas station is, or was . . . That whole thing . . . I mean there was all kinds of other stores on up the streets, but just right there . . . all that. And uh . . . I saw the fire, and I could see the fire from my house, and I thought it was the church; I just knew the church was burning, but it wasn't . . . it was right across the street. Uhh . . . It completely destroyed all that, took all that out . . . Down the street where there is a store now, University Market. There was an A&P there, and across the street on the other side there was a little department store, like, and a drug store . . . those were completely burnt down. And, the thing is . . . the people who set A&P on fire . . . was a white person who lived right next door to me. They caught him! They found out and he got locked up . . . He was taking advantage of the situation. And the store right across the street . . . the market . . . that covered the whole block . . . it was a big store that housed a hairdresser, a bakery, and a fish market . . . a shoe maker . . . It didn't get burnt, it wasn't set on fire . . . but it did get broken into . . . And I watched people go by my house with big shopping carts full of meat. I mean slabs of bacon hanging off of the side . . . and I'm sitting there saying, "All I need is some bread," but I would not go stealing . . . But it was really scary. And you sit there at night with all of the lights off, not knowing if somebody was going to come in. But . . . uh because there were some blacks living among us, there just wasn't any problems between us.

JH: So you didn't feel vulnerable because you were white?

PAT: Well . . . I did a little bit, because I didn't know who might be coming from some other area . . . I didn't know that . . . so there was some fear. And there were guns . . . like sitting around in people's doorways. Across the street from me, they had a rifle sitting there. And they went somewhere . . . they weren't supposed to be out at night, but they went somewhere, and left the rifle just sitting there in their doorway. Boy was that pretty dumb, anybody could have gotten it. And my husband at that time was working at the Krogers on the Boulevard, kind of near Ford Hospital . . . and it was burnt down. The only thing left was the safe sitting there. When they finally said, "Okay, you can leave your homes today. For so many hours you can go out if you need something at the store." I did go to the store to get some bread and some other things . . . And ah, walking down Trumbull with a tank going by you, it reminded you of being in a war movie. You'd seen all of these movies where . . . peasents are walking next to tanks—and that's what I felt like, y'know. I'm walking down the street, and here's this tank going down the street! It was scary!

Although Pat was the only white resident I spoke with who felt unnerved by the possibility of racial violence, she too stressed that the conflict was not "racial." Her concern with being white involved only the possibility that blacks from other parts of the city, who might be racially motivated, would come into the area. That did not happen. She did recognize a danger in the occupation forces that rolled down Trumbull with their tanks to restore order. That display of force unnerved her more than the riot's chaos.

Like Wanita, Pat drew a distinction between whites who participated in the riot and those, like herself, who resisted the temptations. This contrast turns on a matter of status distinction. Both women emphasized the role of whites in the looting and the general biracial order of the event, but neither laid any stress on the race of the particular people they noted for "stealing." Wanita's "complete friend" and the people Pat watched going by "with big shopping carts full of meat" are differentiated because they looted. A keen sense of moral status difference is deployed in an etiquette linked to class differences derived, I suspect, from an intraracial attention to behaviors and attitudes. Race is not absent in their readings;

rather it remains in a passive, momentarily insignificant, mode in relation to class/moral distinctions that interest them more. The significance of whites emphasizing that whites participated in the looting and burning in 1967 becomes more apparent when contrasted with the response of white Detroiters to the riot in 1943. Although whites broadly and violently engaged in racial conflicts on the streets in 1943, press accounts and subsequent official city investigations strove to distance "proper" whites from any connection to the rioters. Again, this involved scapegoating the "hillbilly."

Capeci and Wilkerson demonstrate that despite much evidence to the contrary, "the [popular] image of rioters remained one of black ruffians and . . . white newcomers. Hooligans and bums, said news columnist Kelsey, 'ignorant Negroes and southern whites,' remarked the east-side mayor, evoking images that news photos and, for black participants, official studies would verify. Yet, public beliefs and formal surveys aside, those in the crowd possessed more than criminal faces and few migrant ones. Hoodlums and hillbillies made for easy scapegoats and sensational press, but they hardly reflected the reality of who rioted."[78] This projection of "hillbillies" as rioters masked the character of white participants, who were predominantly northern-born, long-time Detroiters. It was easier for these whites to believe that only lower-class southern whites engaged in such heinous acts, rupturing the public white decorum in Detroit by participating in unruly street violence.[79] Although whiteness was the object of defense, and the basis from which white rioters derived their righteous sense of rage, it was apparently easily compromised or corrupted through an open, public admission of association with indecorous, obviously racialized violence.[80] The figure of the "hillbilly" was deployed to shroud the extent of white involvement in these riotous acts and to set their unseemly behavior apart from the normative realm of whiteness. Interestingly, although white residents in Briggs were prepared to blame "hillbillies" for the area's demise in the 1940s, there was no similar effort or interest in confining the designation of white "looters" or "raiders" to a similar collective in 1967. Instead, their narratives addressed a different set of concerns; they articulated a counter-discourse to the phenomenon of "white flight."

Whites poured from Detroit's deteriorating inner-city neighborhoods for a range of reasons, starting as early as the 1940s. Whites demonstrating their upward mobility by moving to the suburbs were propelled by a tangle of motives; in addition to racial integration, there was the increasing concentration of poor whites in areas like Briggs, as well as the yawning crevasse between media images of "the good life" and the mishmash of residential circumstances in the inner city. But racial concerns alone stand out when this demographic shift is linked with the riot of 1967. It is partly to counter this singular attention to race—and the linked assumption that interracial fighting prevailed throughout the city—that whites in Briggs express the conviction that the riot in 1967 was not a racial conflict.

I was tempted to consider these whites' insistence on this matter as a demarcation of their remove from the normative institutions and social practices of whiteness—as primarily an example of their distance from the class and racial norms of belonging in America. But such a reading obliterates the interesting commonalities between white and black characterizations of the violence in 1967.

The narratives related here operate as instances of what Kathleen Stewart refers to as "backtalk," a form of counter-discourse oriented toward a hegemonic reading of events.[81] White and black residents reject racial readings of the riot in a related manner. In each case, they undercut the way racial versions of events in 1967 are developed into political narratives. Shotgun, Bill, and Howard each undercut readings that valorize the actions of blacks on the streets of Detroit in 1967 as expressly political in nature—"They wasn't doing nothing but burning up and started stealing"; "It wasn't nothing to do with colored and white"; "It wasn't like that. It was looting and tearing up." They did not characterize the local actions of black rioters as expressions of collective racial interests—either in the defense of an assailed and threatened community or in conjunction with a nationwide uprising of a subordinated people. They regard the actions of looters as self-interested and shortsighted.[82] Bill, in particular, expressed remorse over his friend whose business was ruined, and each man lamented the irreparable losses to the neighborhood. Although there are certainly reasons to see in this riot politicized acts that provoked a shift nationally into our tumultuous "post–civil-rights" era, their accounts undercut such readings by emphasizing the negative local effects.

The accounts of whites and blacks commonly counter interpretations that essentialize race or that mobilize a politicized view of race as a contest between two absolute collectives, one dominant and the other subordinate. When residents of Briggs undermine racial readings of 1967, they assert a local view of things, in which the meanings of race are not very clear cut. Whites backtalk the historical narrative that too simply assumes that whites entirely left the inner city; they also implicitly counter the claims of suburban whites who posit the riot as a justification for abandoning Detroit. Of course, local whites' rejection of racial versions of the riot seem to mimic the general tendency of whites to *refuse* to see race at work in manifest forms of social inequality in the United States. Their interpretations do overlook the racist aspects of the incident that sparked the conflagration, the racial targeting of blacks by the armed forces charged with restoring order, and the overall disadvantaged conditions of blacks in Detroit. But, their class position as poor, inner-city whites certainly mitigates against their seeing social disadvantage as a strictly racial predicament.

The basis of backtalk in Briggs to explicitly racial readings of these events strikes me as grounded in a common class predicament. To inner-city residents with memories that reach back to a time before the urban crisis exploded, the riotous days of July 1967 represent primarily the opening of the flood gates of deprivation. For older residents who remembered the area in its most bustling and independent times, the rioters brought nothing but chaos and dependency, obliterating the very resources the neighborhood had relied upon. Unlike the rioters of 1943, who defended and/or attacked racial communities and orders, the participants in the event of 1967 were too disparate in their motives to be read under the homogenizing labels of race. Race is noted in these accounts to make clear that "everybody" was involved. This racial counter-discourse does not assert that race was entirely unimportant but rather that it could not be reliably parsed by depending on homogeneous abstractions, white and black. Rather than emphatically discounting race, their interpretations suggest that the prior means of characterizing conflicts as "racial" were dissolving, leaving an emergent set of criteria to be uncertainly discerned in this unfolding situation. This new order of significance is more diffuse, less communal, than modes through which racialness had previously been experienced and interpreted.

The distinction drawn by residents between the riots of 1943 and 1967 is supported by perhaps the most exhaustively thorough treatment of the later riot. Sidney Fine, in *Violence in the Model City: The Cavanagh Administration, Race Relations, and the Detroit Riot of 1967*, demonstrates that violence and upheaval were "racial in character," though not directly "interracial." This distinction attempts to assess the disproportionate participation of blacks in the riot along with their lack of interest in striking out against any and all whites. "The Detroit rioters, after all, were mainly although not entirely black, the disturbances occurred in black neighborhoods, and it was policemen and firemen, the overwhelming majority of whom were white, and business establishments, mostly white-owned, that the rioters attacked. . . .There was, as a matter of fact, a very small amount of interracial fighting during the riot, and some rioters were very hostile to whites; but the arrestees, it will be recalled, overwhelmingly rejected the interpretation of the riot as 'an anti-white event.' Whites in the riot area were sometimes treated with derision, but they were rarely menaced." As he recounts a number of reported instances of whites and blacks looting together, Fine adds a quote from a black character in Barbara Tinker's novel, *When the Fire Reaches Us*: "The riot was about the most integration I have ever seen in Detroit."[83]

Although whites represented 12 percent of arrestees, they were charged with 27 percent of the arson counts and 35 percent of the assault and battery charges.[84] Thus, although blacks constituted a vast majority of the rioters, those who looted, burned, and fought with police did not form a racially homogeneous group.

Capeci and Wilkerson also document the contrasts between the riots of 1943 and 1967, as drawn by residents in Briggs. There was obviously a racial component to the 1967 riot, if only because the rioters were largely black; these rioters, however, rarely sought out racialized victims. "Participants, regardless of race, gender, or residence, focused on police and property targets and rioted side by side rather than in opposition to one another, as did the 1943 participants." The key difference that Capeci and Wilkerson point to between the riots of 1943 and 1967 is the shift in the latter upheaval from community-based and directed racial violence to class warfare against property and its defenders, the police and firemen. "Unlike the riot of 1943, when black and white Detroiters battled over the color line, rioters in 1967 generally protested an abusive system. Unquestionably a black woman cursing 'whitey' and a white man shooting a black youth were exhibiting interracial passions. Nevertheless most black and white participants attacked white lawmen and firemen or white-owned property, convinced that they shared the same fight." They conclude that "black and white Detroit rioters of 1967 completed the transition from communal to commodity violence begun by their forebears; less interested in interracial combat, they fought more along class lines."[85]

Whether the local character of the riot of 1967 consists primarily of class or racial elements is not as important as the realization that the significance and constitution of race shifted in the interval between these two conflicts. In 1943, racialness seems to have been a given matter, a mode of enforced or required solidarity that made communal links appear obvious. In 1967, in the inner city of Detroit, racialness was no longer constituted in such a manner. The matter that was growing increasingly obvious to residents of this zone was the divide between the "haves and the have-nots." Racialness of the residents did not thereby evaporate, but its significance was reprioritized along a continuum of concerns that stressed class distinctions. Race still mattered, but as the physical structure of the city shifted so did the material organization of their lives, which once provided a sharper context for reading race.

The class contours of this counter-discourse in Briggs to racial versions of the 1967 riot are further distinguished by its absence or underdevelopment in the neighborhoods of Corktown and Warrendale. Few of Corktown's older residents had distinct memories of the riot. There were not

many shops to loot, since the area had been decimated by an urban renewal project in 1958. Also, a contingent of the National Guard was
bivouacked nearby, beside Tiger Stadium. Mary, who had arrived with
her family from Malta in 1923, drew comparisons with war-torn Europe.
"That's because it was like an army camp . . . I thought I was back in
Europe in World War II [laughing] . . . I tell you, they had jeeps, armored
cars . . . tanks even. It was something."

For another Maltese resident, Betty, whose family arrived in 1931, the
riot provides a convenient marker for the emergence of prejudice among
local whites. One afternoon in her kitchen, I asked Betty what led people
to begin leaving the neighborhood for the suburbs. She begain by describing a setting free of racial conflict: "It really had nothing to do with . . .
blacks or browns, because we lived among them all our lives. I had
friends that were black. I had a lot of friends that were black. I had a lot
of friends that were Chinese.[86] My mother and dad never, never once
said, 'He's a black man.' She would say, 'that's Mr. Hill,' and 'this is
Mr. Pace.' I wish children today could be like that."

As she talked, she listed the names of black children with whom she
went to school. Although she granted that "some of 'em are prejudiced
around here, because of the crime," in her opinion racism had not been
active in this zone in the 1940s and 1950s, as blacks began moving into
the area. But she made sure I knew that prejudice informed their larger
context in the city. She told me about a black woman, Nelly, who was
good friends with her mother.

BETTY: One time we went . . . and that's the first time I ever realized that
people are so prejudiced. My mother and I . . . I had just started to drive . . .
and my mom and Nelly and I went to K-Mart's, and they refused to wait on
her! And my mother got mad. She said, "Take everything back and I want a
refund for everything I bought. WE'RE leaving!" And of course Nelly cried,
y'know. But that's the way it was. But when we were kids, there was no prejudice. Y'know when that started, prejudice? During the riots. Then it got bad.
I was here during the riots!

JH: What was that like around here?

BETTY: It was a little frightening, but we were really safe over here. They
didn't bother us. They were driving by with the vans . . . They were breaking
into the Trumbull Chevrolet, and they were breaking in Firestone and this
appliance store over here, and we were sitting on our porch watching them go
by with big TVs, and I was just thinking, "drop one, drop one [laughs]." We
didn't have one at the time [laughs]. "Come on guys, drop one." See at the time
I was here by myself with the kids, because my husband had gone up to my
mother-in-law's in Orchard Lake . . . But it was after that, that's when all the
damn prejudice started. I never knew what the hell a [whispers] "nigger" was.
That's what makes me so mad.

In Betty's account, residents regard the riot as a racial matter even though there were no local instances of interracial violence: "that's when all the damn prejudice started." This version, though, somewhat simplifies a complex dynamic, which I examine in more detail in Chapter 3. Briefly, the process of integration in Corktown followed an initial course similar to that in Briggs. However, urban renewal and freeway projects gutted the areas where blacks were residentially concentrating. As a result, there were scarcely any blacks among the few remaining families in Corktown in the late 1960s. With the scarcity of black neighbors, it seems these residents were as susceptible to racialized versions of the riot as were whites who experienced events solely through media coverage.

In Warrendale, recollections of the riot conveyed a similar sense of being removed from the violence. Here, too, whites did not feel personally threatened by the riot, because they were so far from the core of the looting and burning. They did not experience a sense of racial vulnerability as whites; but they also did not articulate a counter-discourse to a strictly racial view of the riot.

Wally—the president of the Warrendale Community Organization—was a foreman at Ford's River Rouge plant at the time. His parents had come to Detroit from Poland in the early 1920s, and he was born on East Jefferson in 1926. He moved to Warrendale with his wife in 1956 and has lived in the same house ever since. His recollections of the riot began in an exhilarated tone that grew increasingly somber as he talked about a particular friend's store that was burned.

> WALLY: I was working at Ford's at the time. I worked afternoons at the time, so we lucked out. We got sent home every night at 8 o'clock. Everybody got sent home at 8 o'clock because the city had a curfew. So we got sent home at 8 o'clock and we'd come home and party. I had a big pool in the backyard, and the guy across the street had a bar. Yeah, he had a bar down on Elmhurst. So . . . after the riot started . . . matter of fact, it was right around two blocks away from where we [previously] lived on Cherrylawn. Anyway, he had this bar down there, and the police told him to come in and get your stuff out of here, cause we're not going to be sure that it won't either get burned down or broke into, and you'll lose everything. So, we went out there with a couple of . . . I went out there with my station wagon. I must've got nineteen cases of beer. We took shotguns and bats and what not . . . They told us to! The police. They said "Just protect yourselves." And so we went down there in the daytime and emptied the building out. And I'm not sure if they finally broke in and trashed it, or I don't know what. I don't really remember. I don't really remember if they did. But I know I had a guy that uh, he and his brother had a market, on Dexter. He wasn't far from the Boulevard if memory serves me correct. His name was Tommy Fikes. He and his brothers had this fish market down there.

And I'd go down there occasionally and maybe buy a five-pound block of uh shrimp. And I'd BUY it. Just cause a guy works for me doesn't mean he's gonna give it to me or anything like that! I'm sure I got a better price, but I bought it. And he told me . . . I said "Tommy, how you guys making out down there?" He said, "Well, we went in and we sat down . . . and we were handing everything out to 'em so that they wouldn't [his tone of voice grows increasingly slow and morose] . . . just go in and bust everything up and take it." He said, "so when everything was gone, we had nothing to give away anymore . . . we just closed the door and walked away." Well, they broke in and busted everything up inside. I felt so sorry for them, y'know, because they were nice people, they were hard workers. And to have your life-long dream get shot to pieces like that.

JH: What were your feelings about living in Detroit after that? Did you think about moving out?

WALLY: Naw. Naw . . . Maybe if I had lived down closer or had my house burned down, I might have. I don't know.

Wally's recollections are interesting, in part, because of the way that they combine investment and detachment with the riot. His class sympathies are clearly with the small-business owners who, like his friend, had their "life-long dream[s] get shot to pieces like that." Unlike Howard and others in Briggs, he harbors no suspicion of business owners being involved with insurance fraud or other forms of profiteering. But, overall, he experienced the riot at a certain remove, reinforced by his neighborhood's distance from the hard-hit zones. Though he journeyed into these areas and saw the conflagration on the streets, he did not feel a sense of racial threat that would provoke him to leave the city.

Garnett, who was born in a lumber camp in Michigan's upper peninsula and moved to Detroit in the early 1930s, also told me about traveling into the riot zone. In his recollection of the riot, the events were racialized, though without much fear or blame.

GARNETT: That was a bad riot. And one of my friends, his young boy was with a grandmother down on John R. And, he come over and said, would you go down with me, I want to pick up my kid. I said sure. So he handed me a shotgun. Then we went and picked up another guy, and he had a shotgun for him. So we had three shotguns. So we started down on Warren, and we got near Livernois, and the street was . . . there was a surge of people into the street. Well, they were black. And one of 'em threw a brick at the car and broke the windshield, but we had three shotguns. If we'd fired into that crowd we'd of hit kids or women, y'know, they were out for a lark. So we pulled back, we wouldn't do that. But I saw one sixteen-year-old kid walk up in and spit in a cop's face that was standing there; the cop didn't move. I don't blame him, they would've killed him if he'd done anything. So, anyways, we did get downtown and pick up his kid.

In both Wally's and Garnett's account, the riot does not seem to be the racialized conflict that the media portrayed in their coverage; neither one articulates a singular emphasis on race. Yet, neither of them has an emphatic sense that race did not matter, as residents in Briggs insisted. They have no counter-stories to tell that belie the media's versions of this event.

Bonalee's family moved to Warrendale in 1924, when it was first being developed. Her parents had tried farming in Florida but failed, so they moved to Detroit, where Bonalee was born in 1912. Initially, they lived in the Briggs area, and her father worked at the old Detroit Creamery on Grand River. When the landlord at the last place they lived was going to raise the rent, they decided to move out to the new subdivision. In 1967, she was working as a bookkeeper in a real estate firm. Her recollections of the riot were a mix of the bucolic and of terror.

> BONALEE: You couldn't drive or anything. And it was the most peaceful weekend, because by then you were beginning to hear traffic noises on Warren and on Evergreen. And the weather was beautiful all week until it rained at the end of the week, which helped to stop the riot. We sat out in the yard and it was very peaceful. And we didn't go anywhere. I remember, I went to work over off the Lodge expressway, on Meyer, there were offices over there. And we could see the smoke developing—you could look down the Lodge and see smoke coming up in the air at around 2 P.M., so my boss said, lets call it quits.

I asked her about the response of people in Warrendale to the riot.

> BONALEE: Well, we were all very shocked. I think most people, they just went to work; they had to. Then they just came back home and sat in their backyards. They did their shopping before it started. You visited around from next door, you didn't drive! So it was the most peaceful neighborhood you ever lived in—like being in the country. You heard the birds singing. But you read about and you watched it on the TV, and you were scared silly!

For Warrendale's "young people," who were children at the time, the televised pictures of the riots were often their first experience of racial difference. When I asked Claudia, the newly elected vice president of the Warrendale Community Organization, about the first time she thought of herself as white, she recalled the version of the 1967 riots that played out on her family's television.

> CLAUDIA: I remember, because it was on TV. And my dad was telling us that people make judgments about other people based on the color of their skin. And he said that skin color had nothing to do with it. Those people just weren't thinking things through, making judgments based on skin. And that, even though the TV was showing all of these black people doing this stuff like burning buildings, we shouldn't decide to judge all black people on that basis, as if

all blacks were bad. He just told us that we can't assume anything about somebody based on their skin color.

Claudia's response provides an interesting background to the generational shift in racial discourses. Her memories of the riot feature an object
lesson on race that depended on distance, with her father using the media
images to stress the importance of resisting racial readings of events. It
was a lesson that remained with her, a lesson that had to be stressed
strongly since the moral runs counter to the received opinions informed
by reporting on the riot.

In this range of accounts from Warrendale there is a clear series of
difference from how whites in Briggs and Corktown experienced the
same event. Even though the event was recognized as horrendous, for
whites in this far-west-side neighborhood, the riot of 1967 did not bitterly mark a drastic change. In Briggs, residents sadly recalled the loss of
independence that had come from having close, well-stocked stores and
markets. In Corktown, the riot conveniently marked, in Betty's narrative,
the beginning of racial division and white animosity. In Warrendale, the
images of rioters and looters that remain are solely colored black. Residents' accounts featured no encounters in which the significance of race
as allegorized in media images was countered or undermined. Although
these whites experienced little sense of being racialized through the proximate potential for violence, neither did they have compelling experiences
that would counter the national narrative, which locates the events in
1967 in the ongoing clash of racial interests between whites and blacks.

Racial readings of the riot of 1967 solidified quickly in Detroit's "all-
white" suburbs. In the riot's immediate aftermath, experts on civil disorders expressed opinions that the "cause" of the riot was based more in
the problem of poverty than in racial antagonism and conflict. This view
was widely expressed in Detroit's political community, but had little pur-
chase in the thinking of suburban whites. Donald Warren, in his study
"Community Dissensus: Panic in Suburbia," states that although this
view had the potential to be adopted in Detroit's suburbs, whites were
more greatly influenced by "the specter of black militancy" that emerged
in politicized rhetoric of black activists such as H. Rap Brown and Reverend Albert Cleage Jr.[87] Warren found that whites outside of Detroit were
influenced by a community context much more than by a direct perception of events in Detroit. On the basis of his survey of suburban whites'
opinions, he argues that "the climate of opinion in a community affects
what people think and do apart from what the same individual might
think or do if he lived in a different community" (126). Such community
contexts are where whiteness is both reproduced and reinforced, as a condition for which blackness is a distinct embodiment of cultural otherness.

Whites in Briggs, Corktown, and Warrendale did not share this kind of community context and, hence, show interesting rifts and ruptures in the ideological operation of whiteness. Although "racial" readings continued to dominate political discourses in the city and in the metropolitan area of Detroit at large, in Briggs such abstractions lost a good deal of their relevance. The disjuncture between the operation of "racial" readings at the city level and in the neighborhood is the subject of the last section in this chapter.

Franklin School

All of the changes, subtle and complex, reconfiguring the social and economic landscape in Detroit during this century appeared to come to a climax in the galvanizing moment when Coleman Young was elected mayor of the city in 1973. Young was one of a number of black leaders who came to power in the wake of urban riots in the late 1960s, and his victory was achieved by a familiar political alliance between white liberals and African Americans.[88] But Young was the most brash and articulate in engaging racialized political discourses and in asserting stark, plain racial interests. For many whites, he symbolized the fact that the terms of racial identity had irrevocably changed in Detroit. Young's victory, combined with a shift in the city council to a black majority, marked a watershed in the significance of race in Detroit. The geography of race changed drastically: the now predominantly black central city and east side squared off against the overwhelmingly white northwest neighborhoods in citywide elections over school funding and integration measures. In the wake of this spatial reconfiguration, whites increasingly found themselves racialized, either directly in face-to-face clashes with black parents at school board or city council meetings, or indirectly through the new political discourse on race that dominated the city. Their motives and interests were starkly rendered as "racist," and they were no longer able to assume a sympathetic hearing from Detroiters at large for their efforts to keep blacks out of local schools or housing. Through the decade, the white population plummeted, dropping from 838,877 to 413,730, by 1980 constituting just 34 percent of the city's residents. Whites became a minority in Detroit.

The 1970s were a tumultuous time for Briggs, as well. The area continued to hemorrhage residents, white and black. As the decade ended, Briggs's last link to its once "respectable" character was sundered when Franklin Elementary School, an erstwhile stately institution, closed in 1978.[89] Residents I spoke with pointed to the school's closing as a final blow to the neighborhood; the loss of its stabilizing force seemed to assure the area's reconstitution as an isolated, extreme poverty zone. The closing of Franklin Elementary provides a basis for grasping the points of contrast and correspondence between conditions in Briggs and Detroit generally. More important, contrasting white views of Franklin's closing provide an initial example of the way racial aspects of a situation are assessed when whites are faced with black political dominance. The hegemony that blacks attained in Detroit is read in a range of modes by whites in the city, alternately stressing or deemphasizing race.[90] The Board of Education's decision to close the last remaining majority white, inner-city school could be regarded by whites locally as either a "racial" matter or as having nothing at all to do with race. These contrary interpretations derive, in part, from the way whites emphasize class matters in relation to racial identities. They offer a preview of the dynamics at work in Warrendale, where the conflict over the Malcolm X Academy is perhaps the latest battle in a struggle over the significance of race in Detroit's schools that has been waged for the past thirty years.

Franklin was exceptional among inner-city schools in that it stayed predominantly white through the 1960s and 1970s. But it exactly mirrored other Detroit schools as a site of intense class conflict. The ostensible racial features of contests over schools too often obscure underlying class frictions. In neighborhoods like Briggs, middle-class families, white and black, fled the increasing concentrations of the poor of both races.[91] Between 1960 and 1970, the black population in this area dropped by 25 percent (from 5,294 to 3,978), and between 1980 and 1990, the number of blacks was practically halved, from 2,983 to 1,658.[92] Although "white flight" conveys the disproportionate rates at which whites fled the city, it unfortunately masks the class dynamics driving the middle and working classes from the inner city. As historian Robert Conot explains in his study of Detroit, "well before conditions in the neighborhood became intolerable for residents, parents felt that their children were endangered in the schools. Their first response was to transfer their children to schools that continued to be middle class in character; their second was to transfer their homes as far as practicable from the tide of poverty sweeping out of the inner city—in effect, as far as the freeway would carry them back and forth to their work in reasonable time."[93]

The demographic "balance" between the classes in the schools—at least in the 1960s—was as volatile and tenuous as the color line, particularly in an area like Briggs, where residents managed to diffuse the potential for interracial violence during the riot. Anxious parents responded to a class threshold as well as to a racial one when they decided that their children were threatened. When the Boulevard was finally "breached" by residents of the inner city, it was as much through the schools as by residential "invasions."[94] Conot asserts that "as long as children from problem homes had constituted no more than about 20 percent of enrollment, they had benefited from improved facilities, the better teaching, and the atmosphere provided by the middle-class emphasis on education and achievement. But by the time the proportion of problem students reached one in three, a teacher, no matter how well motivated, was overwhelmed. His class lost its homogeneity."[95]

Whether or not Conot's estimate of 20 percent as the line of irrevocable difference in the perceptions of danger by middle-class parents can be regarded as objective, the fundamental point is that a threshold emerges in its transgression.[96] The community context Donald Warren referred to above is affected by shifts in scale of class and racial concentrations in a neighborhood, changing residents' perceptions of and modes for interpreting the significance of race in relation to class. This threshold corresponds to the notion that neighborhoods "tip" in their racial balance, reaching a point at which white residents feel distinctly racialized and decide to move.[97] What is intriguing about Franklin Elementary is that in the 1960s this threshold was crossed in terms of class, without greatly affecting the racial balance in this zone—whites continued to be a majority in the area, partly because black middle-class families were also leaving but also, because a core of poor whites was remaining behind.

Franklin's story reads as a ledger of the classed conflicts emerging in the inner city. The school was featured in Detroit's application to the Office of Economic Opportunity for War on Poverty funds in 1965, as part of "A Proposal to Serve Disturbed and Delinquent Youth and Troubled Families in the Franklin School Area." The key problems in this zone at the time were gangs and delinquency. The application states: "Since September, 1963, the problem of delinquency has become more acute for Franklin School. Gang rivalries have resulted in excessive violence and the malicious destruction of property. School children have become fearful and have been victimized. A delinquent lifestyle is becoming more general. Also, certain children have been exposed to stressful family relationship or crises which have seriously impaired their functioning in school."[98] At the crux of the "problem of delinquency" was an intensifying class divide in Briggs. The "delinquent lifestyle" that concerned school and city officials was not distinctly racialized. I asked residents about the gangs that roamed this zone in the 1960s; they recalled the Stilettos, the Butternuts, and the Mohzam Boys. These gangs were generally not racially homogeneous, neither did they strike at racial targets. Rather, their victims tended to be participants in the broader society that was clearly leaving these gang members behind. A class divide, which had been apparent in the area since the arrival of "hillbillies" in the 1940s, grew wider and increasingly fraught with tension. The application describes the situation succinctly: "Feuding relationships exist between families; i.e. families on public assistance vs. families who are employed." It was this class divide as much as anything that promoted the flight of more respectable families, white and black, from this zone.[99]

My interest in Franklin was sparked while talking with one of the school's community agents, Betty Hogan, who was based there from 1966 until it closed in 1978. Several residents suggested I talk with Betty, since they still admired her organizing role in Community on the Move. Betty was born in Corktown in 1925; her parents came separately from Ireland and met in Detroit. Her mother served as a cook for the Navin family on 17th Street, while her father worked for the railroad at the old Fort Street depot, trucking freight and eventually working his way up to tally man. She recalled his hands cracking and bleeding from the bitter winter cold in the freight yards. Her family eventually moved to the east side, but Betty returned to Corktown with her college sociology class in 1946—a site chosen by their teacher because the area had the largest concentration of social agencies in the city. Betty took up with the *Catholic Worker* and found her niche in the lay Catholic movement inspired by Dorothy Day.[100] After the Westside Industrial Project decimated Corktown in the late 1950s, she found work as a community agent in the Detroit Public Schools (DPS) in 1960. Community agents were established by the DPS to provide a link between parents and the schools. They were charged with establishing programs to help parents receive whatever forms of aid or assistance were provided by the schools or the state.[101]

Although Betty watched as two freeway projects ripped gashes through this zone and residents fled from escalating class conflicts in the school and on the streets, her version of the neighborhood's demise featured a more sinister motivation. For her, the critical moment came when Franklin was closed; she insisted this was racially motivated—an attempt by the predominantly black school board to break up this "white neighborhood" by closing its elementary school. Owen School, a smaller but newer building with a predominantly black student body, was left to take up the displaced students.[102] Surely many factors were involved in the decision to close Franklin, but Betty prioritized the situation's racial aspects. "See when that school closed, people took off. See a good school or a good church stabilizes a neighborhood. You'll notice the block on which a nice school or church is located is usually the prettiest block in the area. Because the example is there. That's why people were concerned about the closing of the [Catholic] churches—even if we didn't have a lot of people, it gives the look of stabilization. Now, what caused a lot of change was the closing of Franklin School. And that was strictly a racial situation. It was a completely integrated school and some people couldn't stand that."

I asked her what race relations were like before the school closed. "They were very good, 'cause they had grown up together. [Lowers her voice] When you get more than 50 percent black, that's it, the whites move out. Now in order to keep Franklin open, we made a big thing about the fact that we had many American Indians here. Now many people with American Indian hadn't declared it before then. So the blacks said, 'That's phony.' See they had to send away for their proper papers. And we proved it! But they were determined to close us. And to say it was an old building . . . it had a gorgeous new kitchen, it had an elevator, y'know. It was a very good building. That was terrible."

Her recall on details of the closure was slipping, but she remembered the general tone of the debate. A key issue was the racial classification of residents. As the DPS began implementing a busing program to desegregate schools, Franklin stood out among the other inner-city schools for its large number of white students. Betty said that Briggs had many groups that passed as "statistical" whites, such as Native Americans, Hispanics, and the Maltese. "Like the Indians . . . They were sub rosa until . . . But some of the blacks said, That's phony, they're not Indian, they're just saying it. But it was true."

> JH: Was it an issue of not having enough funds to keep the school open?
>
> BETTY: No. It was because, if we had enough nonwhites, then we could stay open. And the Indians were saying we are nonwhite. Franklin had perfect balance, racially. Staffwise, about half black; community residents, about 40 percent black. They were still okay.
>
> JH: Were there any racial conflicts at the school?
>
> BETTY: Not really, not really. Not until they got over to Owen, which was black and racist, very anti-white, very anti-white leadership at that time. It became mellow with the next principal, but by that time, we didn't have too many whites going over there.

Her suspicions were fueled by the fact that although Franklin was closed as an elementary school it was reopened the next year as a vocational school with only seventy-nine students.[103] It continues to operate today as an adult education school.

After Franklin closed, Betty was moved from school to school, first to Northern High, then to Butzel Middle School, until she finally retired in 1986. Her cynicism with the school board grew as it became apparent that her job of informing parents and involving them in the operation and decision-making processes of local schools was being undermined. Community agents were not replaced as they retired, and agents were given impossibly large districts to cover in addition to the particular school to which they were attached. While at Butzel, Betty was assigned six schools on the east side and five other schools scattered throughout the city. Board meetings were scheduled at the same time that school community meetings were held in order, Betty felt, to cut down on parental oversight of decisions relating to their schools. "They didn't want them to know too much," she said; the relation of community agents to parents was restricted to "just jollying them along" and "monopolizing them with bullshit." After she quit, Betty was hired to do social work for St. Dominic's Church in 1987, a job which she still held when we spoke.

Betty's interpretation of the closing of Franklin Elementary featured her deep bitterness over the political and social changes that transformed Detroit. She raged about the "brain drain," and how people who had benefited from private and state-supported educational programs for the poor had left the community and the city behind. Whites were as often objects of her scorn as blacks. But what stood out in Betty's recollections of that period was the advent of black political dominance; for her, the lines in all political matters in the city now were racial. She considered Franklin's closing a racial matter: the black-dominated school board had decided to close the school because it anchored what remained of a white enclave in the heart of Detroit: "that was strictly a racial situation."

It is important to remember that politics and the practices of civic government did not suddenly become "racial" when blacks achieved political and social dominance in Detroit in the 1970s. African Americans were being no more "racial" than were whites who previously dominated the city and made racially motivated decisions regarding the operation and development of Detroit. "Racial," in this instance, denotes a point at which previous assumptions about what counts as race shifted, in concert with the massive demographic and political changes in Detroit. "Racial" marks an alteration in power as constituencies respond to a collection of interests articulated in the recognition that social conditions are never equal; "racial" acknowledges a scope of conflict in which collectives will, perhaps, never be neutrally recognized.[104] Betty's reading of race is not primarily keyed to the personal level of anxiety over homes and classrooms; rather, as a participant in the racial transformation of the city's bureaucratic structures, she recognized whiteness as something that blacks had decided to counter actively, as something that became objectified and polemicized in the articulation of "black interests." This reading develops out of the racial conflicts that occurred in Detroit throughout the late 1960s and 1970s.[105]

It is hard to overemphasize the extent to which DPS issues and decisions were racialized from the 1960s to the 1980s. As blacks became a clear majority in both the city and the schools, the articulation of parental and community interests, especially in the inner city, were explicitly and incessantly framed as racial interests. In Detroit, as in other large industrial cities, the movement for civil rights and more militant demands for black power overlapped in challenges to the largely white educational establishment. Already volatile, the racial politics of this period were exacerbated by the decisive economic transformations that irrevocably changed Detroit. As the city lost jobs and the people who filled them, tax revenues for the schools plummeted, setting the stage for the increasingly charged financial and educational crises that continue to haunt the DPS.[106]

Jeffrey Mirel, in *The Rise and Fall of an Urban School System*, recounts the traumatic conflicts that dominated the operations of the DPS from 1965 to 1981. Between 1965 and 1967, the long-simmering discontent over the poor quality of education in largely black schools congealed into a sustained protest from the "black community," supported by the NAACP, the Group of Advanced Leadership, and the Congress of Racial Equality, which resulted in administrative and curricular changes in the DPS. The accomplishments of this political pressure transfigured educational politics in Detroit. As Mirel describes it,

> Prior to 1967, leading civil rights and liberal activists had maintained that "cultural disadvantages," segregation (of both teachers and students) and unequal finances were the main sources of the educational problems of black children. The solution to these problems lay in such compensatory programs as Great Cities, integrating schools and staff, and equalizing educational resources throughout the city. Leaders of the liberal-labor-black coalition believed that there was nothing fundamentally wrong with the system, it merely had to shed the vestiges of its discriminatory past. . . . By 1967, however, that position began to give way before a new set of radical arguments that rested on the premise that the schools were fulfilling their fundamental mission, namely to *miseducate* black children. Advocates of this position declared that the schools were part of the white racist establishment, and, as such, they would never contribute to the meaningful education of black children. Indeed, these militant leaders saw the unequal educational outcomes in Detroit as the result of deliberate policies and practices of the school board.[107]

Subsequent debates over public education in Detroit were relentlessly racialized. Despite a range of moderate voices on many issues, competing racialist interests articulated by black nationalists and white separatists dominated public forums on school-related issues. A group called Inner City Parents (ICP), formed in 1967, insisted that most white teachers and administrators be transferred from predominantly black schools because of their conscious or unconscious belief in the inferiority of all nonwhite students. ICP also demanded changes in curriculum: racially biased textbooks must be removed from the classrooms and, in the inner-city schools, lessons had to be reoriented to provide "Afro-American children a knowledge of their history, their culture, and their destiny." "Meanwhile, white Detroiters expressed their discontent with the school board's acquiescence to black protesters by refusing to support critical tax increases to keep the schools operating. The riot in 1967 heightened the racial polarization over school-related issues, and political extremists of both races came to dominate debates. This polarization reflected conditions in the schools: by the 1973–1974 school year about half of all the schools in the city were over 90 percent black, 27 schools were 90 percent white, and an additional 46 schools were 65 to 89 percent white.[108]

Throughout 1968, the number of violent racial incidents in Detroit's junior and senior high schools surged. By 1969 and through to 1971 violent incidents in the schools were so numerous they were recorded hourly by Deputy Superintendent Charles Wolfe. ICP, along with Rev. Albert Cleage Jr., founder of the Shrine of the Black Madonna, and Dan Aldrige, a leader of the Student Nonviolent Coordinating Committee, organized a series of protests and boycotts of public schools, demanding that white educators be replaced by blacks, who in turn had to prove that they were not "uncle Toms." Black student groups demanded "that the board totally reorient the educational program along black nationalist lines."[109] The contest for racial dominance was waged fiercely in the DPS. There were, of course, other interests involved in these fights—including the State of Michigan and the teachers' union (the Detroit Federation of Teachers)—but racial positions were the most audible. The crux of the impasse was demographic: in 1970, whites still constituted a majority in Detroit; as a voting bloc, they solidly resisted efforts to desegregate the schools. At the same time, blacks made up almost two-thirds of the students in the DPS. Black parents promoted decentralization of the DPS in order to assert black control over black schools.

For many Detroiters, white and black, racial segregation in the schools was not troubling. Betty's claim that the problem with Franklin, in the school board's view, was its degree of "integration" neatly frames the unusual position of whites in Briggs. As a concentration of whites they were susceptible to being read as separatists and racists, while the ethnic and racial heterogeneity of the zone fits disjointedly at best in the polarized schema of the "black" inner-city versus the "white" outlying neighborhoods. In the contest over decentralization of the DPS, integrationists were overwhelmed by separatists of both races who realized that control of local schools promoted concentrated political, representational power. When the school board first attempted to redraw school districts to promote integration in 1970, they were undermined by a contempt for the plan voiced by both blacks and whites across the city. As a state senator, Coleman Young—referring to the school board's efforts as a "chicken shit integration plan"—pushed a bill through the state legislature that nullified the desegregation plan. The NAACP, disgusted by the plan's defeat, sued the state of Michigan to force the DPS to desegregate. The suit,

Miliken v. Bradley, although initially successful, was reversed by the Supreme Court in 1974. When the NAACP filed a second version of the suit, white and black Detroiters from Mayor Coleman Young on down criticized the NAACP for pushing for desegregation.[110]

Following my interview with Betty Hogan, I searched out records of Franklin's closing and of the protests it sparked. I wanted to find any account of public hearings regarding the closing or some documentation of how the decision was reached. I wanted to know if residents also read the closing in the racial terms that Betty used and, if so, how the board responded to such charges. The next day I went to the Board of Education's offices in the School Center Building on Woodward. The building's lobby neatly framed the disjointed history of the DPS. Although its ceiling is ornately decorated by a glittering mosaic, a remnant of the opulence that once characterized Detroit's cultural institutions, the most prominent visual symbol was a large white circle with the letters D-P-S cascading across an outline of Africa, all in black—an emblem of the new world order of the Detroit Public Schools.

I found very little information there, even after talking with the board secretary and the head of Architectural Services. My queries were perplexing to people, and it seemed there was no record of the school's closing.[111] I was directed to the Area A Office—the administrative unit that now includes Franklin—and told this was the only place where such records would exist. The physical plant manager of Area A, Mr. Greene, asked his secretary to go through all the files that they had, but their records only extended back to 1988.[112] There was no information on Franklin School, and he wasn't even sure who the last principal had been. "Anybody who would know," Mr. Greene added, "is probably retired by now." Several times in the course of our conversation he recited the reasons for closing a school; he said it always came down to the number of students in the area and how economical it was to keep them in one school or another. After it was clear that there were no records, and seeing that I was disappointed, he asked me what it was that I really wanted to know. "Look, you can be open with me. I'm from the community, you can tell me what you're really looking for. If you were a reporter I'd have to be more guarded, but, as it is, I can tell you straight up about this." I said that I heard there had been a large protest over the school board's decision, and I was interested in finding out more about the community opposition to the closure. He smiled and replied, "I'll tell you how it is. There is only one school in the city of Detroit! Right? There are two hundred and fifty schools in this city, but there is really only one—mine! I can't count the number of times I've heard that. 'My school needs new windows, and it has to stay open. I don't know why you bother keeping that other school over there open at all.' Anytime you close a school, the

parents are going to be upset. It doesn't matter why you're closing it, and
they don't tend to be reasonable. They will say anything, blame it on
anything, because there is no good reason why you should be closing the
only school in the city of Detroit."

Then I framed the question more specifically, referring to the claim that
it was a "racial situation," that the majority black school board decided
to close the school because it was predominantly white. He told me,
"Look. Say you're on the school board, and you try to close my school.
You're a white man. And I'm going to say you're being racist. I may be
right and I may be wrong—you can't tell. But that school is still going to
be closed. And I'm going to be upset about it." I pressed him on the
question of racial bias on the part of the board, and he replied, "I know
that area, and the bottom line there is that the kids are gone. There were
not enough kids in that area to keep that building as an elementary
school. You can see that just by driving through there. The houses are
gone, the stores are gone. Y'know, my father used to tell me when we
were driving somewhere around the city, 'I remember when all of that
used to be trees.' You know what I tell my kids? 'I remember when all of
that used to be houses.'"

I laughed and told him that my grandmother used to tell me about how
8-Mile Road was just cornfields when she was young. He then elaborated
on the bias issue. "Look. Did racism have something to do with that
school closing? Sure. Did bias have something to do with it? Yes. I know
how these things work, that's part of how decisions are made. But the
reason why that elementary school was closed was because there weren't
enough children to make it economically feasible to keep that program
going. The school board doesn't like to close schools. It is always an
unpopular move, and it means jobs are lost. If there is any way around
closing a school, I guarantee you, they will try to find it. Nobody likes to
be unpopular, especially not an elected official." I thanked him for his
time and resolved to inquire further about Franklin among the residents
of Briggs.

It was shocking to find that there was no accessible record of the past.
Budget cuts and staff reductions were a factor, but clearly the school
board felt no need to preserve records of such decisions. The power structure in Detroit had been drastically transformed in a twenty-year period.
This change was fiercely fought—generally on racial grounds—and now
it was accomplished. There was little need to justify anything that had
happened before or during that transformation. I still do not know what
a record might show or demonstrate—a purity of intent, clear proof that
there had been no racial motivation? Why and to whom would that matter, especially given that race was a central concern? As Mr. Greene said,
"it" was obviously there, but only part of the story.

I continued asking about the school's closing in Briggs. Mothers who sent their children there had detailed memories of the many services available at Franklin, such as a school for the blind and numerous programs for single parents and struggling families. Delores (see "Disgrace to the Race") remembered that "they even had a dentist in the school. And those of us, and there were quite a few people in those days, that were on welfare, we could get our teeth worked on there." I even talked to several of the mothers who participated in the picket-line protest of the closing, but no one voiced Betty's opinion that it was a "racial" matter. Pat ("Riots and Race"), in particular, had detailed memories of the conflict over the racial demographics in the school and the neighborhood. When I asked her about Franklin, she linked it with her suspicions and frustrations over the city's (in)actions and policies in relation to Briggs. She, like Betty, was second-generation Irish; her mother came from Ireland, through Canada, and her father was born of Irish parents in Hamilton, Ontario. They met after her mother had separated from her first husband while living here in Detroit. Her father was never able to establish residency in this country. Pat explained, "They weren't married . . . And he was here in the country illegally, and they would keep sending him back [to Canada]. And he would swim back, and they would send him back. Finally, they sent him back and locked him up. And that's the last I remember of him, and I was only a couple years old, but I remember them putting him on a bus."

She attended Franklin in the 1940s, but her sharpest recollections of the place stemmed from its role in politicizing the community. As one of the parents drawn in by Hogan's organizing efforts, Pat was animated in describing the transformation that occurred for herself and her neighbors as they became politicized by attending meetings at the school. But her experiences in this process returned her to an earlier stage in our conversation when she explained her "paranoid" version of how the neighborhood had been intentionally decimated by city planners, a view shared by white and black residents and, in their minds, substantiated by the rash of fires that were still reducing the dwindling housing stock in Briggs.

> Pat: Again, here's where I'm paranoid. Because of the parents' involvement, we got politically aware. At the regional offices, when they had elections, the people running for those offices would be there, mass meetings. You got to meet 'em and you got to know what they stood for. We had so many people registered to vote who had never voted before. And that was a good reason to squelch us [she bangs her fist on the table], to get rid of us, because we had become politicized. But that's just me and my paranoia again [laughs].

She explained how "blight by announcement" works, pointing out how the city announced it was going to widen Myrtle Street into a boulevard long before they had financing to carry out this plan. The value of homes bordering the street dropped precipitously; landlords refused to do repairs; a rash of suspicious and "systematic" fires burned many of the houses to the ground.

> PAT: The same thing has been going on for years and years and years and years—it's been systematic. And the way I'm talking now, I would have laughed at anybody who sounded like this years ago. I would've said, "You're silly, that's paranoid. You're really talking nonsense." But . . . Now I don't think it's nonsense.
>
> JH: So people used to talk that way when you were younger?
>
> PAT: Yeah. I heard people say these things, and I thought, "Ahh, they're crazy."

She recalled that the initial effort to close the school occurred in the mid-1970s, when busing first became an issue in the city. The DPS apparently decided to close Franklin and bus kids to other city schools, assuming that its white majority was an outgrowth of the racial politics that sustained segregated schools in Detroit's outlying neighborhoods. But the class and ethnic mix suggested a more complicated situation.

> PAT: See, we did a lot of squawking when they put our school up on the block. And we presented a case that it was valuable and that we needed it. They wanted to bus the children somewhere else, and so we proved to them that our school was already desegregated, because they wanted to desegregate other schools because this pocket was so predominantly white. Not . . . there was more whites than anything else, but there was the Spanish, the American Indians, and the blacks. So we had to come up with the figures, we had to go out and get the heritage of people to prove that.
>
> JH: Was that successful?
>
> PAT: Yeah, we kept it open. But after they took out the region [the previous unit of school districting in Detroit], and there wasn't the community involvement, it was just a couple of years after that they closed the school.

Pat and the other parents made their presentation of the revised figures on the racial composition of the students at Franklin to the school board, demonstrating that a social heterogeneity existed in the area which confounded the politics of white and black interests. According to Pat, the members of the board responded favorably to their presentation. She felt the favorable decision was due partly to the fact that the parents had become familiar with the various board members. "We were down there at least once a month for a general meeting. Then, if you were on any of the committees, you were there for at least another meeting. Uh, Title 1, that was federally funded. You had to have representatives for those meetings, and that was once a month, too. So they knew you, and that's a big difference, if they know you . . . It's politics. I don't care what it is. Wherever you go, it's politics, and that's part of the politics. We were down there, and we were aware. We knew what we were talking about."

Betty's and Pat's versions of this same event are quite distinct; they characterize two interpretive modes by which whites assessed the rise of black power in Detroit. Their views are as much products of their social position as of their individual psyches. With so much in common—both women are second-generation Irish Americans, born and raised in a deteriorating inner-city neighborhood—the role of their contrasting social situations comes to the fore. Betty operates in the institutional circuits of the city as a social worker, while Pat lives in and works for one extremely poor neighborhood. They are both openly suspicious of the motives of city institutions and of the bureaucrats and politicians that operate in that realm. Where they differ is in how they prioritize race in their suspicions regarding city politics. Betty's racialized view is shaped by the rhetoric and politics of citywide contests between black and white collectives; she speaks through a discourse oriented around the fundamental role of racial interests. Pat's view primarily stresses class and the sense of her neighborhood's disempowerment in relation to city government; the identifying features she recognizes are the area's poverty and the city's implicit interest in seeing this zone completely deteriorate, making its eventual redevelopment cheaper and more feasible. This difference also involves a contrasting sense of scale (local versus citywide) that each woman employs in reflecting on one moment of Detroit's racial, political, and economic transformation.

At the level of the city's institutions, racial discourse overrides attention to discrepancies and contexts that militate against the stark division of whites and blacks into polarized, absolute orders. The rhetoric of racial collectives with opposed interests, as Mr. Greene explained to me, has a firm basis; there is a "racial" component to most issues in the city. Where he differed with Betty was on the weight that "racial" aspect carried in relation to a more fundamental basis for making administrative decisions. Pat's position as a Briggs resident grounds her perspective in a localized reading of race in this issue. Whether or not the power structure is white or black, residents in areas like Briggs are always going to be poorly represented at the city level and will be at the mercy of larger, more powerful interests. Whether through "blight by announcement" or "demolition through neglect," there are a variety of subtle ways by which a neighborhood can be reduced to rubble and its land made available for redevelopment. For Pat, racial readings of these operations are hardly relevant to a process that has gone on as long as cities have existed. "On the ground," the racial heterogeneity of this place undermines the coherence of a polemicized sense of racial discourse.

"Racial" matters, as assessed by Betty and Pat, are read antithetically, one prioritizing a singular attention to race and the predicaments of whites racialized in a political context, the other subsuming "race" under a host of class-related concerns about the precarious position of this one neighborhood within the city's broad political calculations and operations. Although the positions they occupy are proximate, their interpretive orientations are distinct; their differences indicate a series of discontinuities within the field of white racial identity. Their stories underscore the problems in objectifying an abstract "white view" or "white attitude" about these events; their specific positions, and the scale of perception each entails, ensures that these whites will prioritize race differently in their interpretation of events. The disjunctures in these perceptions should not be regarded as proving that there is no such uniform and homogenizing ideological operation as whiteness. Rather, the significance of white racialness can not be adequately comprehended by relying on abstractions that ignore the differences among whites.

The historical narrative compiled here has tacked back and forth between processes transforming urban geographies and the experience of people in one neighborhood, responding to and (in some cases) effecting those transformations. The next chapters, turn to the contemporary lives of whites in three neighborhoods, examining their engagement with, and deployment of, a range of social distinctions convolutedly linked to race. Each of these neighborhoods features an ongoing questioning of the significance of race—what does it matter, how does it effect social situations, and when does it arise? Rather than analyzing the operations of a generic cultural order, whiteness, the subsequent chapters attempt an alternative view by compiling examples of whites troubling through these questions, querying themselves, the people, and the spaces around them, about the significance of race; more particularly, about the significance of white racialness, of being marked "white" in a time and place where it is not, locally, an unmarked, normative order. Whereas "whiteness" brings ideological operations and the structural role of institutions to critical attention in the maintenance and reproduction of racial inequality, questions concerning white racialness shift attention to the realm of the everyday, where "race" conflates and competes with other registers of concern—not just "class," "gender," or "region," but "homes," "place," and "schools." This ethnographic perspective is not a refutation of whiteness as a critical concern; rather, it provides a repositioning of its conceptual interests toward a broader, more wide-ranging uncertainty: how does race play out in rapidly transforming urban areas; how will it continue to matter in the wake of whiteness?

2

"A Hundred Shades of White"

JERRY AND I were sitting on the front porch when a young black man in a gray Buick Regal pulled up and stopped in the middle of the street. He called to Jerry, who rose, ambled out to the car, and leaned his heavy, shirtless frame against the driver's door. They talked for a few minutes, then Jerry came back up on the porch. I asked him who that was, and he replied, "Aw, that's Curtis. He's the guy I rented that downstairs flat to, next door in the gray house. The ones I had to throw out, the crackheads." The gray house was one of three that Jerry watched over, serving as a sort of rental agent/maintenance man for Frank, the Maltese landlord. Two black couples lived in the downstairs converted apartments: Marvin and Charlotte, and Gale and Fred. Jerry and Marvin had been friends for years and often barbecued together. Donnie, a "hillbilly" like Jerry, lived in the upstairs apartment. My wife Rebecca and I lived in the downstairs flat of the middle yellow house; one of Jerry's several brothers, David, lived upstairs, with his wife and child. Jerry and his wife Jessie Rae lived in the red house, a three-story, massive brick structure, once an elegant home but now broken up into one-room apartments. Jerry mostly rented these rooms to black men from the neighborhood and transients.[1]

I mentioned to Jerry that his conversation with Curtis seemed pretty mild given their rough past. Jerry drawled, "Shit, I've known him for years, since he was six or eight. I've known him forever. That's Mrs. Wade's grandson. She lives right over there, across to the next block, right down that alley. See there, that's her trailer. Curtis is her grandson." He pointed through the empty lots across the street, down the alley, to where her mobile home perched on its concrete foundation. The adjoining lots were vacant and overgrown, but he and Jessie Rae had lived next door to her in the 1970s until the place they were living in burned down. They remained friends as Jerry and Jessie Rae shifted from rental to rental around the neighborhood.

Getting back to Curtis, Jerry explained, "I don't mind him at all. Its just when he gets on the crack, forget it. There's no dealing with him then. See, he's a crackhead. I can't let him back in. He's just looking for a place to start dealing anyways. He's a crackhead." As Jerry described the "last time" and why he could not let Curtis move back in, he stressed, "See, that's why they respect me around here. 'Cause I've been knowing them

Figure 6. Hillbilly Jerry

since they were little babies most of 'em. Him, I had to literally throw out of the house. I had to drag him and throw him out of the house. But he knows me—it ain't like I'm fucking him over." Jerry had done his own share of dealing, mainly cocaine, which he used excessively for a time. When Jessie Rae finally threatened him—either he stopped or she would take the kids and leave—he stopped cold. His objections to Curtis's dealing were not on moral grounds. At one point, when he and the landlord, Frank, were fighting over his responsibilities and compensations as manager of the houses, Jerry not only stopped all upkeep work on the places, he also let several black men who he knew were dealers and "crackheads" move into the red house. Frank finally yielded to Jerry's terms for defining his role and begged him to clear the dealers out of his place. Jerry's subsequent confrontation with the black men was quite tense, he told me, since he and the men had lengthy personal ties. They told Jerry to "stay out of it," that "it wasn't his business" to evict them for Frank. Jerry saw it differently. In a standoff, each "side" gathered local supporters and faced off in the street in front of the house. After pushing and threats, the dealers relented and left, but they returned later and shot up the front of the house.

Less than three weeks after Curtis first asked about the flat, Jerry let him move into the gray house. Curtis had stopped by several more times, asking Jerry to let him move back in. Whether they worked out a kickback for Jerry or he just felt like doing Curtis a favor, I never knew. Jerry explained his reversal by saying that Curtis only wanted it so his pregnant sister could have a place to stay, too. The day after Curtis moved in, a friend of his sitting out on the front porch was spotted by a passing undercover officer who knew he had outstanding warrants. As the cop approached, the kid drew his handgun and ran up through the house, busting through Donnie's door, scaring him with the brandished pistol as he scurried out the window and escaped through the alley. Donnie ran out of his apartment, through the front door, and into the gunsight of the officer. Nobody was hurt, and Curtis soon returned to dealing from the house, though on a low-key basis, given this kind of attention.

The racial differences between Curtis and Jerry were grounds on which the situation could have been racialized. Curtis could have read Jerry as a "white motherfucker" for refusing to rent to him, and Jerry could have asserted categorically that "niggers are all crackheads." Such volatile and summary assessments were by no means infrequent in this zone, as will be seen below. But neither reading materialized in their exchange; they knew each other too well to invoke racial absolutes to characterize this situation.

When Jerry first explained why Curtis did not get upset, it was hard for me to fix the "they" to which Jerry referred: "See, that's why they respect me around here. 'Cause I've been knowing them since they were little babies most of 'em." He could have been speaking of the young men, white and black, who have grown up in the neighborhood, or those who are now dealing drugs, or those who are "crackheads." I assumed at the time that he meant black kids in the area. Eventually I learned to resist such assumptions, because what goes unsaid in this articulation is as intriguing as what is stated. The racial subtext is there, but it was not something that Jerry tried to explain away or elaborately counter. This type of statement conveys how difficult it is to consider the racial aspects of a situation without affording them a fundamental, determining effect—instead, letting "they" stand for what it will.

Although the exchange between Curtis and Jerry was not racialized, other incidents in Briggs were—some arbitrarily, others by intention. In such "racial situations," the significance of race was overdetermined and out of control. Countervailing factors, from friendships to personal histories, mattered little; the volatile meanings of race consumed the nuances of those marked by its difference. But there were many more situations in Briggs in which the racial aspects of an exchange or encounter were unremarkable, there to be read if one pondered the matter long enough (as I was prone to do), but not substantive enough to have been stressed or noted by any of the actual participants—that is, nobody decided to "make something" out of these racial subtexts or contexts.

Racialness, in this zone, is a function of indelible markings, poignant, irrevocable histories, and unavoidable proximities. For most Americans, racialness, as an order of clear identity and difference, is based on distance. The operations of racial identity, the privileges and the disadvantages, are predicated on the spatialization of epidermal difference, which, in turn, informs and reproduces modes of social differentiation. In Briggs, there are very few means by which racial difference can be "properly" spatialized: whites and blacks both occupy this extreme-poverty area where jobs are scarce; their paths cross daily on the streets, in the corner stores, and in the bars. Racial difference remains significant because these people are problematically and uncertainly connected to larger collectives, both through their personal histories and through their awareness of broad, popular cultures and political orders. Racial markings are fairly indelible in this zone, but what remains an ongoing question is what significance those markings will have: What kind of difference will they make, and what forms of stability or boundedness pertains to the identities they suggest?[2] These questions are potentially raised in an array of social interactions in Briggs.

My attention to the conditional significance of race draws, in part, upon the work of Henry Louis Gates Jr. Gates asserts that to understand signification, we have to see its distinct operations in "two parallel discursive universes: the black American linguistic circle and the white."[3] In the latter, significance involves a fairly direct correspondence between any term and the meaning it conveys or is intended to convey. In the former, signification supplants simple semantics with elaborate rhetorical relations, in which meaning is constantly shifting between figurative and literal modes, tangled in "the free play of these associative rhetorical and semantic relations."[4] Alhough he generalizes this contrast in terms of racial absolutes—the "language of blackness" on one hand, of whiteness on the other—Gates admits that these two relations to meaning collide and overlap, constituting an ambiguous, symbiotic relationship.[5] This linguistic contrast, however, is useful for conveying how whites in Briggs engage the significance of race not as a semantic field where meanings are clearly denoted and established; they treat it rather as a variety of "ways of meaning," in which the play between surface and latent meanings is active and unstable. In particular, they attend to the way context influences the shifting movement of surface and latent possibilities of meaning. Gates succinctly renders this disposition with a quote from Claudia Mitchell-Kernan: "A particular utterance may be an insult in one context and not in another. What pretends to be informative may intend to be persuasive. The hearer is thus constrained to attend to all potential meaning carrying symbolic systems in speech events—the total universe of discourse."[6]

Residents of Briggs know that at one extreme, the significance of race is constituted in a charged, polarized (often violent) rhetoric of absolute distinctions; at the other extreme, it forms an unremarkable aspect of the daily lives of whites and blacks in this inner-city zone. They navigate between these conditions, knowing both that they are susceptible to reductive racial readings and that they are obliged to be vigilant for situations in which they must apply such readings to others. In particular, the significance of white racialness is primarily framed first, by their remove from the suburbs, where investments in whiteness are manifest but largely unmarked; and second, by their position as poor whites in the inner city of Detroit, where their motives or actions can easily be read as racist, and where they are subject to being reductively read as "whites," out of place, vulnerable, and suspicious. In this latter register, they are compelled to represent condensed versions of the tradition of white racism and supremacist ideology. Because it is subject to the variableness and uncertainties of sociality as constituted in conversation, gossip, rumors, and stories, the significance of race is often ambiguous and indeterminate.[7] Residents have developed means of interpreting the racial aspects—potential or expressed—of situations through an array of discursive categories that they deploy in different settings to make sense of race. But novel settings and the instability of the neighborhood often undermine the reliability of these categories. Hence, residents also must rely on a mode of attention that allows them to prioritize and judge the relevance of racial subtexts or suspicions in relation to competing frames of interest in everyday life, such as the relative importance of class or regional difference or gender distinctions.

This chapter features a very specific focus on the larger question of racial significance in this zone. Inner cities (or ghettos) and their residents are too often regarded through generalized figures—"blacks," "Puerto Ricans," and sometimes "poor whites"—depictions that simplify and homogenize diverse social settings. The following discussion aims at counterbalancing this tendency in social-science representations of the urban poor. Although some generalities may be posited of whites, blacks, and Latinos in this neighborhood, there are too many distinctions and discrepancies active within these groupings to make such comments worthwhile or intelligent. The emphasis in the first section, "Hillbillies," is on conveying the heterogeneity of the white population in Briggs, and relating how they assess intraracial distinctions through this charged rhetorical identity.

"Hillbillies"

In the 1940s and 1950s, "hillbilly" was applied as a strict act of boundary maintenance, shoring up an imperiled sense of white identity that was challenged by the way shared traits of white and black southerners undermined northern convictions of a qualitative difference between the races.[8] Like any cultural matter that threatens an established symbolic order, the dirtiness of "hillbillies" caused great anxiety among native white Detroiters.[9] Today in Briggs, "hillbilly" still carries these connotations, but as a racial category its uses are more plastic. Previously, "hillbilly" rather strictly designated a regional identity and marked those so described as being "out of place" in this city. But now it signals a more fluid, unstable disjuncture between the status of whiteness nationally and the significance of white racialness locally. In current usage, I heard "hillbilly" misapplied, being used of whites who had no southern ties but who did embody a lifestyle that clearly transgressed the mores associated with, or evidencing a desire for, the upward mobility that is so integral to ideological constructions of whiteness.[10]

One such case of misapplication arose when I was talking with Wanita (see "Riots and Race") about people who had caused her trouble in the neighborhood. She singled out "hillbilly Pat," even though she, like Wanita, was northern-born with no southern ties. Pat's Irish heritage also did not disrupt this designation. What registered as significant for Wanita seemed to be the fact that she had raised a large family mostly on her own, with her alcoholic husband making sporadic appearances, creating disruptions and turmoil. Pat herself used the term "hillbilly" only in reference to "low-down" whites, those who occupied a space animated by class contempt and loathing. When I asked her if there were many "hillbillies" in the neighborhood when she was growing up, she replied, "Well, most of the people owned their own homes and were stable . . . were . . . well, I'd never . . . I wouldn't refer to them as hillbillies, because to me, a hillbilly is the people who are dirty and they shuffle back and forth and all . . . So I've always compared it to southerners and hillbillies. That's how I tell which is which [she laughs]."

Such objectifications, used by whites to inscribe a classed distinction between themselves and more contemptible whites, existed side by side with the term's usage as a means of self-identification, as an actively claimed identity by (mostly) southern whites. As a self-designation, the term named a history, an origin, a style of manners; as a reference to others, the term deployed a tradition of stigmatization, a comical or offensive collection of traits, dimly keyed to a regional identity or, more precisely, a lifestyle. These two modes of usage were often overlapping and contiguous; they are in strange agreement. "Hillbilly" also marked an interesting dynamic of proximity and distance between whites and blacks, more elaborate than that entailed between "proper" or unmarked whites and blacks in this zone. As a group, "hillbillies" were the whites most frequently and elaborately engaged in interracial social ties in Briggs.[11]

As with any rhetorical identity or discursive objectification, "hillbilly" is difficult to pin down and define.[12] This difficulty derives from the mediating work such terms perform in clarifying the shifting correspondence between social spaces and collective or personal identities, each susceptible to varying degrees of instability. This is especially so because of the duty the term performs as a racial label, drawing together a range of critical white intraracial distinctions primarily keyed to class. This section features two views of "hillbillies." The first is a spatial crosscut of Briggs—from one street, Cochrane (which runs parallel to Trumbull), I draw together examples of people who fall under its marking and instances when the label is used; these are mostly centered in one of the few remaining local bars, O'Leary's. The second involves a dense rendering of a particular "hillbilly" family, Jerry and Jessie Rae's. I lived next door to them and developed my social relations in the neighborhood through their extensive ties in this area; I use their engagements as an example of the repertoires mobilized making sense of sociality in this location. Jerry, in particular, is interesting because he embodied a volatile set of features that were often the subject of projected intraracial distinctions from other whites; he also had more developed interracial associations than any other white that I knew in the area.

As a conflated racial and class category, "hillbilly" could be applied quite loosely at times, by both whites and blacks.[13] The term's rhetorical status was evidenced by its often meager ability to refer to an objective condition: The "fact" of southern heritage did not make the application of "hillbilly" either proper or assured. As with ethnic identities in the United States, the meaning of "hillbilly" follows generational demarcations. I never heard either of Jerry and Jessie Rae's two adult children—little Jerry and Jean—ever use the term in self-reference, though other "third-generation hillbillies" in the neighborhood did. The clarity of the category primarily stands out in relation to the degree of assimilation into the "mainstream" of white, middle- or working-class cultures. For these "hillbillies," the designation was a way of marking (and being marked by) their difference from whites who left Detroit (often including their

own kin) or from those who had stayed but who were of a slightly higher
class status, either as homeowners or as steady employees at one job. As
an intraracial marking of otherness, "hillbilly" objectified the collapse of
clear spatial arrangements of racial and class difference and identity in
this zone, differentiating whites who embodied a degraded form of whiteness—that is, whiteness without key forms of individual supports (striving for upward mobility) or institutional ones (from homeownership to
political activity)."[14]

Implicitly, "hillbilly" entailed a difference between whites and blacks:
I never heard the name applied to southern-born blacks, who, in this area,
were almost entirely from Alabama, Mississippi, and Georgia.[15] But
blackness was not the term's primary source of difference or otherness.
Indeed, older blacks in this neighborhood would refer to "whites" and
"hillbillies" as not quite synonymous categories.[16] The term's primary
contrast inscribed the difference between whites who "assimilated" successfully in this northern industrial town and those who retained behaviors or lived in conditions that were somehow improper for whites.
It seemed to me that it was the "hillbilly's" very proximity to blacks
that often heightened this sense of impropriety. After all, the central feature of achieved assimilation was escape to the nearly all-white suburbs,
something which these "hillbillies" were largely not drawn to pursue.
In applying the term "hillbilly" as either a form of distancing or self-
identification, whites are evaluating who belongs, both in this decaying
neighborhood and in the space of whiteness.

On Cochrane

Cochrane, like the rest of the neighborhood, is missing most of its houses.
In their stead a veritable riot of biomass rules: grasses, saplings, bushes,
and trees. The street once hosted a mechanic's garage and a half dozen
stores and "confectioneries." Every lot was built up, and during World
War II most were overcrowded by the massive influx of migrants. Now
there is only one "party store" (liquor store) on Cochrane. The garage
was transformed into a community center that has since gone bankrupt.
O'Leary's bar, though, still does very good business. The street is nine
blocks long and dead-ends at the freeway. Most of the forty-odd houses
still standing on these blocks are occupied, while the encircling empty lots
surge with grasses that, in the summer at least, cover the tires and other
refuse in the fields.

Floyd (see "Introduction") lives at the south end of the street, near the
freeway. Most of the houses at this end have long given way to parking
lots for Tiger Stadium crowds. His is one of four houses—each clearly

rotting—still standing on this block. Floyd likes to remember the days in the 1950s and 1960s when the "hillbillies" became something of a dominant cultural presence. Floyd has been here, up from Kentucky, since 1948. He was ten years old when he arrived and has lived in this neighborhood ever since. For him, "hillbilly" refers to a general regional identity; he did not use it to denote specific class divisions. There was an inclusive air to his descriptions: "Well there's hillbillies all over here. Most everybody around here's a hillbilly." As he characterized this amorphous group, he talked most intensely about fighting in the bars as the particular cultural pastime of people like himself. He told me, "The worst place to be on a Saturday night is a hillbilly bar. Especially if you're not a hillbilly, cause they'll beat you up first. Course, if there's just hillbillies in there, then we turn on each other. We'll just beat each other up."

He laughed and related, eyes gleaming, accounts of reckless nights and big brawls, describing the bar on Temple where he had been shot and others over on Cass that have long since closed. He showed me the bullet scar in his chest, three old knife wounds, and where the knuckles on the right hand, four of them, had been busted down to nothing from punching people. He had lost all of his teeth.

But things are different now. "It didn't use to be so crazy with the guns. We would fight all the time, but it wasn't this stabbing and shooting. We'd beat on each other and bust each other up, but that was it. And when you got done fighting, it was over. You'd each get up and start drinking again, you'd see each other next week. It didn't matter if I had beat you or the other way. It was just that one guy that was stronger had beat you. It wasn't calling each other 'punks' or 'asshole' on account of being beat."[17] About the neighborhood in general, he said, "There's only one rule around here, if you mess with somebody, they're gonna shoot you." He said right off that he was old now, so he had to rely on guns instead of fists. Pointing at my chest, he let me know that "I'd have to shoot you, rather than fight you now. That's how it's gotten." This attitude, he suggested, had produced a kind of racial equilibrium in the area: "We don't have trouble with black people around here 'cause the white people are meaner and crazier than them. They some mean, crazy people 'round here. They know people around here would just as soon shoot you if you mess with them." He assured me that nobody would "mess" with me once they got to know me, and if I minded my own business. After describing a killing that he witnessed—though he reported nothing about it to the police—Floyd concluded that, "If you don't know nothing, you live longer."

Near the other end of the street, one afternoon I stumbled into a conversation about tomatoes with Justin, an old white man who often sat with his wife on their front porch. I stopped to admire the large green plants and their ripening bounty. After sharing loose conversation about planting strategies, I asked them where they were from—he is from Kentucky and she from Tennessee. They had just returned from a stay in Kentucky, he told me: "We got a little trailer down there." I located myself by saying that I had just moved into one of the places Jerry took care of. He said, "Yeah, you got a lot of hillbillies over there." "Yeah we do," I agreed. But he then observed that "Just about everybody up and down this street is hillbillies." She added, "Yeah, they're from Arkansas, Tennessee, Kentucky, everywhere."

Justin had found a job at Jefferson Chevrolet almost as soon as he arrived and he kept it for thirty years, then retired, living off the pension, whereas Floyd keeps scraping together work from his repertoire of skills, including window washing and car repair. Justin parks his new Chevy van on the empty lot next to his house—"they" stole his battery a couple of times, so this is a preventative measure. Floyd has no car and bums rides downtown or to the store as necessary.

Although Justin and his wife, like Floyd, loosely regarded all the southerners in the area as "hillbillies," their next-door neighbors were more exact in their usage of the label. I met Roscoe Howell and his wife on another day—they too were sitting out on their porch. When I mentioned having moved recently from California, they recalled working there forty years ago as migrants, picking fruit for five years. They were both born in Arkansas. One of their daughters, Retha, lives on the next block down Cochrane, and two live outside the city. When I told them where I was living, she gasped and asked distressedly, "With hillbilly?" I chuckled and replied with Justin's sentiment that it seemed to be "all hillbillies around here." They each winced and turned their faces, cringing at the implication, though they politely let it pass. As I learned through later conversations with them, southern heritage was not synonymous with the term that they used to denote a rude minority of whites.

Roscoe had known Jerry's daddy and a few of his uncles from the time when they all lived by Canfield and Cass, about a half-mile north of this neighborhood in an area where "hillbillies" also concentrated. By his estimation, they were "a good family—they don't bother nobody." Of Jerry, in particular, he generously noted that "He's a good fellah. He don't bother nobody." But she found Jerry dreadful and recalled the yellow house before Jerry and family moved in some years ago, before shifting over to the red house. "That used to be such a beautiful house. It was all painted and kept up, until they moved in. They just let it go down. They don't care about nothing over there." She remembered the old couple who had lived there; one of them died, and the house was sold. Instead of blaming Frank, the landlord, Mrs. Howell fixed the blame for the decay of this place solely on Jerry's family. She animatedly told me how they let the trash just pile up and never once cleaned the windows. "She had such beautiful drapes in those front windows. They were beautiful. Well, when they moved in, they just threw them out and put up rags. Ole Hillbilly don't care about nothing. They just let that place go down."

There were clear class lines involved in the difference between the Howells and Jerry. They were homeowners and Jerry has always rented; Mr. Howell got a good factory job when he arrived in Detroit over forty years ago, while Jerry's work record is sporadic at best.[18] Such class distinctions mattered in the delimited and derogatory applications of "hillbilly" among the broader collective of southern migrants. The extension of "hillbilly" as a common identity in the way that Floyd deployed it, however, was most frequently undermined by the type of rowdy, reckless lifestyle that Jerry maintained. The difference discerned and stressed by Mrs. Howell intriguingly mattered more than any ethnic difference from Frank, the Maltese landlord who owned Jerry's place and who could easily have been held accountable for the decrepit condition of the house that we moved into.

Jerry was widely known locally as "Hillbilly Jerry," a designation observed by other "hillbillies" as well. His unquenchable willingness to fight, his stints in jail, the fact that he was always broke, surviving on various scams, and his unerringly profane and often vicious use of language, made him for most people the apotheosis of the category. During a party at O'Leary's on Halloween night, I was drinking with Larry, a white man in his mid-thirties, who lived two houses down Cochrane from the bar. We were talking just before he picked a fight with several other white men in the bar and was stabbed (he survived, though the house where he lived burned that night—in connection with the fight, most suspected). One topic in our conversation was a recent robbery that he had carried out with "little Jerry," Mr. Howell's grandson; the target was a local church. When I asked him something about "Jerry," he questioned whether I meant "little Jerry," or "Hillbilly Jerry." I clarified that I was asking about "Hillbilly Jerry," and Larry replied, "Don't get me wrong, I'm a hillbilly, too! No doubt about that, I'm a hillbilly too." And even though "little Jerry" counted, too, as a "hillbilly"—being the Howells' grandson allowed him to claim the identity "legitimately"—the designation went to "big Jerry" instead, since he so publicly performed the dirty, reckless role of this figure.

The Howells' daughter, Retha, lives with Steve, across the street from O'Leary's. Steve is one of Larry's two brothers living in Briggs. Although they were all born up north, they identify themselves as "hillbillies." Their other brother, Jeff, lived just around the corner from the bar. He moved back to Tennessee during the second summer of my stay. When we first met at O'Leary's, he asked me, "So what part of the South are you

Figure 7. O'Leary's (background). A baseball game is under way on the corner lot. Mrs. Wade's trailer is in the foreground. Steve and Retha live in the white house on the left.

from?" Their mother lives on the other side of Trumbull and worked parking cars around Tiger Stadium when her health allowed, or running a rather constant "yard sale" during baseball's off-season. Steve and Retha made O'Leary's their first stop when they brought their newborn baby home from the hospital. It was the middle of the afternoon; several black women and two old hillbillies sat in the cool, shadowy confines, and the baby was a big hit.

The bonds between "hillbillies" were susceptible to the forms of volatility that underlie all social relations in this neighborhood. "Hillbillies" crossed paths more often than other whites in the neighborhood, operating in the same social spaces, thus increasing the chances of stumbling into some type of conflict. Also "hillbilly" kin groups were quite extensive. Following the "feuding" stereotype, family loyalties often outweighed individual relationships, and conflicts between two people escalated into animosities that extended across the kin groups. One afternoon, I asked Jerry about a large white family living around the corner from us on the last block of Cochrane. There were half a dozen children, several big adult brothers, parents, and at least a couple of grandparents living in the one house, supplemented by a steady stream of visitors. I asked Jerry if there was a good way of introducing myself to them. He just growled, "They're a bunch of assholes—all of 'em. Well, Tommy's all right, and so is Billy if he ain't drunk. They all hang out at O'Leary's some, but they just down there looking to fight. They get stupid drunk, then make trouble. They're a bunch of assholes." He had fought a couple of times with one of the brothers and regarded the whole family with contemptuous detachment.

I was surprised to hear Jerry describing another family in a manner similar to the way some of his friends had described him and his family to me. Jerry kindly introduced me around to people in the area, and told me that if anybody was giving me trouble I should tell them that I was his brother—that would settle matters, he assured me. But as soon as Jerry was out of earshot, his "friends" consistently warned me to watch out for him and "the whole damn family. None of 'em can be trusted." Jerry, they all took pains to warn me, was dangerous and mean, which certainly proved true. Jerry and I had a protracted dispute over the gas bill for the house we were renting; he had assured me the landlord would pay half of the bill, since there was only one meter for the two flats—this was a scam, though. He won the argument by having his brothers slash the tires on our car; then Rebecca and I moved out.

What became apparent through all of these cautions and distances was that there was little or no sense of racial solidarity among whites in this area. The social connections between whites were no more stable than those that existed between whites and blacks, or than the relations between blacks in the area. Although they could drink and party together at the corner bar, or share a word or two in passing on the street, sociality here required a developed sense of caution and guardedness with all people, even among one's own family members.[19] Like broad racial collectives, regional identity was fraught with ambiguities and differences, providing only a tenuous basis for developing or maintaining social relations. Generally speaking, broad projections of collectivity are an unstable basis of identity in this neighborhood.

O'Leary's: A Public Space

O'Leary's is one of the last of many "hillbilly" bars that were once scattered across the core of Detroit. Such bars were, and remain, a prime reason why "hillbillies," particularly the men, stayed in Detroit. They may have come north for divergent reasons, and found varying degrees of success here in Detroit, but one common strand ran through their stories about why they remained here: There was nothing matching these bars "back home."[20] Bars such as O'Leary's provided a voluptuous mix of immodest urban culture along with the familiarity of other rural folk raised with "down-home ways." From these bars emerged the "urban hillbilly," a cultural fusion of the city and the country.[21] Several of the old "hillbillies" made regular, extended trips "back home," flirting with the idea of moving back. But in listing their reasons for returning to Detroit, they stressed that there was nothing like this bar in the rural, sometimes "dry," counties that they had come from. O'Leary's allowed for racial, class, and gender mixing, too, which is still uncommon in other places.[22]

On most nights, there are more whites than blacks in the bar, but it was not unusual for the reverse to be true on other nights. Men usually outnumber women of both races, though a rough gender balance was quite frequent. The jukebox ratified the heterogeneous racial setting by interspersing the latest offerings of Prince or Sir-Mix-Alot, Silk, Salt-N-Pepa, Boyz-II-Men, Tony Toni Tone, Snow, Whitney Houston, and Bobby Brown, alongside recent and older tunes by George Jones, Merle Haggard, Dolly Parton, Loretta Lynn, Conway Twitty, and cuts from the newer country stars like Dwight Yokum, Vince Gill, Trisha Yearwood, Mary Chapin Carpenter, Mark Chestnut, and big favorite Billy Ray Cyrus. On any evening, Prince's "Sexy-MF" might follow Dolly Parton's "Romeo"; Sir-Mix-Alot's "Baby's Got Back," precedes Mark Chestnut's "Prop Me up beside the Jukebox if I Die" or John Anderson's "Honky Tonk Saturday Night," which in turn might be followed by Silk's "Freaky." The jukebox epitomized the synthetic crossings of racially marked musical genres that Detroit has long been known for.[23] Selecting tunes was often a public matter, especially late in the evening. I heard black patrons warn a white about playing "too much of that hillbilly shit"; whites, in turn, would sometimes draw loud attention to their rhythm and blues choices. White and black patrons made selections with an understanding of what racial orders the musics affirmed or blurred, and men and women of both races operated the jukebox with an aesthetic sensibility that encouraged selections across perfunctory or "mainstream" racial lines.

Tyrone, a black man in his thirties, and I met taking turns at the jukebox one night. After gabbing about Prince and Dolly Parton, we carried our conversation back to the bar. He helped run one of the area's "after-hours" joints and invited me to stop in sometime.[24] In passing, I noted that people got along well here. He agreed, pointing out that, "most everybody around here I went to school with. We all come up together. Most everybody here, we all went to school together." He pointed out Jerry and half a dozen of the other whites in the bar as people he had known since he was a kid. Others had emphasized the basic fact that people get along in this neighborhood, but I only then appreciated that this degree of familiarity was predicated on more than twenty years of social interaction.

Afternoons in O'Leary's, the old "hillbillies"—usually about four or five of them—gather to talk and drink, sipping slowly from their beers, carefully stretching social security or pension checks to last through the month. This afternoon routine was stabilized, in part, by the bartender, George, who came up from Kentucky in 1961. Several of the old "hillbillies" bragged about how they had followed him from one bar to the next, changing their status as regulars as he moved between jobs. He had worked in more than a dozen bars all over the area, most of which have long since burned or closed. He lives only a block away from O'Leary's. The participants varied from time to time, depending on how the checks were holding up or what other diversions were available. During the first few afternoons I spent there, conversations were steady but almost impenetrable to me. Not only did they speak with "thick" accents through often toothless mouths and garbled memories, but their fleetness with common references was so developed that, though I might be able to make out the words and the general sense of action that they conveyed, I was oblivious to the specifics of the scenes and the people they were discussing.

Events in the neighborhood composed the prime topics of conversation: what kind of trouble so-and-so was in, who was working and who wasn't, and what type of car repairs or trades were under way or just completed. Gardening was also of keen interest to these men. In the spring, discussions centered on what was being planted, whether it was early or late for which plants, and who was giving away what kind of seeds. Summer conversations shifted from this detailed attention to the ground and moved back to cars, gambling, weather, and occasionally problems with squirrels, raccoons, and other local wildlife. Over the course of the fall, the bar top became cluttered with the harvests, large and small. People brought in particularly good-looking vegetables or those that were in surplus from overplanting or good luck with weather and rodents. The knowledge they employed in assessing the bounty of harvest, or the judiciousness of planting tomatoes in April, derived from spending their early years in rural Tennessee or Kentucky, working on their families' plots. Allusions were made to "secret" techniques that somebody might have used to get those great cucumbers, but this seemed largely a form of banter.

In general, they teased each other heartily over lost poker games, bad binges, and foolish choices regarding cars, property, or people. Several men had lost their driver's license here but picked up new ones "down South." There was still a steady traffic between the two places. This shared regional origin also provided them with a common reservoir of knowledge about that both real and imaginary weakness of "hillbillies"—moonshine. One afternoon, the men were discussing a rash of minor acts of "vandalism." Some guesses were made as to the identity of the culprit, but, whoever it turned out to be, all were convinced that the villain(s) must be "on the shine," referring to a batch of "moonshine" circulating in the neighborhood. The men giggled as they discussed its ability to "make you do some stupid shit."

This conversation led quickly into a string of moonshine stories, each located in different "hollers" down South. Personal accounts gradually shifted into jokes about "hillbillies," each centered on buffoonery. Then George told a story about a stranger who came looking for moonshine; he found the old "hillbilly" who was selling the stuff way back in some "holler." When the man asked about his moonshine, the "hillbilly" whipped out a pistol, held it to the stranger's head, then ordered him to "drink it or I'll shoot you." The stranger gulped down a swallow, choked, gasped, retched, and reeled—then was surprised to see the "hillbilly" handing him the gun, saying, "Now you hold it on me and make me drink it." They chuckled for a while over that one.

The "hillbilly" in this and other jokes or stories displayed a degree of detachment from "their" own cultural identity. Although all of these "hillbillies" at the bar would use the name as a means of self-identification, they also stood back from it and laughed at its comic aspects and the dubious antics associated with it. They could laugh at "hillbillies" because of their intimacy with the stereotype, having been marked by it often enough that the designation was comfortably self-inscribed.[25] The comic aspects of "hillbilly" were a performative matter, too, in the very public space of O'Leary's. The use of "hillbilly" here was often played out in widely broadcast, stereotyped affections for certain jukebox tunes or in brash, "ignorant" behavior. The first time Jerry took Rebecca and me over there—on the evening we moved in—we met Donnie, seated by himself at the bar. Donnie was in his thirties and already toothless. At one point, he led me to the door and pointed out the grassy lot across Cochrane where the house that he grew up in once stood. His parents had come up from the South and, when he bothered with such things as collective identity, he referred to himself as a "hillbilly." When Lorreta Lynn's "Coal Miner's Daughter" started playing on the jukebox, he and Jerry joined in singing along all the way through. Their fathers had both been coal miners. Donnie's suffered from black lung—such hazards had provoked Jerry's dad to leave for Detroit as a young man in 1941.

Three days later, early in the evening, Jerry, Sam, Leroy (Jessie Rae's brother), and I went to the bar. We had to drive the two-block distance because of Jerry's bad leg, which he had recently broken but never let properly heal since he would not stay off it. That afternoon he had dramatically reinjured it with a sledge hammer while trying to remove a tire from its rim for his brother David. Jerry had the tire propped against his knee while swinging the sledge hammer. (This technique of separating the tire from the rim was devised to save him the $2 charge for having it removed at a gas station.) On the second swing of the hammer, he missed the tire completely and smashed it into his bad leg.

Orin, who had directed me to Jerry's when I first inquired at the bar about places to rent, was propped up on a stool.[26] While Leroy and Sam struck up a game of pool, Jerry and I talked with him. Jerry told him how his leg was still messed up, explaining that it never healed quite right. I jokingly told Orin that the doctors had put a cast on his leg but that Jerry had beat the cast off with a sledge hammer. They both laughed, and Orin said, "Ain't that just like his dumb-ass hillbilly self." Jerry, smiling, thundered, "That's right I'm a hillbilly! From West by God Virginia. That's right." He strutted about, his massive arms swinging in the air, roaring his affirmation—"That's right I'm a hillbilly," while Orin just laughed some more.

Later, after Leroy knocked Sam off the pool table in a close win, Sam took up where Jerry left off, recalling the enthusiasm with which people in their state of "origin" insisted upon their difference from Virginia proper. "That's how you got to say it down there. They really do say it just like that, 'West BY GOD Virginia!' West BY GOD Virginia, hand over your heart and everything. They're crazy down there." His eyes were animated as he related this and described their trips "every summer" back to West Virginia to visit their daddy's family.

Jerry joined us. He asked Sam why his wife, Earline, had not come along. "She's not coming," he answered. "She doesn't like city bars. We're suburbanites now," he grinned. The bars in Detroit had always made Earline nervous, but since they had recently moved to the downriver suburb of Taylor—her hometown—she was even more uncomfortable in these places. I said it was hard to believe Earline was not a real "hillbilly." Sam nodded, "Yeah, but I made her into one." By bringing her down to his class level, it seemed that she could be included as a "hillbilly," even though she was northern-born, of German-American parents.

Such extensions of this marked or stigmatized identity were not uncommon in this zone. Where heritage was not in question or of interest, the status of "hillbilly" was assigned in strictly behavioral terms. O'Leary's got a bit of traffic from the nearby Teamster's Union headquarters. Various officials who wanted either to avoid an afternoon in the office or to have a rendezvous with a secret lover would hang out at O'Leary's. One such couple was in the bar when we entered that afternoon. They sat at the far end of the bar, alone, immersed in amorous fondling. Leroy felt compelled to bother them. "Ahh, we got some lovebirds here," he announced loudly, proceeding to annoy them with questions and unremitting, lecherous attention, until they finally left. The man, though, over the course of my stay, gradually became a "regular" in the evening hours as well as during the day. He still wore his office suit and tie, but he eased into a string of friendships. By the next summer, he as easily ended up dancing to the jukebox as any other drunk at the bar. For that accomplishment, I heard Urvena—George's wife and fellow bartender—holler at him one night, "Well, look, we made a hillbilly out of you after all." He beamed a boozy grin and swerved blissfully across the crowded floor.

This inclusive extension across class lines suggests the great degrees of plasticity to this name, which has clearly exceeded its initial usefulness as a term of boundary maintenance for a threatened sense of whiteness. But its derogatory aspects continued to be close at hand and could easily be wielded by people who used the term incautiously or maliciously. As a rule of thumb, more intimate settings let the recipient of this label decide to take offense at or ignore the remark. But in public places like O'Leary's, the epithet's charged meanings were often as unruly as the patrons. Although I never saw a fist fight provoked by somebody using "hillbilly" as a slur, I did hear people warned when their usage crossed the line into clearly derogatory connotations. Part of what undercut a visceral immediacy to the demeaning implications of "hillbilly" is that whites so marked, or who chose the term as a means of self-designation, evidenced little interest in the forms of "management" that Erving Goffman described in relation to other stigmatized identities.[27] "Hillbilly" as a collective label carried a double-edged signification; it cut alternately inclusive and exclusive lines. Not wanting to be caught unaware by its exclusive, stigmatizing uses, Jerry and others outperformed them, playing out the most bufoonish associations preemptively. Emphatically drawing associations between his actions and the degrading stereotypes of "hillbillies"—rather than controlling the features of disrespectability that arose in various situations—Jerry and other whites in this zone seemed to wallow in these conformational moments.[28] But these performances also involved a complicated engagement with the social distance from a normative sense of whiteness that informed the marking practices objectifying these poor whites.[29]

This matter bears a bit of unpacking and will become clearer in the following discussion of how family members used "hillbilly," but basically it was the stereotypicality of "hillbilly" that these whites found useful in negotiating their social environs. Two points are key here: First, the social signifiers of respectability (in class terms) generally exceed the grasp of these inner-city whites; and second, the types of ambiguities that Goffman found arising in encounters between "normals" and stigmatized individuals, rather than being exceptional moments, define sociality in this zone. In refusing to manage properly their identification as "hillbillies," these whites seem to have stumbled upon a discursive means of negotiating both their ambivalent remove from the norms of whiteness—cleanliness, upward striving if not actual social mobility, and distance from black people, to name just a few—and the uncertainties that permeated the social relations encompassing their lives. Inscribing themselves with this objectification of racial ambiguity (a marked form of whiteness), "hillbilly" performed usefully as a rhetorical device and as an interpretive means for assessing the significance of race (generally) and white racialness (specifically).

This function of "hillbilly" is made clearer by drawing upon Phyllis Chock's analysis of the interpretive work that stereotypes perform in the construction of ethnicity, where "stereotypes are used by the very people they encompass. This is a classic double bind. When a Greek American uses a stereotype, his discourse is directed both at himself and at his audience. When he uses 'Greek,' he confronts American classification schemes and ponders whom they may include; at the same time he confronts himself as one of their possible objects. He tries to connect, and sometimes disconnect, a particular ethnic category and the multitude of images of 'Greeks' available."[30] Such self-deployed stereotypes, of either Greeks or "hillbillies," open a gap between the forms of social signification where the contours and contents of racial and ethnic categories are assumed and the space of daily life, where the inconsistencies that complicate or undermine stereotypes are manifest. For whites like Jerry, "hillbilly" made tangible the distance between his situation and the decorums supporting the normative status of whiteness. These whites used stereotypes in this way not to ratify or insist upon certain static meanings and presumptions, but to engage the discrepancies between the signifying background of established, broad social norms and their own uncertain predicaments.[31] As Chock underscores, stereotypes "bring to talk about something many nearly ineffable traces of their connections to other domains of meaning," thereby drawing "attention to larger, usually hegemonizing, discourses and the sociocultural contexts of use and understanding that are essential to their production of meaning." In the clash between the indeterminate flux of sociality and the determinate power of structures of classification that stereotypes represent, self-inscribing this marked identity allows "hillbillies" to undermine the absolute opposition of self and other that such a category maintains as part of a broadly functioning racial ideology. "That is, the rhetoric constitutes the social categories and their structures by assembling, disassembling, and reassembling not so much the categories as the structures in which they fit. It is these structures that make constructed selves so uneasy, because they fit untidily into notions of personal identities."[32] Although not managing the respectability of his personal identity, Jerry's usage of "hillbilly" allowed him dexterity with charged, collective (racial) identities, and an open-ended, boisterous, and often ugly interrogation of the relevance or relationship these structured identities ("whites and blacks") bore to the fluid, volatile realm of sociality in Briggs.

"Hillbilly Jerry"

The kind of ironic ambivalence that Chock finds integral to ethnicity was a constant at Jerry's. Family members alternated between invoking "hillbilly" as a heritage and trying to fix each other in the stupefying glare of its inscription as a comic image. Rather relentlessly, they played with the stereotype. They had little interest in dignifying the identity. "Hillbilly" was affixed to any sort of makeshift repair or any kind of not-quite-sufficient effort or resource. When a lost or damaged car bumper was replaced by a piece of 2 x 6 lumber, they called this a "hillbilly bumper." Jerry replaced a missing muffler on his brother David's car by lashing a tin can with numerous punctures in it to the end of the exhaust pipe, announcing that now he had a "hillbilly muffler." When he jimmied up a poorly aligned headlight with a small twig, his buddy Willie commented right away, "Nice hillbilly headlight." The circumstance of such naming did not have to be actual; they were also projected in jokes and riddles. One joke they savored was picked up by Jerry's brother Sam at a free country music concert downriver in Wyandotte; it asked, "What is a guitar case?" "Hillbilly daycare."

In these namings there was both humiliation and pride. The ineluctable basis of all such appellations was the lack of money that made such makeshift repairs necessary. But, there was also pride in the basic innovation, the cheap, money-saving design that outwitted the economic system and the stigmatizing condition of constant poverty, subverting the connotations of stupidity that dogged them. Hence the significance of the prefix "hillbilly" depended on the emphasis of the speaker and the mood of the receiver. This made for a volatile mix.

Earline thoroughly disliked being called "hillbilly"; she was also miserable most of the time that she and Sam and their two kids lived with Jerry and Jessie Rae. Sam was out of work, and rent was "free" as long as Jerry could conceal from Frank the fact that they were staying in one of the vacant rooms. They stayed for months, even though Sam had to drive over one hundred miles a day, taking the kids to and from school in Taylor, taking Earline to work at a fast food restaurant, and trying to find himself an occasional part-time job (usually involving roadwork, like spreading tar). When family members referred to Earline as a "hillbilly," she usually made a point of proving them wrong. One of the first nights after Rebecca and I moved in, Sam was teasing Earline about something, then he called her a "hillbilly." Earline reared up in a huff, and sharply hissed, "I ain't no hillbilly—I'm German!"

Sam chimed, "That's right. You ain't got any hillbilly in you."

"No, I don't," Earline snorted.

She smiled, raising her nose in the air while Sam snickered. Later that night he emphatically pointed out to me, "I'm a hillbilly. I got a lot of hillbilly in me. My dad was from West Virginia and my mom was from Kentucky. I'm all hillbilly." The fact that he was born in Detroit did not seem to be a mitigating factor.

Although I was surprised at first to hear "hillbilly" used in comparative contrast to an ethnic identity like "German," there are interesting forms of equivalence at work here, besides the discursive uses of their stereotypicality. The question of the "ethnicity" of urban Appalachians has been the subject of intense scholarship for over two decades.[33] Although the majority of whites who migrated to the industrial Midwest from Appalachia successfully assimilated into the suburban, white middle class, a significant portion of this group remains mired in the impoverished conditions of inner-city neighborhoods, and many were also forced to return home, after finding conditions in the North to be unaccommodating and too alien.[34] Those still mired in urban slums closely resemble the residual effect of stalled or failed assimilation that is central to the sociological conception of ethnicity. William Philliber demonstrates that urban Appalachians match seven of eight categories of ethnicity: They are "found to share a common origin, to have socioeconomic homogeneity, to show intergenerational inheritance [poverty], to have a separate process of achievement, to experience differential association, to identify with other Appalachians, and to experience rejection by non-Appalachians." Intriguingly, the only category this group lacked "was the existence of unique cultural traits."[35] The equation between "hillbillies" and ethnicity is also suggested by that most telling realm of jokes and insults. In cities from Pittsburgh to Chicago, "hillbillies" are the subject of numerous retreaded ethnic jokes, keyed around images of ignorance, laziness, uncleanliness, and immorality.[36] Such stereotyping—currently and historically, as recounted in the previous chapter—highlights the crux of the matter: that residual groups, like white "hillbillies" in Briggs, are characterized by the type of intergenerational poverty that has been largely associated with African Americans in the inner city.[37]

Whether or not it can be considered an "authentic" ethnic identity, "hillbilly" demonstrates how loosely and with what little reverence such categories and identities are considered in this zone. Larger collective orders are unstable reference points in Briggs; the operation of poverty is such that, apart from family, there is little else to rely on for help in crises, and appeals to a larger collective are rare. People simply do not invoke "community" as a means of making sense of local relations or conflicts; the designation is too abstract and individuals' ties, given the transient housing and often volatile neighbors, are too tenuous. Rather, ethno-racial categories and names are used more synthetically and specifically for their stereotypical connotations. Ethnic labels resolve the immediate problem of finding a means to locate or objectify someone culturally. From there, specificities regarding individuals and families are elaborated. Derogatory ethnic labels, in a sense, generate a common social field: If everyone can be stereotypically marked, then their shared class predicament is emphasized.

Frank, the landlord of Jerry and Jessie Rae, is Maltese. His family came from Malta in the 1940s when he was a child, and he grew up on Cochrane. Although several Maltese families lived in the area, and Jerry and his brothers knew that they were Maltese, as an ethnic group they were largely innocuous. "Malt," their identifying tag, did not draw on a cultural reservoir of charged meaning. Jerry and his brothers found it more interesting to locate Frank using other ethnic identities. Sam, who was disgusted with Frank for being "money-grubbing" and refusing to let him stay for free in one of the vacant apartments in Jerry's house, one day described Frank to me as "your typical Arab-Jew." This synthetic inscription of ethnicity mobilizes two more familiar and emotionally charged categories for positioning and making sense of Frank. Since the majority of the businesses (liquor stores) are owned by Arab Americans, this naming "fit" Frank because he was a landlord. He reaped profits by over-charging residents and took the money out of the neighborhood, back to the suburbs where he now lived. The "Jew" tag was surely drawn from a pervasive and enduring anti-Semitism not confined to certain neighborhoods or regions; this usage attempted to locate his "money-grubbing" tendencies.[38] The difference that Frank embodied was subtle, but rather than objectify this difference for its uniqueness, they chose to describe it within a more reliable, charged currency.

When they analyzed Frank, the key points they emphasized were class markings: his late-model Lincoln Continental; his refusal to invest money on upkeep for the house; and his increasing fear of, and contempt for, residents in the neighborhood.[39] In this regard, the prime connotation for "Arab-Jew" was not an ethnic heritage so much as an economic identity/position.[40] Sam made it a point to stress the typicalness of Frank's fusion of Arabness and Jewness: "your typical Arab-Jew." In part, this underscores the perception that Frank's personality is familiar. This naming designates an ethnoclass, a position of difference that was indelible and absolutely distanced from their own social position. Among members of his class (property/business owners) certain "ethnic" features had simply become fused, from Sam's perspective, in a seamless equation of class and ethnic difference. This fusion is not surprising, since Frank embodied many of the critical elements of the ethnic success story.[41] What is a bit unusual here is that it seems his ethnicity obliquely "racialized" Jerry and his brothers, a matter examined in the next section.

The important point was that Frank held economic power over Sam and Jerry and their families. In the conflict over Sam's "free" rent, Jerry eventually sided with Frank, throwing his own brother out on the street. For Jerry, it was an economic necessity: If he wanted to keep his situation with Frank he could not get away indefinitely with letting Sam stay rent free. In this situation, not only was whiteness not a bond of common solidarity, neither was family or kin. It is in this regard that collective identities are not overly invested with significance, since they had scant material to bring to bear on such poignant conflicts.

As with "Arab-Jew," there was little interest in establishing refinements or adding subtleties to any of the charged, derogatory markings that ethnic names entailed. Ethnicities were regarded racially, as a set of characteristics, the significance of which varied from context to context. Jerry was waxing nostalgic one afternoon over a friendly family that had once lived across the street. He was saying to me, "There were some Puerto Ricans living there, and they were from Puerto Rico . . . ," when Willie, standing nearby in the yard, interrupted to deftly note, "Oh no shit, they're Puerto Ricans."

Jerry roared, "Fuck you, not all Puerto Ricans are born there."

Willie, undaunted, rejoined, "Then they aren't Puerto Ricans! They got a name for it. Like African Americans, Italian Americans . . . "

Jerry, with bemused disgust, interjected, "Yeah, and then there's Asshole Americans." Facing me, he rolled his eyes and cocked his head toward Willie, indicating him. Willie laughed when he caught Jerry's implication, and returned the favor by cracking a joke about Jerry's huge gut. The two broke into charged banter, teasing each other back and forth until Willie tried to return to the "serious" topic.

Willie said, "It'd be like blacks. They call themselves African Americans 'cause they weren't born in Africa."

Jerry, though, refused to adopt the serious mode. "Yeah well where do Asshole Americans come from? Tell me that, huh!? Where do Asshole Americans come from?"

Jerry was in Willie's face, menacing him with his mass, while Willie convulsed in fits of laughter, scurrying and again eluding Jerry's shirtless torso. After another round of cussing and fat jokes, they moved on to other subjects.

Jerry's stance both acknowledged an indelible quality to ethnic identity and refused excessive refinements to such identities. This position is similar to his use of "hillbilly." He considers himself a "hillbilly," even though he was born in the North and never lived in West Virginia. Like "Puerto Rican," the point with "hillbilly" is to mark a broad collective background, one to which not much can be emphatically attributed, but which provides a means of placement in this heterogeneous and unstable social zone. Jerry also refused to define "hillbilly" with great rigor or elaboration. Such rigor would likely preclude the comic or performative aspects of the designation, insisting that it be taken seriously and commonly recognized by everybody. It was the very performative aspects that were vital for defusing tensions and undercutting possible provocation, which always seemed plentiful. Taking these designations seriously would involve an untenable policing of the term's usage and require a dangerous defensiveness. On this latter point, too, Willie was attempting to "correct" Jerry's use of language. Implied in this posturing was Willie's assertion of greater sophistication with language and culture. Jerry reacted to and rejected this assertion as much as he did the ethnic elaboration Willie proposed by insisting he specify "Puerto Rican-American."

A key difference here between "hillbilly" and "true" ethnic identities is that the former operates as an inclusive designation, and one which is additionally a matter of class distinctions and lifestyle. Later during the evening when Earline insisted on being "German" rather than a "hillbilly," Jerry teased Rebecca when she came out on the porch to join in one of our sporadic efforts to play music. He bellowed, "What are you doing out of the house? A good hillbilly woman stays in the house working all the time."

Jessie Rae answered for her by punching Jerry's arm, as he giggled to himself. It was clearly a joke; he was playing with the stereotype of "hillbilly," knowing that for him and Jessie Rae it was untrue but wanting to see how Rebecca would act both to the extension of a marked, common identity and to the implicit transgression she was enacting upon its "tradition." Rebecca just laughed. Jerry continued this tack of teasing when Rebecca started playing the washtub bass, which impressed him. He demanded to know from Rebecca if she was a "hillbilly" or not. She replied that she guessed she was now.

"That's right," said Jerry, "and proud too!"

"That's right," she laughed, "damn proud."

Jerry grinned with glee and called for another song.

Earline, however, was too close to the stereotype to enjoy being marked by it. Earline was the most "social" of all of them in welcoming us. She came over while we were moving in and clued us in to everybody's quirks and problems. Of herself, she noted, "Some people don't like me because I talk too much and I'm too damn loud." In this regard, she did fit right in. But her discomfort at having to live in such close quarters was read relentlessly by Jessie Rae and Jerry as contempt or arrogance, so any conflict that arose quickly escalated into hard feelings and cold shoulders.

They called her "hillbilly" to watch her squirm in discomfort at its points of accuracy, catching just enough of her predicament to imply that she belonged here as much as any of them. Earline responded by brooding in their one-room apartment, while Jessie Rae would tell everybody that she just had "her nose stuck up in the air."

One final note on "hillbilly": its comic debasement or performative aspect, detached from any refined content, was apparent when they talked about music. They mostly referred to country and western music, their music of choice, as "hillbilly" music. When it was played on the jukebox at O'Leary's, a wide range of stereotyped behaviors, mostly excessive, were justified. They contrasted it with "mountain music," a revered object they had "lost" in the move north. "Mountain music" survived in ballad form, as a few "old-timey" tunes that would be sung with great reverence. When I played music with Mike, another "hillbilly," he and his mother would sing "Knoxville Girl" and other tunes she had taught him as a child only late in the evening and with much fanfare.

One late evening Jerry insisted that I bring out my guitar and Dobro and play some songs. He and two of his other brothers had formed a country music band years ago, playing in the local bars, so Jerry took up the guitar while I played the Dobro. His fingers were too mangled to play well, but we made it through a number of 1950s country numbers, like Web Pierce's "There Stands the Glass," and several of Hank Williams's songs. Then we moved on to more current tunes. Jerry, Sam, and Leroy got around to talking about their daddies. Jerry and Sam's dad played just about everything, but especially the fiddle; Leroy's father played guitar. They reeled off memories of how the two of them would play "mountain music," old fiddle and banjo tunes, all night long. They recalled the parties when their fathers played, and Jerry said, "If they were still alive and playing on this porch, they would have people standing all the way across the street to hear them play." When his other two brothers, Barry and Drew, stopped by on occasion—inevitably because they needed him to work on their cars—Jerry would talk them into jamming with me. And always the talk got around to their father, who played so well and got them all started, but they retained very little of the "mountain music," being more familiar now with the songs on the country stations from the last twenty years.

"That White and Black Shit"

The subject position of "hillbillies" is shaped by the intraracial dynamics informing the local significance of white racialness, but inevitably the contours of this rhetorical identity are fleshed out in interracial relations. The process whites engage in when they judge who among them is a

"hillbilly"—and the significance of the identity as a self-inscribed label—
is a function of the ongoing necessity of figuring out how differences between "whites and blacks" matter. The volatility and provocativeness of
"hillbilly" partially reflects the charged and uncertain potential to all
local racial matters.

Social interactions in Briggs reveal the wide gap between the clarity of
racial abstractions and the often confusing contingencies of everyday life.
Residents, black and white, recognize that their daily interactions are removed from the institutional contexts, political debates, and cultural exchanges wherein "race" is expressly engaged by most Americans. When
they grapple with racial implications and influences, they confront and
express uncertainties over how these local matters relate to national collectives, "whites and blacks." Subsequently, the local mode of sociality
treats racialness as subject to indeterminacies. Residents' ideas and assumptions about race are prey to what Kathleen Stewart refers to as the
constant possibility of misinterpretation, transgression, and betrayal animating the realm of everyday life. Rather than a set of fixed beliefs, "race"
is negotiated through rhetorical identities and labels that hold "open an
interpretive space in which everyday events are taken as a test of principles, and . . . 'meanings' are asserted not in the certainty of an indicative
mode that claims to represent fully objects but in the indeterminacy of the
subjunctive mode of 'as if.' "[42] The indeterminate aspects of race do not
undercut its volatility, however, because racial categories like "hillbilly"
and "nigger" bear the ability to maintain or collapse this subjunctive
mode alternately in various social contexts.

Race remains a provocative matter in this zone for many reasons, not
the least of which is that life here is full of uncertainties. The potential for
violent conflict is a constant in Briggs. This is not to suggest that people
live under siegelike conditions or that a stroll down any street is an invitation to be attacked. But in that strangely mundane way of inner-city
zones, the possibility of sudden outbursts—from robberies to fist fights
on the street or the frequent play of gunfire from the kids selling crack
who, when boredom sets in, try out their "toys" in fields and alleys—
requires a state of edgy watchfulness.[43] Add to this the anxieties of life on
the economic edge, with its often unpredictable moments when there is no
money to shop or wash clothes, and you have a context providing people
with both an array of excuses for venting their rage and a substantial
interest in defusing such situations to prevent them from escalating dan-
gerously.[44] Race is interwoven in the social textures of this charged setting, but its significance exceeds containment by invocations of abstract
social collectives. Whites in Briggs do not attribute "crime" in the area
generally to blacks, but many of them relate stories of being victimized—
often violently—by blacks, in situations where they felt selected on the

basis of their race. The interpretive choice of stressing race faces whites continually; just as their motives, comments, and actions are susceptible to being read for racist intent by black neighbors and strangers.[45] "Race" provides both pretext and context in a powerful, reductive fashion for locating the meaning in an unkind remark taken "the wrong way," or a misstep, an abrupt impropriety, read as a racial slight.

Their ability to think through or negotiate the significance of race, subsequently, develops out of *recursive* readings of events in everyday life; that is, what they find out about race in one situation shapes how they engage in subsequent social interactions.[46] Rather than relying on stock certainties about "whites and blacks," they continually sound out the disparate meanings these categories imply. They encounter racial significance as distinctly composed and contoured in different social situations, shifting from foreground to background according to dynamics that involve both the exteriorized, inevitable meaningfulness of race and the uncertain, unfixed interior realms of personalities, which few people can estimate with certainty. The labels they ascribe or claim meld the meanings of race alternately into stark relief and muddled contradictions.[47] Their discursive objectifications of race do not treat it as a stable reflection of absolute difference or fixed beliefs, nor as something that if dissolved or properly contained would leave behind neutral, uncolored social beings. Indeed, the means they deploy for negotiating racial difference often have double-edged effects, antagonistically inflecting racial terms in already tense situations.[48]

The provocativeness of race is something residents approach through an array of rhetorical means for defusing a racialized situation or to undermine assumptions that racialness inherently involves eternally clashing, polarizing collective orders. The ability to deflect racial instigations usually involves depersonalizing the context and demonstrating a disinterest in polarizing rhetorical ground—this tactic served as a general style for defusing a range of potentially explosive situations. George, the bartender at O'Leary's, described using this type of response when conflicts arose in the bar. We were talking the day after he threw Jerry out of the bar for causing trouble. He complained that Jerry acted like he could "make up his own rules" and expected that his personal ties with George would allow him freer reign than others. George didn't "take it personal" when Jerry cussed and threatened him; he characterized his detachment as a requisite stance for getting by in this zone. I asked him how this worked when "race" was at stake. After stressing how well whites and blacks socialized together in O'Leary's, he added, "There's a lot of black people who come in here real regular. Oh every now and then you get some blacks come in here, trying to be prejudiced, talking that white motherfucker crap. Like the other day. Over at that table [in the front corner], there was about ten or twelve of 'em sitting there, maybe two or three of us whites. Well one of 'em starts talking shit, 'Lets show these white motherfuckers who's boss.' I told 'em, 'Hey, you black motherfuckers can just get your asses the fuck out of here. Don't you come in here trying to start that black and white shit. I won't put up with it.' Well one of the women there jumps up and gets in his face, 'What you talking about white motherfuckers? My momma's white.'"

George laughed and said that everybody "cooled out." The crowd at the table stayed and drank through the afternoon. He told of other instances, in the bar and in his life in the city generally, where people were "making something black and white when it wasn't like that at all." He complained that "they'll make it black and white when you're calling 'em on making trouble." On this point, he drew a connection with throwing Jerry out. George was still upset that Jerry had tried to make it a "personal" issue when all he was trying to do was keep a mean drunk from getting out of control. The same dictum held in the racial incident as with Jerry: "Hey, I try to show everybody respect, but they've got to do the same. You can't take shit off nobody. Once they see they can get away with it, then they won't ever let up." George routinized or relativized the volatility of racialness by placing it in context with the array of modes of manipulation that people commonly use on each other. Whether accurate or not, the imputation of racial motivations had powerful and almost certain effects. In explaining how Jerry was mistaken in taking his ouster personally, he underscored, too, how it was important not to take "that black and white shit" as a personal affront. It was largely how people talked and acted when they were looking "to start something."

For all of the ways their lives, bodies, and speech brushed and ground against each other, whites and blacks in this zone were compelled to find means of qualifying the significance of race, or diffuse its power to polarize. Although an attention to race was a fundamental aspect of everyday life, people looked for moments when this attention could be objectified in seemingly neutral exchanges over the (in)significance of racial markings. Nobody ever expressed the view to me that race should be ignored. Rather, they found forms of recognizing its presence in offhand ways that neither exaggerated nor denied its importance. Indeed, an attention to racial markings could easily constitute a common social ground instead of asserting a polarized field of difference. I found that residents, white and black, were much more adroit in negotiating and effacing the social importance of racialness than they were at manipulating the class divisions between themselves and the broader society. On Labor Day, Billy Lee—one of Jessie Rae's brothers who lived nearby—had a barbecue at his place right across the street from a cluster of Teamster's buildings that includes the headquarters of Jimmy Hoffa's old local. The Teamsters, too, were barbecuing, and they had sent people around twice to Billy Lee's house to make sure that he knew people in the neighborhood were all invited. When I got there, Billy Lee and his brother Clarence and his nephew, Little Clarence, were raptly watching the proceedings across the street, where a couple hundred people had gathered to celebrate. They told me about the invitation, but all agreed they would never go over there. Billy Lee explained that they get invited every year, but he has never gone, nor would he ever go. Instead, they joked loudly about whether or not they would later steal the huge mobile grill, or what other trouble they could cause if they did show up. Despite their brave banter, they were unnerved by the idea of having to socialize at that party—what would they talk about if somebody tried to start a conversation?

By contrast, when June, a black man who was one of Billy Lee's neighbors showed up, these men adroitly played with the significance of racialness. Billy Lee had sent one of his sons down the street to tell June they were starting to drink. When June showed up, Viki, Billy Lee's daughter, ran up and hugged him around the legs, greeting him as "grandpa." June asked Billy Lee and Clarence if it was still just "grandpa" or if he had advanced yet to "great-grandpa." Clarence told him that he was indeed "great-grandpa" now since his daughter, Teresa, had just given birth to a boy. This extension of kinship across racial lines was just the beginning of a series of cross-racial gestures that characterized the afternoon, with the men commenting on or backtalking movies that featured racial objectifications. They looked for extensions that disrupted racial abstractions. Clarence ridiculed Wesley Snipes's line in *White Men Can't Jump*, about how Woody Harrelson couldn't "hear" black music; June sang along to a Led Zeppelin tune on the radio and after hitting a high note in tandem with Roger Plant, he said, "Well I guess I've got a little white in me." The point in their exchanges never seemed to be that race did not matter, but rather that its importance hardly lay in static, emphatically bounded identities. So they all cracked up when one of Billy Lee's boys came down the street, crashing into the yard in a swirl of dust and motion, and June said, "Well that's the first white Buckwheat I've ever saw"—referring to the black character in the Little Rascals movies.

Food, music, movies, jokes, all provided constant fodder for whites and blacks both to acknowledge the "fact" of racialness and manipulate seemingly inert racial categories or play with their meanings. It was the very stereotyped and predictable quality of these materials that made them useful for transposing the relevance of racialness or undermining its quality as a conventionalized set of understandings. Conveyed in this reliance on stereotyped matters was their disregard for "race" as equivalent with fixed identities or absolute social divides, assumed to be an indissolubly significant matter. However, every stereotyped feature or label bore a visceral charge and potentially involved the large-scale discrepancies between whites and blacks, blunt reminders of the historical injustices and hatred or the broad landscape of social inequality in the United States. The state of detachment that George described, whereby racial invocations can be regarded rhetorically, is not easily maintained—just as the connotations of "hillbilly" were sometimes too biting for certain whites to tolerate; the distinctions involved were too emotionally forceful to be joked about. At times, the terms and gestures residents relied upon to stress the plasticity of racial significance instead worked bluntly to reinscribe the color line.

No term better condenses this dynamic than whites' uses of "nigger." Whites and blacks use "nigger" with a number of inflections and a range of purposes; neither social collective's usage can be generally characterized here. Indeed, many whites that I met refused to use the term at all. "Hillbillies" used "nigger" frequently—but then, too, they had the most developed interracial social networks and, occasionally, kin groups. They invoke it in a range of settings—on other whites as well as in reference to certain blacks—that warrant close analysis. The ambit of its uses by "hillbillies," from white-on-white to white-on-black labeling, conveys the dense spaces of interpretation and sociality in this zone through which residents sound out and engage the significance of race. But discussing their usage first requires some attention to the problematic gap between the political and scholarly realms, where the opprobrium against the term "nigger" is absolute, and the murky, convoluted social settings in Detroit where poor whites strive to make sense of race in the inner city.

Instances of scholarly examinations of whites using "nigger" are quite limited, which is somewhat unnerving given the term's broad circulation in this country, historically and contemporarily. Since "nigger" has been effectively banished from polite public discourse in the United States, instances of usage of the term are subject to fairly immediate condemnation—its use is regarded as a certain indication of racist sentiment, proof positive that a white person is wholly animated by racism. Critical race theorists are the only scholars I have found who systematically address this subject; they argue that "nigger" can simply have none but racist connotations nor reveal any other disposition than racism.[49] I found this perspective difficult to apply in analyzing whites' usage of "nigger" in Detroit, though, because it regards race as a matter of moral absolutes and asserts that the operations of its logic are clear and consistent. This stance distorts more than it reveals of tangled, swampy, and uneven social terrain of Briggs, as evidenced in uses of "nigger" and "hillbilly." This is a landscape scored by ambiguity rather than certainty.

Judith Butler, in her work *Excitable Speech: A Politics of the Performative*, develops a theoretical framework for analyzing uses of "nigger" that has bearing on the social life of Briggs. Butler challenges the assertion that words like "nigger" and "spick," even when used among friends, are solely "badges of degradation" that can have "no other connotations." While conceding that an injurious content is retained in any use of such terms, she asserts that in their various uses "they become a kind of linguistic display that does not overcome their degrading meanings, but that reproduces them as public text and that, in being reproduced, displays them as reproducible and resignifiable terms."[50] Butler asserts that we need to think through the "power to race" that precedes the subjects who make such utterances, structuring (through institutions and political organizations) the unequal social terrain where race remains significant. Additionally, she challenges the emphasis on locating the subject as a singular, delimited "origin" or "cause" of racist speech and structures.[51]

Butler analyzes the resignification and productive reiterations of terms like "nigger" in rap songs, arguing for a more nuanced view of the contexts of such utterances. She states the conundrum in these disparate views of uses of "nigger" succinctly. "To argue, on the one hand, that the offensive effect of such words is fully contextual, and that a shift in context can exacerbate or minimize that offensiveness, is still not to give an account of the power that such words are said to exercise. To claim, on the other hand, that some utterances are always offensive, regardless of context, that they carry their contexts with them in ways that are too difficult to shed, is still not to offer a way to understand how context is invoked and restaged at the moment of utterance. Neither view can account for the restaging and resignifying of offensive utterance, deployments of linguistic power that seek at once to expose and counter the offensive exercise of speech."[52] In analyzing the "patterns of verbal conduct" of white speakers in Briggs, I follow Butler's example and consider that in their usage, racial labels "not only mean or communicate in a conventional way, but are themselves set forth as discursive items, in their very linguistic conventionality and, hence, as both forceful and arbitrary, recalcitrant and open to reuse."[53] Whether or not readers consider the following examples as deft or crude restagings of this offensive utterance, I argue that these local white uses of "nigger" operate as part of the recursive stance—sounding, marking, and transposing—that characterize the engagements of "hillbillies" with the significance of race.

The remainder of this chapter presents a series of examples of situations in which "nigger" arises in Briggs. My purpose is not to develop a definitive case broadly characterizing white usage of "nigger." Rather, I render a continuum of specific instances in which this label was voiced, in order first to understand the way race infuses this social landscape and is actively engaged by white and black residents; and second, to undertake a consideration of how to assess when racial matters need to be analyzed in terms of social contingencies and uncertainties, rather than absolute judgments. "Nigger" is perhaps the ultimate racial allegory—its intense, overwhelming meanings are impacted and frozen in a stark figuration of an absolute divide between whites and blacks. The epithet embodies the long-standing white conviction that there are or must be racial absolutes and a clear distinction between whites and blacks. To the extent that "nigger" retains this singular significance—that whites mean only one thing when they use it—a host of other racial allegories will continue to go unchallenged in public and private discourse in the United States. The following discussion is necessary because the self-evident status of "nigger" as a representation of white racism supports a disturbingly limited understanding of the extent to which race informs the experiences and perspectives of whites in this country.

Bill (see "History of the 'Hood"), Donnie and I had a morning routine, sipping coffee in the alley behind a local church, where Bill worked as a custodian and opened the building for alcoholics coming in for their AA meeting. One morning the sky started to spit a light rain, so Donnie went to get his jacket. He came back wearing a green windbreaker with "Wes" stitched over the right breast. A suburban bar's name was loudly emblazoned across the back. Since it was green, Bill asked him if he was Irish.

Donnie answered, "Yeah, I'm an Irish hillbilly."

As we laughed, Donnie added, "I believe I've even got some nigger in me, too." Bill, still laughing, told him, "No, wait a minute, you lying now. Don't start your lying." He insisted that Donnie was clearly "crazy," announcing, "they broke the mold when they made him." Donnie, instead of countering Bill's assertion, rather accentuated it, pointing out that two of his brothers were even crazier. He told us one of his brothers just put in his garden with "nothing but Poke salad." This caught Bill's attention and he stopped Donnie. "Poke salad?! Well that's some good shit. You get that with some turnip greens and some mustard greens and some swamp seed and some ham hocks, then you're eating." Donnie added to the list, "Yeah, you need some chitlins too."

Bill exclaimed, "Chitlins too! Well then I believe you are kin of mine." They both laughed.

Bill's extension of racial "kinship" to Donnie was possible largely because there was little of a collective order to be compromised by such inclusive gestures. But what also makes Bill's extension of racial connection possible is that Donnie posits race in one quite plastic medium—food. When people demonstrated an interest in finding common ground across racial divides, food was usually where they started—it mediated racial identities to the extent that it was both mobile and stereotypical. In actuality, local diets featured copious cross-racial commonalties, since both whites and blacks savored a variety of fried foods and greens. The diets in this zone were similar, in part, because they derived from regional sources in the South. But there were stereotypical items for each race: "Hillbillies" were known to love pinto beans, while blacks ate chitlins. Rather than attempting to debunk the stereotyped usage, people emphasized these foods as crossing points, interpreting them as "making" somebody racially mixed. In recognizing Donnie's use of chitlins, Bill both admitted the stereotype of chitlins as a "black food" and allowed that its usage extended, however tenuously, a marked form of racial kinship to this white man. Donnie asserted the "fact" of shared racial material with Bill, not based on a desire to *be* black, but rather a desire to have race not differentiate absolutely, allowing instead for a shared materiality. Such extensions were certainly enabled by their shared class predicaments as poor, inner-city dwellers.[54]

Donnie's claim to have "some nigger" in him succinctly conveys the term's dynamics in Briggs. In trying to breach the allegorical divide between whiteness and blackness, he uses a label that resonates with the fiercest declarations that the two must be kept distinct. Instead of expressing a generalized sentiment to the effect that "we are all the same inside," he incorporates a stigmatized racial term as part of his identity. By inscribing himself with "nigger," Donnie implicitly marks certain discontinuities within whiteness that make the significance of white racialness an uncertain matter here. This was one more case of the local enthusiasm for marking whiteness, from the use of "hillbilly" as a self-designation to the claim of having "some nigger in me." And since "hillbilly" had limited effects when "hillbillies" used it on each other, they seemed to have taken up "nigger" as its supplement. This racial marking of whites was facilitated by the cross-racial commonalties in this zone. It was as if—through brute proximity, the collapse of proper forms of distancing and spatialized racial distinctions—the coloredness of whites necessarily emerged. As one white resident (described below) explained to me, "There's about a hundred shades of white. We're all colored." Although quite obvious differences remained active between whites and blacks, their collation into projected collective orders was continually undermined through sheer proximity and the heterogeneity of those categories locally.[55]

One of the prevailing usages of "nigger" by "hillbillies" was to express or underscore intraracial distinctions. This form of usage was varied, but it consistently entailed a double operation, one of denigrating certain whites while gesturing toward effacing the significance of interracial divisions. Surely, whites calling other whites "nigger" was at times no more than a simple transposition of a term of racial contempt into a different setting. But the "hillbillies" who used the term this way often made a point of explaining to me the rationale of such a labeling practice. These explanations conveyed a disinterest in assertions of white solidarity through the deployment of a term for policing racial boundaries to breach certain decorums associated with whiteness. Billy Lee insisted several times that Willie, one of Jerry's white friends, was a "nigger." When Billy Lee used "nigger" in this way, he felt compelled to explain to me the conventional basis for such labeling. I mentioned Willie once in a conversation with Billy Lee and his wife Barbara. They both snarled contemptuously and listed a number of his social transgressions. Then Billy asserted, "He's a nigger, man, and you know what I mean by that. He's an asshole, and it doesn't matter whether a person's black or white, orange or plaid, he can still be a nigger if he runs his mouth like that asshole."[56] Billy Lee's explication suggests that one convention guiding its application is a regard for undermining any basis for asserting a qualitative divide between the races. He explicitly states that you can "be a nigger" no matter what your race.[57] In this convention, the historical content of the term is ignored in favor of the effect achieved by marking whites with this racial term. This form of usage is not a self-naming, nor is there an explicit claim to using the term "like blacks do"; rather the ascription marks the racialness of whites or whiteness. This became clearer to me when I spoke with a "crazy" hillbilly, Tom, who liked to fly his large Confederate flag from his front porch. When I met him, he told me that his door is always unlocked. "Anybody is welcome in my house, as long as they come in the right way . . . I'll shoot a white man quick as I'll shoot a black man—I ain't prejudiced." I asked him how blacks and whites got along on his street and in the neighborhood in general. He answered, "They don't bother you, you don't bother them. The only ones that bother you are the ones that you let bother you. If they know they can bother you, they will. Niggers'll do that. And see, you don't have to be black to be a nigger. Niggers come in all colors. We are all colored, everybody's colored. Don't forget that. There's about a hundred shades of white. We're all colored."

Tom felt that "you got to be crazier than they are" to keep from being obliterated by the spasms of inner-city violence. When I asked him about an incident that I had heard about, involving his brandishing a shotgun on the porch, he smiled proudly: "Yeah, I've built up something of a fearsome reputation around here." I couldn't help but recall James Baldwin's comment that "to be colored means that one has been caught in some utterly unbelievable joke. . . . One's only hope of supporting, to say nothing of surviving, this joke is to flaunt in the teeth of it one's own particular and invincible style."[58] His particular "style" was to play out stereotyped features of white racialness in a deranged manner. Whether his "style" reflected "true" racial sentiment or whether it was an old man's means of building up a protective space, I could not tell. Clearly, for both Tom and Floyd, race is a "fact." But, in their view, there is nothing about white racialness that makes it qualitatively distinct from blackness or that would preclude the transposition of "nigger" onto other whites. The nonsuperiority of whiteness is suggested by the "fact" of white "niggers." The racial readings of both of these men are permeated by their potential to be racialized in all kinds of ways, often with violent ramifications—a condition unusual for whites generally, but a commonplace of life in this zone for the last twenty-odd years.[59]

When they explicated their uses of "nigger," Billy Lee's and Tom's accounts seemed meager in relation to the density of the social significance embodied in these ascriptions, and certainly not adequate to the kind of dexterity they evidenced in such exchanges. I pushed and prodded them, and others, for more detailed explanations, but this only produced more succinct reiterations of previous statements—attempts at rule-like formulations or conventions: "You don't have to be black to be a nigger." I began to suspect that perhaps they did not have a fixed idea of what they were doing or meant. It occurred to me that they were, rather, using the term as a sounding for the significance of race, finding out what it meant from the way their uses were received and responded to, in the reactions of whites they marked or blacks who overheard their uses. As with other local terms or modes of calling attention to race, the meanings of "nigger" are indelible but subject to inflection by shifting contexts, making precarious any extrapolation toward certain essential truths or fixed identities. I assumed, at first, that in such usage they were asserting that race did not matter. It would be more accurate, I realized later, to say that this usage reveals a complicated social position. Marking whites as "niggers" quite obviously transposes the stigmatizing and degrading connotations of this racial label—such uses do not dissolve them nor rid them of their histories. In this regard, there seems to be an implicit acknowledgment that "race" will never be insignificant, that it will never go away, but that its key signifying components can be actively used to disrupt the conceptual segregation that supports beliefs in separate racial communities. Calling whites "nigger"—especially in the presence of black friends and neighbors, as we will see with Jerry—made the term's degradations present and forceful, but importantly reused and reapplied in ways that tacitly assailed the term's polarizing inscriptions.[60]

Whites' uses of "nigger" were informed by black practices in applying the term, which involved certain conventions and context-shaping inflections. "Nigger" is used so pervasively by blacks in this zone that it often seemed routine, ranging from affectionate bemusement to hard-edged derision.[61] Although "hillbilly" did not have the lengthy history of contempt and degradation that "nigger" entailed, the two terms shared a key linkage: they could be used intraracially to inflect class differences. "Nigger," though, bore a wider range of connotations; social differences beyond a strict sense of economic class were also inscribed by "nigger." I can scarcely convey the range of inflections here, but at least one example of this usage is perhaps warranted, accompanied of course with the cautionary notice (though it should be unnecessary) that this example is not considered representative of black usage of the term generally.

Gale and Fred, the other black couple besides Marvin and Charlotte who lived in the gray house, were disgusted when Jerry decided to let Curtis move in. Marvin and Charlotte didn't mind, but Gale in particular was contemptuous of Curtis and his friends, a contempt that reflected her predicament of downward mobililty.[62] Gale used "nigger" in a range of contexts, but an instance of intraracial marking of the type to which "hillbillies" seemed most attentive stands out. She woke me up one morning, pounding on my front door and wailing inconsolably, yelling, asking if I had seen her cat. Shaking, she told me that it was missing. In the midst of her panic she decided that it was Curtis or his friends who had taken the cat. She said, "I know them niggers took it. Them fucking niggers took my cat. I know they did, them drug fiends took it." Fred was outside looking up and down the street, and Ricky—a drinking friend of theirs who slept on the floor in their apartment—was standing in the yard, confused. We surveyed the outside of the house to see if the cat could have crawled out one of the other windows or just slinked off some place. But Gale, still sobbing, kept insisting quite loudly that, "them niggers took her, I know they did." She went on about how "I don't do drugs and stay up all night screaming. But he let them move right in next to us. He don't care, he'd let anybody move in here. Even these fucking drug addicts. How could those fucking niggers take my cat?" I said that she should tell Jerry when he got up, and she replied that she would make him "get them niggers out of there." Fred, also in a fury, was saying how he was "gonna fuck them up," and again, complaining that Jerry would "let anybody move in there."

She came back happy, about twenty minutes later, with her cat in her arms. The cat was hiding behind the stove or somewhere, and came out when they began frying bacon for breakfast. Curtis never commented about her display. It was hard for me to distinguish the way that she and Fred, Ricky, and Donnie stayed up "all night" drinking, hollering, and carrying on from Curtis's occasional revelries, but for Gale it was very different. After all, she had come from a "better family," and she was not a "drug dealer."

Whites were aware of the various inflections of the term "nigger," as well as its range of connotations, and that its meanings were not absolute and had to be found out in each context. Whites seemed to incorporate these by stressing the term's interpretive plasticity, while treating the significance of race as a variable matter, dependent on oft-changing settings and situations where the degrees of familiarity and shared assumptions among participants were often unfixed.

Although whites were aware of the charged content of the word, they saw little point in forsaking it for the sake of politeness—that emotional charge made it a useful term. "Nigger" fills one of the key aesthetic interests in the various elements of language in this zone: it is powerful and it regularly produces an effect. Using "nigger" is guaranteed to draw attention or provocation, if that is the desired result. People here use strong language exactly for that purpose. And Jerry's uses of "nigger" illustrate its conflation of provocation and ambiguity. Jerry's uses of "nigger" were more varied than those of any other white I met; he applied it with vigor, often gearing it to approximate black uses, but at times with all the mean, blunt force of its racist connotations. Although more excessive than representative of whites' usage of this term—again, some whites refused to use "nigger" under any circumstances—Jerry's usage encompasses the range of its deployment by "hillbillies."[63] He used "nigger" sparingly in Marvin's presence and singularly applied it to whites. Jerry referred to two of his brothers as "niggers" in different contexts, but each time with an eye or ear toward Marvin's reaction. In one instance, Jerry, myself, Charlotte, and Marvin were going down to the bar in Marvin's car. While we were all still in front of the house, Jerry and Charlotte were discussing their respective collections of Motown tapes, when Jerry recalled that his brother Sam had one of his tapes. Jerry started hollering out the car window to Sam, demanding back his Supremes tape. Sam at first acted as if he didn't know where it was; Jerry called him a liar, plus a few other names, then Sam remembered. When Sam handed over the tape, Jerry announced, "See, that nigger was trying to steal my tape." While Jerry continued to cuss Sam, Marvin slipped the car into drive and offered no comment. At the bar, while Jerry was shooting pool and I was sitting with Charlotte and Marvin, I asked him if Jerry's use of "nigger" bothered him. "That's just Jerry," he answered. "He don't bother me." He did not elaborate further, so I won't speculate on his "true" sentiment, but it seemed that Marvin had either allowed for Jerry's personalized usage of the term or he felt that Jerry's usage reflected an adequate sense of the term's context-dependent inflections.

The other instance occurred when we were jamming one afternoon with his brother Barry, who was there to pick up Sam for their annual deer hunting trip up north. Barry played through a slew of sixties rock tunes, just wailing away. Jerry, thrilled that Barry and I were finally getting a chance to play together, beamed and turned to Marvin and said, "That nigger sure can play." "Hell yeah," Marvin replied. Barry seemed to become somewhat more animated in his gestures and vocalizations, I suppose undergoing a form of "minstrelization," inflecting both his "hillbilly" roots and racialization by Jerry.[64] Later, I suspected that Jerry's ascription of "nigger" to his brother was also purposefully ironic, since Barry had used "nigger-lover" to characterize Jerry's daughter, Jean (see below). We played on, with Barry impaled by this rhetorical gesture.

Both of Jerry's comments were received by his brothers without indignation; neither brother took any more umbrage at being called a "nigger" by him than they did when he called them "motherfuckers," "assholes," "cocksuckers," "shitheads," or any other numerous offensive but routinized names. Jerry's ascriptions operate on two axes—one orienting his variously strained relations with his brothers, another hinging on the way local blacks like Marvin responded to the usage and the context.

As with Billy Lee's labeling of other whites as "niggers," this mode of naming blatantly ignores or almost willfully undermines the "purity" of whiteness, both as a material and a cultural condition. In the other two neighborhoods examined in this book, whites find plenty of names to call low-class whites, but they never use "nigger." It strikes me now that I cannot even imagine similar instances of this white name-calling practice in the other neighborhoods, where decorums prevail that sequester "nigger" into a silent, prohibited realm, perhaps thought but never spoken. In Briggs, however, whites' uses of "nigger" are one aspect of the rhetorical efforts at blurring the demarcations of supposedly static racial orders.

Jerry's usage of "nigger" was also distinct from Billy Lee's, simply because he deployed the term in the presence of some of his black friends. In this regard, it is worth considering Jerry's actions as a form of social performance more than as expressions of a racial world view. This distinction suggests a critical challenge to the oft-repeated assertion that race is socially constructed. The central limit to the social constructivist perspective is that its fundamental premise posits race as a form of false consciousness, an illusion that needs to be dispelled. From this perspective, Jerry is only perpetuating the myth of "race," rather than engaging an unwieldy social material that people must make sense of in their daily lives. An alternative view—drawn from the performance model in anthropology—is that in such speech acts Jerry may be actively assessing the meaningful structures of a situation, not simply reflecting a form of social conditioning. That is, he may be constructing a meaningful sense of race—interpreting, postulating, or revising his racial orientation rather than passively reflecting a fixed racial belief system.

Richard Bauman and Charles Briggs describe performance as providing "a frame that invites critical reflection on communicative processes. A given performance is tied to a number of speech events that precede and succeed it (past performances, readings of texts, negotiations, rehearsals, gossip, reports, critique, challenges, subsequent performances, and the like). An adequate study of a single performance thus requires sensitive ethnographic study of how its form and meaning index a broad range of discourse types." From a performance view, Jerry's use of "nigger" turns on an implicit call to his audience to assess the significance of his statement and on its indexical relations to similar utterances, by whites and blacks; he and his "audience" are engaged in "interpreting the structure and significance of their own discourse."[65] Jerry seemed to be motivated by an interest in Marvin's opinion. I suppose that he was performing a mode of behavior that might be considered acting black.[66] Since he and Charlotte had just been comparing music collections, and had entered into a playfully competitive comparison of who had better Motown selections, his use here might have been an attempt to extend the common ground further by demonstrating a practiced sense of the "proper" name to call his brother. With the other brother, Barry, Jerry received a clear affirmation from Marvin. This situation was less ambiguous, if only because the possible connotations were less offensive. Whereas Sam's act of "stealing" appeared to be the connection that brought "nigger" to mind for Jerry, with Barry playing so well, and slipping in and out of Chuck Berry-style tunes, the connection perhaps seemed to Marvin to be more tolerable. Certainly, Jerry was pleased with Barry's performance and the extension of sociality it achieved in generating a cause for gathering and hanging out in the yard; it also mattered to him that his friend Marvin was enjoying the performance.

Whites' awareness of the variety of black uses of "nigger"—some disciplined, others promiscuous—did not lead them to attempt to sanitize the term's most vicious connotations; its provocative aspects were inevitably present. Instead of trying to purify the term, they developed a range of circumspect approaches to its usage. Whether it was from observation of the distinct uses that blacks made of the term, or in recognition of the overdetermined history of whites using it, "hillbillies" developed an elaborate sensibility about deploying this form of name-calling. It was one of the most routinized and volatile terms available to whites and blacks, capable of both inscribing or effacing racial difference. And it was the one word that could instantly ignite a racial brawl. Hence Jerry, his kin, and other whites in this zone actively policed the use of "nigger," personally and collectively.[67] Like dismissals of invocations of "that white and black shit," whites policed improper or excessive uses of this term by disparaging instances of "nigger talk."[68]

The discursive category "nigger talk" was distinguished from the uses of "nigger" per se; it was applied to situations in which whites would be "going on" *about* black people, describing them or categorizing them in a generic, derogatory mode. "Nigger talk" could arise from friendly banter that went too far, or by being purposefully initiated. The core characterization of this mode of speech was its intention to draw absolute racial lines between whites and blacks. In whites' efforts to police against the activation of "nigger talk," the texture of gendered patterns of speaking roles became evident. Among Jerry's family, it was the men who consistently used the most viscerally abusive labels (racial or not) and the women who typically called first for some restraint to be exercised. This gendered division of truculent linguistic labor loosely correlated with gendered relations to public spaces like street corners and bars—the settings where aggressive displays were often linked to defensive posturing around place and masculinity.[69] Men were most active in these settings, where the ability to use "hard words" played a critical role in maintaining a social identity as strong rather than vulnerable.[70]

A variety of situations prompted Jerry or his brothers to start in with "nigger talk." Any number of problems or conflicts could provoke the charged naming that "nigger" entailed. On a hot afternoon, we were sitting out on the front porch: Old Eddie, Jerry, Rebecca, and I. We had friends visiting, and I took them up to the store to get a few things. When we got back, Jerry was in a suddenly irritable mood, cussing easily and throwing in "nigger" often and loudly, projecting it recklessly around the yard and out into the street. Since no blacks passed by, nothing came of this, and he eventually went inside where he sulked for the rest of the day. I asked Rebecca what had happened and she said that a black man had come down from Trumbull Avenue, hollering belligerently at Jerry, who was having a hard time recognizing the man—his eyesight is poor and he claims to be "legally blind." The man was yelling a string of phrases keyed to race, like "what's your fat white ass doing out here?" Jerry hollered back, "Do I know you?" As he drew near, the black man reminded Jerry of where they knew each other from, then Jerry recognized him and relaxed a bit. The man continued in an abusive mode, though, vigorously attempting to "bum stuff" off of Jerry. "Give me some beer," he demanded. Jerry refused, saying he was down to his last bottle. Then the man demanded cigarettes. Jerry got mad and shouted, "Every time you come through here you're always bumming something."

The man ignored him and started asking Eddie for beer and cigarettes. Jerry turned his head and back to the man, who finally left, walking back onto Trumbull. Although Jerry is generous with many of the black street people daily passing by the house, this encounter set him off into a mode of "nigger talk," cussing "niggers" as rude and ignorant. The combination of the man's racializing Jerry ("what's your fat white ass doing out here?") and abuses of the tenuous basis for sociality unleashed all the meanness that Jerry could throw behind his guttural snarl of "nigger." Any ambiguity the term entailed in his other uses evaporated in this hard-edged, racial inflection.[71] The restraints Jerry usually observed in using the term dissolved in the wake of this man's rudeness. His subsequent withdrawal into the house suggested, also, that he had gone too far with this usage. It was just this kind of outburst that Jessie Rae, Earline, and others would try to defuse with the demand that he "cut it with that nigger talk."

In policing the use of "nigger" or the emergence of "nigger talk," Jerry and his kin did not relate such uses to a core of personal opinion: that is, its use did not indicate to them that a person was racist. The gender differentials in the term's deployment were never addressed or expressed as an indication that men were more inclined to racism. Rather, it seemed to be regarded as a function of their greater activity in the public spaces of the street, where the potentials for conflict were legion. People were recognized as having distinct tolerances for racial conflict and differences, but the act of using "nigger" was not a certain reflection of somebody's inclinations on matters of race. In developing an elaborate series of qualifications and restraints on the terms, contexts and relationships were primarily invoked, not a sense that some equation existed between the word and the personality revealed in a white's usage. Indeed, whites who used it often made eloquent statements to the effect that they harbored no sentiments of racial hatred or sense of inherent superiority and inferiority. Jerry made this kind of profession often. Circumscribing one instance when he used, "nigger," Jerry went on to explain, "I've got nothing against blacks or any other race. I've got blacks renting from me, living in my house. It don't make no difference to me. If you respect people, well, then they respect you back. If you're good to people, you're just being good to yourself, 'cause it'll come back to you. However you treat people, it's gonna come back to you. That's how people are. You've just got to treat 'em with respect."

Part of what prevented an automatic or permanent equation between instances of "nigger talk" and personal prejudice was the fact that this mode of speech had reciprocal aspects, which were lodged under what George referred to as "starting that white and black stuff." The black verbal counterpart to "nigger talk," when blacks would start "going on" about whites, featured "honky," "whitey," and "white motherfucker" as the most routine forms of racial rants; the latter term was the most favored locally. These rhetorical modes were so familiar and active that in Jerry or Jessie Rae's descriptions of past racial fights, they summarized tense interracial conflicts animated by verbal exchanges that preceded the physical violence as, "It was all nigger this and honky that." Jerry and his brothers had a long memory for instances of often random violence in which they been racialized by blacks.

It is incredibly easy for people to find provocation in this zone. It seemed to me a mark of restraint that such charged racial language could be neutrally demarcated and regarded with some detachment in a decision as to whether the challenge would be accepted or ignored. Jerry described one fight that occurred in their house during a birthday party he was throwing for a friend. A black guest started verbally antagonizing some other people. Jerry asked him to leave, then physically threw him out when he refused to go. "Then he's just standing out there on the porch, hollering shit, shooting his mouth off, cussing everybody. Then he started on honky this and honky that. I warned him. I said 'James, it's time to go home.' And he keeps it up. I told him ten times, 'James, it's time to go home'. He kept it up, and that was it. He says to me, 'You white ass bitch honky motherfucker.' Bam, I was over the rail and in the street pounding his ass. I was slamming him and punching him—he was all fucked up. I was going, 'Say something now motherfucker! Say something now!' He just went too far."

Jerry and other "hillbillies" used "nigger" or "black" depending on who they were talking to or about. The usage varies according to contextual concerns rather than a static inner core of opinion regarding blacks. Some make an effort to follow black usage and to avoid slipping into the generic use of "nigger" to describe an amorphous, threatening "they" or blacks as a collective. Amid these cautions, certain tendencies became apparent, like the gendered differences in relation to its excessive use. But, as with other semblances of rule-like formulations in this zone, they are contingent and easily disintegrate in the face of changeable circumstance. When someone used "nigger" uncharacteristically, disrupting personal conventions, this provoked comment and exclamation. These discrepant moments, I would suggest, do not reveal a "true" self or a hidden core of racist sentiment as much as moments of greater susceptibility to reductive readings of racial matters. They convey, as well, the brittleness of conventions regarding speech styles in this inner-city zone, and their inability to assure stability or formality in everyday life.

On a hot Sunday afternoon, we were sitting around in the yard letting the effects of Saturday evening's trip to the bar dissipate. Jessie Rae was in a foul mood; Jerry was restless. He suggested we get a game of horseshoes going, and he looked about, unsuccessfully, for their horseshoes. They had dug two good pits in the vacant lot alongside their house. The shoes were always left where they last fell until the next game. But this time, because Donnie had moved them when he mowed the tall grass in the lot, they were "missing." Jerry asked if anybody else had seen them—nobody had. Jessie Rae snapped angrily, "The niggers probably stole 'em."

Jerry slowly broke into a broad smile, realizing that she had broken her characteristic resistance to using the term. In an educated, lofty tone, he succinctly informed her that "They aren't niggers, they're black people."

Jessie Rae snapped back in an exaggerated, "backwoods" accent, taking up his positioning of her as the rude and ignorant hillbilly. "Anybody darker than me is a nigger," she announced, crossing her arms abruptly. Jerry, looking down at his tanned, shirtless chest, grinned broadly and replied, "Well I guess I'm a nigger then."

Jessie Rae smirked and muttered, "Well, I guess you are one."

Jerry, with a wry laugh, concluded, "Well, I guess that makes you a nigger-lover then." He roared laughing and Jessie Rae followed suit with her first deep belly laugh of the weekend.

In addition to the reversal of gendered positions regarding the use of "nigger talk," Jerry inflected his "correction" with class distinctions as well. They were all familiar with the interest most whites have in locating racism stereotypically among poor whites. Through numerous interactions with professionals—largely the police, social workers, and doctors—they were aware of their objectifications as rude and uneducated "hillbillies." In this case, when Jerry "caught" Jessie, he carried out his coup by invoking the air of class superiority in correcting her language use. It was an easy "voice" to mimic and use against each other at choice moments, such as when Willie corrected Jerry on his use of "Puerto Rican-American." A similar mimicking of class distinctions occurred a couple of weeks later, also out in the yard. It was another Sunday, and Jerry and Sam had dragged two televisions out into the yard so we could all watch the football games outside in the pleasant fall weather. David made an exception to his customarily aloof stance and joined us in the yard. David refused to socialize on the porch, in the bar, or anywhere in the neighborhood. He was contemptuous of his brothers' poverty— David took every opportunity he could to point out that he was "going to school" to better himself—but the racial mixing also bothered him a great deal. When he did come down, he used "nigger" freely and was regularly chastised for all his "nigger talk." But there were interesting moments when he enjoyed straying from that tendency.[72]

This Sunday, the Detroit Lions were playing and doing quite poorly. In particular, Rodney Peete, the black quarterback, was having a typically sub-par day. After cussing him through most of the first half, Jerry finally included "nigger" in the string of profane appellations he was using to describe Peete. David immediately jumped on this usage. As with Jerry's prior coup, David beamed as he informed him, "No Jerry, it's African Americans. That's what you should say, African Americans."

Jerry snapped, "Well I call 'em niggers."

David patiently instructed him, "No Jerry, it's African Americans. You have to call them African Americans."

Jerry finally shrugged and muttered, "Yeah, yeah," relenting to the fact that he had been caught by David, the one who typically set others on edge by his excessive indulgence in "nigger talk." The correction David offered was "mannered," in a style that closely mirrored Jerry's challenge to Jessie Rae's use of "nigger." The difference was that David's sense of class distinction operated full time, whereas Jerry's momentary assumption of superior airs over Jessie Rae played out as a joke. It was interesting to see how stymied Jerry and the others could become in response to the classed inflections in such exaggerated object lessons on race.

It is difficult to generalize about the role that "nigger" played in whites' negotiation of the local significance of race. Their uses varied by context, mood, and sense of social identity or standing. I am not sure how its usage reflected the true beliefs of anyone there, let alone all of them taken together as a group, as poor whites. These instances reflect the ambivalence, contradictory sentiments, and muddled feelings held by particular individuals and within this extended family generally.[73] To reduce all this to a neat sociological object, such as "white attitudes" or "white perceptions," would obliterate the interpretive engagements that marked each usage of the term.[74] If there is an overarching point here, it could be that such confusions and variability are often lurking behind "white attitudes" about race, shifting with the phrasing on a survey, the "stability" and "character" of one's neighborhood, or the changing patterns of social interaction—each entailing forms of specificity that generalizations overwhelm.[75]

Are the uses of "nigger" by "hillbillies" forms of restagings or resignifyings of an offensive term that Butler describes? Or are they essentially, regardless of context or inflection, a ratification and extension of the structural subordination of minorities through derogatory namings?[76] Both assessments seem too certain and overstated, given the contingency of sociality in this zone. There is also an intermediate view. "Hillbillies" use "nigger"—on themselves, on other whites, on blacks—recursively, using a racialized term, not primarily motivated by an interior set of beliefs or reproducing a social structure in which they are considered social refuse, but as a device for sounding out the significance of race in the continually shifting settings of this inner-city neighborhood.[77] Whether their uses provoke fierce reactions, bemused acquiescence, or even frustrated confusion, they are a means of figuring out how contexts matter and where racial lines cohere statically or are characterized by plasticity. "Nigger," in these instances, is neither generated solely by an internal set of convictions about race nor is it a completely detached assessment of conventions and contexts; it is used as a function of the ongoing need to understand the unstable ways that race matters. Because white racialness can be inflected from so many social positions, the local significance of race remains open-ended. Underlying all of their uses is the fact that, as whites in the inner city, they are continually racialized—not uniquely by black neighbors or strangers (situations that are examined in the next section), but by whites who have left the city and consider whites remaining behind in Detroit to be racially suspect.

Although these whites assumed varying positions in relation to "nigger talk," it seems that they were uniformly susceptible to being regarded by suburban whites—at least those who made occasional forays into this zone—as racially suspect, that is, as "nigger lovers." The common thread among the instances I recorded of this label being applied locally involved the strained or ruptured assumption of racial solidarity experienced by whites who considered themselves "above" racial mixing. Simply by residing in the inner city, their white racialness was compromised, a position heightened by their precarious class circumstances. Judging from Jerry and Jessie Rae's dexterity with this label, they were familiar with this marking and not overly concerned by the implication that their lifestyle challenged white solidarity. Certainly, their sense of belonging in this part of Detroit inflected the significance of their white racialness.

Late one evening, after it became too dark for Jerry to keep working on the ruptured fuel line on his Gremlin, we slipped into a long conversation about family. At the moment, he was furious with his brother Sam over the rent dispute with the landlord. That night, this conflict led Jerry and Jessie Rae to talk about strained family relations and the problems with raising kids in the city. Jerry explained how he tried to combine discipline with restraint. "Those kids got only five whippings between 'em their whole lives. That's it. Just five. That was enough. After that I could just raise my voice and they listened. Just five whippings. I never beat them up or slapped them around 'cause that ain't right. And they minded too. And my brothers and sisters were all the time giving me shit, saying they were gonna grow up all fucked up 'cause we lived in Detroit. Barry was the worst of them. He was saying, 'your boys gonna be in the Pen, and your daughter's gonna be a nigger lover.'" His face drew into a sneer as he repeated his brother's predictions.

Jessie Rae added, "That's right, he said she'd grow up to be a nigger-lovin' whore."

Jerry reiterated, "That's what he said. And everyone of them have given us shit about staying here. They all live in the suburbs and they shit on us because we never left. We never left the inner city of Detroit. We never tried to either. We've never lived any more than a few blocks from where we grew up. Those kids grew up between here and Third and Alexandrine. We never left this city. And those kids all went to the Detroit schools and they all turned out fine."

There is a glimpse, here, of the anxiety and animosity that compelled most whites to eschew any contact with blacks. The schools, in particular, unnerved his brothers. But intriguingly, the sentiment was not homogeneous within the family. Two of Jerry's brothers left the city; three stayed. He and Jessie Rae gloated over how their nieces and nephews had turned out. Barry's oldest daughter just turned twenty, has three kids, another on the way, and is still unmarried. Several of his boys, they noted, "are knocking on the door" of jail. Barry's conviction that suburban life was better for white kids, they suggested, turned out to be ill-founded.

In another instance, Jerry was called "nigger lover" by Mike, one of Willie's friends from the suburb of Hazel Park. Jerry did not care much for Mike. He had been to the house once before and managed to infuriate everybody within a half an hour. That day, he was trying to lure Jerry and Willie into a scheme he had concocted to make money off of public pay phones, but both men declined. Months later, Mike returned and almost as quickly sparked a conflict. We all went to O'Leary's, where Mike proceeded to get drunk and obnoxious. He said something rude to Lynn, a black woman regular at the bar, and Jerry furiously threw him out of the bar, literally dragging him into the street and then shoving him into Willie's car. Mike kept hollering that Jerry was a "nigger lover," and tried to fight, but he was too drunk. After Jerry stuffed him in the car, I never saw him again.

Mike's outburst points to an important aspect of the operation of racial categories in this zone. Whatever whites may "truly" feel about the varying significance or insignificance of racial identities and matters, in this city and in this neighborhood they are regularly in situations where the significance of race is out of their control. Indeed, I intentionally forego an analysis of their various personalities, in favor of letting the compilations of situations act as articulations of a certain class position and the racial predicament it entails. In the incident with Mike, Jerry responded in a fashion that removed all doubt about his racial sensibilities. In other contexts, such emphatic responses are not always possible. Whatever intricate modalities for negotiating the significance of racialness, these whites were susceptible to unpredictable circumstances and contexts in which racial difference was no longer negotiable, as the next section illustrates.

The Wicker Chair and the Baseball Game

The whites of Briggs could not control the significance of their racialness with certainty; they had not shaped social space and discourses into interlocking structures that could respond to and diffuse their objectifications as whites, although such structures are variously developed in the neighborhoods of Corktown and Warrendale. Whatever discursive means they

developed within kin groups to dampen the riotous play of racial significance, these hardly matched the range of circumstances in which they
could be reductively read as whites in terms of intentions, interests, or
vulnerabilities. Whites in Briggs were continually susceptible to being
marked by the arbitrary logic of racial violence. The men, in particular,
all had stories of being "jumped" by blacks, either mugged or randomly
beaten. For Jerry and his brothers, the incidents began when they were
children and have not ceased to loom as a potential threat. The possibility
of being read simply as "white"—that is, as out of place—increased with
their distance from their home base; the further afield they went in the
city, the greater their chances of being racially objectified. Even in the
neighborhood, the "fact" of their racialness was always present as a
means to ground a number of possible readings of their intentions or
motivations. Their engagement with certain modes of racial etiquette
were meager in comparison with the range of ways that white racialness
was signified in the inner city of Detroit.[78]

Right after we moved in, late in the afternoon of a windy day, I heard
Jerry come storming into the yard. He had just returned from a ride with
Willie and his wife Paula (Jessie Rae's niece), whom I had not yet met.
They were all upset, but Jerry's fury was the most daunting. Willie concentrated intently on trying to calm him down. I came out into the yard
and asked what had happened. They all spoke at once, repeating the
event and trying to figure out the situation.

They were over at Billy Lee's house; a few people hanging out, black
and white, and everything was fine. They were unsure what set things off,
but two black men asked for a ride to the store. Paula and Willie said that
they would take them up there and back—they had driven their blue
Nova over to Billy Lee's. When the two men were getting into the back
seat, they started acting rude. Willie said one of them, while he was climbing in, excessively pressed the seat back down on him. Although he did
not take offense, Paula got mad because they started throwing things
around in the backseat, scattering stuff all over the place. When Paula
said something, the men got mad and started calling them "white motherfuckers," accusing them of not wanting blacks riding in their car.

Both Paula and Willie started yelling at them. Jerry heard this, decided
his friends were in trouble, marched down the street and proceeded to get
into the middle of the dispute. A tense round of name-calling ensued, and
a fist fight was only avoided because other people on the street intervened,
including Billy Lee and his wife Barbara. After their accounts, I was vague
on how this situation developed, but they all remained so upset—and I
did not yet know any of them well enough to pry—that I could not get
them to clarify matters further. Jerry continued to pace around the yard,
and they stormily sorted out who said what and when. The little more

that I caught was Willie insisting that "They were just trying to fuck with us. Some people are like that, they just want to fuck with you. They want to make something out of nothing just to start trouble."

Jerry then went over to the gray house and talked with Marvin for a while. They drifted back over to our yard, where Jerry got some beers and they talked as the sun sank. As Jerry slowly calmed down, Marvin, too, offered the interpretation that "They were just trying to fuck with you, Jerry. Some people are like that." I heard only snatches of their talk, as I was too shy to go over and directly intrude. But, I was surprised when I later stopped at my back door to listen that they were now talking about the "next riot." Jerry asserted that "The next time, it's gonna be white and black against the Arab, and it ain't gonna be about race, it's gonna be about getting back all they took from us. And they the only mother-fuckers around here makin' anything, so you know we're gonna be taking from them." Marvin tends to be soft spoken. He offered Jerry nods and muttered affirmations. It sounded as if Jerry's resolution of the matter was a displacement of race onto an ostensibly "classed" event that would finally join whites and blacks together.

This incident was retold and reexamined by the participants at least twice. The next time I heard the story was about three weeks later. It was Jerry's mother's birthday, and a big party was planned over at her house on the southwest side, in an area known as "Vernor-tucky." The main street in the neighborhood is Vernor; "tucky" is an affix labeled to numerous sites that still host large concentrations of "hillbillies."[79] Relatives arrived at Jerry's through the morning, then headed over to his mom's house. One of them, Bobby—a brother-in-law of Leroy (Jessie Rae's brother)—stopped in and stayed a while, out on the porch, drinking and catching up with Jerry. One of the stories Jerry told was about the incident over at Billy Lee's. In this version, the purpose of their visit to Billy Lee's became clear to me: Willie and Paula had gone over there because they heard one of the black families down the block was selling some of their furniture. Jerry had stayed and talked with Billy Lee while Paula and Willie went across the street, looked over the furniture, and picked out a large wicker chair. The man said he wanted $6 for it. While they were considering the price and looking at the rest of the furniture, another black man in the house asked if he could get a ride to the store, saying he would give them $3 for gas money. His friend, who was selling the chair, said he would take the $3 off the price of the chair if they would give both of them a ride to the store and back. Willie and Paula agreed.

The two black men went next door to get something while Willie and Paula looked at the rest of the furniture. A black woman in the house soon followed the two men down the street and told them that after they left Paula said she "don't want no niggers riding in the car." All Jerry knew was that he heard the black men lashing out at Willie and Paula, calling them "white motherfuckers." He rushed over to stand up for his friends. One of the black men, who knew Jerry, told him, "Jerry, you ain't involved with this," but he insisted, "Oh yes I am!" This led to the shouting match, which Billy Lee helped to break up.

Jerry did not dwell on what had actually been said by Willie or Paula; he was primarily concerned with justifying his action of jumping into the conflict. He explained to Bobby that he had not been standing up for anything Willie had said, but that since he had brought them over there he was responsible for their safety. He had placed them in a situation that turned out to be dangerous and felt responsible for getting them out. He did not dwell on the origin of the conflict. In this version, he surmised that the black woman was just trying to cause trouble, supposing she was "naturally mean." There was nothing mentioned about the physical contact in the car, which now seemed unimportant, and he was perplexed by the allegations about Paula using "nigger," since she never seemed to use the word.

Jerry said it was not just the black woman, but a group of blacks living on that block were aggressive and mean. He was telling Bobby and me about the incident as much as he was warning us, "You got to watch yourself over there." The moral he found in the story was that the block was a dangerous site for whites, where pretense for a conflict could be drawn arbitrarily. Willie said he was never going over there again, on account of "all the niggers over there." But neither Jerry nor Willie related the incident to behaviors or attitudes of blacks in general; their racial reading of this aggressiveness was strictly localized to that group on that block.

Hours later, driving back from the birthday party, we stopped at Billy Lee's. Jerry and Bobby were very drunk by then. I rode them over in the back of our truck, and they rolled about, hollering and laughing as I made tight turns on the wide, deserted streets. When we pulled up in front of Billy Lee's house, he was across the street with four black men shooting dice. He came over as soon as he recognized Jerry getting out of the back of the truck. Billy Lee—tall and gaunt, with dirty blonde, ragged hair, a broad mouth, and glaring eyes—got up in my face and hissed, "Don't any of you start in with that nigger shit. This is family here and I don't want you fucking it up." I told him that I didn't use the word, and he relaxed a bit, but still hissed at Jerry, who assured him that he wasn't "gonna start nothing." Billy wanted to make sure that Jerry was getting the message, so he repeated, "This is my place here man, and I don't need no shit starting up." I went with him back to the porch where the crap game continued, while Jerry and Bob played with Billy Lee and Barb's kids off the back of the truck. After a while, Barbara came over to the truck and talked with Jerry, while the kids went off down the block with some of the black kids from across the street.

Apparently, Jerry had been sent to convey Jessie Rae's dismay that her brother, Billy Lee, had not spoken to her for more than a month. This was largely due to Billy Lee's crack binges, which had grown more frequent over the summer. Jessie Rae told me a couple of times that it had been a hard year—their mother had just died, and her brother, Herschel, became her second brother to die from alcoholism. She was worried that Billy Lee, too, was going to end badly. Jerry's efforts paid off, though, with a visit a few nights later; both Billy Lee and Barbara showed up with their three kids. The women, in practiced manner, set a table up in the yard, gathered chairs, and sank into a game of cards for penny stakes. Jerry and Willie did not play, and Billy Lee was out quickly after losing the little change he had. Then the men talked against the porch and took great pleasure in observing aloud how it was the women and not the men play-ing. Willie noted that "They always say that men just love to gamble, that we *have* to do it. Well look who's gambling now. I want to take a picture of this." The men laughed and the women ignored them and went on playing. The game and our talk ran late into the night.

The name-calling incident was again recounted the next day. Barbara and Billy Lee came back around noon. She wanted to win back the money she had lost, while he just sulked along grumpily. Billy Lee was carrying a lush, fiesta-style dress that he had bought for Barbara at the liquor store (Sharkey's) on the way over, apparently to "make up" for spending so much of their money on crack. Barbara assured him that she would never go anywhere in "that thing," and none of the other women was interested in it either, when he offered it up for grabs. Willie and Paula were back as usual, and Jerry was on the second "jumbo" (a 40-ounce beer) of the day. The table and chairs had sat out in the yard all night, so the women fell quickly into the game. The men lolled around the yard, shirtless as usual in the summer.

Jerry was fuming because he had asked Leroy for help putting a new refrigerator in upstairs. He had worked with Leroy on a number of jobs and recently promised to help him put in a furnace. "Man, y'know what he told me? 'Today's my day off.' I just said, 'Right, don't help me, that's fine.' Just like my next day off is when he's trying to put in that furnace." Billy Lee was also disgusted with Leroy, whom he worked with doing demolition jobs for a contractor. He felt Leroy had messed up on the last two jobs by showing up too hung over to work. They took turns telling disparaging versions of Leroy's lack of reciprocity or sociality, in what I was recognizing as a familiar mode of talk. Willie and Billy Lee were alternately subjects of similar rounds between Jerry and other visi-tors. I remained amazed at the way they could so angrily denounce each other, and yet avoid severing these critical but tenuous, aggravating, and usually disappointing social ties.

When Billy Lee announced that he wanted to go back up to Sharkey's, Barbara started yelling. They argued loudly over why he was "really" going. She relented, finally, and gave him money to buy her four packs of cigarettes. I drove him up there. As soon as we left, he acknowledged that he just wanted to smoke in the crack house behind Sharkey's. I bought Barb's cigarettes while he went to smoke. There was the usual contingent of large black men on the front porch; greeting each in turn, he went in. When he finished, we went back to the house.

Back in the yard, I gave Jerry one of the jumbos I had bought, since he screamed at Billy Lee for not thinking to bring him some beer. Willie was trying to line up deals with some people he knew, going in and out of our place using the phone (we had the only phone in all three of the houses). Once the initial focus on the game relaxed somewhat, Billy Lee brought up the name-calling incident. He said he hadn't received any flack from his neighbors over the incident. Figuring it had been forgotten, he said that we shouldn't worry about coming over there. This sparked the third review, and the participants took turns breaking down what had happened.

Jerry started out, still concerned that his jumping into the conflict not be construed as a form of provocation or standing up for the use of "nigger." He recognized that he had acted out of place, getting into a fight at Billy Lee and Barb's, but he also felt responsible for Paula and Willie. "He [the black man who knew Jerry] kept saying, 'This ain't your fight Jerry. It ain't involving you.' I told him, 'The hell it ain't! These are my friends.'" Jerry repeated that he felt responsible for bringing Willie and Paula over there, even though Willie had driven them, and Paula was the one who wanted to see the furniture.

Jerry's effort to explain his role was framed around what emerged through the discussion to be everybody's primary concern: that Billy Lee and Barb's place had been marred by a racial incident. Jerry, always prideful of his brash, vulgar behavior around his own house, wanted to make it clear to Billy and Barbara that he had not acted in the same manner over at their place. Although he enjoyed his fearsome reputation for "crazy" behavior and the charged space it created around his place, he also savored a sense of appropriate action. But even though he distanced himself from whatever Willie or Paula might have said, he could not afford to make an elaborate distinction at the time because he felt responsible for taking care of them in this neighborhood.

Then Billy Lee described his perspective: "I didn't know what happened when I went over there. But they were saying that Paula said she didn't want no niggers in the car. I didn't believe it. I figured they must've got it wrong." Willie had finished with his calls and was now listening to the discussion. Billy Lee said to him, "If they had said that you had said it, I could've believed it, 'cause I know you slip sometimes." Willie, who does use "nigger" often, acted hurt by this insinuation. He immediately responded that "I would never say something like that at somebody else's place, man. That wasn't my place, I wouldn't have said that, no way."

Billy Lee snapped back, "Yes you would, man. I've heard you before."

Willie was insistent. "No way! If it's not my place, I aint' gonna start going on about niggers."

As they debated over past instances of Willie's use of "nigger," his position remained that whatever he might or might not say was strictly determined by context. He did not just "go around talking about niggers all the time," and his sense of spatial etiquette would have prevented him from using the term in that situation. After arguing back and forth they asked Jerry what he thought, but he could not (or would not) decide who was right. It was Barb's version that finally settled the matter. She had talked it over with Paula previously, and had developed the clearest sense of the situation. Barbara was down the street waiting with the two men who were going to the store. She repeated that the deal had been $6 for the wicker chair, with $3 off if they would drive the men up to the store. Barbara said that the black woman in the house overheard Willie and Paula talking about how they were going to get the chair into the car and mistook "wicker" for "nigger," then came down the street and told the men waiting for the ride. "And what gets me is that she didn't even check it out, she didn't stay around to find out if she had heard right, or nothing. She just marched down the street, shooting her mouth off." Barbara was upset that the woman had chosen to believe the worst instead of checking to confirm what had actually been said. Being neighbors with the woman, Barbara felt this fit her style, which was racially antagonistic. "There just ain't no use for that shit," she concluded.

This version was mulled over and evaluated by everybody. Jerry repeated aloud Barb's version as he was thinking about it. When he said "wicker" with his thick, slurry voice, it sounded remarkably similar to "nigger." Recognizing how the two words could be indistinguishable with a similar inflection, they decided the incident must have been a misunderstanding.

In these retellings, several features of life in this zone stand out. Primarily, this was an incident in which the ability to negotiate the terms of racial significance was out of their control. An "innocent" word had triggered a racial offense and racialized a mundane exchange over a chair. In reexamining the situation, nobody pondered what they could have done differently. This was a situation where race mattered beyond anybody's intention. Although they had developed an elaborate sensibility for policing uses of "nigger," this hardly mattered because the woman heard the term anyway. Additionally, their attention to context and place, fundamental aspects of how racial matters were evaluated and articulated, had not prevented such an incident from occurring. In a sense, their white racialness signified apart from all of the discursive forms of etiquette they had fashioned for avoiding racialized conflicts. Etiquette is perhaps an improper term to use in this setting. Their reflections on labeling practices and the attention they paid to contextual determinations of meanings, even their regard for moralized spaces in which racial conflicts are situated, do fall under the sign of etiquette.[80] But they clearly cannot invoke the reliability and certainty that such forms of decorum imply. Instead, they posture in the subjunctive mode that Stewart referred to, acting as if there were rule-like formulations guiding racial actions and speech, maintaining clear roles and positions, even though the novelty and uncertainty of situations such as this incident overwhelm the possibility of stabilized social routines and identities. This neither leads them to voice a deep cynicism regarding race relations nor does it lead them to generalized opinions about blacks as a result of their racialization. Rather, the situation was calmly marked up as another instance in which, as whites, whatever they said or did was susceptible to reductive racial interpretations.

In assessing whether or not the word "nigger" had been used by Paula or Willie, there was interestingly no talk about racism or being racist. Indeed, very little was made of the fact that Paula does not use the term, and no consideration was given to whether or not she had suddenly expressed a repressed core of racist sentiment. Billy Lee came closest to assessing Willie's character in relation to the possibility that he had said "nigger": "I know you slip sometimes." This upset Willie, it seemed to me, not because of the implication that he was a racist but because he felt his sense of racial etiquette was developed enough that he would not have used the word out of context. Nobody in these evaluations expressed a conviction that "nigger" was an absolutely unusable term. "Nigger" remained part of a repertoire for objectifying racialness, clearly charged but not uniformly prohibited. The questions never concerned what either Willie or Paula "really" felt about blacks. Even Billy Lee, who put a great deal of care into his relations with blacks, did not pursue this question. In dealing with Willie, he did not argue about an abstract set of beliefs that Willie held, but only his personal knowledge of Willie's naming practices. This reflects their regard for the significance of racialness, but it also stems from the fact that, like the blacks around them, they each used "nigger" at different times—the term itself was not absolutely contaminating, just in certain situations and instances. Billy Lee did not even object to the name itself, since he used it, particularly on other whites, like Willie. I also found it interesting that both Willie and Jerry, who would bandy "nigger" about fairly frequently, would be so distressed that they would be accused of either using it or defending its usage in this particular situation. Both of them were at pains to establish that they did not condone, let alone act out, such careless disregard.

Racialness was evaluated as an exteriorized matter, something that did not revolve around an individual's core beliefs or sentiment but was negotiated in a social world of changing contexts. Interiors were bracketed as an uncertain, inconsequential realm. Whatever Paula "really" felt about blacks had not made any difference in this situation. Racialness was clearly, too, not a matter of solidarity. Jerry had come to Paula and Willie's defense because he felt responsible for putting them into a situation where trouble developed. He did not question the black men's rights to be upset or defend the use of the word "nigger" by dismissing the allegation that it had been used. Rather, he stood up for his wife's niece and her husband so he could get them out of harm's way. He was frustrated that the incident had been racialized, but his defense was not predicated on racial solidarity. Billy Lee, as well, did not take sides; he tried to calm both parties down. He certainly did not rush to help Willie, a man whom he disliked immensely. If it had been Willie alone, I suspect he would not have done anything more than watch the conflict unfold.[81]

For these whites, their racialness remained indelible. Read as whites, their words and actions—scrutinized for racial intent—became the basis for a "misreading" of the situation. The black woman listened to Paula speak with the assumption that she could say "nigger." It was in this regard that Jerry had warned me and Bobby that you have to "watch yourself over there." This was a site where extra care was required to assure that no racial situations developed. He did not read blacks in general for their potential to read whites racially, but he did indicate that, as whites, there were situations in which the potential for racial animosity outweighed the ability to control it. Hence, you have to "watch yourself."

The Baseball Game

The family's summer Sunday ritual was to play baseball at a field up at Trumbull Avenue, close to the apartment building where they all grew up. They invited Rebecca and me along, incorporating us into the overlarge teams. By the time we had finished breakfast one Sunday, a large crowd of family members was forming. Leroy and his wife Grace were there, with one of their daughters, Erika, and their son, little Leroy. Then Jerry's sister Mabel arrived with two of her boys. While we were all sitting out on the porch, Jessie Rae explained to those who had missed the previous game that today we were playing for a case of beer. Last week, with fewer people, they played as a team against some black men who were also at the field. By the game's end, several people from both teams decided to have a "real game" next week—hence, the wagered case. Jessie Rae also said that, on account of this arrangement, Jerry's brother David would not be playing this week. She explained that when he heard the racial arrangement, he announced that "no way am I playing with niggers." Jessie Rae added, "And I just told him, well screw you. Who wants you anyways?" Mabel laughed and Erika said he was stupid. Leroy wanted to know what his problem was with "colored people," and "what's he afraid of?" Jessie and Mabel took turns telling stories about how "weird" David is; they centered around how "he thinks he's better than the rest of us," rather than examining his racial opinions. The two women stressed how he never "hangs out" or drinks with any of them; that "he never works a day in his life" (especially not on cars); and his very unconventional choice of going to school to be a hair stylist. David teased his brothers about how, once he had his degree, he would never have to do any work on his car.[82] Leroy summed the matter up by saying that "he's a faggot."

Jessie Rae later called a friend in the downriver suburb of Taylor, where David had gone to play baseball with some of their extended family members. By the time he had arrived in Taylor, no one was around who wanted to play. Jessie Rae told us that while she was on the phone to her friend, David had walked into her place. She explained, "I was on the phone with her and I heard a door slam. I said, 'What was that'? And she said, 'Oh that's just David storming out all mad.' I said, I bet he's gonna go crying to momma. 'Momma, they won't let me play.'"

Everybody laughed, while Erika and Mabel repeated the sentiment, "who needs him," adding that he was "being a baby." They responded to his refusal to play with blacks by characterizing him as "childish," infantilizing his behavior, and questioning his masculinity. When another relation, Tommy, showed up from Taylor, Leroy filled him in. Tommy was also disgusted to hear about David, and also decided that "he's a faggot."[83] But they did not consider his disposition in racial terms; rather, his actions were a reflection of his inability to socialize in this place.

One of the last arrivals was little Jerry and his fiancée Becky. By this time, the group was breaking up into gendered orders: The women stayed on the porch talking, while Sam and Tommy tossed the ball in the street, and Leroy went to look at little Leroy's carburetor. Becky stood by the porch, noticeably uncomfortable about hanging out. She did not want to actually sit on the frayed particle board covering the rotting steps. Earline had "warned" us about her in our first conversation, describing her as "pretty different. Everybody tries to be nice to her and all. We try to tolerate her 'cause little Jerry likes her so much. But she doesn't fit in. And you can tell that she don't want to. You'll see what I mean when you meet her. She's really different." She is from Trenton, a largely white and wealthy suburb. Jessie Rae braced herself for Becky's arrival that morning with a few choice comments about her being "spoiled." "She's always had everything handed to her. And she's making little Jerry take care of her the same way." She claimed that Becky was also spoiling Jerry, pointing out, "Like the other day, he was saying something about wanting a new glove. And she just went out and got him one. Just like that! You can't be doing that all the time. She's just trying to make him as spoiled as she is."

Little Jerry works at a steady job as a meat packer and spends as little time as possible in the old neighborhood, unlike his sister Jean. Part of his attraction to Becky seems to be her insistence on maintaining distance from his family, too. He was the first man I met who made noticeable use of deodorant and after-shave; his face was clean and his hair trim. Although his efforts at hygiene inscribed a clear sense of remove from the others, he quickly fell into sync with the men's teasing, rough play, and conversations about cars.

Several runs were made to the store for cigarettes and beer, while people scrambled to find bats, mitts, and plausible bases. Mabel went to several houses over a range of a few miles to gather these. After an hour and a half of waiting, we got under way. Marvin and Charlotte were playing, too. He drove a carload that included Earline, Paula, and Louise over to the field. Jessie Rae gleefully noted how low the rear of his car was riding. "There some fat women in that backseat," she laughed. Her daughter Jean pulled up with her boyfriend in a big, rusted-out, burnt-red Cadillac. Erika and Jessie Rae were making fun of the car before it was even parked, calling it "a yacht" and commenting, over its loud exhaust, what a good muffler it had. Jean leaped out yelling at them, her big pregnant belly only somewhat slowing her. "Don't none of you make fun of my car." Jessie Rae kept laughing, until Jean got right up in her face. "Say something now! I'll slap you! I'll slap you bitch." Jessie faced her down with an icy stare, glaring until Jean backed off. But they continued to ride each other verbally, in the animated, vicious public mocking they relied upon to break down people's pretensions. Jean went on to pick on Erika. Later, Jessie Rae made a point of assuring Rebecca and me that "You'll get used to us all in a while and find out that this is just normal."

The field was across the Lodge freeway, just the other side of the nearby housing projects, and in front of Jefferson High, the school the adults had all attended—it has long since closed. Sam talked a lot about the school and the building where they grew up. "We all lived in the same building on Cass and Canfield. You'll never have another building like that. 'Cause everybody watched out for everybody else. If somebody lost their job, their rent was paid and their groceries was bought. Then, when somebody else lost their job, their rent was paid. Nobody went without there, ain't that right Jessie Rae?" She confirmed this, as did Tommy, saying, "You'll never have another place like that again. People took care of each other there." He and Jerry, Tommy, and all of Jessie Rae's siblings grew up in that building; it was where Jessie Rae and Jimmy met as teenagers and fell in love. Before that, they had lived across the Lodge in another building. Sam recalled, "It cost me a nickel to get across that bridge. The black kids would make you pay to cross it." About the high school, he only noted, "Man, there was a lot of greasy fights in that place. There was a lot of fights there."

We parked by the field and slowly unpacked the supplies and equipment. The place was empty and Jessie wondered aloud where the other team was. Since they were not around, we chose up teams, with Leroy and Sam picking sides. Jerry was made the pitcher because of his bad leg—he could barely walk now. Twenty people were formed into two teams, and the small kids or those not interested in the game settled in the bleachers around the cases of beer, pop, and assorted bags of food.

Teasing and heckling were constant for the batter, the outfield, and anybody in the general vicinity of the game, often between members of the same team. The men were subjected to teasing about their guts or about stupid plays in last week's game. The women were heckled about batting stances and other technical aspects of the game, but they dished out most of the verbal abuse. Men carried beers along when it was their turn in the outfield, and batters threatened to hit the array of big and small bottles with a grounder.

The background was impressive. Behind us was the abandoned hulk of their old high school, surrounded by the devastation of old, empty apartment buildings, their interiors exposed by collapsing outer walls or missing window frames, stripped by salvagers. This site was even more desolate than parts of Briggs. A fire started during the first game, somewhere to the north. People casually noticed, watching the large black column of smoke steadily rising, but not commenting until about ten minutes later as the cloud grew enormous and the first fire engines were heard. Then, several people remarked on how slow the fire department was, and wasn't that "just pathetic." When Erika said something to her mom about how it was still burning, her mom said, "Don't you worry about it, you just let it burn."

Several young black men were playing basketball on the court adjacent to the field. At least eight or nine ragged men, mostly black, drifted by through the course of the game, checking the dumpsters or looking for bottles along the fence. One black man came by and asked Jerry if we were keeping the growing pile of cans. Jerry said we were. He asked for a cigarette; Jerry gave him one and they talked for a bit. Before the end of the first game, two black men left the nearby basketball court and sat watching in the bleachers. Jerry asked if they wanted to play, and Leroy and Sam each chose one for their team. By the time the first game wrapped up, two more black men stopped by. They were the ones who had made the arrangement for the game this week. Jerry told them to decide who wanted to bat first and who would field first. That left the teams at twelve a side, but Jerry encouraged them to get into the game anyway. After a couple of innings, Sam said to me while we were waiting our turns at bat, "Now this is family—black people and white people playing together. This is what it's all about. This is family." Since one of his brothers had chosen not to play because of the racial mix, his repeated reference to "family" was quite striking.

But there was a problem, and neither Sam nor I noticed it developing. During the break between games, while the sides were being increased, little Jerry and Becky went to the store. We were just starting and their team was already out in the field when they returned. She noticed right away that one of the black men was using her glove. She asked loudly and repeatedly, "Has anybody seen my glove?" She posed this question while looking right at the black man nearest where she had been playing. He gave her the glove and the game resumed, while somebody from the sidelines offered him an unused glove. I did not pay much attention to the matter, until I noticed her complaining to little Jerry about something. He seemed to be trying to ignore her. I found out later that she was upset because the same black man was playing "too close" to her. It was a crowded outfield, and little Jerry told her not to worry about it. She remained visibly bothered by the presence of the two black men in the outfield, but the game ended rather quickly, due to the preponderance of outfielders.

As it wrapped up, a few people thought about leaving, but most wanted to stay and start a third game. Little Jerry and Becky, though, were through for the day and started packing up their things. Jerry asked his son to leave their gloves, but little Jerry said they needed them both. Jerry got mad. "What, don't you trust me? You think I'm just gonna leave it here?" Little Jerry said they played baseball every day and they would need them tomorrow. Becky was already walking to the car with their equipment, but Jerry just kept asking out loud, "Don't you trust me? Don't you trust me?" Jerry followed them to the car, and it was unclear what was being said. Jessie Rae hollered to Jerry that they did not need the gloves, there were plenty. Then Jerry exploded and really began shouting, "Just take your shit and get out of here. I don't need you and I don't want to see you no more. Don't be coming back here. I don't need your cheap ass shit."

His face went bright red and the veins bulged in his throat as he screamed at them. Jessie Rae tried to calm him down, thinking it was just about the gloves. "She said they use it everyday Jerry, let it drop." "Naw, that ain't it," he snarled, storming back from the car. "That ain't it at all! Y'know what she said to me? You know what she said!? She said, 'I don't want no nigger using my glove' Can you believe that bitch? How could she act that way? She had the nerve to say, 'I don't want no nigger using my glove.'" Jerry stomped the sidelines in a rage, dragging his bad leg and kicking empty cans with his good one. "Fuck her! That does it! I don't want to see her sorry ass no more. We don't need her." As Jerry raged, the gathering slowly dissolved. Two of the black men went over to play basketball. The other two waited to see if another game would start. Marvin asked aloud as he watched their car roar out of the lot, "Who's she calling a nigger?"

The momentum for another game dwindled as Jerry's fury continued unabated and his curses toward Becky and his son were fired with un-dimmed passion. Leroy and Grace went off with their kids, and those of us who lived in the three houses ended up back there shortly. Sam got a barbecue going and we ate well after dark in the unlit yard. While we ate, Jessie Rae elaborated on the incident in the field, saying that Becky had tried to provoke little Jerry into a fight with the black men, trying to get him to say something to the man nearest her. Jessie Rae noted that even though the man could hear her prodding little Jerry, "He had the respect enough to just let it drop. He could have started something but he had the respect enough to just drop it."

Not much more attention was given to the incident, but it was reexam-ined that next Friday, when Marvin, Jerry, and Sam were sitting out in the yard. Talk eventually turned toward the baseball game. Jerry told us that his son called and said he was working long hours for the next few weeks and would not be coming out for any more games. Jerry reiterated how sick he was of Becky, and that he wished little Jerry would "come to his senses" and leave her. Marvin said she was lucky she didn't get hit for her bout of "nigger talk," stressing, "They'll hit you for shit like that down here." While Marvin reflected on the incident in the field and Becky's discomfort at being too close to a black man, Jerry brought up the glove. "She said, 'I ain't gonna let no nigger use my glove.' Well she can just keep her ass out in Trenton. You can't come down here talking like that. That's like calling me a honky." He noted that the name was not illicit but had to be used only in certain circumstances. He illustrated this point by recalling a black friend of his who lived across the street. "We were always talking like that to each other. He'd be calling me honky and

I'd be calling him nigger. If you know somebody, you might joke around like that. Like Jingo, when he lived across the street. It was always nigger this and honky that, some people don't mind it. Marvin, here, does. He don't like to ever be called that. And I don't ever use that word with him." Marvin nodded and pointed out, "She was the only one using that language. She's lucky that Charlotte [Marvin's wife] didn't hear her. She'd a really been hurting then."

The two men shifted to the topic of women fighting, bragging on Jessie Rae's and Charlotte's past exploits, and said nothing more about the game. The only time in the next year that little Jerry stopped by was when Jean had her baby.

This racial situation was clearly shaped by the play of class distinctions among these whites. This scene of interracial mixing brought into sharp relief the class rifts within this extended family, and also makes clear the discontinuities in whites' racial thinking. David and Becky, the two whites who made an issue out of race by expressing their disdain for or discomfort over socializing with blacks, both also strove to distinguish or distance themselves from the poverty that characterized this family. Their striving for upward mobility and higher class standing was articulated through an assertion of the need for careful racial boundary maintenance by avoiding interracial situations. Although the contours were easily blurred—David, after all, was living off of government loans while he was going to school, and it was unclear what occupational status Becky held—the classed inflections of their unwillingness to socialize were sharply read by Jerry and Jessie Rae. This is underscored by the fact that neither David or Becky was challenged for being racist. Rather, they both were regarded as being pretentious.

This spatial setting highlights the contrasting racial sensibilities between Becky and these other whites. She attempted to follow a racial decorum that did not apply. Becky found a couple of outlets to signify her discomfort; first over her glove, then over her proximity to the black man in the outfield, and finally her quiet use of "nigger" with Jerry. These ranged in degrees of subletly, but they were all cues that it appears she felt other whites should be able to read, responding to her discomfort supportively. To the extent that they noticed the cues, these whites let them pass in favor of maintaining a scene that Sam considered as "family," despite his own brother's loud absence. In turn, she was criticized for not being able to "read" or maneuver in this context without creating a disruption. Marvin criticized Becky because her comments were inappropriate in that setting: "She was the only one using that language." He implied that there are contexts, largely reciprocal situations, where that "language" would not be out of line. Becky's comments effectively disrupted their place, the site where they played baseball regularly; as a result of her outburst, they did not return to the field for over a month after this incident. The space where such interracial socializing is possible is very precarious.

The role of "nigger" in this and the previous situation over the wicker chair underscores the ambiguity and context-dependent nature of white racialness in this zone. Even when the term is not "spoken"—Paula did not say it, and Becky tactfully whispered it to Jerry—"nigger" sounds potentially in white speech as something that might be said; that is, the weight of white racism, traditionally and in the national context, reverberates with white racialness. Perhaps this echo effect is intensified in the inner city, where the fallout of the investment in whiteness is palpable in the environment of material and social devastation. Jerry and Jessie Rae are located in an area where face-to-face confrontations are frequent. This class predicament shapes the significance of their white racialness in a matter that will appear in sharp relief against the background of the second half of this book.

The use of "nigger" in this context demonstrates an aspect of how class shapes racial meanings in this setting. Neither Jerry or Jessie Rae rejected usage of the term out of hand; it fit with the abusive mocking they used on each other. Jean tried hard to insult her mom, and Jessie Rae just ignored her. It was part of how they played with language—very roughly. They did not preclude the use of "nigger" for the sake of refinement. But the further point is that the term was manipulated in the classed inflection of this situation. Jerry insisted on broadcasting Becky's use of the word "nigger" to the whole gathering. Considering how angry he was, maybe he could not have kept it to himself. Jerry was no master of discretion, and no one in the family seemed surprised that he announced so loudly what Becky had said. But judging by the effects his comments had and the certain way they played to an already polarizing situation in which he and Jessie Rae were interested in severing little Jerry's relationship with Becky, it is fair to speculate on whether or not his actions strictly addressed the breach of racial decorum. If he intentionally relayed her comments with a desire to bring out their utmost divisive effects, then it is possible to see Jerry's desire to drive Becky off as more important than his wish to maintain racial harmony. If he had treasured the interracial connections that were enacted by the game more highly, he might have kept Becky's words to himself. What he achieved by publicizing his anger was to keep her from coming back again for quite a long time. Maybe he hoped to split the couple up. All this is speculation. But whether he emphasized Becky's impropriety in order to highlight the obvious class differences or whether he acted purely out of frustration and disgust, there was no sense of racial solidarity for which he would have shielded her rupture of decorum from all those present. Even though it meant repelling his son, Jerry was compelled to objectify her lack of tact and her inability to negotiate in this heterogeneous racial zone. The point I want to stress is that the evaluation of the significance of race did not occur in an abstract manner. On the one hand, it melded seamlessly with the volatile conditions of their everyday lives; on the other, the role of "race" was evaluated in terms of whether or how class matters. The racial reading was a function of how Jerry prioritized the importance of the animated class distinctions between himself, his son, and Becky.

These two situations convey a great deal about the local dynamics that shape the significance of race. Both were unpredictable, involving sudden and surprising outbursts that racially polarized the social interactions. The social instability of Briggs makes the significance of race fluid and dangerous. It also undercuts whites' interest in assertions of or associations with a larger racial collective—whiteness. Its not the ideological conditioning by whiteness that is most significant, but the multiple ways their words, actions, and interests—as whites—can be objectified and interpreted. What matters is how they prioritize, mobilize, or manipulate "race" in relation to others' concerns, such as class distinctions and family matters. "Race" is read through these other frames, not as an abstraction and not from a unified core of beliefs.

3

Eluding the R-Word

THE SIGNIFICANCE of race for whites in Corktown is generated from a confusing array of sources, including the neighborhood's historical and political position in Detroit, its current degrees of social heterogeneity, and the ambiguous role of intentionality among whites who are reshaping the recalcitrant housing stock in this zone. The area designated as Corktown today is a remnant of a much larger zone that followed the parish boundaries of Most Holy Trinity, which extended along Trumbull Avenue through what is now the Briggs area. Like many old urban neighborhoods, it developed before racial and class homogeneity was expected of northern residential zones; its architecture—matching what remains standing in Briggs—blends small worker's cottages, built cheaply by the Irish in the last century, with brick rowhouses and two-story homes constructed in the 1910s and 1920s. Until 1958, when demolition began for the West Side Industrial urban renewal project—over 70 percent of the houses in Corktown were razed—the two areas featured similar racial and class demographics.[1] Although more blacks moved into Briggs over the subsequent decades, the class composition of the two zones remained similar until the early 1970s. Today, although proximate, they are antithetically positioned in the city: Corktown is a model of "revitalization," while Briggs stands as an example of the "worst" effects of deindustrialization in Detroit.

This chapter focuses on the means by which whites assess and control forms of racial significance in this neighborhood. As is true of whites in Briggs and Warrendale, the racialness of whites in Corktown is not often "unmarked." As white professionals taking up residence in the inner city, they cannot elude the sense that their racialness is significant. Indeed, I found them engaged in an ongoing, if limited, assessment of what role race played in their efforts at reconstructing and reinhabiting this neighborhood. But, in a manner that is more or less sharply drawn in contrast with the situations of whites in Briggs and Warrendale, they have developed means of controlling the apparent significance of racialness in their actions and desires; they have synthesized a nuanced racial etiquette that both melds and is reinforced by the interplay of material structures and their distinctively classed interpretive repertoire.

Figure 8. The varying roof lines of these houses in Corktown—rising with a homeowner's social status—reflect the class heterogeneity that initially character-ized this neighborhood.

Although there are clear racial and class contours to the way whites have occupied this zone, it is not the case that their efforts or interests can be confidently characterized as socially uniform. Whites in Corktown are varied in their economic circumstances. Although lawyers, bankers, and architects seem to predominate, there are whites who can barely afford to renovate or maintain their homes. What they do generally share, in terms of class, is some form of professional training and higher education, whether or not they achieve salaries they consider to be representative of what professionals should earn. Corktown can also seem alternately very white and very heterogeneous. In terms of demographics and political activity, whites are a dominant presence in Corktown. According to the carefully demarcated boundaries of the neighborhood, Corktown is 64 percent white, 21 percent Hispanic, 8 percent Maltese, 4 percent black, 2 percent other.[2] But taken more broadly, the demographics of the encompassing census tracts closely resemble Briggs in being 52 percent white and 33 percent black. The fluctuating image of the area's racial "character," however, is rendered static and stark when you consider the composition of the area's representative body, the twenty-four-member Corktown Citizens District Council (CCDC). During the period of my fieldwork, this board was composed of eighteen men and six women; it had just one black member and one Hispanic member. The black board member attended only one meeting while I was there, and the Hispanic representative quit after a bitter fight over the board's refusal to extend further support to the Casa Maria Family Services Center (a community center offering a range of recreational and support programs) in its effort to obtain a vacant building.[3]

I concentrated my interviews on these board members, both because the CCDC is such an overwhelmingly white collective and because it is the representative civic body for the area. The following sections feature their versions of debates over whether the neighborhood was being gentrified and how the whiteness of Corktown mattered to city officials and to themselves. But before proceeding, I will sketch briefly the contours of other versions of Corktown, those features that alternately annoyed and disturbed or went unnoticed, removed from the attention of white board members. In doing so, I want to underscore again the social diversity of inner-city zones. Corktown hosts one of the largest concentrations of social programs in the city, which are anchored by two churches, Most Holy Trinity (established in 1834) and St. Peter's Episcopal (established in 1859). St. Peter's operates a daily soup kitchen, Manna Meals, and Alternatives for Girls, a program designed to help teenage girls get out of prostitution. Trinity, along with the League of Catholic Women, initiated the Casa Maria program in 1943, and it continues to operate a health clinic for the indigent. A previous, more expansive program to help homeless people, the Open Door, was discontinued after a sustained protest engineered by some white members of the CCDC. When the pastors of both churches describe the neighborhood, their characterizations—emphasizing these programs or referring to the steady sociality developed through weddings, funerals, baptisms, and other events—are quite different from those drawn by the whites I interviewed about the area's "revitalization."[4]

Various "ethnic" versions of Corktown also complicate a view of the area's whiteness. Latinos are numerous here, but quite removed from the decision-making forums that affect the community through the CCDC. They are primarily involved with Most Holy Trinity, sometimes engaging in the community-building efforts in the Hubbard-Richard area (a neighborhood directly to the southwest of Corktown), which has a larger Latino population and features the popular "Mexican Town" conglomeration of "ethnic" restaurants and shops. Then, too, there are the Maltese-American Club and the Gaelic League Irish-American Club on Michigan Avenue, each operated by a small core of resident members of varying generational removes from their cultural "homelands." The Maltese ranks are being increased slightly by a "return" of grandchildren who were raised in the suburbs but now find themselves drawn to the neighborhood where their families lived when they first arrived in Detroit in the 1920s. Although the numbers of the Irish and Maltese are dwarfed by Latino residents, I found them emphasized more often in conversations with white CCDC members, who pointed to these people as embodying the distinctive and identifying ethnic aspects of the area.

The neighborhood's name, Corktown, derives from the county most represented in the surge of Irish immigrants who poured into this neighborhood in the 1830s and 1840s.[5] The Irish immigrants came to Detroit following the opening of the Erie Canal; the Maltese and Mexicans came following the lure of Henry Ford's five-dollar day.[6] This neighborhood, abutting the riverfront and surrounding the towering (but now vacant and abandoned) Michigan Central Station, was where newcomers to Detroit often first settled. Many of the Maltese crossed the river from Canada—as residents of a British protectorate they could enter Canada easily and then make their way into the United States. These "ethnics" are distinguished from recently arrived whites, certainly by their lengthy experiences in this zone but, most important, by their sense of history—they do not recognize these whites' aesthetic valuation of the area's "historical" homes. This contrast surfaced sharply in a story related by an old Maltese resident, Joe Micallef, in a heated community debate over applying for a historic designation for Corktown. I heard a couple of versions of his comments—featured below—but he also told the story to me one afternoon, sitting at a table with two of his old friends in the Maltese-American Club on Michigan Avenue.

Their talk had turned to stories of the caves and catacombs they explored as children on Malta. Tom, who had brought me to the club that afternoon, told of his uncle who "never had a job," but always managed to travel to other countries—he had found gold idols in a catacomb and was selling them in Egypt and Greece. Then Joe told his story, about how one day he and his friends were trying to sink a post for a fort they were building. They accidentally drove the post completely down into the earth, opening a gapping hole, which they all ran away from immediately. Eventually, though, they went back to investigate. They fashioned a ladder of rope with broom handles for rungs: "A lot of mothers had brooms missing their handles after that," he declared. They went down and wound around, coming upon a walled room where the wood of the door had long since crumbled into dust. In the room was a stockpile of weapons. There were spear points where the shaft had long disintegrated, and swords and armor. "Everybody got something. We all got something out of there." He got a broadsword, and rushed home excitedly to show his mother, who was disgusted and told him to "get rid of that thing." He hid it instead, and kept it for years. They covered the hole over, and later, when he went back to Malta, a building had been built on top of it. Years

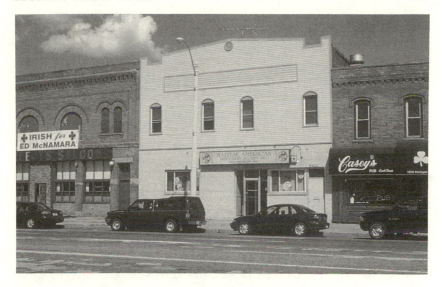

Figure 9. The Maltese Club and two Irish bars

later, relating this tale to his Corktown neighbors debating the neighborhood's historical designation, he concluded by saying, "Now that's historical. These houses here, they're just shacks!" This sentiment is not shared by the whites who pour hours and precious, at times scant, funds into lovingly restoring Victorians and Federal townhouses.

Yet another "version" of Corktown is constituted by the lives and stories of the "street people" who circulate through this zone. Their movement is quite regular, following a route down Trumbull from the shelters or the Plasma Center on Cass Avenue, coming for the soup kitchen or the health clinic located in Corktown, or to panhandle fans at Tiger Stadium. Recently, the Roosevelt Hotel on 14th Street, which has been a shelter for decades, increased its capacity to three hundred beds. This provided a rallying point for members of the CCDC, who lobbied the City Council to close the facility (described in more detail below). Apart from this contest, white residents demonstrated a bemused or frustrated tolerance for these "street people." The class divide between residents and these transients was more of an existential given in Corktown than it was in Briggs. The same "street people" pushed their carts and ragged bodies through both neighborhoods, but they were not objectified as the "problem of the homeless" in Briggs.

The contours and material importance of white racialness in Corktown is both obvious and deceptive. The degree of intentionality with which this predominantly white zone has been constructed and main-

tained, the conscious or unconscious recognition of racial and class interests by these whites, is difficult to assess with certainty. Ostensibly, these
whites have little interest in politically or socially asserting a sense of
racial solidarity. Despite the historical links with Briggs, members of the
CCDC, both formally and informally, reject the idea of working in concert with whites in that neighborhood; indeed, they actively try to de-
emphasize the extent of white concentration in this area. Perhaps more
significantly, they have chosen to live in a racially heterogeneous zone
near the core of a city that is nearly 80 percent black. Coming from small
towns and suburbs, mostly throughout Michigan, these whites demonstrate no desire to live in a racially homogeneous zone similar to the ones
in which they were raised. Finally, the coursing movement of black
"street people," though a mild irritation, does not present an unnerving,
uncertain encounter with racial otherness and all of its threatening men-
ace; the difference embodied by these "street people" is effectively managed as a strictly classed sense of uneasiness.

Whites in Corktown are positioned uneasily within a nebulous racial
and class collective. Commonly their backgrounds are in middle-class
families, and their youth was spent in overwhelmingly white small towns
or suburbs. Some combination of two desires or interests brought them to
this zone: either they love (and can afford) "historical" houses or they live
there because the neighborhood is so close to the businesses downtown;
many expressed an elaborate mixture of both motives. In terms of class,
their collectivity is more ambiguous. Although there is a common basis in
some form of professional training, not all of these whites are financially
successful or accomplished. The "historical" characteristics of the houses
neatly encodes an equally important register of affordability; they are
much less expensive than suburban "starter" homes. Racially, these residents were anxious about the appearance or fact of white solidarity as a
motivating force in their individual actions. In the process of constructing
a "revitalized" community, these whites would grudgingly acknowledge
that they were engaged in a class contest; they resisted, however, granting
any importance to race in their efforts to improve the appearances and
financial viability of this area.

This chapter is divided into four sections, each based on a critical mode
of addressing race and class in this zone. The first, "The 'Fact' of Whiteness," features assessments by these whites of how race matters in Corktown. The reasons and the explanations for the concentration of whites
in the area tended to blur in the accounts of residents, who stumbled over
issues of intentionality and responsibility when we discussed the racial
aspects of their neighborhood. They drew sharp contrasts between their
neighborhood and the white residential suburban communities carefully

crafted through racial and class exclusions. Whites in Corktown were gradually assembling the means for keeping racial others out, but in any situation where race seemed to matter they opted for coding conflicts in strictly classed terms, for instance between the race-neutral terms "homeless" and "homeowner." But for all of the understated aspects of whiteness in Corktown, the types of interracial encounters experienced by residents are quite distinct from those that occur in Briggs, as related in the second section, "Encounters."

The third section, "Gentrifier," tangles with the difficult matter of how racial and class identities are discursively conflated. Members of the CCDC share a common anxiety and experience of being marked as "gentrifiers." Their anxiety over the term's applicability involves its extensive, charged connotations: "gentrifier" objectifies an apprehension of naming whiteness or identifying and acknowledging white interests. Their experiences with "gentrifier" have been confusing, too, because the term is used largely by other whites—it operates like "hillbilly" as an intraracial category. Whites use both terms to assess and efface the extent of their racialness and of their classed markings. But "gentrifier" is rarely ascribed as a form of self-description; it remains an unredeemed term of intraracial otherness. If, as an other, "gentrifier" embodies racial motivation, then the unmarked self could pass as nonracial or free of racial significance.

The final section, "History," treats the discursive and aesthetic category that these whites posit in place of "gentrifier" when assessing the possible presence of a shared collectivity between themselves and their white neighbors. They largely assume "history" to present a neutral register, a frame of reference through which their interests can be articulated without the hint of racial content. However, "history" operates as an efficient, if not intentional, mode for culturally distinguishing between whites and blacks.

The "Fact" of Whiteness

How does whiteness speak? How does white racialness remain a significant material fact that informs or provides the background for social interactions of whites, quite apart from their personal sentiments, beliefs, or intentions? These questions arose as I listened to whites in Corktown appraising the role that race played in their community. In interviews, I posed questions along the lines of "what is it like being white in Detroit?" People responded with varying degrees of articulateness and engagement. I asked one white woman in Corktown, "What is it like . . . ?" She tersely told me that she encountered "no problems" being white in Detroit. We were sitting in her kitchen on a cold, dreary morning in March; the interior of the house scarcely showed signs of "renovation," remaining largely in the dilapidated condition it was in when she bought it in the early 1970s.[7] When I elaborated on the initial question, asking more particularly about the neighborhood's political interactions with black city administrators, she fell silent, reached to the center of the table and seized the refulgent white buds of the flowering plant sitting there, then sharply snapped off two of the three stems. She said nothing more until I changed the subject. At the other extreme, two white men openly and comfortably told me that the main reason why they lived in Corktown was that it was predominantly white and there were not a lot of blacks around.

The rest of the whites I talked with fell somewhere within this range of articulations. Whites described the area to me as a tolerant, racially diverse neighborhood; the most common opinion expressed by whites in the area was an assertion of racial equanimity and a general acceptance of, and even preference for, diversity among the residents. Yet they continually stumbled over the disjuncture between this ideological sensibility and the "fact" that the concentration of whites in this area potentially implied racially interested motivations. Objectifying white racialness often proved difficult for them and for me because it was distended between their individually professed sentiments and the exteriorized residential structures in which they participated and belonged. What they confronted, in describing this place to me, was the troublesome task of both acknowledging and neutralizing their racialness, naming its presence but effacing its influence.

Glen spoke to me in his home one afternoon, talking about his role on the CCDC and his residence in the neighborhood. He is a portly man, of medium height, with a smooth gentlemanly voice, crisp inflection, and soft eyes. The house was built in the 1850s and once served as a funeral home. The interior resembled that of many other homes in the neighborhood that I visited in the course of interviewing residents. The "historical" house was filled with new, technological paraphernalia for both work and entertainment. The first room we passed through had been made into an office where Tim, his partner, ran his own business. The room bulged with an impressive array of computer equipment. An elaborate stereo system stretched through the rest of the house; the phones were cellular and the walls were adorned with contemporary works of art. The interior design, though, did manage to incorporate "antique" elements drawn from the wreckage of Detroit, largely furniture but also wall decorations. The exterior of the house, too, was redone with "historical" bricks salvaged from a demolished restaurant.

When I asked Glen to assess how race played a role in the thinking of his fellow council members, he measuredly replied, "I get the sense that . . . I get a real strong sense that . . . the people who live in Corktown are very open-minded about race, sexual orientation, anything. And respectful. And people tend to mind their own business very much, fairly much. People down here tend to be . . . to mind their own business, but still be very friendly. I don't see any evidence of prejudice in any way." Glen's characterization of community members as "open-minded" and accepting was widely asserted by other whites, who amplified his account of residents' predisposition for tolerance. These whites expressed little nostalgia for the homogeneity of their hometowns or what they sometimes characacterized as the "close-minded" thinking of their previous neighbors and friends. I asked Glen how this attitude developed, and he suggested it was simply part of the disposition of people attracted to this kind of neighborhood. Pointing out that physically the area "looks tawdry in a lot of ways," he concluded, "I think it takes a special kind of person already, to even consider moving into Corktown. So the attitude is already there, preformed, even before they meet the other people."

His confident assessment relied upon a particular mode of attention that scanned the professed statements and intentions of his white neighbors. Clearly, I had not been the first to ask him about potential racial interests at work in Corktown, and just as apparently, it was the kind of question that he and others seemed to continue to ask themselves. What they inevitably decided was that, lacking any "evidence" of blatant forms of racist exclusion, people like themselves are as they avow themselves to be, not racially motivated in their choice of a place to live or their concerns about who else moves through this zone. However, the fact that "the other people" they predominantly meet and socialize with here are white was a more difficult matter for Glen and other whites.

Most of the CCDC board members underplayed the extent to which, as whites, they had achieved a very local racial dominance. During interviews, I asked people about the racial demographics of the neighborhood.[8] Significantly, most whites underestimated their majority status as 64 percent of residents. I talked with Phil, one of the first members of the CCDC and a federal attorney, amid the wood shavings and sawdust in the living room of a house that he was refinishing. It was the second he had acquired in the area. He and his partner, Harvey, were drawn to Corktown by their interest in and desire for historical houses. When I asked him what he thought the racial demographics of the area were, he answered, "I'd say that it's . . . uh . . . I think that there's a big racial and . . . an economic mix . . . in the area. And racially, I guess, . . . it's maybe . . . about 10 or 15 percent Hispanic, maybe about 20 percent

Maltese, maybe about 20 percent black . . . and maybe . . . the rest is various . . . well white. I don't think we have very many Orientals. And then economically it's really . . . y'know, . . . we don't have a lot of millionaires . . . or corporate magnates, no! But there are some people that are very comfortable, and there are others . . . that go down . . . I mean there are homeless people in the neighborhood."

The concentration of whites in this zone is hardly apparent in Phil's rendition of the demographics of Corktown. Its presence is partly dissolved through an attention to the "mix." He emphasized the racial and economic diversity of the area. Whether or not he felt uneasy about acknowledging the extent of white concentration in this zone, he was hesitant to say "white" at all, as if naming such a collective asserts a faith or investment in its reality. Aside from underestimating the number of whites, Phil's account demonstrates an interested distortion. In his estimation there are more Maltese and many more blacks in Corktown than actually reside there, and he undercounts the Latino population. Though inaccurate, Phil's attention to the "ethnic" residents in Corktown is indicative of a general perception that stresses the heterogeneous aspects of the racial demographics in interesting ways.[9] That Phil underestimated the number of Hispanics in the area was not unusual for whites who were not affiliated in any way with the church, and reflects an important aspect of the construction of perception of race in this zone. Although there are twice as many Latinos as Maltese, they were grossly underrepresented on the council; thus it was easy for members not to notice them. There were two Maltese members, though, so they stood out more for Phil and for other "whites."

Phil draws a distinction that I heard often repeated, referring to the Maltese as distinct from "whites" while estimating the racial demographics, counting them as a separate entity.[10] It was a distinction that I found unevenly maintained by the Maltese I spoke with, both in Briggs and Corktown. When I asked Maltese residents to describe the neighborhood in the "old days," they distinguished between "Maltese," "Mexicans," and "American" people. Some recalled the few "southern people" (Appalachians) who lived in the now long demolished apartment buildings by the river. But when speaking in contemporary racial terms, the Maltese and their descendants were content to express matters in black and white. Charlie, a third-generation Maltese-American—his grandparents moved to Corktown from Malta, and his parents moved out to Livonia, where he was raised—succinctly described the area as "almost 100 percent white. Well, there are two black families. No, there's three." Two older Maltese who related stories of being mugged or harassed by black men put a racial interpretation on the matter, explaining that "they were just looking for somebody white." The Maltese, if compelled to position themselves in the binary system of racial identities, marked themselves as white. But whites tended to maintain a distinction around their racialness and the "ethnic" difference embodied by the Maltese.

This distinction allowed for effacing attention to the concentration of whites in this zone. By stressing ethnicity, the dimension of white racialness in this zone becomes less obvious. I talked with Gene in his home, which he uses as an office for his architectural projects. He, too, stressed the ethnoracial "mix" in Corktown. "Well we haven't had any problems with racial matters at all. We have a good mix . . . a high percentage white, but we do have Hispanics, we do have Maltese . . . people, very high stronghold for Maltese, and we do have some Irish people, but not too many. Blacks seem to be a low majority, but my neighbor here is black . . . uh . . . she's fixed up her house . . . No. It seems like a good mix. Its not segregated like the suburbs are. We knew that . . . uh, moving into the area."

> JH: Was that a plus?
> GENE: Oh, I think so, I think so. Many people do ask that question. Now I have to say that our neighborhood, compared to other neighborhoods in Detroit, that we're a much more high percentage of white over black. And I'm not saying that's good or bad, I'm just saying that it's a fact. We DO NOT have a lot of black people moving into the neighborhood. But we do have people here who LOVE it.

Except for a couple of blunt speakers, the question of the racial composition of the neighborhood caused many white residents to fumble with their words. Gene's description of the 4 percent of the neighborhood that was black as "a low majority" is one of the quainter examples of this confusion. His characterization follows a key dynamic of racial discourse in Corktown. The comparison he draws in acknowledging the degree of whiteness of this neighborhood is that "it's not segregated like the suburbs." If anything could be broadly attributed to whites living in Detroit, it is an awareness of their differential position in relation to suburban whites. This contrast underscores their disinterest in segregating the area and the fact that the presence of blacks does not simply unnerve them. Gene here refers to his black neighbor, something that most whites in this country cannot do. But, in actively choosing "diversity" and the "mix," he haltingly discerns a vague collective: "We knew that . . . uh, moving into the area." Whether through concerted actions or commonalties of desires, whites grudgingly observed, if only to dismiss, the relevance of the designation "racial" to their collective interests, usually on the grounds that the allure of the "mix" was strong for them.

Whites regularly told me how much they appreciated the social heterogeneity of this area. When I asked Herb, another white Corktown
resident, to describe the area's demographics he laughed and said, "Mix.
That's it, that's all I can say. Y'know? Counting it, I don't know. Y'know
I read something the other day at the [CCDC] office that it's 58 percent
black and Hispanic. Okay."

> JH: Yeah? It's a pretty interesting area.
> HERB: And y'know, that's quite honestly one of things I like about it.
> Y'know, I like the mix. But that also says something about the current situation
> in the States right now. Most people don't like the mix. That's why they moved
> out. They don't want to mix it up. They want to keep it . . . uhh . . . religiously
> and culturally and ethnically clean—isolated. This is a product of it, y'know.

Like Gene and others, Herb knows that whites, for the most part,
"don't want to mix it up," preferring and requiring racial homogeneity in
their residential settings. As Gene also stressed, this is not a *purely* white
area: "We do have Hispanics, we do have Maltese." His stress on ethnicity goes so far as to point to the "Irish people," who, by most accounts,
have long ago dissolved into the larger collective order of "white." Although Corktown is certainly not homogeneous, the "mix" here is distinctly racially imbalanced—the diversity includes very few blacks. Although he tries to assess neutrally the absence of blacks as just "a fact,"
he still gives his tacit approval of the racial composition, twice referring
to it as "a good mix," a "high percentage white."[11] It is unclear whether
Glen would regard Gene's concluding statement as "evidence" of prejudice: "We DO NOT have a lot of black people moving into the neighborhood. But we do have people here who LOVE it." Even though the absence of blacks is implicitly linked to the pleasure that "people" find in
this area, Gene does not seem to be consciously drawing the connection,
especially since he made an effort at neutrally portraying the racial imbal-
ance as just "a fact." What is clear, though, is that the interpretive repertoire these whites rely upon to evaluate the presence or absence of racial
interests on their part—collectively or as individuals—is not quite sufficient to the complex questions posed by their concentration in this neighborhood over the last two decades.

Their perspective on race seemed to equate whiteness with an active
spatial policing of viscerally coded and charged differences, whereby
blacks embody a naturalized, stigmatic condition. Part of what made it
difficult for these whites to grasp the racial aspects of the concentration
they formed is that they had not encountered a clear black other in this
zone. In addition to having black neighbors, these whites refused to rely
upon the animalistic imagery of racial stereotypes to express their discomfort with black "street people"; rather, they submerged their un-

easiness with this collective through an overwhelming emphasis on class differences articulated in a sanitized public discourse, observing a strict decorum concerning racialness.[12] If they were not pursuing intentional segregation, and they expressed a purposeful disinterest in asserting racial interests—indeed, they maintained a very broad, liberal open-mindedness about race—how could these whites be suspected of racial motivation?

The answer—one that occurred to them with varying degrees of clarity and frustration—is that their racialness is significant in ways that exceed traditional registers for judging whether or how race matters in a situation. Generally, whites in Corktown would prefer to have race not matter. They seemed to operate under an assumption that if race did not matter to them then it should not matter to anybody else either. But, given the kind of attention that others in the city drew to the racial demographics of their neighborhood, this was impossible. Gene related an example of how the significance of their white racialness became an issue or was objectified: "I've had a couple of people from the city ask me, how come you don't have any blacks on your board? You've got twenty-four members, and no black people. And . . . at one time it was kind of an issue. And, I was kinda mad that they brought it up. But we do have a black member now [his voice trailed off into a barely audible mumble]."

> JH: Was it city officials who asked you about this?
> GENE: Yes, but they brought it up informally, y'know. They said if you want to retain your power and image with the city of Detroit . . . the influence of the black administration . . . [He gets up for the first time, goes to get coffee] . . . [his back turned to me] you have to have blacks on the board . . . [long pause] And I had to show them that it's not like we have . . . ah, it's not like they aren't being represented. I mean we aren't trying to represent . . . you want some more coffee? . . . we're not trying to be representative of any . . . any ahh, ethnic background. Including Irish, which we have a long heritage with the Irish people.

He shifted topical gears as I pondered what he meant by representation. Again, the ethnic "card" was laid counter to a racial reading. He deployed "the Irish people" as a marking that should discount the whiteness of the board: "I mean we aren't trying to be representative of any. . ."; they are not trying to represent themselves racially, so why are these people bringing up race? ("I was kinda mad that they brought it up.") Opposite interpretations of the significance of the whiteness of the council results from two distinct understandings of racialness. The black city officials seem to be suspicious that the practically all-white board is excluding blacks—whether intentionally or not—either through tactical maneuvers of the board members or by some strategic effort to keep blacks out of the residential area. In this sense, whiteness is read through the absence of blacks. But Gene refuses the implication, and wonders instead—since "white" interests are not being articulated, just the interests of some whites—how this could be a racial matter. "We aren't trying to be representative . . . "; we are not trying to construct and police a racial identity here, it just turned out that way: "I'm just saying that it's a fact." Without expressed intention, he dissolves the significance of white racialness into a neutral factual status.

Resisting the readings by blacks in the city government, stressing their distinctions from traditional forms of white racism, Gene and other whites in this zone tried to let their racialness stand as a mute, unmotivated fact. They were fairly successful in managing the appearances of how their racialness mattered, partly because of the classed character of the social contexts in which they circulate and the material settings they occupy. Whites in Corktown are rarely directly confronted or engaged interracially on the street, so they can continue to be inarticulate and uncertain about the significance of racialness. The distinction between their position and that of whites in Briggs, and the contrasting orders of racial significance, is apparent in the dissimilarities in interracial encounters in the two zones.

Encounters

The sense that race did not and should not matter—to them as whites or to anybody evaluating their actions, as a collective or as individuals—was ratified by the type of interracial encounters in which they engaged. These were of a much more limited nature than the range of encounters whites experienced in Briggs. Rarely violent or ambiguous, their stories of interracial situations were preeminently benign; the instances that have been antagonistic were few. These whites socialized in more formal settings, where expectations and decorums were well established. But rather than affirming the insignificance of white racialness, their stories indicate that their class position is critical to how race matters in this zone.

Most white residents of Corktown can point to instances in which they were the "only white" at a social gathering, meeting, or event. In these situations, by their accounts, race has not seemed to matter, especially if they made no effort to raise it. Their stories emphasized both the absence of prejudice toward themselves and their personal lack of discomfort around black people. Absent from these stories is any expressed desire to be (or indication that they were) accepted by the blacks who surrounded them. There seemed to be no aesthetic mode for blending race differences through active consumption of overly significant cultural elements as often occurs between whites and blacks in Briggs.

While Gene and I were talking, I asked him what it was like "being white in Detroit." Was it ever a problem or an issue? He replied, "In this neighborhood it's not. I mean, I see that we haven't excelled in a political nature because we're not black. Again, that doesn't . . . slow us down . . . We tend to do on our own. The city likes to promote this neighborhood as a successful neighborhood . . . we can't really . . . they seem to want to take it [Corktown] as a success on their part. But we know that's not true. But we don't go out and say that." I asked him further if he had any racial encounters in the city generally, and he said,

> I never had a problem. I mean, I've been in meetings with the city, where I'm the only white guy. But I've . . . That doesn't hamper me from making my point. A couple of years ago the mayor [then Coleman Young] invited all of the leaders from the CDCs with him in his office. I went. And I was the only white guy there. And each of us had an agenda. I knew I wasn't going to be first, and I knew I wasn't going to be last. And I got my point in, and actually it was resolved. It was a real funny meeting. It was a political year, it was the last time he ran for reelection. Every problem that was brought up, he got on the phone and called up the department head, and took care of it . . . I . . . What it was about, he was trying to impress us, so we could all go back and say, "Look, the mayor has resolved this for us." We all knew that. But it was an opportunity to get a problem resolved.

The striking core of this story of Gene's encounter with the local master of racialized discourses, Coleman Young, is that the significance of his whiteness seems to be neatly effaced. As with other "only white" stories I heard in Corktown, nothing ostensibly "racial" ever happens. Young avoided calling on Gene either first or last; if he had been first, it would seem that the mayor was privileging him because he was white, just as calling on Gene last might have indicated racial contempt on the part of the mayor. Hence, his order of being called upon was innocuous; it had no overtly racial implications. I first assumed that Gene was expressing the opinion that race did not matter in this setting, but I suspect his point was that the significance of his white racialness was deftly managed so that nothing even accidentally "racial" occurred. Whatever the actual motivations behind Young's choice of speakers, Gene related this encounter as an example of how a form of etiquette effaces the significance of whiteness; "race" is something to be thoroughly managed.

The overtly formal aspects of this encounter are distinctive, but the basic situation is quite common and the genre of being the "only white" is an active one in Corktown. The residents enjoy relating such instances because they stand as examples of how race can be rendered insignificant. But not all Corktown whites have dealt well with such situations.

Hazel told me a similar story of an evening when she and her husband, Avery, went out on the town. She and Avery lived in a narrow worker's cottage that they thoroughly refurbished in a "period" style from the 1880s. I asked her the same question I had asked Gene, about whether she got into situations in the larger city when she felt "particularly white."

> HAZEL: Y'know, I don't know . . . I suppose, but I think that it's become . . . so . . . normal for me to be in that situation. As a matter of fact, when we go to Belding [her small hometown in western Michigan], it feels real strange because there are no black people in Belding. It feels very strange not to see . . . There are Hispanics . . . because that's farm country. We have some semipermanent migrant workers. But Belding has an extremely low black population.
>
> JH: Was it difficult to make the change to Detroit?
>
> HAZEL: Oh yeah, it was real hard for Avery . . . when I worked at the Y [she laughs]. I worked at the YWCA when we first came here in 1982. And we went to ahh, we bought tickets and went to ahh, they had this . . . outing . . . going to a play at the Attic [Theater], when the Attic was still in Greektown. And they had a dinner at the Y ahead of time, and then bussed everybody to the Attic and then bussed us back. And it was a delightful evening and everybody had a great time. We were the only two white people in a crowd of about eighty black people [laughs]. Avery felt real uncomfortable, but I worked at Interim House at the time—it was at the Y. And the majority of the people who worked at Interim House were black. So I didn't even at first notice it, that we were the only white people in that group. I'm not usually uncomfortable with that. Avery, on the other hand, is real uncomfortable with that.

Hazel attributed their differing degrees of comfort around black people to contrasting family backgrounds. Avery's father, she said, was "real racist" and often made derogatory remarks about blacks. Her family was quite different. "We were brought up to respect everybody. That was the bottom line." She said this upbringing, rather than encounters with her fellow workers, had enabled her to not "notice" her racialness. Avery, on the other hand, has changed little in his uncomfortableness with blacks over the course of the ten years that they have lived in Detroit. Nothing in his encounters in Corktown has undermined his upbringing. He works in the suburbs, and so his contacts with blacks are fairly limited, even though he lives in this overwhelmingly black city.

Hazel went on to explain, "I'm not particularly uncomfortable being the only white person in a group. Though, now that rarely happens. In Corktown, as you know, the majority is white." However this zone has been fashioned, it offers whites living here a context in which their fundamental opinions and sentiments can remain unchanged. There were few conflicts of the type that occurred in Briggs, where race mattered in a way that these whites could not control. In these well-managed public settings, racialness is either innocuously dismissed (as with the mayor) or neatly compartmentalized (as with "homeless" people), but rarely is it subject to the uncertainties that informed situations in Briggs. Though they might find themselves a minority in other contexts, in their own neighborhood this possibility was forestalled: "In Corktown, as you know, the majority is white."

The absence of racialized exchanges in this neighborhood is partly a function of the greater concentration of whites, but it also hinges upon the material circumstances of these whites. Although there is certainly a range of occupations and educational backgrounds represented in Corktown, whites share key social activities. In particular, they invest time in the care and upkeep of their homes, rather than in the forms of socializing oriented toward the street—barbecues, hustling, car repairs, or porch sitting—that typified daily life in Briggs. As a result, there were few of the ambiguous exchanges between whites and blacks that were common in the adjacent, underclass zone.

Interestingly, the only stories of charged racial encounters that I heard were related by a white couple that live on one of the boundaries of Corktown, across the street from the Clement Kern Gardens [CKG] Apartments. In their generalizations about the neighborhood, whites almost invariably made qualifying statements as to whether or not they were including the apartments—the concentration of black residents there greatly affected their estimations of the area's "character." I talked with Peter and Yolanda one evening after they had put their kids to bed—they were one of the few white couples with children—and we had settled out on their back porch to talk in the warm evening.

One topic they raised was the difference in how race mattered in individual interactions and the situations in which people in organized groups clashed over conflicted issues. Peter offered, "I think people on a one-to-one basis are willing to ignore race. But, when you get to organizations, then they start to . . . rub each other the wrong way."

Yolanda added, "I think that's largely true, but y'know, there was that weird . . . It's always the little . . . Y'know there aren't too many black families here in Corktown. And . . . yeah but y'know, last summer, Barbara [a black woman who lived across the street in the CKG] made that weird comment to me."

Peter asked, "Oh, about Freddy?"

She replied, "Yeah, about Freddy and like, 'other people' there. She would be . . . She would talk to me, and I was talking to her and I . . . over there, just across the street. And she told me that everybody says to her, 'why do you talk to the white pregnant bitch?' or something like that. And after that, like, I don't really talk to her any more. It was too weird for me. Like, that she would even think . . . They might say that, but that she would think that it's okay . . . to even let me know like that. I'm sitting there like, 'Oh. All of the sudden, I'm like this white woman.' I'm just this white woman . . . So, I just don't talk to her any more really. It's too weird. I thought it was pretty strange."

Yolanda's reaction suggests how quickly, once race (and particularly whiteness) is raised, situations and relations become untenable for whites who are not accustomed to such explicit or reductive assessments of their racialness. This story also indicates how rare such encounters are in Corktown. Yolanda was completely unprepared to hear, even at second hand, the racial comment about her: "All of the sudden, I'm like this white woman. I'm just this white woman." Being racialized in this manner was an unfamiliar event for her. Yolanda was not familiar with means for diffusing this inscription as "just" a rhetorical matter, as whites in Briggs are able to do. Her reaction conveys something of the way "race" is experienced for this class—"yuppies."[13] Race appears as a polluting force that marks individuals. She felt contaminated by even being told that somebody had reductively referred to her as a "white pregnant bitch." This feeling was so intense she could no longer even speak to the black woman who had related the name-calling to her.

Peter immediately related an encounter of his own of being racially marked. He was more cavalier about the name-calling.

> And what was it, last year, or the year before? There was this drunk laying on the lawn next door. And I was ready to just let him lay there, until he whips his dick out and starts peeing. Well . . . So I grabbed a big stick . . . And he starts pulling this 'white boy, white motherfucker' stuff . . . "Get out of here man! Does it make any difference what race you are as long as you've got your dick in your hand?" Y'know. So there's . . . but generally I think that people are willing to . . . I mean, there are racists on both sides. But generally, on a one-to-one basis people are willing to be friendly, but as soon as they get organized . . . I mean, myself, I have no use for black politics. Black people are okay, but their politics stink [laughs].

This distinction between black people and black politics brought us back to the contrast he earlier noted between individual encounters and organized politics. Peter detects an "objective," detached discursive positioning involved in racialized politics. His account is worth quoting at length to consider the form of detachment that this distinction entails.

> JH: Is that a detachment you can maintain pretty easily here, with black politics dominating the city?

PETER: Yeah, I mean . . . I think . . . there's no real . . . no real invisible black politics. I mean it is the city government. So, y'know, it's kind of an objective thing. Now last year, when we were having trouble with the basketball [earlier he described their annoyance over a basketball hoop that a family behind their house had placed on a telephone pole in the alley and the boys that played under it late at night], one of things I tried doing . . . was . . . I tried to find out where these kids lived. They were from the neighborhood. So I went and knocked on their doors and tried talking to their parents . . . And that worked pretty well . . . people were really . . . I said "look, I'm not accusing your son of anything, but we're having some trouble with the boys in the alley, and I'd just like to ask you to talk to him . . . to give us a little bit more respect." And it worked! I mean they were having these parties here . . . Oh, at the same time, this graffiti appeared in the alley.

So . . . one of the families . . . What I gathered was that they were gone for a weekend and the son was home alone and he had a party and it got a little out of hand. And that's when the graffiti appeared. And so, I didn't know this! I just, I just . . . Somebody said, "Oh yeah, I think one of those guys lives over there." So I just knocked on their door and started talking to her, and she said, "Look! My son isn't in a gang." I said, "I don't know what your son looks like. I don't know who he is. I couldn't pick him out!! [loud voice]. I have no idea who your son is." As a matter of fact, I thought it was somebody else, y'know. And then when I actually saw him, I said, "No, I've never seen this kid before [laughs]." Then when her husband came home, and he heard about it, he got all bent out of shape. "AHH This happens just BECAUSE WE'RE MEXICAN, blah blah blah."

And he came over, and we had to explain to him, "I never saw your kid before in my life. Somebody told me that he was a kid that played basketball here" [exasperated].

From this chain of instances, it should be apparent that in this zone "racial" conflicts occur along more axes than that of black and white. His story of the Mexican family, though, was the only such incident that I heard related; and it was secondary to the more pervasive and, for these whites, more troublesome awareness of the dominant politicization of black interests in this city.

Peter ended his account exasperated and confused. This encounter with the Mexican family stands in stark contrast to the realm of Detroit politics, where race and racial interests are just "an objective thing." In contradistinction, this local situation was an ambiguous matter that became more befuddling the more he tried to straighten things out. He is able to regard the racial aspects of Detroit politics as objective because the discourse is explicit. Arguably the most powerful political action committee in the city is called the Black Slate; it is the political arm of the

Shrine of the Black Madonna. Such "objective" racializations, to Peter, might "stink," but they do not produce the ambiguity and uncertainty regarding race that arises in more personal encounters. Whether the modes of racial significance are explicit (the Black Slate) or implicit (as in Gene's meeting with Mayor Young), in the political realm the meanings of race seem to be effectively managed; some common understandings are established that allow these whites to see "race" as a political function, removing them from the potential of being personally racialized by these discourses at home. But when Peter and his Mexican neighbor become tangled in each others' racial objectifications, there is little "objective" ground to which they can appeal for clarification and to stop the unintentional play of racial significance.

Peter's neighbor responds to the stereotype of Mexican youths as belonging to gangs and vandalizing property. He reads both Peter's whiteness and his concern as an area homeowner; Peter is not prepared for the signifying onslaught that his request for "a little bit more respect" unleashes. But his depiction of the neighbor—"all bent out of shape" and screaming—attempts a containment of the riot of racial signification, and Peter's efforts "to explain to him" convey an image of patient tolerance, rather than opening up a questioning of how race mattered in this dense series of exchanges. There is an interesting contrast between his account and the wicker chair incident recounted in the previous chapter. Peter concludes, at one point, that "there are racists on both sides." In this estimation, the unnamed black man on his lawn must be a racist, because he uses racial language: "this 'white boy, white motherfucker' stuff." Although he imparts a sense of common racialness, that both races have a similar propensity to be racist, the black man's attention to race is regarded as contaminating. In debating the incident of the wicker chair, racism was never raised as a possible explanation for the black woman's response to the situation. In Briggs, racial name-calling involves elaborate patterns of positions and mood; such names are recognized rhetorically for their power and for their inflammatory quality. A person uses charged racial namings mostly because they want to "start something," or to respond in kind to someone who is "shooting off" their mouth, not because they are "racist." The difference is that in Briggs name-calling is just one way that racialness is acknowledged and objectified. In Corktown, where the repertoire of references to race is somewhat more limited, the simple act of calling attention to race can be considered racist.

The one type of incident that regularly had the potential to be read for racial significance in Briggs was crime, particularly violent crime involving interracial perpetrators and victims. The majority of violent crimes that whites encountered in Briggs involved black perpetrators. It was easy for whites to assume a racial motive for the crime, though few did. Such incidents are not as common in Corktown. Residents often told me that the neighborhood was much safer than most people realized. I heard only one story in Corktown in which a white man was physically assaulted by black men, and it provides an interesting glimpse of how whites in this zone reflect upon the significance of race.

As I noted in the opening, Glen was similar to many other whites in Corktown in expressing a sentiment that race was not an important factor in people's attitudes. He also voiced a common sentiment when he articulated how racist thinking was something that he actively avoided. When I asked Glen if he felt racialized by being white in the city at large, he conveyed the following story and the act of ideological will that it entailed. He answered sharply,

> No! I don't, and I don't allow myself to think that. I was mugged by five blacks in '71. On the Fisher freeway in fact [which divides the neighborhoods], on the service drive. I was walking home from a gay bar, to Woodward to catch a bus. I had no car at the time. I was only twenty-one. I'd just been working for one year so I was still in debt. So it was 11:00 at night and this car pulled over, five of them jumped out and got me . . . broke my jaw . . . But I did not become prejudiced . . . towards blacks . . . because of that event. Even though, in my opinion, I had every good reason to [very angry voice]! . . . So, I realized that I have to work with these people . . . I mean I've had black employees work for me, I always have had. And worked with them, side by side. And it's just never become an issue for me any further. Even though I was born and raised in Virginia. Y'know, that southern heritage.

As with Peter, white racialness comes into view in a limited manner and is tightly managed: "I don't allow myself to think that way." The temptation to "prejudice" is broad and emotionally charged. In his rational mind Glen decides against holding such feelings, "even though I had every good reason to!" This decision, though, also flows against "good reason." His restraint regarding an assumption of racist sentiment is perhaps not as impressive as the base sense of certainty that assuming such an attitude is easy and obvious. But then, Glen is aided in this discipline by his class position, having always had "black employees." In a sense, it would be beneath his class position to harbor racism.

The class positioning of these whites, which allows them to maintain a remove from the street and the type of ambiguous situations that are common in Briggs, comes more clearly into view in relation to the uses they make of the public board, the CCDC. These meetings—where participants, often arriving directly from work, are formally attired and deft at deploying their educational capital—succinctly convey the material

class distinctions between these two groups of whites. But a more important distinction lies in the forum presented by assembling the board; it
provides these whites with an opportunity to develop a means for transposing the vagaries of racial matters into the dense obscurantism of bureaucratic discourse. In part, the CCDC provides them with a "neutral,"
official voice for speaking back to the black administration downtown
and for countering "black politics." Just as important, though, board
meetings operate as a proving ground where they can articulate tricky
frustrations with like-minded individuals who understand how some
statements can convey unintended racial expressions. In these meetings,
they shape anxious matters into collective concerns that conform to an
etiquette devised to manage racial appearances.

Members move matters out of the personal realm by objectifying their
issues as concerning the "community"—subjects that threaten or are of
interest to "everybody" and not simply personal or individual concerns.
When the Roosevelt Hotel shelter reached three hundred occupants, several of the whites who lived nearby became upset. Hugh, whose term on
the board had just expired, brought their concerns to a meeting of the
CCDC. Some members were interested in trying to get the city council to
close the Roosevelt, but most realized that they had little or no chance of
accomplishing such a feat given the political and economic nature of the
situation: The residents were predominantly black and the city had a
shortage of low-cost shelter programs. Through the next several meetings, members tried to articulate their interests in closing the Roosevelt in
the most politic terms possible, in phrasings that would avoid the impression of racist interests on their part.

After the administrator of the CCDC had been given a tour of the
Roosevelt, he reported back to the board that the building was clearly in
violation of numerous fire codes and health ordinances. They could, he
suggested, get the building closed just by pressing for strict code enforcement. If the city did not comply, they could carefully document the
charges and take their complaint to the proper state agencies. He further
proposed that they apply "reverse psychology," and argue that the "clients" at the Roosevelt were being poorly served, because the Salvation
Army was "taking them into a drug-infested area."

Various board members considered and elaborated on this interpretation during the rest of the meeting, further developing the "victim" connotations. Gene eventually suggested that "these people living in the
Roosevelt are getting screwed to some extent. Instead of being real anti,
we can say, 'why aren't they getting better services? They should be
getting a lot more for all this money that's being spent.' We can make
the case for closing it, just by showing concern for the clients." It was in

the best interests of the occupants, he concluded, to get them out of that building.

Over the next couple of weeks Gene continued to develop this line, and included it in his speech before the city council during a hearing on whether or not the Roosevelt would remain open. At this council session, several residents spoke against allowing the hotel to continue its operations, whereas a host of black ministers from around the city supported the Roosevelt. The council in the end decided that they could not close the facility. I asked Gene about his approach after the hearing. He explained that his reasons (which also emphasized the strain on the neighborhood of having three hundred additional people residing there) had been carefully constructed with the understanding in mind that, as a white man, his opposition to the hotel would most likely be construed as racist. He told me, "I knew they were going to bring up the r-word eventually."

When I asked him how he dealt with the charge of racism, he replied, "You've got to always be prepared for when they bring up race. You've just got to have your facts in line. Just keep getting back to your point and don't get sidetracked." The key "fact" in this case was that the Roosevelt was not safe for the poor blacks who lived there; he transposed the issue into a bureaucratic register. By his account, this had nothing to do with race. Whether or not Gene or any of the other residents who spoke in favor of closing the Roosevelt was racially motivated was not discernible in the texture of their verbal protests. As students of the political process in Detroit, and as participants in this process through their membership on the CCDC, these whites had grown quite sophisticated in controlling both their language of interests and their perception in the eyes of their black fellow Detroiters. They have developed a very active means of effacing any ostensible evidence of racial motivation in their speech and in their actions.

Their success at managing the appearance of racial motivation should not be taken as a measure of cynical adroitness nor as proof that they are repressing or occulting racist motivation. They have observed "race" as a subject of political discourse in the city and followed the conventions they presume are its basis of operation.[14] At the same time, they remain troubled by the possibility that their interests and actions are racially motivated, and they actively examine the racial implications of their position in Detroit's inner city. They do not simply block all racial matters from their view. Although these whites successfully manage the impression that whiteness has influenced how they have constructed their neighborhood, the significance of their racialness and its implications has haunted them in another form. Their cognizance of less-conscious aspects of possible racial influence surfaced in their energetic discussions of "gentrification."

"Gentrifier"

> I feel that the gentrification tag, number one, that
> it's incredibly misunderstood, y'know, and it's a
> word I avoid using, and try to cull down to what
> are you really talking about. Because you have
> to be very careful about how you use the term.
> It's a very threatening word to a lot of people.
> It's a very confusing word, and when I hear it,
> I try and say, "Hey, what do you mean, what are
> you saying when you use that word?" A lot of
> people are confused about what it means, and in
> general it's not clear what the term really means.
> I don't think we've had gentrification.
> —*Hugh*

From the first to the last, "gentrifier" surfaced in my conversations with white Corktown residents. Whether or not I asked about it, the question of "gentrification" inevitably arose in our discussions. Descriptions of this figure were freighted with anxiety and antipathy. Although the accuracy of the designation "gentrifier" in relation to the action of white Corktowners was a subject of great debate, the label bore a correspondence to the general economic and racial contours of the situation in which they found themselves. As white professionals living in the inner city of Detroit, "gentrifier" maintained a spectral power and tenacity for these residents as a figure of the racial and class interests that might appear to animate their actions; they recognized but refused to identify with this figuration. Instead, they easily ascribed it to other neighborhood whites.

"Gentrification," in national and a variety of place-specific discourses, is a complicated and emotionally charged subject. The term has been applied to a disparate range of contexts and processes, without much consensus on what constitutes this phenomenon.[15] "Gentrification" is used to describe processes as diverse as the redevelopment of historic rowhouses in Philadelphia's Society Hill—an outgrowth of an urban renewal project—the transformation of working-class neighborhoods in San Francisco by gay men, the turbulent speculation and displacement on New York's Lower East Side, and the conversion of warehouses along the waterfronts of Boston and Baltimore. In each case, the term "gentrification" highlights the general movement of people and capital into these areas, while simplifying or obscuring the specificity of local actors and forces.[16]

Figure 10. "Gentrification" is an uneven process in Corktown.

"Gentrification" remains a subject of theoretical debate and is a contested term when applied "on the ground" in various inner-city neighborhoods.[17] The ambiguity of the term lies in its application to novel processes whereby the basis of class identity seems increasingly grounded in spatial practices rather than in obvious relation to the means of production.[18] This uncertainty brings to the fore the discursive aspects of class identity and distinctions, a matter often overlooked in objectivist definitions of economic interests and social belonging. As Neil Smith writes, in the face of the surprising "return to the city" of suburban whites, beginning in the 1970s,

> The language of "gentrification" proved irresistible. For those broadly opposed to the process and its deleterious effect on poor residents in affected areas, or even those who were simply suspicious, this new word, "gentrification," captured precisely the class dimensions of the transformations that were under way in the social geography of many central and inner cities. Many of those who were more sympathetic to the process resorted to more anodyne terminology—"neighborhood recycling," "upgrading," "renaissance," and the like—as a means to blunt the class and also racial connotations of "gentrification," but many were also attracted by the seeming optimism of "gentrification," the sense of modernization, renewal, an urban cleansing by the white middle classes. The postwar period, after all, had intensified the rhetoric of disinvestment, dilapidation, decay, blight, and "social pathology" applied to central cities throughout the advanced capitalist world. If this "discourse of

decline" was most acute in the US, as perhaps befitted the experience of decline and ghettoization, it nevertheless had a broad applicabillity and invocation.[19]

The emotional valences and the range of social or political meanings that Smith delineates in the term "gentrification" make for a fluid and charged means of characterizing transformations of urban space. In this regard, I treat "gentrifier" as a rhetorical identity, as a means of articulating a range of anxious and ambivalent matters for whites in this inner-city zone. As with "hillbilly," it is more revealing to consider the term's uses than to assess the relative accuracy of its application; insisting on delineating a limited form of correct usage makes static the dynamics by which the evaluative process operates—through shifting criteria and discrepant prioritizing of local examples—and precludes an understanding of the rhetorical effects the labels achieves. Whites in Corktown are obsessed with the question of whether or not they are "gentrifying" this neighborhood. The instability of their ascriptions of this identity to other whites—the uncertainty over whether such labels will stick—encompasses the aspects of their social lives that both reflect the significance of white racialness and exceed containment by the previously discussed social etiquette.

The objective evidence of "gentrification" in Corktown is ambiguous.[20] Although median rents in Corktown ($217) were similar to those in Briggs ($213) in 1990, the median value of homes in the area that includes Corktown had almost doubled in the previous ten years, from $12,700 to $23,400.[21] In 1970, the median values of homes in Briggs and Corktown were fairly close (just over $7,000 in Briggs and just under $9000 in Corktown). Since that time, the value of homes in Corktown has steadily increased, a few renovated cottages are selling for well over $100,000 and new, "historically" styled condos built on several vacant lots cost between $150,000 and $180,000. In Briggs, the average home value has yet to crack the $10,000 level.[22] During these two decades, a less ambiguous social transformation occurred in Corktown: Whites have steadily been buying homes in the area. Whereas Briggs has remained a community of renters (75 percent of residents are renters), the majority (53 percent) of residents in Corktown now are homeowners.[23] Of the 147 owner-occupied units in Corktown, 122 are owned by whites, only 8 by blacks.[24] Whether or not the whites who moved into the area since 1970 qualify as "gentrifiers" is unclear. What is certain, though, is that these whites are intensely concerned that their actions and interests not be equated with gentrification. Equally apparent is that in using the term "gentrifier" they project an identity marked by class and racial interests that they feel more comfortable ascribing to other whites than in accepting as a form of self-identification.

One of the first interviews I conducted in Corktown was with Gene, who was then president of the CCDC. He quickly raised the issue of gentrification and gave an example of the kinds of situations in which whites in Corktown are confronted by this charge.

> We still have some blight. A lot of people have accused . . . the board, and people in this neighborhood, and myself . . . we're gentrifiers, that we're trying to push out the poor and the elderly, and we don't give them a chance, that we're trying to bring up the neighborhood with the wrong sense of values. I just can't understand that. If it wasn't for people moving back into the neighborhood, such as myself, this neighborhood would look like many of the other neighborhoods in Detroit. People try to present to us that we're gentrifiers. But I think that people moving into the area, trying to fix up a home, such as myself, and just bring up the whole community, is an added plus. We still have a lot of elderly, we have a lot of low-income people. I only see that we're making their property values . . . uh . . . even better, and providing better community over all. That's one issue. And to deal with blight. Trying to deal with it, you see we probably have eight to ten vacant homes. And that bothers us, even though it's low. We'd like to get 100 percent occupancy.

Gene's characterization of the charges of "gentrification" reflect the rhetorical stances that Smith delineates: He shifts the focus of this naming practice from the vituperative to the anodyne. In this shift, though, he is compelled to grapple with the uneasy matter of the collective aspects of his and other whites' involvement in Corktown. Although "gentrifier" marks individuals it also names and refers to a process, a collective order of actions recognizable in local and national situations. Whites' resentment of the term was multifaceted, but they focused on how this ascription collapsed the social space in which an unmarked individuality was possible, reducing their standing as individuals into a swirl of racial and class stereotypes. As with any rhetorical label, "gentrifier" involved an elaborate contest over positions and associations, through identifying and differentiating claims and counter-claims.[25] Whites in Corktown tried to keep their associative designations sparse and neutral. But "gentrifier" placed its object in two collectives simultaneously, one classed and the other racial. In resisting "gentrifier," Gene did not counter that he has no social affiliations; rather he tried to account for his social group in sparse, generic terms. Twice in this account, Gene used the phrase "people . . . such as myself." He used "people" as an open-ended referent, only parenthetically connected to himself. In this phrasing, he acknowledged the rhetorical assignation of a social position to him but, in turn, referred to it without characterization or content. Of course, in Detroit, and perhaps in most other places, it is hard to resist fleshing out that collective and sketch a characterization of the group to which he is linked. "If it wasn't for people moving back into the neighborhood, such as myself, this neighborhood would look like many of the other neighborhoods in Detroit." There are two contrasts drawn here between Corktown and Detroit. One surely is intended, and the other most likely is not. Unlike many Detroit neighborhoods, there is not a large number of abandoned houses; also, unlike most other neighborhoods in Detroit, there is a large number of whites. The connection between these contrasts is overdetermined in terms of class and race.

What Gene and other whites end up contesting as they talk through the relevance of ascriptions of "gentrifier" is what larger social group they can be identified with, without falling prey to charged labels that polarize matters in terms of class conflicts—"gentrifiers" versus "the poor," or, for that matter, "white" versus "black." The whiteness of "people . . . such as myself," comes into great relief with "gentrifier"; when they contest whether or not Corktown is being "gentrified," it is the significance of white racialness that they are assessing, evaluating, and fundamentally disputing.[26]

"Gentrifier" first came into use in Corktown as whites began arriving in the late 1970s and early 1980s. What I find striking about the term's career here is that whites are the most active users of the term. Among the area's "old-timers," largely Latinos and Maltese, the term has little relevance—in my interviews with these residents, I never once heard it used. The Maltese seemed to consider the recently arrived whites as part of a process that was also bringing their grandchildren back to the area. There was no grassroots, politicized, defensive response or resistance to the white inmovers. This is partly due to the scale of events in Corktown. No more than a few dozen whites have moved into the area over the last two decades. And, fairly it seems, these whites argue that there has been little or no displacement of "old-timers" on any significant scale. The term "gentrifier" is active here because it is used primarily by whites to label other whites in relation to the overdetermined significance of their racialness and class status. "Gentrification," in Corktown, orients an intra-racial discourse through which whites position themselves and each other through a charged, racially marked objectification of class identity.

Although the assignation of "gentrifier," or the relevance of "gentrification," is contested among these whites, they share a general recognition of the connotations that go along with these labels. As most whites in Corktown understand it, "gentrification" involves the displacement of prior residents. In nationally circulated representations of gentrification, this process of displacement is characterized as a racial conflict, with white members of the gentry evicting poor, black inner-city residents. This racial coding is central to white Corktowners' understandings of the term. They also agree that "true gentrification" involves an escalation in the value of housing stock and in the cost of rents. Additionally, they feel that "gentrification" implies a shift in the class composition of an area, and that a clearly wealthier class of people (the "gentry") clash with "the poor" over how a zone should be used socially. Although whites debate whether or not there is or has been gentrification in Corktown, they seem to be agreed that the answer depends on whether or not there has been racial displacement, a major shift in property values, and a clear emergence of class conflict.[27]

For these whites, the matter of racial displacement is most critical. As whites reoccupying the inner city of Detroit, they are quite susceptible to this charge. In countering the assumed connection between "white" and "gentrifier," they pointed out that few blacks had been displaced. Indeed, one of the reasons why people felt that the term was misapplied in Corktown was because the few people recently dislocated were white. Since they recognized that little obvious class conflict had appeared in the neighborhood, it was easy for whites to assume that "gentrifier" was inappropriately used in this area.[28] A conversation with Phil conveys this interpretive process. He was describing how he and his partner, Harvey, acquired their first house in the area—a place they paid about $10,000 for, then resold for over $80,000 more than a decade later—and the procedure involved in evicting the family living there.

> The house hadn't been chopped up too badly. It was built in 1864, and it stayed in the same family for ninety years. And then it went through a few owners, but it never really got gutted, or chopped, or altered, and a lot of the original architectural details were still there. And that was the big appeal.
>
> JH: Who were they renting to at the time?
>
> PHIL: At the time, the people in there were squatting, basically. I think they had started out renting, one person about ten months previously, paid maybe one or two months rent and that was it. Then the rest of this extended family, from little kids to the grandfather, had moved in. So . . . part of the sale was that we were the ones that had to see that they left the property. Usually the seller does that, but in this case the buyer had to.
>
> JH: What was that like?
>
> PHIL: Well, they broke in. They were living downstairs. At that time it was divided by floors. They broke into the upstairs where I stored some stuff and the other guy stored some stuff. Took that, and then just left the grandfather there. It was a snowy day, I remember, and the grandfather was running around in his bare feet, and two attack dogs, the rest of them just vanished. So . . . [laughs].
>
> JH: How did you get rid of the dogs?
>
> PHIL: The dogs . . . Well when I came back and saw them, I was really angry.

I didn't really worry about the dogs, I just sort of went at 'em. I called the pound to get them. I told them to get rid of them. I don't know what happened to them. And that grandfather just sort of took off into the snow . . . in bare feet. I mean he was gone, I don't know. So, yeah, they were a pretty rough crowd. The mother was the worst but the daughter was turning tricks and the son was selling drugs. I mean, having lived upstairs for a few weeks while they were still down there . . . I mean they pulled out the eviction process to the nth degree. So we got a little taste of what was going on. So, anyways, I didn't feel guilty like I was some gentrifier. I mean these people were criminals, and they were squatting on the property, and they were white . . . , y'know, frankly just, . . . well . . . well, y'know . . . [long pause]. Anyways . . . They were just bad actors.

"Hillbillies?" I asked with a smile.

"Yes! [With a great release of breath and satisfaction.] That's my guess."

Phil's story clarifies the racial stakes of "gentrification." If his object of economic and residential displacement was "colored," then he would reasonably be susceptible to feelings of guilt; he would be open to accusations of acting racially. But since the family he displaced was white, the matter, by his reading, does not involve race; therefore, "I didn't feel guilty like I was some gentrifier." He also preferred to mute any problematic valorizations of the class difference between himself and the squatters. Rather than referring to them as "poor" or "underclass," he stressed their criminality and read them as unfit in moralistic terms, as "just bad actors." In the absence of any class conflict, the relevance of "gentrification" to his actions seems meager. In such examples, whites in Corktown addressed implicit charges of "gentrification," finding the racial and class divisions too insubstantial to support the term's pertinence—as if white racialness was insignificant in an all-white circumstance.

They ably elided the label "gentrifier," because it was other whites who most often used the term.[29] Whites who had been called "gentrifiers" expressed bemused frustration over the fact that someone who was also white, and who may have arrived in the area only a few years earlier than they, would be charging them with "gentrification." Gary, an architectural consultant who had worked on a variety of restoration projects for the CCDC, had been living in an apartment in Corktown since 1978. In his renovation work, he had been labeled as a "gentrifier" by several whites in Corktown. This frustrated him, especially since in other neighborhoods, where he has assisted nonprofit groups in restoration projects, he has encountered "no opposition."

And here, it's just a weird neighborhood, but . . . I can name the people on one hand that have a real problem with progress. It's just a handful. And I'll tell you, none of them were born here. They came in at a time . . . and they remember a neighborhood . . . and either they . . . I don't know, I don't know what . . . I can't figure out exactly why they do it. But you have people like Shirley and Lou . . . The people who claim that outsiders are coming in as gentrifiers are people who have been here as long as I have! But they seem to think of themselves as . . . BEING BORN HERE! Or OWNING this area! It's amazing how they'll look at you with scorn and demonize you, until they find out that you've lived here as long as they have, even if you've done nothing, had no contact with the neighborhood for the past ten years. Suddenly, because you moved in in '78 and they moved in in '78, you're okay, you're okay. Y'know, who makes up these RULES? But it's funny because I've shut up a lot of people by telling them when I moved here.

When we spoke again, at a later date, he returned to this same discussion, elaborating on his frustration over the term's intraracial usage. Referring, again, to the people in Corktown who use the term, he fumed, "And they give you this attitude . . . They look at you and scream, 'Intruders,' and 'What are you doing here!?' and all this bullshit, *and they're white*! And I just look at them and I say 'Why don't YOU go back where you came from, to like Royal Oak [a suburb], or wherever?'"

As a racial label that largely refers to whites displacing blacks, it is indeed confusing to hear the term operating intraracially. But racial matters are not strictly a function of interracial otherness and difference. As with "hillbilly," "gentrifier" distinguishes between those whites who are susceptible to being marked by their racial and class condition. "Gentrifier" objectifies racialness and class position and that is uncomfortable for these whites, who seem used to controlling representation of their social identities, and are able to undermine racial readings by diffusing invocations of the "r-word." As Gary points out, there are only a few whites who aggressively use the term in public denigrations; many more whites in Corktown feel marked by the term than employ it against others. In this regard, it is the reservoir of anxiety which is tapped in the use of "gentrifier" that opens up a view on the local significance of white racialness.

I suspect that there are two evaluative axes to intraracial uses of "gentrifier"—both assess matters of belonging in this inner-city zone. They each turn on the uncertainty these whites faced in articulating a sense of normative space in Corktown; they are also practically inseparable because of the muddled significance of race and class. Succinctly, what I found is whites displacing the connotations of racial motivation and class privilege onto other whites. Ascriptions of "gentrifier" follow an unfixed demarcation of relative economic advantage, while also distinguishing between whites based on length of tenure in the neighborhood—more recently arrived whites are most easily so labeled. Perhaps, in the latter regard, this reflects these whites' interest in establishing and maintaining an unmarked racial identity. If so, their charged exchanges of "gentrifier" indicates that this is complicated and compromised by the subtle distinctions of class advantage that score their common social space. Despite their numerous similarities of background, economic and social differences among these whites are active and mitigate against any assumption of unmarked identity, whether in terms of race or class. Granted, their position as whites in a city that is almost 80 percent black undermines the substantive basis for assuming an unmarked racial identity. But the active play of class distinctions in this zone, which undercuts their ability to establish a normative sense of belonging, I think reflects a process that whites engage in consistently and should suggest caution to analysts relying on the theoretical assertion of white identity as simply unmarked.[30]

In the rest of this section I relate instances of how Shirley, Lou, and other whites hurl the label about. My emphasis is on the way these exchange reflect individuals' interest in positioning themselves as part of what Benjamin DeMott refers to as the "imperial middle"—that is, as unmarked in terms of class. The emotional charge and the relative uncertainty over the applicability of "gentrifier" suggests that the distinctions between whites make a normative sense of class identity difficult to establish. In the subsequent section, "History," I relate how this instability affected their reflections on how race matters. But here I present a detailed account of how "gentrifier" was first used in Corktown and sketch its subsequent career in this neighborhood.

Shirley Beaupre, a white woman from a French family in Detroit for two generations, was widely identified as the first white "newcomer" to the area following the urban renewal demolition. She was drawn to Most Holy Trinity in the early 1950s, working as a volunteer while she was getting her teaching degree. She left Detroit "and went overseas," then returned in 1970 and became reinvolved with Most Holy Trinity. In the process, she acquired some property from a young catechist who was leaving for California. As she tells it, "And then I was a PROPERTY OWNER. And nobody was doing anything about the housing in Corktown. And this was a first-class slum in 1970. It was a SLUM . . . straight up. Over on Church Street and Leverrette, those were pretty good. But in this area, what we call area A, and area C, they were slums."[31]

Beginning with Most Holy Trinity Housing Committee (formed in 1972), Shirley worked on assessing housing conditions and needs in the neighborhood; she was a cofounder of the Most Holy Trinity Non Profit Housing Cooperative (MHTNPHC) in 1974. Their initial goal, based on the findings from a survey of housing needs in the neighborhood, was to get co-op townhouses and apartments built in the area. They asked the

Michigan State Housing Development Authority (MSHDA) to consider building such a project on a site that remained unused after renewal project demolitions, but they were told by MSHDA that the neighborhood was far too decrepit for such an undertaking. Then as now, MSHDA tries to be involved primarily in suburban and rural projects; the notion of supporting a townhouse development in the inner city seemed untenable.

Subsequently, MHTNPHC decided to find funding to improve the housing stock in the neighborhood with an eye toward providing a more feasible setting for a townhouse development. Their first step involved strategizing how to obtain the newly announced Community Development Block Grant (CDBG) funds initiated by the Nixon administration in 1974.[32] Since Corktown was tiny and underrepresented, they were unsuccessful in this attempt. In 1976, when the Neighborhood Opportunity Fund was established in Detroit to let smaller groups get some of these monies, MHTNPHC was successful. They obtained NOF grants each of the next three years (in 1976, $60,000; in 1977, $100,000; in 1978, $300,000), and in 1979 they graduated to line-item status in the city budget and received $400,000 in CDBG funds directly. The first grant was used to rehabilitate five houses. One of these structures turned out to have "historic" value. Shirley commented that the last house they worked on was "this Federal townhouse next door. Which is a very significant structure. Very significant."

> JH: Is it?
>
> SHIRLEY: It's Thomas Jefferson's design, his adaptation of an English row-house to the United States. So when that became publicized, we started getting a lot of people interested. We became . . . The gentrification process started just like that. As soon as we got houses. Then they discovered that five of the seven existing Federal townhouses [in Detroit] are in Corktown. And the National Register of Historical Places said, "WHAT!! YOU HAVE Federal townhouses?!"

She points to Mike Clear as the first "gentrifier," because he was the one who both "discovered" the Federal townhouses in Corktown and notified the National Register of Historical Places. At the time, Mike was a student dabbling in architecture and radical politics who had been drawn to Corktown while taking pictures of old buildings. As Shirley tells it, "One day he was coming home down Michigan Avenue, he lived out further. And he said, 'Oh my god, that's a Federal townhouse.' So he turned his car in, he was looking at the one on the corner . . . and he went down the street and said 'Oh my god, there's another Federal townhouse.' And he looked further and he said, 'Oh my god, there's another Federal townhouse.' So he went around the neighborhood . . . Unbeknown to me, he had taken pictures of every house in the neighborhood. And he said, 'It's a historical lexicon.' Well this was all unbeknownst to me."

Shirley equates the recognition of "historical" houses with the beginning of gentrification: "The gentrification process started just like that." Her version is interesting because, ostensibly, she and the other members of the MHTHPHC were undertaking the same type of rehabilitation efforts that would come to characterize the efforts of the "gentrifiers"— they both were restoring old houses. The difference she recognized between these "same" but contrasting efforts is in the emphasis on "historical" value alone rather than on the "needs" of the particular residents occupying these structures. At first, the two were difficult to distinguish, but the difference evolved into a key political battle in Corktown.

Mike was indeed drawn to the area, at least initially, for its "historical" aspects.[33] He became a member of the MHTNPHC several years before he finally moved into the area in 1978. He met his wife Grace, a Latina born and raised in Corktown, through the MHTNPHC. They bought a house and lived in the area until their children were old enough to start attending school. Mike was motivated to save the neighborhood from further erosion through demolitions of houses for parking lots or businesses on Michigan Avenue, and he saw the area's "historical" value as a basis for developing zoning protections. Shirley did not see such a threat, because it was not the historicity of the structures that concerned her. Rather, she wanted to draw investment into the area to develop new housing. Although demolitions were not a boon to her larger project, they also did not present the same keen sense of threat that Mike felt.

Mike went from photographing old houses in Corktown to researching the history of the area. While the MHTNPHC was trying to develop an application for CDBG money, Mike argued that they could build a strong case based on the neighborhood's "historical" status, which would counteract the handicap he perceived in the neighborhood's racial mix. Mike explains, "I told them, 'what you need is an angle.' What's going to distinguish you . . . First of all, you're not black, by the way [laughs]. And most of the other contenders are. And you're little. So you're white and little. I mean, you need an angle."

Although the "angle" he suggested was not adopted by MHTNPHC, it became the basis for forming the Corktown Historical Society (CHS). Mike wrote a proposal for designating the area as an historic district and sent it to the state of Michigan. They passed it along to the national office, which designated Corktown a National historic district in 1979. But Mike did not feel the Historic Designation provided sufficient protection against future demolition, especially given Mayor Young's aggressive interest in making land available for reuse by businesses. Mike and Grace quit the MHTNPHC because of conflicts with Shirley over strategy, and started working on getting a Citizens District Council (CDC) established, which would give the neighborhood an official voice in city government. Shirley read their efforts to establish a CDC in the area as a move to diminish the influence of Most Holy Trinity in the neighborhood. Seeing the CDC as a means of promoting a contrasting mode of development, Shirley cried "gentrification." As Mike relates,

> Her public argument against what we were doing was gentrification. And that was unfair. The threat was there, but this was no Annapolis. This was no . . . We weren't pushing out black people, or Hispanic people, or anybody. And uh, there were a couple of dislocations but they were kind of incidental. P. G. threw out this little old lady, and she went to the Parish Council and they set her up I think [long pause]. I was really concerned about this . . . because if I had been involved in gentrification, I would've backed out. I have a conscience, and I would have felt that was wrong. What I argued was, "This neighborhood is too weak. It's going down the tubes. If we don't do something, we're going to lose it. I think, if we're lucky, we'll stabilize it. I don't think we have a snowball's chance in Hell of gentrifying this area, that's really out of the question." And so far, I've been pretty much proved correct. It could've gone the other way, though.

He emphasized the rhetorical edge to the use of "gentrifier" and challenged its bearing to the situation in Corktown. "It was their best argument against what I was doing. And I don't think they would've raised it . . . That was their best argument." Grace noted that "It wasn't the people who lived there forever and ever that were calling the new people gentrifiers. It came from Shirley, who was herself new to the community, calling people who she saw as in essence trying to take away her power and her territory, and all that. And so she called names." Mike allowed, though, "The gentrification argument is not without merit. Sooner or later it will happen. Class struggle will not go away. It will go on forever. And indeed, that will happen. So it was their best argument. It was the one I would've taken if I was on their side."

Mike regards "gentrifier" ambivalently, pointing simultaneously to the term's racial irrelevance and obvious class connections to Corktown. He allows that Shirley was not wrong in using the term, complaining only that her use asserted a moral high ground in a political contest over the neighborhood's representation. Her argument, though, had little effect on the Maltese who strongly supported the move for a CDC, due largely to Mike's effective canvassing. He acknowledges that the substantive differences between himself and Shirley are modest, since he could see himself in her position: "It was the one I would've taken if I was on their side." In this account of the origin of the term's usage in Corktown, clearly "gentrifier" does not arise from absolute ontological oppositions, but only inscribes public positions as such. The malleable rhetoric of "gentrification," although easily mobilized, however, is not easily contained or delimited, nor does it serve to establish a normative sense of class belonging—its valences are too charged and its criteria unstable.

Another white who was involved early in charging "gentrification" is Lou Deming. Several white "newcomers" on the CCDC pointed him out to me as one of the principle users of the term. Lou lives in a deteriorating Federal townhouse on Labrosse, probably built in 1853. He bought it in 1978, and was greeted by Shirley, who told him he had just "ruined the neighborhood by paying too much for it." He paid $22,500 for the townhouse, which the owners—three Polish brothers who worked at the nearby IRS building—had paid $14,000 for in 1973. (He still has not finished paying off the land contract.)[34] They had decided to sell out of concern that Corktown's designation in the National Register of Historic Places would curtail what they could do with their property.

Like Mike, Lou was drawn to the area by his interest in history; unlike Mike, Lou is, as he snidely notes, a "real architect" and continues to do consulting and freelance work. He had worked for the renowned urban planner Charles Blessing in the City Planning Department for a summer in 1955, just long enough to become convinced that the notion of urban planning was both "corrupt" and "absurd." He moved to Greenwich Village and participated in the Greenwich Village Plan Study Group, which pushed for zoning codes to restrict developers from building structures taller than four stories. He came back to Detroit with a desire for old houses, Victorians or Federals. While working as an architectural consultant at the State Building down the street in 1974, he found himself parking in front of the Federal townhouse he ended up buying in 1978. He told me, "I just admired it, I didn't knock. If I had, I probably could've bought it." It was the house, rather than the neighborhood per se that attracted him: "I got the house and the neighborhood came with it."

Several of the houses on his block were built prior to 1890. A couple still stand on the pine posts that originally served for foundation blocks. The interior of Lou's house continues in the full-blown state of deterioration it was in when he bought it in 1978. Plaster crumbles everywhere, paint peels in large swaths, and the flooring is warped and loose. Lou only heats the downstairs sporadically with a gas heater in the dining room; there is another one in his bedroom study. The stairs are unsteady and rickety. Although the interior reflects the fact that Lou lacks the necessary capital to renovate his home, he stressed to me that the cracked plaster remains because he plans to restore it fully, instead of gutting it all; the chipped paint endures because he is "carefully investigating the original colors." Rather than mimic the (Colonial) "Williamsburg restorations" undertaken by his neighbors—where the integrity of interiors is compromised, in Lou's estimation, while the façades receive elaborate emphasis—he is forgoing any renovations until he can attentively follow the National Trust guidelines for historical preservation.

Lou took me on a tour of his block on a frigid afternoon, and noted proudly that the people living there were divided between those who were here before the 1940s and those who arrived around the time he did. He knows everybody by name. From the corner closest to his door, he pointed out three empty lots and referred to another a block over. Each of these had featured grocery stores in the 1930s. The population density of this neighborhood in that period still impresses him.[35] There are several Mexican families that moved to the area early in this century.[36] Their children and grandchildren mostly live in the suburbs, though a couple have recently returned to this street. On the other corner is a vacant lot crowded with several cars and a large pick-up truck. The number of vehicles varies as Emillio—living there with his parents who moved onto the block in the 1930s—finds wrecks to disassemble and sell for spare parts. The administrator of the CCDC regularly calls the police to have them all towed away. Then Emillio has to find more wrecks. This use of empty lots is prevalent in Briggs and draws no public censure; that whites in Corktown find such utilizations offensive suggests the distinct class aesthetics at work in these two zones. The contest over proper and improper uses of this empty lot also conveys the kinds of transformations these whites require to make this place livable and their willingness to impose their naturalized aesthetic sensibility forcefully on this recalcitrant urban zone. Two of the houses on the block have been bought by a landlord who owns a large amount of property in the nearby Woodbridge area. A little blue worker's cottage across the street just sold for $48,000. Another house on the street recently had $68,000 worth of renovations done on it. To Lou, this means the block is on the verge of becoming relatively lucrative property; other whites scoff and consider such prices for housing as "cheap."

Lou does enjoy ranting about "gentrification" and "gentrifiers." His comments on the matter vary—sometimes they are detailed but often, too, they are framed as generalizations. One of the various "signs" that indicates "gentrification" is under way, he told me, is that "people start worrying about dog shit. My pivot is the dog shit. They're worried about dog shit now." He affects a whiney voice and shrieks, "'Your dog's been shitting on my lawn.' If you're sitting around worrying about dog shit, then you've got too much time on your hands."[37]

He can be vague in his estimation of when "gentrification" started here. He first told me it "begins with displacement," but by his account there was none in the neighborhood until 1986 or maybe even 1990. Before that, he said, "people bought houses but let the current residents continue living there. No poor families were pushed out. People gently inserted themselves into the area. They came in, they fell in love with the neighborhood, and they bought houses. I bought my house because I wanted a house, not because I wanted to make money renting it out."

The problem, as he sees it, is that people move in with a sound enough financial base to improve their properties and hence their values substantially. He thus distinguishes between a "pioneer" phase and subsequent "gentrification," though, in Corktown, the two phases seem to run concurrently. He also recognizes another "type": those who came in as either "pioneers" or "gentrifiers," struggled for a few years, then left the neighborhood. Their reasons for leaving varied, but Lou pointed out bitterly that Mike and Grace were in this category. "People like Mike, they come down here, raise hell, and say why don't you do something with your house. I tell them, 'Why don't you hire me as your architect so I can afford to do something to my house?' They say, 'Well, I have a drafter who does that for me.' And that's as far as it gets. Then they go away."

Lou points to one of his neighbors across the street, Geoffry, a pastor, as "the first gentrifier." He sharply contrasts Geoffry with a couple who were, to Lou, "the kind of people that I thought were just gorgeous to have in Corktown . . . Kinda . . . Greenwich Village kind of writer, and poets and intellectuals . . . and artists . . . particularily artists. He was a sculptor and she was a lawyer, and she was also very liberal, y'know, Legal Defense Fund . . . Politically correct [laughs]. Politically more than correct." They bought their house—three lots down from Geoffry— from a Mexican-American couple, but left after a few years. The house next to Geoffry's was briefly occupied by another couple, a painter and a graduate student. They bought the house for $3,000 and began trying to fix it up.

> LOU: It was a mess. There was nothing in it. For the next two years he killed himself . . . he killed himself that whole summer putting a heating system in. You should have seen his face when he was told all his used furnace needed was a $75 set of controls. I thought . . . I thought at that point he was going to break down and cry . . . To make a long story short, she divorced him . . . or she was going to. And he flipped out . . . and tried to kill her. And set the house on fire . . . And it was reclaimable at that point—they just left. And it went for taxes.

Geoffry bought his house from Mike Clear (whom Shirley identified as the "first gentrifier") in 1981, and paid, according to Lou, $8,500 for it. What makes Geoffry the "first gentrifier" in Lou's mind is that he immediately refurbished the property. "He put the patio on in the back, and he put the sliding glass door on, and he put in stairs that collapse. He rewired, he replumbed, he did everything under the fucking sun . . . expecting to get thousands of dollars in grants and loans. He told me he put that whole $6,000 on his plastic! And he couldn't get any more money, so it sat there since '81. See, Geoffry has done no work, except tear things out, but everything is bought and paid for. So he may . . . he was the first gentrifier, but since then he had this hiatus . . . I think it's funny that this Episcopal priest is a gentrifier, especially in an extremely poor parish."

In addition to the specific example he found in Geoffry, Lou also provided abstract definitions of "gentrifiers." "The people who were there at inflated prices. The usual earmark of it, as I understand it, is that the pioneer's investment is sweat equity. The earmark of the gentrification, it is no longer sweat equity, it is cash. They use cash. They buy it, they pay, and you can see it." In these examples and definitions, he settles on no specific set of criteria; they seem to shift in relation to the status of the whites to whom he ascribes this identity. The connotations are linked, but the significant class features vary, as do the whites in Corktown. Although Shirley charged that he had ruined the neighborhood by paying "22,5" for his house, he returned the favor by including her in his list of "gentrifiers," pointing out that she has put about $40,000 of restoration work into her house over the years. He listed other white residents of Corktown who turned their houses into investments. In particular, he named Hazel and Avery, who lived on the block behind him. But when I talked with Hazel, she too railed against "gentrification." In her discussion of gentrifiers, Hazel invoked an analytic of attitudes, "groups of thought" as kinds of people, a mode of reference that elided indelible categories such as class and race.

I asked Hazel if she thought that people in Corktown shared a similar mind-set. She answered,

> No. No. We have . . . We were talking about this the other night, Shirley and I. We seem to have three distinct . . . groups of thought, or philosophical . . . ideas going on in Corktown. One is, at the very top maybe, I don't know . . . are the gentrifiers, who want to get rid of all the poor people so their property values will go up a whole bunch. Then you have the ones who would like . . . to keep the mix . . . so that we have . . . the whole broad spectrum of people here. They don't want to see anybody pushed out necessarily . . . They're working at improving their houses and the neighborhood as a whole. Then there are the old-timers, the people who just want everything . . . to stay the same . . . who really don't like all the changes that they see going on. They remember the neighborhood like it was when they were growing up . . . They don't care for all this fixing up of exteriors, the paint jobs and such. I think they feel threatened by all this new activity.
>
> JH: Of the people who want things to stay the same, is there any overlap of old-timers and preservationists, say?

HAZEL: Uh . . . I think it's probably mostly all old-timers. I think it's very much, heavy on the Maltese end. They really don't want the neighborhood to change very much. Uh they fought . . . My understanding is that they fought very hard against the historic designation, because they didn't want . . . anybody to tell them what they could do with their houses [laughs].[38] And I hate to say this, because it is going to sound so bigoted [laughs] . . . But the person I heard this from is Maltese, so maybe it's okay. George. did you talk to him?

JH: Yeah, I did.

HAZEL: He calls it Malcheesing [laughs]. Y'know, when they fix up their houses, they tend to Malcheese, y'know, put up aluminum siding and fluff off all the details and just weather proof it so they don't have to spend very much money [laughs].

JH: Why are the gentrifiers only one of three groups? Why haven't they just taken over completely, as I assume gentrifiers do?

HAZEL: Yeah . . . true gentrification scares me, because that drives out the long-term residents. I don't want that to happen. My neighbors next door. Dennis and Judy, are very, very poor [and also white]. They are very poor. They both work.

JH: The house next door?

HAZEL: Yeah, it's exactly like mine; it's a mirror image of mine. They were probably both built about the same time. Judy grew up in that house. She was born and raised in that house. And her father still lived there when we moved in. He died in '86 I think. Then she rented it for a couple of years, but then she and her husband and her son moved back in. So she's back in her house, y'know, her girlhood house, which I think is wonderful. They can't afford to do anything to the house. You see, they are very, very poor. Most people would like to see them gone. Many people, not most of the people. Because then somebody would buy the house and fix it up. Y'know, I covet that house, because I would attach it to this house [laughs]. Then I would have a big house, and I wouldn't have to find a bigger house. But I don't want to see her driven out of the house because of gentrification. That's what often happens. Because as property values rise astronomically with gentrification, so do taxes. And that drives out the old-time, poor residents.

Although Hazel could be marked as a gentrifier from at least one vantage point (Lou's), from that same position she used the term "gentrifier" to distance herself from a type of economic activity undertaken generically by whites in the inner city. In this way, "gentrifier" was used by whites as a volatile objectification in a chain of distancing marks that could always be displaced on to other whites. The "same" material activities carried different significance for whites assessing what type of activities were proper or improper for other whites living in the inner city. The lack of direct interracial conflict also let the term's racial connotations seem unfixed or irrelevant. Neither Hazel nor Lou had been racialized in acquiring their properties; that is, neither was confronted by a person of color accusing them of "gentrification."

Hazel's use of "gentrifier" highlights the critical classed divide between the "gentry" and the "poor." In dismissing the significance of race as an aspect of Corktown's transformation, residents perhaps grew more attentive to the classed terrain upon which these whites maneuvered socially. "Gentrifier" was useful for marking the actions and interests of someone who had attained a slightly greater degree of economic opportunity.[39] In addition to an ability to make substantial renovations on their own homes, whites were also labeled as "gentrifiers" if they acquired more than one piece of property or if they protested against the social programs operated by either of the two churches. Such actions were marked as inimical to the "poor" and read in a mobile register highlighting subtle class-based differences between whites: "that drives out the old-time, poor residents." "Old-timers" are alternately regarded as "poor" or "ethnic"; the emphases shifted in relation to the contrasts whites were interested in developing. Since the "ethnic" designations are closely linked to their racial articulations, I leave that to the next section and conclude here by considering how these whites positioned themselves through the polarized class figures of "gentrifiers" and "the poor."

In contesting the accusation of being "anti-poor," whites both recognized and returned the uncomfortable attention to class—the kind of attention that provoked the performative sensibilities of "hillbillies." They responded to being marked for aggressive class interests by ascribing similarly classed motivations to those who were advocates for "the poor." They invoked a rhetoric that insisted that "everyone" was defined by base economic motives. When I asked Phil about the racial composition of the neighborhood, I questioned whether he felt that there were conflicts between different groups. He pointed out, first, that "the black population is mostly in Clement Kern Gardens." The few blacks who lived in houses down the street got along well, though they never participated in the CCDC in any way. He told me, "It just doesn't seem like . . . there's any racial tensions or whatever."

> JH: How about between old and new residents?
> PHIL: Well, y'know . . . to me, if there's a tension, then I think it's between some of these . . . what are they . . . these people that think they're sort of ministering angels or something . . . the social . . . well, not the social activists. We're all social activists to be down here, but I mean the social . . . uh, program workers or they uh . . . the people connected with the church to some extent. Some of them have formed up into little blocks, and uh . . . again, these are people that regard themselves again as the true voice of Corktown . . . And they

take a kinda tunnel-vision view of things at some times. And uh . . . feel that . . .
for some reason, that they have greater authenticity or whatever it is . . . You
really can count on them to be really anti-business . . . or to be suspect of the
motives of anybody that might have a little money or might be fixing up a place
. . . Some of the hard-core ones, you think that you might as well leave it
crummy looking because otherwise you'll be accused of gentrification.

JH: So they charge that real quickly?

PHIL: Yeah, I think that there's definitely that. And I think that it's still kinda
of a . . . ongoing dynamic here.

Phil scrambles here for a label: "Some of these . . . they're sort of minis-
tering angels . . . well, not the social activists." No label is as evocative,
though, as "gentrifier." As an attorney being so labeled by an advocate of
"the poor," this vituperative term invoked a troublesome terrain for Phil.
Instead of effacing class altogether, Phil pursued what I found to be a
common mode of response: he in turn labeled the classed interests of
those supporting the "poor." Rather than cast the conflict in a more apparent, but probably disconcerting, contrast of secular versus religious
interests ("the people connected with the church to some extent"), Phil
turns to the economic stakes these advocates have in maintaining "the
poor" in Corktown. This response undercuts any party's ability to be
unmarked in relation to class interests. Also, in recouping the activist
identity—"We're all social activists down here"—he neatly acknowledges their collective ties without making any reference to white racialness at all. The core of his disgruntlement, however, seems to be that "you
might as well leave it crummy looking because otherwise you'll be accused of gentrification." The aesthetic of "revitalization" sharply informs
the targeting of "gentrifier," and it is precisely the aesthetic mode of activity that Phil and others dearly wish to routinize and naturalize as an insignificant activity.

Hugh responded similarly when Father Kohler from Most Holy Trinity labeled him and others who opposed his Open Door program for the
homeless as "gentrifiers." Hugh moved into the area in 1981. He was
born in Detroit, but his parents had moved to the suburbs when he was
still young. Hugh chose Corktown because he prefers an "historical"
house to any of the new developments in the suburbs. He owns a couple
of other properties, which he rents out; he considers himself "underem-
ployed," since he only works part-time as a bartender, but he maintains
a steady income from his rentals.

Although I'm not anti-poor people, like, the reality is, most of the people who
live in and really work to maintain the neighborhood are a very working-class
type of people. They're not looking for any type of handouts. But they're also
not looking to be abused. So I think that in the neighborhood, we have a few

personalities that have really latched onto that star of "We're here to help the poor." Y'know, and my response to that is, "Don't help the poor at the expense of the rest of the neighborhood." Like, you keep drawing in homeless people, and . . . you reach a saturation point of what, indeed, you shouldn't step over . . . We can't constantly have this bleeding-heart attitude about helping, because in the long term that will kill the neighborhood.

Hugh's response negotiates the discursive terrain of "gentrification": reinterpreting his portrayal by others as being "anti-poor" or hating poor people. He resists the stigmatized identity by invoking a solidarity with the "working class" in the neighborhood. Rhetorically, this achieves a remarking of the issue as a matter not of likes and dislikes but of fundamental, clashing economic interests. If being marked in terms of class was unavoidable, some class positions were preferable or more highly valorized than others. Hugh depersonalizes it for himself—while he personalizes it for his opponents, referring to "a few personalities"—by reinscribing the issue as a matter of the viability of the neighborhood. If "they" are allowed to help the poor without being unresisted, "that will kill the neighborhood." In this version, his crusade is also to help an ennobled class, the "working-class" homeowners.

I asked him to specify whether this "bleeding-heart attitude" fell into either of two "mentalities" he had earlier contemptuously referred to— the "religious" or the "social worker." After suggesting that each is "tied up into the other," he stormily asserted,

You don't run your programs and they overrun my homestead, y'know what I mean. That's one part of it. The social-worker mentality is similar in that they have a status quo to maintain. Obviously, social workers keep their jobs when there's a need. In my experience with the social worker's mentality, they have personal needs to maintain this stuff, to keep their job. So I have a little problem with that. Also with the social workers, the bigger, overriding problem that I always have with them is when their job ends, they're out of here. Y'know what I mean? When the job terminates, their investment is done. Whereas, whatever havoc they may wreak with what they present or create to the people, the people that live here were kinda stuck with the ramifications of it. . . . Y'know, so I've seen this time and time again, where the social worker is always beating the drum of more and bigger programs, more services, and let's expand this. And I'm like, well . . . I mean, that certainly paints you as a wonderful person. But the reality is, that's the way you keep your job: you expand this concept. And clearly, when you can't expand it, and it's a done deal, you're out of here. You move back to Grosse Pointe Woods, or wherever the hell you live. And then here, whatever that's created, we have to live with the effects of that. So I'm very critical of that. It's like I don't think either one of those mentalities is ever broad-based enough for my liking. I think if anything, there's not a wanton, but almost certainly a disregard for people who are here and maintaining their homes. It's almost like, "well, what's your problem? Are you an inhumane person?" NO! But . . . y'know . . .

The rhetorical contest over the classed aspects of "gentrification" is clearly drawn here. There are the subtle shifts in valorization when Hugh claims he is defending his "homestead" or when he notes that advocating for the "poor" "certainly paints you as a wonderful person." But the prime discursive tack involves dissolving the classed divide of "gentry" and "poor" in favor of a more ambiguous ground of equally interested class identities. At the core of his response is an attention to the classed interests of those who advocate for the poor: "Obviously, social workers keep their jobs when there's a need. . . . The reality is, that's the way you keep your job." In this exchange, the "poor" disappear from sight in this contest between two similarly classed racial entities. And the difference between whites in the city and in the suburbs is again involved: When the program ends, "You move back to Grosse Pointe Woods, or wherever the hell you live." Hugh suggests the whites who are most animated by an interest in helping "the poor" are those who are the most well off economically.[40]

Hugh assured me that the difference in income between himself and the "social workers" was not great. Other whites made the same assertion— another resident labeled as a "gentrifier" insisted that the nuns at Trinity made more money than he did. In this tack, the valorized classed divisiveness dissolves in an assertion of an equally interested position.[41] When the extremes of class difference dissolved, and the "poor" were lost from view, the charge of "gentrifier" could be regarded as simply a matter of somewhat capricious interpretation by eccentric "personalities" and, hence, dismissable. Although no whites I spoke with appreciated being called a "gentrifier," they contested the assignation from different tacks. Some insisted on the term's misuse on racial grounds, other rejected it by dismissing the substantive basis of class differences. In each approach, what was left unresolved and remained a prime concern was the difficult matter of collective identity and how that was to be acknowledged and inhabited. They refused to allow those who invoked class rhetoric to escape the implications of economically interested actions and motivations; they insisted that those who used this term were equally caught by the logic of class relations. They could not stabilize a local etiquette that moderated or guided proper applications of such charged labels. Their presumption of a normative sense of belonging was continually troubled by any blunt attention to class.

The means that whites in Corktown employed for resisting the term "gentrifier" suggests certain contrasts between this intraracial category and that of "hillbilly" in Briggs. What perplexes whites charged with "gentrification" is the underlying commonalties between themselves and those who launch the accusation. However the difference embodied by "hillbilly" was assessed or valorized, whites in Briggs recognized a certain cultural rift that the term demarcated, a critical class and regional divide. In Corktown, despite the use of "gentrifier," whites continually detected an extensive degree of class homogeneity among themselves. In responding to the charge of "gentrification," it was this confusing but palpable sense of a shared collective background that whites emphasized, while eluding its ostensible racial markings.

Although their interest in restoring and occupying or renting out "historical" homes in Corktown opened these whites to what most of them felt were disingenuous charges of "gentrification," this activity irrevocably drew them together in a mode of sociality that seemed to develop unintentionally. They did not want to acknowledge the class and racial significance of such concerted social actions; they just wanted to be regarded as individuals who were brought together by their common interest.[42] Herb and his wife were drawn to Corktown by both their interest in "historic" homes and the area's location so near downtown. Herb, among other sundry occupations, defined himself as both a "developer" and as "working-class poor."[43] He had been labeled a "gentrifier" for turning out the old men who lived in an apartment building that he acquired and then renovated. Herb's description of the social order of Corktown holds out a flickering image of commonality, which was threatened by shifting "interpretations" and the capricious use of "gentrifier" to inscribe class distinctions.

> HERB: There's a couple of different kinds of people who are here. The people who are the core of Most Holy Trinity Church. There is the church, there is that Irish-Spanish involvement with the church. Uh there is the recognition that . . . this neighborhood was . . . they . . . uhh . . . the haven for . . . the poor [he tries, after all that to just say the name, simply, matter of factly, but finally throws it out just to get it over with]. That uhh "those [slips into monotone] people are the most important citizens of Corktown." That's a quote from one of the people involved in the church, okay, and the poor. Uhh, there were the people who lived and worked in this city, who grew up here, and sent their kids to school, and those families worked hard and held onto their property and didn't necessarily adhere to those particular values of helping the poor. But yet they were participating in the parish and the school, so they . . . silently bent to the wishes of those church people. And then there were the people who were part of the church group, but got active in the community to SAVE the neighborhood from the onslaught of urban planning and tearing down houses to build low and uhh uhh uhh medium sized manufacturing and industry like what's down in the industrial complex . . . So there was those folks, And then . . . even some of those people in the late '60s early '70s, who came in. They wanted to

help the poor, so they came to this neighborhood. They wanted reasonable housing and they wanted to live in an interesting place, so they came in, and they renovated. But they had those values of . . . helping the poor, giving to the poor. So they came in, kinda landed, kinda gentry, and kinda yupped it up in the '70s, and . . . to help the poor. Now the '80s interpretation is . . . y'know, folks like us are interpreted as being the yuppies, coming in and GENTRIFY-ING, uhh, not necessarily concerned for the poor, but wanting to help in other ways, y'know, want to have a different agenda in terms of helping. Y'know, some of the problems come from the misinterpretation of each group, okay. People thinking that the latest round of quote gentry coming in, is we're bootin' out, we're raising prices, uhh, we're trying to make it a trendy . . . uh . . . upscale . . . uh Birmingham, Michigan-type place, for lack of a better comparison, y'know. Urban-wise, I don't know . . . what to compare it in another urban area . . . So there's a little bit of friction with that kind of, of uhh that kind of activity and what has happened here historically.

In this lengthy description, all the critical registers for assessing "gentrification" were mobilized. Herb narrated a history through which two kinds of groups emerge. First, there were the "church people" and those working-class people who "silently bent to the wishes of those church people." Then, an ambiguous shift in class identities occurs, one that never mentions race. The "church people" meld into the "yuppies": while they had "those values" of helping the "poor," their mere presence "kinda yupped it up." The difference between himself and those whites involves only a "misinterpretation" of intentions and values. He was confused, though, over how this continuum could be so emphatically interpreted as being sundered by an absolute social distinction, across which lurked the "gentrifier." Instead of trying to stress differences between himself and the earlier whites, he claimed the "content" of the groups is not as critical as the fact that interpretive orders shifted. The interpretive tendencies of various people is seen as being as constitutive of group divisions as are actual cultural contents such as "values."

But what is objectified in the various interpretations of the actions of these whites? Circulating at the core of Herb's and the others' responses to being labeled as "gentrifiers" is a constellation of values and aesthetic desires that are variably read by "old-timers" (ethnic or poor), black city officials, and other whites. This core is the basis by which these whites differed from the Maltese and blacks; it was also how they were inevitably and often uneasily linked as a social collective. At stake with charges of "gentrification" was their ability to be objectified racially and in terms of class, to have their cultural condition read through the registers of intentionality and interest. They most keenly addressed class, trying to obfuscate its distinctions while leaving white racialness unfocused.

"Gentrifier" objectified an anxiety over whether or how they belonged in Detroit and their ability to "discover" and enforce their ("historic") aesthetic sensibility in this inner-city neighborhood. Although they resisted the implications of "gentrification," they did grapple with the anxious implications raised by their racial commonality. When they talked about themselves and about their sense of community, they relied on a different term, "history." An interest in "history" covered many of the same activities as did "gentrification," but without the burden of an assumed nefarious motivation to establish a hegemonic, collective order. It provided a seemingly race-neutral position. They could identify with other whites in Corktown based on a shared interest in "history," and although they could describe in great detail the extent of this common connection, they gave no indication that they assumed that this also indicated a shared collective order. "History" directed attention "out there," onto the material objects and activities, whereas "gentrifier" kept attention on the people engaged with these objects. This difference is explored in the next and final section of this chapter.

"History"

The architectural and internal decorative esthetics
of gentrified buildings and neighborhoods have
attracted only passing attention. This lack of
attention is particularly surprising in that the
esthetics of gentrification not only illustrate
the class dimension of the process but also
express the dynamic constitution of social class
of which gentrification is a specific part.
Indeed, the esthetics of the process are the
most immediately visible aspects of its
constitution; etched into the landscape in the
decorative forms of gentrification is a picture
of the dynamics of social class.
—*Michael Jager*

In Corktown, "history" is a locus of desire, the material means of socializing, and the unstable substance that inexorably links these whites and divides them from their Maltese neighbors and black, fellow Detroiters. However hesitant they were to be objectified as belonging to a collective order that implied forms of racial or class exclusivity, in their sensibility regarding "history" these whites stumbled upon a common ground, a vantage point from which they could express their social ties in a seemingly neutral manner. The racial and class-specific contours of this collective desiring of "history" were easily obscured. Though they effaced any ostensible interest in whiteness, the social order they cohered to was predominantly white. How their racialness signified in this collective lies in the intricate diversions and inattentions that "history" allowed.

Corktown residents' historical sensibility involves anxiety and aesthetics. The recent history of the city was an anxious matter, because of the tumultuous shift in racial hegemony and the uncertain position they now occupied in relation to dramatic battles and devestation in Detroit. Their desire for the "historical," though, neatly effaced most current events and the recent past that had transfigured the city and their neighborhood. "History" returned them to the cusp of the last century; it did not raise contentious issues or assert a host of unanswered questions about racial interests or inequalities. The "historical" was a solid "fact," aesthetically interesting, susceptible to reanimation through intensive struggle with the recalcitrant and receding materiality of this vulnerable housing stock; most critically, though, it let them dwell in a dream of racelessness.[44]

Recently arrived whites were singularly engaged in rehabilitating their houses. They contrasted the scale of these actions with what they posited as "true gentrification," which entailed the wholesale removal of "old-timers." Whatever the actual extent of displacement, working on their own homes out of a desire to restore "historical" houses seemed to these whites to be of greater relevance and importance than any connection with "gentrification." They preferred to be called "preservationists," "antiquarians," and "urban pioneers," names revolving around a core connection with an interest in history. Houses formed the dense nexus of their interests in "history" and, subsequently, produced a basis for socializing with others of their kind.

Martin and Heidi moved into the area in 1987. He has a shop in their garage where he restores and refinishes art deco furniture from "midcentury." They shared a long, simmering interest in old houses that finally coincided with an ability to buy one here in Corktown. The house they are living in was only built around 1900, which was a source of some disappointment for them.

> MARTIN: Once you get into it, we kinda realized that, after a couple of years, some of the things that we could've gotten, just buying a house thirty years older, we put into this house.
> JH: Like what?
> MARTIN: Fixtures, slate mantles . . . that kind of thing. And prior to 1880, 1890, they wouldn't have used oak, they would've used pine. And the baseboards were bigger . . . so this place doesn't have that. Once everything became

oak, that was it. But there are some in the neighborhood that are beautiful . . .
Walnut woodwork, things of that nature.

As with many other recently arrived whites in Corktown, his approach
to restoration required a synthetic practice, melding a desire to reestablish
a particular historical style with the often partial or imperfect material
remains from an earlier period. The push for extremely purist modes of
preservation was short-lived in Corktown. Initially, the area's historic
designation was strictly enforced as a preservationist ordinance rather
than a conservationist statute; this distinction is suggested in the contrast
between rehabilitation and restoration. As the preservationist craze
surged across the country, spurred largely by events surrounding the nation's bicentennial and subsequent tax revisions that made restoration
economical, codes were assembled to dictate proper methods for repairing or replacing plaster, fixtures, and siding. Regulations, too, were ratified concerning the colors people were allowed to use on their exteriors.[45]
When the city's budgetary constraints resulted in staff reductions at the
Historic District Commission office, enforcement of the regulations was
severely curtailed. People then synthesized their materials and periods
with fervor. Martin described the improvisations required in contending
with imperfect remains.

> We've always been, whatever was there or left, we used. Someone had broken
> in during those twelve years [when the house stood vacant before they bought
> it] and stole the stain glass, and stole the mantle, and all the light fixtures . . . It
> was all gone. So we spent a good portion of that time trying to put things back,
> not necessarily to 1900. Ours actually . . . well the lighting would be art deco,
> from the '20s. But certain other elements, like plaster medallions and such are
> 1880s which is before our house—they're more elaborate than what would've
> been used. There are a couple here on the block . . . I used to own the house
> next door, and it had plaster medallion work in it, but not as ornate as what
> we put in. So you kind of . . . Because the house is scaled down quite a bit. Some
> of these from the 1880s would have ten-foot ceilings, but over here, their line
> is nine foot. So they drop down a foot, so things get scaled down. The rooms
> aren't really quite as big, the windows aren't as elongated, the woodwork isn't
> as elaborate. Things get scaled down. I really like that look, though. And it fits
> some of our house, so it's been put in.

Martin contrasted his and Heidi's approach to that of other couples in
the neighborhood who were driven by a more purist attitude, restoring
their homes in a rigorous approximation of their original condition.
These couples, too, he noted, are driven by a competitive interest in having "the oldest" houses still surviving, rather than being drawn to the
styling of certain periods. Although there are clearly differing approaches

to restoration projects, among whites in Corktown any interest in old houses offered an intense basis of socializing.

When Herb and his wife moved into the area, they were drawn largely by the "history" of the neighborhood and its proximity to downtown. Their interest in "historical" homes drew them into social contact with other newly arrived whites, but uneasily insulated them from socializing with the Maltese. They found making extensive contact with the "old-timers" difficult, even though they were keenly interested in developing such ties. When I asked him if he knew any of the people who had lived in the area for a long time, he replied,

> Only a few, only a few really. Uh, just coming from the activities we would participate in the neighborhood. Uh, we didn't come across too many people . . . the home tour. We were on the first home tour, that uh, at that time, it was really interesting because there were some of our neighbors that came on the tour. They'd participate just to see what was going on. And so consequently you had an opportunity to meet people. Now, of course, these would be the people who would be a little more sociable, a little more interested in getting out to meet people. They wouldn't be the people who would . . . uh . . . never open their doors, y'know. Those people who it will be difficult to contact. Uh, it is my understanding that there are some families who have tremendous photo collections, y'know, old photo collections of Corktown. But they will not share those. They just keep it. I think they understand the value and they don't want to share it necessarily, y'know. So it's going to be difficult to get to those kinds of people. Unless you live right next door, unless they begin to understand you and your quote AGENDA! y'know.

Herb did not present this difference in modes of socializing—"the people who would be a little more sociable," versus those who would "never open their doors"—as a racial or ethnic reading. He chose, instead, to draw descriptive orders in terms of those who are comfortable with public displays, such as opening one's home to a general procession of strangers, and those who are so private that they would deny to the collective order of the neighborhood their portion of the historic record, materialized in family photos. Herb assumed that the pictures were of Corktown, rather than of family members with the neighborhood as a backdrop; he also assumed that they must "understand the value" of these photos as "historical" objects and have obstinately decided "they don't want to share it" with others by making it part of a public display or record of the neighborhood's historicity. Such people are prey to a politicized paranoia regarding "AGENDAS." Although he draws no explicit lines between ethnic or racial groups, the register of "history" objectifies the ethnic "old-timers" as part of the neighborhood's "authenticity," as material ratifications of its historicity rather than as consumers of or participants in its aesthetic delights.

Herb's social experience was replicated in the later wave of whites arriving, as Martin explains, "There was a big influx around '87, '88. People in the early '80s [Herb, for example] were finishing up their homes, and there was a whole influx of young couples moving in and getting started, and they were being urged on by the beginning . . . and there were some people getting out and some people moving in . . . It was . . . actually, last year it sort of had that same feeling because there were a lot of cool things happening in the neighborhood, a lot of people taking the asbestos siding off of their houses, and getting it down to the wood, y'know. Heat gunning it. And, y'know, there's always people asking about what colors, and where . . . it just, everyone's feeding off of each other for ideas."

This mode of socializing, with its free-flowing exchange of ideas and swapping of materials, also developed an exclusive edge. As the years passed, a critical social difference emerged among these whites, based on a couple's or a person's ability to maintain steady progress on their homes. Like others in Corktown, Martin and Heidi's initial sense of the length of time and amount of energy and cash required to restore their house was wildly optimistic. They began with an assumption that their efforts would be complete in a year. Seven years later, although the house is close to where they want it to be, they have yet to finish their plans. The house was in worse condition than they realized, and a lot of their money had to go into weatherproofing the house first. They went through a stage of depression that is common to these couples; theirs eventually dissipated. But their steady progress on the house inevitably inscribed a social distinction that marked them off from others of their "class." Martin related, "What's depressing on some people is that . . . We've moved further along than some people that, y'know, started at the same time. And y'kinda . . . y'kinda move into a different . . . category, y'know. You don't kinda fit in with what's really going on with some of them. There's some that are just struggling."

Martin explained this as we were talking about a couple that tried but failed to restore an old home they bought nearby. The failure ended their marriage, not an unheard-of outcome in this neighborhood. This story emerged obliquely from a question I asked about the racial demographics of the area. He said,

Uh . . . [there's] a lot of Maltese. A lot of Maltese! A few Irish. Lots of Mexicans. There's a few blacks, but not many, not many. And I always wondered if it really had more to do with not being interested in homes that were in need of $50,000 worth of repairs [laughs]. There was a courageous couple over on

Wabash . . . It ended up ending their marriage . . . They camped, they really just camped. They tore everything out, and then tried doing a big cathedral ceiling type thing, y'know, in a cottage! . . . They put a tin roof on, and blah blah blah, y'know. They had to get a foundation, then they wanted hot water tubes for heating, running through the walls, it just got crazier and crazier, and they did all the work themselves, and I think it just got to be a HUGE, HUGE strain . . . But they were perfectionists, and they wanted things a certain way. They couldn't have dry wall, it had to be wet plaster, everything had to be perfect . . . As a result, they could never meet the uh . . . they could never reach what they were trying to do. Nothing stands still. As you're trying to do that, you're also evolving . . . to stay interested in a project for six or seven years is very hard [laughs].

This story, ostensibly, is not about race; it is about the stresses and strains connected with this desire for restoring historical houses in Detroit. But a racial logic permeates this narrative; he displaces an attention to "race" onto the seemingly neutral matter of who can afford or is interested in paying the hefty price tag that accompanies "history." What precludes blacks from living in Corktown, Martin suggests, is brute economics, the financial divide between those who will undertake "$50,000 worth of repairs" and those who won't. The whites drawn here, who have survived the financial stresses and emotional turmoils, were not attracted by an assertion of racial solidarity, nor have they felt compelled actively to assert such a solidarity now. What keeps them together and provides a basis for assembling a shared social space is their engagement with "historical" houses and the problems and threats that they collectively face in inhabiting these structures and this zone. In this mode, "history," while attracting whites from small towns and suburbs, deters blacks from moving into Corktown. This very material impediment, though unmotivated, is substantial. Their desire to restore houses to an originary moment, or to renovate them in a pastiche of "historical" elements, also differentiates their physical and social activities from their Maltese neighbors. Whites' interested similarities correspond with an unnerving and inarticulate sense of ethnic and racial difference. The lines of differentiation are subtle and need to be examined in turn: first the racial divide and then the ethnic differences.

White residents considered "history" as a barrier to black residency in Corktown in aesthetic as well as financial terms. The complex of impediments involved political and philosophical aspects of "history" as well. When I asked Glen for his estimate of the racial demographics, he suggested, after excluding Clement Kern Gardens, that Corktown, "is probably 75 percent white . . . Well, 75 percent white and Hispanic . . . at the most 25 percent black, if that. It certainly doesn't match the rest of the city."

JH: Why do you think that is?

GLEN: [long pause] Probably again it goes back to . . . the 1800s. The people that originated in this community . . . The blacks were slaves then! Back in the 1850s and 1860s. So they weren't homeowners! And I think maybe that that heritage is just carried through. Again, y'know, . . . And Tim [his partner] has a philosophy . . . that you always end up very close to where your parents were . . . And if you take that into consideration, and think about it that way, then there wouldn't be any blacks in this neighborhood because they weren't here to begin with . . . Whereas if you look at other neighborhoods in the city, well those neighborhoods were developed in the twenties and thirties, for example . . . and blacks were perfectly fine and working in factories. There weren't that many factories back then, in the 1800s . . . It's just a theory.

In Glen's account, the history of Corktown effectively encapsulates this neighborhood in the antebellum era. "History," here, is a projection across the recent past to a less problematic moment when Corktown was formed, a moment when blacks were not present because they were largely confined on plantations in the South. What this history neatly ignores is the more recent past, the times since "the 1800s" and "the twenties and thirties," the period of the Great Migration when neighborhoods throughout this part of Detroit rapidly and tumultuously shifted in their racial composition. Unbeknownst to Glen, blacks began moving into the area in the 1930s. By 1950, the area had its highest number and concentration of blacks; there were 733 living in the two census tracts of Corktown.[46] This number was halved by 1960 as a result of the Westside Industrial Project. Blacks composed 18 percent of the population in Corktown at the time of this project.[47]

Glen and others took it as an article of faith that blacks had never lived in Corktown. From this perspective it did not seem odd that, as Detroit's black population approaches 80 percent, there would be so few black residents in the area, even though they are such a presence in Briggs, across the freeway. This history also overlooked a more obvious economic reading of their situation. Over the last twenty years, both whites and blacks have steadily left the inner city of Detroit as the factories in and around Briggs and Corktown closed and rental properties were demolished through "urban renewal" efforts. There simply are not enough accessible jobs to sustain lower-class people here. But what has fueled the influx of whites to this inner-city zone is its proximity to downtown's government and financial offices. Their economic viability in this zone is predicated on professional skills and training, which translate into job opportunities not available to their neighbors across the freeway.

When I spoke with Herb, I chanced to hear another version of why "history" deters black interest in Corktown, when one of his fellow developers stopped by as we were finishing the interview. This white man,

Bill, was older, a self-styled "veteran" of the "wars" in the city fought over various development projects. Bill began talking about a renovation project he was trying to get under way over on the east side; it was running up against resistance. Bill told us, "We had a meeting with the [community] board last night, and all they could say is that this is a white project! They're all black. They wouldn't listen to anything else we had to say." He tossed his arms upwards in discouragement.

Herb commiserated and commented that, "Blacks think differently about these kind of houses. They don't want to have anything to do with any of this restoration stuff." He lamented all the structures that were being lost by this stance on the part of blacks in power in the city, adding, "They love stuff like Victoria Park [the first new housing subdivision built in Detroit in about thirty years], because that's new, that's just like Livonia. They want what the white man has now, and to them, that's the suburbs, moving out, getting brand-new houses. When they look at places like these, they just see the white man's history and they don't want to have anything to do with it. They want what the white man has, not what he used to have."

Bill agreed and insisted that what they were trying to do on the east side was in no way exclusive by race. While rejecting the racialization of his development efforts, he concurred with Herb that blacks did not seem to appreciate the aesthetics involved in "historical" restorations. Herb pointed to a current national revival of "historical" architectural styles that was being completely ignored by city planners. He summed up the whole frustrating matter by insisting that "they just think differently about these projects."

Herb's summation seemed strangely abbreviated: "they just think differently." He does not add, "from us." Although they were perhaps astutely reading cultural difference between whites and blacks, only blacks were racially objectified in this exchange. Herb could point to black desire in terms of "the white man," but he, like Bill, felt misinterpreted when they were read racially by their interest in "historical" renovation projects. Herb's reference to the revival of antiquated architectural styles was stated as a general aesthetic phenomenon that was taking place across the nation, bearing no racial marking whatsoever. Blacks, in ignoring this phenomenon, were either acting out of ignorance or racially, out of spite, but either way they were missing out altogether. In contrast to the racialized reading of this renovation project in political terms, Bill and Herb posited a neutral, apolitical interest in aesthetics that seemed to have no racial core.

Herb demonstrates an ability to objectify whiteness, but as a caricature. His reference to, and usage of, "the white man" largely mimics black usage of the referent; he seemed to feel that a lack of caution with this

stereotyped depiction was warranted by his past engagement with blacks
in settings similar to that described by his friend. He recognizes the
"black" interpretation of whites and allows it some objective basis—"the
white man." But his acknowledgment does not recognize white men as an
interested racial collective to which he belongs, only as a gross stereotype
of "his" political and social position. The racial interests of the "black"
community in question in no way posit a form of equivalence by which
this "white" community should also be accountable.

Herb's familiarity with this "black" interpretation of the "white man"
points to an interesting aspect of white Corktowners. They are in a pos-
tion where they watch whiteness, in both a collective and personal sense,
contested by blacks. Although they are cognizant of modes by which they
are read racially, it seems difficult for them to do more than simply mimic
these readings by racial others. "History," in this contest of interests, is
a racial matter, but neither Herb nor Glen pushed that recognition of
racialness to the point that it would be an aspect of their, perhaps unintentional but very motivated, interest in moving to Corktown and constructing the type of community that they have. They could read racial
significance in blacks' disinterest in history; they did not similarly read
their own interests in terms of race.

Although the rhetorical figure of the "white man," in Herb's rendition,
crudely falters as a means of objectifying the link between their communal ties and their racialness, these whites are clearly susceptible to the
observation that they share a cohesive set of interests and behaviors. It is
their common sensibility and modus operandi that Shirley noted when
she referred to the "newcomers" as gentrifiers. She had been relating the
efforts of Mike and his allies to "take over" Corktown, when I asked her
if they were acting with a clear intention of "gentrifying" the area.

> SHIRLEY: Well . . . I don't think that they consciously wanted to make it
> gentrification . . . Uh . . . They didn't even know what gentrification was then.
> But their value systems were different.
>
> JH: How would you characterize their value system?
>
> SHIRLEY: Well they . . . uh . . . they had a keen appreciation of the beauty and
> dignity of the historic structures, and they . . . uh . . . had a lot of . . . comrad-
> erie . . . at the meetings, everybody would say, "YOU DID WHAT! You
> knocked a hole in a bearing wall and the house didn't fall down? How did you
> do that?" And they would share all of this, and there was a lot of enthusiasm.
>
> JH: Were these neighborhood people?
>
> SHIRLEY: These were all the new people moving in. The neighborhood peo-
> ple were very poor. They didn't have the money, they didn't have the sophisti-
> cation. They lived in historic houses and they had ten kids. That was their
> priority, never mind that the porch is falling down. They were raising the kids.

They didn't have an historic appreciation of . . . Well, the Maltese said, what do you mean you want to declare this thing historic?! It's only a hundred years old. That's not HISTORIC!! They come from Malta! That's nothing. [Here she relates Joe Micallef's story and his statement in a planning meeting on historic designation.] "Why we fell through this hole . . . in a road, there was this hole, and we fell through into this cave. And there was all this Roman armor, and swords and such. And there was these chests full of Roman coins. Now that's old. What you got here is nothing but a bunch of shacks!" 'Cause you see in Malta, some of the walls are seven-foot thick. Seven-foot thick STONE WALLS. So what you got here, ARE shacks! To the Maltese these are just shacks.

Not only were their definitions incompatible, but whites' investment in "history" also ran counter to the interests of Maltese residents, who did not see historical value in these ephemeral structures; they saw only regulations imposing limited options on what they could do with their property and the threat of higher taxes that could follow from historical designation. Whites moving into Corktown felt self-conscious about their differences from Maltese neighbors. Primarily, they recognized that their basis for socializing around "historical" renovations was not shared with the Maltese, but they also sensed that their interests in "history" actually antagonized the Maltese "old-timers." Although not anxious to admit to the possibility that their shared interests were based in their common racialness, they were willing to assume that the Maltese were racializing them.

A few whites who discerned a sense of resentment toward them assured me that the Maltese seethed with disgust, though they admitted that they rarely expressed such sentiment either publicly or directly. I found this perception intriguing since, in speaking with many Maltese and their second- or third-generation offspring, I was unable to detect any animosity toward the recently arrived whites. Rather, the Maltese saw the influx of young people into the area as a general relief. Most of the Maltese community had long since left the city for the suburbs, partly from their own desire for outward mobility and partly due to the urban renewal project that decimated the neighborhood. Those who remain see the young whites as a stabilizing influence in the area. The current Maltese residents largely characterized the influx of young people as a "return" rather than an "invasion." They repeatedly pointed to several Maltese grandchildren who moved back from the suburbs, preferring an urban existence. These grandchildren were moving into and renovating the old family houses. For the "old-timers," this was the most notable social trend, and "gentrification" was a word I never heard them use.

But Martin explained to me the suspicion and contempt with which he and the other recently arrived whites were met by the Maltese residents.

> MARTIN: It's funny, some of the older people in the neighborhood are starting to get into kind of putting their houses back, but a lot of them are really resentful. To them, it's just a bunch of young people, coming in here, and dictating . . .
>
> JH: Dictating in what sense, like through the historical society?
>
> MARTIN: Yeah. They just feel like they've been walked over.
>
> JH: Is that something you run up against personally, or do you hear about it from others? Is it more of an underlying tone?
>
> MARTIN: Kinda underlying. Not . . . they don't come up to your face [laughs].
>
> JH: Is it a sense of, "this is gentrification," and they know what that is, or is it more vague displeasure around generational difference in seeing a bunch of young people moving in?
>
> MARTIN: Uh, they'd say gentrification. Unfortunately though . . . On one hand, they know it has to happen, on account of the state a lot of the homes were in. But on the other hand, I think it's just that thing of change, they just don't like seeing change.

Betty (see "Riots and Race"), a second-generation Maltese-American, lives around the corner from Martin and Heidi on Leverette, just a few doors down from the house where she was born in 1932. She was the only member of the Maltese community who actively resisted the move for historic designation. As we talked in her kitchen, she reeled off names of Maltese families who lived here when she was a child; then she listed the grandchildren of these families who are now returning from the suburbs where they were raised. One of her daughters lives directly behind her house on Church Street, the other lives two doors down on Leverette. When I asked her about changes in the neighborhood, she referred primarily to the returning generations. Her husband wanted to sell the place, but her daughters said that they would stay behind. So she convinced her husband to stay. "They told me, 'We're not coming with you Ma.' So, y'know, this is their home, the only home they ever knew, just like me. Are you kidding, go out to the suburbs? No one would talk to you. I walk down . . . It takes me a half an hour to get to the store, and it's only a block away. Because you've got to stop and talk to this one, and to this one . . . [laughs]."

The exterior of her house is still clad in aluminum siding, and some of the "gentry" have spoken to her about removing it, but she just laughs at the thought and their audacity at treating a private matter as a public concern. She rants and enjoys backtalking "history." "I'd have to insulate my whole house then, and this is a big house. No way am I taking the siding down. My mother put that up y'know. See, everything outside on the house is just the way it was when my mother did it. My mother did everything that was done outside on the house, everything."

Her personal sense of history did not register the aesthetic valuation of "historical" that white renovationists employed. And although the exterior retains a working-class look from the 1940s, the interior has zipped along with new wallpaper and other decoration, and plenty of recently acquired kitchen appliances. She said she dropped her opposition to the historic designation after she was convinced that it would not raise their taxes and thus force out "the old people." But she laughed at their color requirements for painting the houses. "These colors were not the colors [crinkles her face in disgust]. . .The colors they have now, they're not the colors we had. They were either gray or white, yellow and white, gray and white, gray and green . . . I've never seen the colors that they're putting on them now!"

I asked where the colors came from. She laughed and mimicked a "dumb peasant" demeanor, shrugging her shoulders and fairly bellowing, "I don't know [points to her head, and laughs], I don't know. I don't know where," implying they were just thought up. Still, she finds the newcomers amusing rather than annoying, and is convinced they have had a positive impact on the area. Interestingly, she thinks that the "newcomers" are being molded by the neighborhood, rather than the other way around.

> JH: There seems to be people moving in too that aren't from the neighborhood . . .
> BETTY: Yeah
> JH: Have they changed the feel or the character of the neighborhood?
> BETTY: No, we're all very friendly. We just kind of mold them into our way. Like with Halloween, they give out candy now . . .
> JH: Yeah?
> BETTY: Oh yeah, we've got kids all over here.

As she proceeded to list the number of kids on this street, pointing to over thirty, I was wondering how this Halloween ritual counted as "mold[ing] them into our way." She returned to that point directly. "On Halloween we get all the kids from Kern Gardens, and on Labrosse, from all over. We really enjoy it. This one girl just moved in, and I says [pause, serious face], 'tomorrow's Halloween.' [pause] 'Yeah,' she says, 'do you get much kids?' 'Buy about five bags [of candy]' [laughs]. And she was out there going, 'I don't believe this. I don't believe this' [laughs, mimicking hysterics]."

The instance that came to mind for Betty when she was describing the process of molding the "new people" into the area had little to do with anything ostensibly "ethnic." She was amused at the woman's unfamiliarity with social settings in which children are a central focus. Perhaps assuming there were only "old-timers" here, the childless newcomer did not notice the kids in the neighborhood—perhaps because many are from Clement Kern Gardens. The difference Betty highlighted had more to do with how people socialized than with detecting a distinct set of "values" that were delimitiable by ethnically drawn identities, lines that the "gentry" used to distinguish between "whites" and "Maltese." Following up the topic, I asked her if she felt that the historical designation had encouraged other people to move into the area.

> BETTY: I think so, I think so. Definitely.
>
> JH: And has that been positive?
>
> BETTY: Oh yes! If it wasn't, I don't think this place would still exist. Because it's historical . . .We not only got the kids who lived here when they were younger, but we got people from other neighborhoods and other places to move in here.
>
> JH: And have those people changed the feeling of the neighborhood?
>
> BETTY: No. They keep up their places very nice, they keep 'em up very, very nice. It's really been a lot of good for this area. Because I think it would have been diminished if it hadn't happened.

In white "newcomers'" perceptions of the Maltese, a complicated sense of race is played out. Whether or not there are Maltese "old-timers" in the neighborhood who do actually resent the incursions by newly arriving whites, the "newcomers'" sense of difference from the Maltese entailed an important benefit; it allowed them to delineate a convenient dumping ground for "race" and "racism." When I asked questions about why the neighborhood was predominantly white, the "newcomers," with great confidence, pointed to the Maltese as a racist ethnic group who purposefully kept blacks out of the area. This conviction among whites was quite pronounced, but it seemed dubious, especially given the earlier integration of the area and Betty's account of how the 1967 riot was viewed in Corktown (see "Riots and Race"). Accurate or not, this assumption alleviated any implication that their own, more recent actions, which have fundamentally shaped the demographics of this neighborhood, could be implicated in the fact that very few blacks lived in Corktown. This image of the Maltese displaced an interrogation of the racial structuring of their neighborhood to decades before and onto a convenient "blue-collar" ethnic collective.

I asked Hazel why she thought that Corktown was so white in contrast to the rest of Detroit. "I think it just always was. It always was, and they made sure it stayed that way . . . Heavy racism on the part of the Maltese

[laughs]. Oh yeah, heavy racism involved. Of course, that's changed
somewhat, but I don't think it's changed as much as it should've. There
has not been as many changes as many of us would've liked to have seen.
This is still a blue-collar neighborhood. Basically, it's always been a blue-
collar neighborhood, unlike Indian Village or Boston-Edison . . . always
very wealthy."

This account performs an intriguing series of displacements, relying on
a past that flies under the radar of "history"; an ethnic, class other—the
area was notably a "blue-collar neighborhood"—emerges as the effective
container of any implications of racism on the part of current residents.
As with the assertion that the Maltese were upset about "gentrification,"
I pursued this matter with older Maltese residents and others who held a
somewhat longer perspective on the area. I spoke with Maltese who
fondly recalled black playmates in this place when they were children.
Although there was some uneasiness and initial opposition by Maltese
residents to the "low-income" Clement Kern Gardens housing project,
this was hardly a pervasive (or a uniquely racialized) position. As with
any social group in the United States, the Maltese were and remain a
heterogeneous lot. But in whites' perceptions, this group, especially with
regard to race, was an homogeneous entity. Blaming the Maltese for
being racist effectively relieved whites of assessing how their own desire
for a certain sense of community might be implicated in reproducing a
particular racial order in a neighborhood where only 4 percent of its residents were black. Whether or not the Maltese were racist, there remains
the question of complicity on the part recently arrived whites in maintaining, intentionally or not, the community structures that make the area
unappealing to blacks.

The one couple I talked with who brought up the matter of complicity
and were concerned with thinking the matter through was Peter and Yolanda. When they described the Maltese, they noted an interest more in
ethnic solidarity then racism. We were discussing why "yuppies" seemed
to fit into the area without causing any social friction. Peter said, "Well,
I think the Maltese are happy to have us move in . . . because they've been
moving to Dearborn, and as more of them move out, they start to wonder, who's going to take their place. Like, the lady who lived next door.
When we first moved here, there was an old lady living there, she was
about 90, or 85. She was GLAD to have us move in! We were better than
what she used to have. There were junkies living there" [laughs].

Yolanda offered, "Still, I think for the Maltese-owned houses, before
they would go up for sale to anyone else, the Maltese community knew
they were up, and that's how they preserved the community for all of
these years. They really kept it to themselves."

Peter said, "Y'know how they list in the paper the houses for sale? I've never seen one listed for this area. So that's how this neighborhood has been preserved in a lot of ways. On the other hand, there are some old-time white people . . . and I use the term loosely, that were instrumental in organizing the official body of Corktown."

Peter then listed the residents, Irish and Maltese, who put together a political effort to represent the neighborhood in dealings with the city planners and bureaucrats who tried to demolish the whole area. The term "white" is used "loosely" because the people in question are marked as "ethnics," and because the effort to organize the neighborhood was separate from efforts to preserve it as an ethnic enclave. When I asked Peter whether or not he thought that blacks were now interested in living in Corktown, he answered, "No, actually . . . Well, I feel kind of bad because the Maltese have effectively kept them out. And that's another thing. They refuse to rent to them and they refuse to sell to them . . . And you feel bad, in a sense, because that's kinda what saved the neighborhood. But in another sense, it's . . . I feel it's wrong! . . . It's really complicated."

That was where they left the matter, noting the complexity of how their desires and the actions of the Maltese have overlapped into a social construct that is predominantly white in the heart of Detroit. But I can add that the several Maltese landlords that I met, including the two I rented from, all rented to blacks and claimed to have done so for as long as they owned rental properties—they clearly are not all adamantly disposed to keeping blacks out.[48]

Although many of these whites easily assumed that Maltese motives were racial in content, a few saw their actions in what they posed as a contrasting ethnic mode. The difference in these modes of explanation were based on a distinction between a positive assertion of and interest in preserving a form of (ethnic) sameness and an opposite, negative reaction to (racial) otherness. Part of what kept these modes distinct for these whites is that they preferred to feel suspended in this divide. Since they did not act out of a fear of otherness, their actions did not appear to be racial in nature; neither did they ostensibly assert an interest in sameness. These whites did not perceive ethnic or racial categories as relevant to the composition of their own interests and actions. But it is in this ability to maintain a conviction of racelessness, the race of no race, that the significance of white racialness signifies most tellingly.

A few were more blunt in recognizing a racial basis for both their own actions and those of other whites in this zone. Hugh was one of the few whites I talked to who had grown up in Detroit. Like Shirley, he also came from the east side. He recalled how his neighborhood had shifted from all white to all black in the 1960s. I asked him what kind of conflicts or situations produced racial interpretations in Corktown. He could not think of any at first, but as we discussed the question further, he offered,

> the only way that I would really see it as a factor here, is since this is a scrappy little neighborhood, we've gone to bat over a lot of things and we do kinda come together on the real important issues, like fighting the prison or getting historical designation. All the groups manage to find common ground on those kinds of issues. I think if there's anything that I would interpret as racial . . . noncommunication about anything, it would be probably that the city . . . The city as it now stands, as a black entity, has not . . . appeared to see much value in an historic neighborhood, y'know, maintaining an historic neighborhood. Whereas I think a lot of the newcomers do see a value in the historicity of the area, and the experience and why that's important . . . to support. And I don't feel that I've seen much from the city administration that really supports that idea that there's any particular value in an historical neighborhood. On the contrary, I can sense that some . . . there's almost an antagonism towards an historic sense of things. Whether that's because of the obvious thing that black people felt disenfranchised from the history of the city so they don't care about it, and that white people don't feel so disenfranchised from the history of, or whatever. That seems to be . . . maybe a source of conflict. No obviously, this neighborhood, not counting Clement Kern Gardens, is 99.9 percent white, y'know. That fact is not lost on anybody, whether it's the people who live here or the city administration; this is basically a little white enclave, and how did it survive as such?
>
> JH: Good question.
>
> HUGH: It's the Maltese again. They just weren't going anywhere.
>
> JH: Do you think that maintenance of the neighborhood is racially motivated?
>
> HUGH: It's not, and it is. It's not in that the ethnic Maltese were just staying in their neighborhood, with each other, okay. I mean their basic thrust was ethnic, in that they wanted to be around ethnic Maltese, and this happened to be their area. But probably with the newcomers, and certainly part of the attraction to me was that, y'know, it was a . . . safe neighborhood and a white neighborhood, y'know. Part of the reason why I chose this over Woodbridge was that number one, it seemed safer, and number two there's not a lot of black people that I can't quite understand what their value systems are in terms of this property. Y'know, you're pouring your life into your house and the people next door are kicking their windows out.

Hugh's comments are no more the "true" voice of white Corktown emerging than are the reflections by Herb, Shirley, Lou, or any of the other whites. But they do frame the range of conscious articulations of the significance of white racialness in this zone. These whites are very conscious of differences between themselves and blacks and Maltese. They invest heavily in houses and see black people in adjacent neighborhoods showing disregard for the "same" structures; they watch the Maltese repair their homes with cheap, on-hand materials rather than carefully aestheticizing their property. How these differences add up is a matter of great anxiety. What these whites are anxious to avoid is the impression that they are purposefully constructing an exclusive racial/ethnic community. And indeed, ostensibly they are not engaged in such a conscious construction: Corktown is ethnically heterogeneous—not to a massive degree, but certainly to a greater extent than the hometowns of many of these whites.

The question these whites were concerned with was how to characterize the collective order materializing in their social relations in this zone. Where "gentrification" was seen as implying a conspiratorial intent, a desire for old houses and "historical" materials was regarded as a more natural, or at least neutral, matter in which aesthetics and longings operated apart from racialized or class modalities. Their attention to "history" suspended a more careful attention to how their values and interests cohered along racial lines. The difficult question to assess is how white racialness is unintentionally significant, apart from conscious efforts on the part of those whites who resist or refuse racialized notions of cultural superiority. The answer, in part, is that as whites their racialness connects them to a national and historical order of privilege and power. This connection, though attenuated by their ambiguous class status and social positioning, seemed to provide momentum for their anxious displacements of the charge of "gentrification" onto whites with relatively better economic means.[49] They read the significance of their racialness in a complicated interplay of self-reflection and intraracial differentiations. Although they sought to distance and differentiate themselves from other whites who (in their eyes) more accurately embodied the loaded objectifications of "white culture" with its implied racism, they were never able to efface the twinge of uncertainty that rose when they encountered in unexpected situations the fact of their own racialness.

Whiteness, of course, does not bestow power and privilege generically; the contours of advantage that white racialness structures depend on class position and social location. "Privilege" is also not a homogeneous condition; rather, it is as varied as the uses of "gentrifier" implied. These whites' privilege lay in their investment in a realm they considered and deployed to be apart from race and racial concerns; they poured sweat and money into this material and imaginary space—their homes—which, in turn, removed them from many of the ambiguous exchanges and uncertain encounters in which their racialness could have come to the fore. Their class position—however heterogeneous, unstable, and distended—

served as an entitlement to suspend an interrogation of racial matters in their most intimate spaces and lives.

It is not the case, though, that "history" simply disguised a seething, influential core of "racism" or racist sentiment. While they seemed oblivious to many of the privileges of their position, they did not loathe or demonize a black other. Moreover, it is not as if "history" purchased them a complete escape from racial matters. Their anxiety over "gentrification" and the possibility that each of them could be so marked, objectified by its conflation of race and class a nefarious image of whiteness, suggest otherwise. With "history," I have not discovered the core of how race truly motivates their thoughts and actions, inhabits their fears and desires. Rather, "history" names the etiquette by which they contain, delimit, and police the relevance of race in their lives, its ability to stand as a point of reckoning from which they can be called to account for their relations, sociality, and the coloring of their interests and contentment in this zone that is largely empty of blacks. Their investment in "history" allows the imbrications of race to be fantastically suspended; it provides a means for shunting the operation of "racism" onto blue-collar ethnics, in the process removing from view, leaving uninterrogated, the racial aspects of their structure of desire. They assume that race matters only if "racism" is evident; they do not consider that race includes the subtle, dense fusion of their desires, interests, and anxieties, expressed variously through the sensations of "comfort" and "uneasiness," not solely generated by a disconcerting view of the Other, but rather through their disconcerting sense of sameness.

4

Between "All Black" and "All White"

In 1985, the Board of Education of the Detroit Public Schools (DPS) closed Leslie Elementary in Warrendale. The summer before the closing was made public, Karen Soper, a white woman, moved into a house across the street with her husband, a machinist, and their young children. She picked the house because of its proximity to the school, and was furious when she realized that the real estate agent had neglected to mention the impending closure. In the summer of 1992, the empty school was chosen by the Board of Education to house one of the city's three African-centered academies. Along with the other two, Marcus Garvey and Paul Robeson, Malcolm X Academy was originally intended to be an exclusively male school. The rationale behind this was that, since young African-American males were disproportionally prone to the debilitating and lethal effects of urban life, they required an educational program that would help them counter their circumstances. A sex-discrimination lawsuit filed by the American Civil Liberties Union and the National Organization for Women successfully contested the male-only designation. By 1994, the academies had female enrollments ranging from 10 to 15 percent.[1] The academy features an Afrocentric curriculum that stresses civilization's origins in Africa and the continued contributions of Africans to civilization's ongoing development.[2] The school's curriculum is designed to counter what its founder, Clifford Watson, has described as an "orchestrated, quiet conspiracy to make sure that only a small percentage of African-Americans will succeed."[3]

Residents of Warrendale found out about the Board of Education's plans in 1992 in a variety of ways. People living around the school noticed the start of renovations and asked construction workers at the site about the planned use of the building. Most people, though, were informed about the academy's arrival in mid-July by an article in the neighborhood paper, the *Warrendale Press & Guide*.[4] From that point on, word of mouth and rumors filled in the picture for residents. The general impression residents formed was that the DPS was reopening a neighborhood school under the name of a "racist" and "radical," Malcolm X, for the exclusive use of black students who would be submitted to a separatist, black nationalist curriculum. Concerns among residents gelled and became the focus of the city's media by the end of the month.[5] The president of the Warrendale Community Organization (WCO), Wally Serylo, requested that principal Watson and Detroit schools superintendent Dr. Deborah McGriff hold an informational meeting with residents to address their concerns and uncertainties. This meeting, held on August 3 at the Warrendale United Brethren Church with over five hundred people attending, forged the spectacle of "racist Warrendale" that riveted Detoriters' attention for several months.

The meeting was rancorous and the crowd was rude. The residents were furious over a range of issues: Some had repeatedly inquired about getting the school reopened because of overcrowding at George Washington Carver (the remaining area elementary school) and had been informed that the DPS did not have funds available to reopen that school; many residents were upset about the academy's name and were concerned that the curriculum promoted race hatred; others were furious over the lack of input from residents and the fact that they had not been informed regarding the school board's plans; then there were people who were deeply disturbed at the thought of black children being bussed into the neighborhood. Some white residents expressed a fear that the academy would lead to a rise in crime in the area. Blacks attending the meeting and some of the white residents commented on the racist nature of peoples' comments; journalists referred to "racially-tinged remarks" used to shout down the school officials, like the suggestion that the school should be opened in a crackhouse instead.

Scenes of the meeting, played on the evening television news, were disturbing enough; but reporters doing on-site, live broadcasts from the school noticed for the first time that there were several swastikas spray-painted on one of the school's doors. An uproar of indignation and disbelief rose across the city. Numerous editorials condemning the graffiti followed, in the newspapers and on radio and television programs. The swastikas were read as the racist expression of white separatist hatred.[6] Since none of these people had paid much attention to the vacant school building prior to this media surge, it is quite possible that, as many residents insisted, the swastikas had been painted on the building by neighborhood kids earlier in the summer, before anybody local knew about the reopening.[7] But the context in which the graffiti were "discovered" proved irrevocably, for Detroiters at large, that the resistance and the concerns of the white residents of Warrendale were racially based and motivated.[8]

Residents, who were divided over supporting or opposing the academy, engaged in a protracted public debate, featuring rallies outside the schools and arguments in school board meetings. Residents opposed to the academy insisted that their primary concern was overcrowding at nearby George Washington Carver Elementary.[9] But school board mem-

Figure 11.
Welcome to Warrendale

bers generally refused to believe that the concerns of upset residents did
not derive from essentially racist interests; school officials pointed to the
fact that no residents applied for any of the 25 percent of registration slots
reserved for neighborhood children. But, as in all these matters, this was
a point of some contention. I spoke with three residents who requested
but never received applications for their children to attend the academy.
Other residents pointed to a letter printed in the *Warrendale Press &*
Guide by a mother (a white woman married to a black man) who had
withdrawn her two sons from the academy because they were being
taught that whites were all "racists" and "killing machines"—reason
enough, they asserted, not to send their own children there.

At the initial, informational meeting in August, Dr. McGriff apologized for not informing the residents earlier of the school board's plans.
McGriff and other board members admitted later that the selection process in this situation had been flawed. As a result, the board passed a

resolution that future openings and closings of schools would be preceded by notifications to residents living within a mile and a half of the particular school.[10] McGriff also acknowledged that Carver Elementary was 133 children over its capacity.[11] At the time, there was a waiting list to get into Carver Elementary, and although school officials asserted that no classes exceeded the maximum of 35 students, parents insisted otherwise.[12] The matter of overcrowding continued to be contentious, but the school board soon reversed its acknowledgment of overcrowding; thereafter, complaints about class sizes at Carver were regarded by school officials as a "smoke screen" for simply racist sentiments.[13]

Opening day at the academy was a spectacle. Helicopters circled over the school building, while the grounds were patrolled by police officers with bomb-sniffing dogs, and camera crews captured it all for television audiences. But only a handful of residents were present to protest the school's opening. Although the day was "uneventful," comparisons to Little Rock in 1954 were repeatedly drawn by commentators.[14] This spectacle of Warrendale and the Malcolm X Academy unfolded in a tense city and stood as a simmering example of white racial animosity in Detroit throughout the school year. The protest was one of several stories that would not go away that winter. In the beating death of Malice Green in November, the long process of bringing the two white policeman to justice featured intense reflections by Detroiters on what, if anything, had changed in the twenty years since blacks achieved political control of the city. Then too, the mayoral election proved to be racially divisive. Even though the two major candidates were both black, one, Sharon McPhail, stridently depicted her opponent, Dennis Archer, as a "tool" of white, suburban interests trying to reassert control over the city. In this context, it was easy for commentators to read "Warrendale" as one more instance of racially based fear and anger in Detroit. Although white residents' concerns over the school were multifaceted, in public debates they were reductively equated with simple racism.

This reading of residents' concerns was buttressed by threats made against the school and the students, which received a great deal of attention in the media. The potential for violence was cited by Dr. McGriff in her decision to act on the request of staff members and parents eventually to move the academy out of Warrendale; a new location, however, was not settled upon until 1996.[15] People involved in the conflict, both from the neighborhood and from the DPS, generally asserted that the threats were made either by scattered people or by "outsiders" who were looking to provoke racial aggression. But when an alleged shooting occurred on the playground, the threats became almost the sole focus of the conflict. One afternoon, at the end of April, two teachers told fifteen students on the playground to go inside immediately after they heard "popping noises." White residents who were sitting on their porches across from the school that afternoon claimed to have heard nothing resembling gunshots, and police did not find bullets or casings at the scene. Although the specter of violence was a singular, consuming aspect of the conflict, it was not at the core of what distinguished supporters and opponents of the school. This incident embodied the ambiguity and uncertainty at the core of many racial conflicts, if not the disjuncture between "white" and "black" versions of what motivated protests over the academy.

The debate over the Malcolm X Academy became, in fact, a contest over the significance of white racialness. In their statements and arguments, whites struggled to articulate a range of interests and concerns that they insisted were not "racially motivated." The persons in positions of authority with whom they jousted did not face this same difficulty. Black school officials generally were regarded as racially unmarked in the sense that, as voices of bureaucratic power and authority, their versions were acknowledged as official positions.[16] Whites who opposed the school were frustrated to find that the "blackness" of the academy (represented for them by its curriculum) went unexamined by the media, never becoming an "issue" the way the whiteness of residents' protests did. Although the anxieties and concerns of whites were read almost solely in racial registers, the tenets of the academy's novel curriculum were not regarded as a suspect assertion of racial interest.

The white voices recorded in this account are of people who participated in some way in the Warrendale Community Organization. This local organization, established in 1979, served initially as a means of coordinating various neighborhood block-based groups attempting to police the area from growing incidents of crime and vandalism. But, in the few years preceding the controversy, the WCO seemed to serve primarily as a social club for senior citizens in the area. Young whites joined the WCO to seek representation in raising their concerns over the academy. The WCO, however, resisted their entreaties, and officially welcomed the school. The new white members continued participating in and prodding the WCO for a year and a half, raising contentious issues about the role race played in city institutions and school politics. But, often as not, they found fellow members more concerned about aesthetic signs of the neighborhood's decline and indications of a shift in the area's class status heralded by an influx of "renters."

The following sections are organized around the central objectifications of racial interests in this contest: The characterization of Warrendale as a "white enclave" and its residents as "racists," and the curriculum that whites who were opposed to the academy desperately tried to make into an issue. The difference between the objectifications "white enclave" and "racist," on one hand, and the "curriculum," on the other

hand, involves a subtle contest over who will remain unmarked in this
discursive terrain. These objectifications were produced in a series of
statements by black city officials and white residents; the dynamics of
their discursive exchange, featuring both familiar and unique aspects, require a summary description before proceeding further.

Statements

> "What would be the problem with them [white
> Detroiters] paying their tax dollars to educate our
> children the way we see fit, when for years we paid
> for educating our children the way they saw fit?"
> —*Tandrea Black, president of the Local
> School Community Organization for the
> Malcolm X Academy*[17]

Many whites in Warrendale made public statements about the Malcolm
X Academy. They spoke either in support of or opposition to the school
in public, neighborhood spaces, and their most inflammatory comments
were recorded by print journalists from the two Detroit newspapers and
television crews from the four local stations. Only fragments of what they
said made it into print or went out over the air waves. Reporters and
editors were interested in certain kinds of comments or incidents. Statements that did not fit this mode of coverage, such as two prayer vigils
organized by local churches and an anti-racist protest that was held outside the school, received no coverage.[18]

The comments that were reported revolved around a tight core of racial concern and fear. White supporters and opponents of the academy
grew increasingly frustrated at their futile attempts to control the ways in
which they were objectified and their interests reduced to caricatures.
What opponents of the academy, in particular, could never quite manage
to speak over was the fact of their racialness, which formed a signifying
background that surmounted the nuances of their "personal opinions" or
experiences. As whites resisting a black school in their predominantly
white neighborhood, they found their actions, comments, and emotions
were read immediately as racially significant. Their class position encouraged this reading. In their talk, bodies, and perceptions, these whites evidenced a fairly obvious class conditioning: Their articulations were not
sophisticated nor, largely, were they adept at manipulating the supposedly neutral apparatuses of bureaucratic power and political office.[19]
They looked and spoke awkwardly on television, and their comments
resonated with an historical continuum of "blue-collar" racism.[20]

My account of this controversy in Warrendale serves neither to confirm nor to discount representations of blue-collar racism; rather, the point here is to understand the ways in which whites responded to objectifications of their interests and actions, how they succumbed to racial readings or attempted refashionings of their objectifications. Both opponents and supporters of the school maintained ambivalent and at times contradictory understandings of race and racial matters; the ambiguity of their positions was usually obliterated by the interests of observers in making this racial situation "fit" historical precedent of radical white defense of neighborhoods and schools.[21]

But historical parallels between this contest and disputes over busing or white opposition to blacks moving into all-white neighborhoods, apparent to commentators and participants alike, often threatened to subsume the novel stakes in this situation. White opponents of the academy, speaking from personal experiences in Detroit, tried to stress that the issues here were different from those that had characterized interracial conflicts over the past two decades, in this city and across the nation. The conflict over the Malcolm X Academy featured transpositions of orders "traditionally" assumed in racial disputes. The prime reversal involves the roles of authorities and protesters: Blacks were in charge of the civic institutions being contested, while whites opposing the academy accused school officials of "resegregating" black children. More than the school itself, though, what white opponents found themselves actively contesting was the limited roles through which the significance of race was assessed and understood. The assumptions that informed both media coverage and the political statements of supporters of the academy suggest that for most observers historical precedents outweighed the aspects of this contest that differed from those in the 1970s.

Generally unacknowledged in this contest was that residents' opposition to the school had neither been articulated as a communal assertion of white solidarity nor had it rallied broad support as such. Maybe this is because such political articulations of whiteness are untenable in Detroit; just as likely, the distinctions between whites in this neighborhood were too great to be subsumed in any communal representation. Also, whites were racialized in a very uneven manner in this conflict; those who ignored the whole issue, either because they did not have school-age children or because they were simply uninterested in being involved in any politicized conflict, escaped being racially objectified.[22] But whites who opposed the school, engaging in a protracted challenge to the class elitism and racial separatism they saw embodied in the academy, were subject to an interesting transformation. Responding to comments like the opening quote from Tandrea Black, these whites were drawn into a discursive exchange in which previous presumptions of racial meanings collapsed.

Not only were they thoroughly racialized, depicted as "racists" by school officials and so represented in media coverage, but objectifications of their racial interests developed in a manner that let the racialness of other participants elude critical attention.

Whites who spoke in opposition to the academy fashioned their statements in response to comments by black officials, as much as in expression of their beliefs or convictions. Opponents of the school attended meetings of the Board of Education, where their comments were greeted by sneers of "white devil" from the predominantly black audience. These whites also raptly tuned in to the "black talk shows" featured on WCHB and WDTR (the radio station of the DPS).[23] On these shows, they listened to guests and experts explain theories linking concentrations of melanin to black cultural and intellectual superiority, and to descriptions of the separatist nation that self-proclaimed black revolutionaries like school board member Kwame Kenyatta talked of establishing in the southern United States. Kenyatta was a lightning rod for these whites; his notoriety grew when he put forth a resolution that the school board discontinue presentations of the flag of the United States at meetings, insisting that he would not stand for "that which has no honor." His daunting, uncompromising defense of the academy unnerved and enraged whites.[24] Kenyatta's response on WCHB to the alleged shooting at the school left whites listeners quite fearful. "We're no stranger to fighting, we know how to fight. . . . It's not a question of running. It's not a question of we can't fight. It's not a question that community cannot be leveled to the ground. It's not a question of any of that." The implied threat that their community could be leveled resonated with whites' fears that another "race riot" was pending and could explode at any time. They wondered how a school board official could make what they considered to be a threat of violence without provoking any rebukes from other official voices.[25]

Although the racial conflict over the academy was the most dramatic issue facing residents in Warrendale, whites there were at least as concerned about an emerging class divide as they were about obvious and inevitable shifts in the area's racial composition. Signs of looming changes in the economic character of Warrendale were quite apparent: Rates of home ownership were dropping significantly, and the increased presence of rental homes unnerved many of the older or more well-off residents; also, poverty rates doubled or tripled in sections of the neighborhood after 1980.[26] Although the issues raised by the academy were more dramatic, the sustained concern of a majority of members of the WCO was the need to stem the increasingly frequent appearance of "junk cars" on the streets and in yards. In a sense, whites opposed to the academy—who often embodied the economic and demographic shift that made older residents anxious—had to speak over these classed concerns to articulate their frustration with the school board to their neighbors.

This shift in economic orders was not preeminently a racial matter. Blacks were moving into the Warrendale area, but they were largely settling in the northern half of the community; whereas poorer white renters were cropping up seemingly on every other block. According to residents, whites moving into the area had grown up in the suburbs surrounding Detroit where they found the cost of starter homes to be prohibitive. Unable to buy a house in the suburbs where they were raised, they were moving into this corner of northwest Detroit. Several opponents of the academy that I spoke with fit this pattern. Diana and her husband, a construction worker, bought their house after the conflict over the school had exploded, but for four years previously they had rented a house down the street from where they now live. Her good friend Joyce was the only member in her family who lived in Detroit; the rest lived in the suburb where she had been raised. But Joyce, also, had owned a house in Warrendale for ten years. "I'm looked down upon as the poor one of the family," she laughingly explained. Her husband works as a gravedigger.[27]

I met these two women after a cantankerous WCO meeting. They wanted to know if I thought the place matched its depiction in the media. They offered to arrange a meeting at each of their homes so I could talk with people who were active in opposing the schools. The first meeting occurred in Joyce's basement.

Joyce showed me a notebook in which she had been keeping all the news articles that involved the academy or the teacher's strike that fall. She had already started a third volume of clippings. When she handed me the first notebook, she said that it had a lot of coverage of the only informational meeting held by the school board. Diana asked, "Even the picture of you standing there? [laughs]" Joyce replied, "Even the picture of me standing there with my hand flying in the air saying, [loudly] 'What about the white kids?!' "

She physically slipped into a caricatured pose of the picture in the paper and laughed about her response. "No, that was only because some guy was going on about the black kids deserve this and the black kids deserve that, and this and that, and he had interrupted me. So . . . I just had enough. I should've said what's wrong with equal . . . but, I didn't." Diana added, "Everybody was pretty hot that night, though, everybody was."

As they thought about what they had said and heard in this contest, Diana and Joyce, like other white opponents to the school, assessed the excess of signification unleashed in their comments that contrasted with the reserved management of "racial" appearances by their opponents, white and black. Looking back on the connotations invoked or latent in her comment, she wished she said something more neutral—not mentioning race explicitly—and less emotional, which would not have left her open to the charge of being a racist. Diana suggested why stating things more neutrally was not possible: "Everybody was pretty hot that night." The debate generated by the academy and its curriculum was emotionally volatile for everybody involved. The emotionality of white opponents, amplified their loud clumsiness with language into a resonating image of unadulterated racism.[28]

Whites speaking out about the academy did so from a variety of positions, but they shared a range of frustrations stemming from their precarious position (economic, political, and social) in a difficult, dangerous city. It was hard for observers to believe that the intense emotion generated by these frustrations was not spawned by a seething core of racial hatred and anxiety. Rather than indexing their relative lack of power in this situation, their emotions, distilled into ugly images on the evening news, stigmatized these whites in the city at large but especially within Warrendale. Whites in this neighborhood, generally, were interested in limiting the significance of their racialness; the excessive emotionality of certain white speakers—those, incidentally, most sought out by reporters—allowed other whites to assume these were the "racist" whites and thus effectively distance themselves from these "hostile few."

It was disturbing for residents to see their neighbors loudly arguing or shouting on the TV news. This coverage rendered the most frequently quoted speakers, like Jeff Testa or Kevin Malczyck, the object of anxious avoidance.[29] Jeff was shunned by almost everybody in the WCO. People described him to me with an ebullient repulsion that seemed to permit no basis for personal relations. He was the example that supporters turned to most often to characterize the "flagrant racists" that opposed the school.

Very few people took Jeff seriously when he claimed to be an "integrationist" or insisted that the school was "resegregating children by race." Yet I found his views, apart from their emotional depiction, to be shared by many Warrendale whites. He was one of several whites who had roots in Detroit's inner-city neighborhoods. His mother lived in Corktown when her parents first arrived from Malta. She married a Maltese man who entered this country from Canada; they were introduced by mutual friends, and discovered that their parents had been neighbors on the same street in Malta. When Jeff proselytized about the "melting pot" and "integration," it was from this second-generation perspective, using the Maltese as a model since they had in turned been Romanized, Arabicized, and Anglicized. "We're the mutts of the world," he boasted. "Who ever had power had us. It's [Malta] been a real human melting pot since humans learned how to sail." On the wall in his home office is a large montage of scenes from Martin Luther King Jr.'s life. Across the room is a bust of the dead Kennedy brothers. Jeff is dedicated to a moment of the civil rights movement that now seems quite distant. But when his statements appeared on the TV or were broadcast over the radio, people were appalled at the "racist" who spoke them.

Jeff joined Diana and Bonnie, a white woman with three children at Carver Elementary, in a meeting at Joyce's house. Talking about how the media depicted their position on the academy, they referred to Kevin Malczyck, whose face had become part of the stock televised images of Warrendale.

> DIANA: Kevin is just basically known as a big mouth.
>
> JEFF: He's been one of the forerunners of the opposition. His heart has been in the right place, but his wording of certain things has come out wrong. Ahh. Y'know, he lives right across the street from the school. And a lot of people have labeled him just because of the way he words things. Put it this way, before I met Kevin, I was really leery of him, just by what I heard and what I'd seen on the news. Once I met Kevin and got to know him . . .
>
> DIANA: He's a nice guy . . .
>
> JEFF: I tell you, I've got a lot of respect for the man. He's done a lot of work for this, and his motivation is not racist. It is not at all, in any way shape or form, racist.
>
> JOYCE: He sponsors black basketball teams. He sponsors black basketball teams where his business is. Not in this neighborhood, but where his [auto parts] business is.
>
> JH: So what kind of quotes were they getting off of him to put on TV? [irruption of simultaneous voices]
>
> JOYCE: The wrong ones . . .
>
> BONNIE: 'I'm going to tear the name off the school' . . .
>
> JOYCE: And as many times as they put it back up, he's going to tear it off again.

When we spoke—at a meeting Diana arranged at her house, which also included Karen Soper—Kevin, too, was upset over how he and his neighborhood had been represented by the media. He, like Jeff and other residents who spoke with reporters, expressed frustration at how long, detailed discussions of residents' concerns had been reduced to brief sound bites that, in reflection, seemed to have been carefully manipulated to fit prefabricated story lines about racism. "The first time I was on TV, when I told them that I'd tear the Malcolm X sign down if they put it up there, they interviewed me for fifteen minutes and talked to me about schools, and where my kids go to school, and all of this stuff. And the only thing they showed out of that fifteen minute interview . . . I mean, by this time, the guy's got me going [Karen: 'yeah, yeah'], he's got me going. And then he says, 'What do you think of the name Malcolm X?' And I said, 'I don't like it.' Then he said, 'Well what are you going to do about it?' I SAID, 'If they put it up there, I'll tear it down!' That's the only thing they showed!"

DIANA: That's what they showed.

KEVIN: To me, they were looking for that racism, they were looking for racism. On the Sally Jessi Rafael show, they were looking for racism. And the Jerry Springer show, they were looking for racism . . .

KAREN: That's why Montel Williams didn't . . . They had Montel Williams' director out here, she flew out here to talk to us when we were going around the school, and, uh, I guess our issues were too . . .

DIANA: It wasn't hot enough.

KAREN: Yeah. It wasn't hot enough. Wasn't inflammatory enough. Because we were really concerned about our kids. And that's what we're talking about, nine hundred kids at Carver . . . when there's . . . Now you tell me why this school only needs four hundred kids in it when Carver has nine hundred [Carver only has two more classrooms than Malcolm X Academy].

Classroom sizes, requests to the school board, informational meetings—none of these matters is very photogenic. Joni Hodder, the producer of the Montel Williams Show, frankly told the *Press and Guide* that rather than arguments over enrollment limits "they wanted more heat."[30] Not finding sufficient "heat," they lost all interest in the dispute. Local reporters also found residents' concerns uninteresting when they were not explicitly focused on race. Nor did they find whites' assessments of black racial interests worthy of coverage. White residents were unable to turn attention to what they felt was the main issue—the "separatist" or "racist" curriculum. As Karen put it, "The [black] children ain't the issue, it's what they're teaching in there. . . . But that issue has never been looked into by the media . . . that part's just glazed over and we're just a bunch of racists complaining about nothing."

These whites encountered an overdetermined discursive terrain when they tried to speak about these matters; their concerns, already emotionally laden and resonating with historical images of violent defenses of white supremacy, were authoritatively rendered as "racist" by the calm, objective voices of black officials. But the racially unmarked status of comments by black representatives of the academy or the school board derived from more than their professional status or their position as officials in this matter; they seemed to speak apart from any attachment to place, as well as maintaining an air of cool rationalism. It was this link

Figure 12. Development in the 1940s and 1950s in Warrendale filled in around existing farmhouses (on the right)

with place—presented in images of aluminum-sided tract housing and fervent residents—that demonstrated and delimited the significance of race; this link was carefully honed through editing and citation techniques that disturbed local white supporters of the school as much as its opponents.[31]

Although the WCO tried to stay removed from the conflict, the organization was compelled to protest the coverage of Warrendale. In March, as the neighborhood continued to be a staple news story, the WCO produced a press release that called for station managers and editors to stop emphasizing the community of "Warrendale" in their reports on the academy.[32] To WCO members, it seemed that stories set in other parts of the city were not *about* neighborhoods, and that the few other predominantly white areas were always highlighted for their social diversity whereas the homogeneity of Warrendale was stressed. Not only did the posture and speech of residents signify "blue-collar racism," the image of the neighborhood itself ratified and assured this impression.

I asked the group at Diana's house, "What is it about invoking a community that keeps it a race issue? Is it because it's about homes and kids?" Diana replied, "Because everybody was so hot when this whole thing started that they said things they really shouldn't have said. Like Sue, when she went after that lady when the picketing was going on. They keep showing her, Sue S—. Y'know who I'm talking about? She was screaming at that woman. They were holding a rally, an anti-racism rally. And Sue S—, 'It's not about racism!' And they, this woman kept baiting her and baiting her, until Sue just went nuts and the cameras went on, and here's this SCREAMING WOMAN [rage in her own voice], y'know, and that keeps being shown."

> JH: What was she saying?
> DIANA: "It's not about race. It's not about race." "Yes it is or you wouldn't be so hostile! What are you getting so mad about? What are you getting so mad about?" And there's Sue, just screaming, y'know.

In such instances, these whites felt themselves betrayed, on one hand by what they had assumed to be an objective media and, on the other, by their own intense feelings of frustration, which held a singular significance for observers. They could not speak about charged issues concerning their neighborhood without becoming loudly emotional. Hence their racialness, too, betrayed them, and signified in a manner that proved to be beyond their control: If whites were this upset, it must be the expression of a throbbing core of hatred rather than an inability to express the complex stakes they perceived in this conflict. There were others, aside from journalists and school officials, adept at manipulating the statements and emotions of residents. "Outsiders" were drawn to Warrendale by the conflict. In addition to the Workers League, the Aryan Nation had representatives in the area trying to incite racial violence. Residents noted that a lot of people making the most inflammatory remarks were strangers to the area.[33] To whatever extent this might have been the case, there were certainly some whites present who tried to provoke rage in their fellow whites. They were referred to by calmer whites as the "hostile few," a designation that Jeff and company were marked by, though he, in turn, referred to others in the same way.

> JEFF: I think that at the start of this thing, there were people coming in from outside the community coming into the meetings and what not. There were a few . . . uh . . . community residents that they pushed to blow up. They'd just pull strings . . .
> JH: How would they do that?
> JEFF: Well, like when you're trying to make a point and every time you make that point they twist what you say and say "Well, you mean this, this, this." And they do that three or four times and sure enough your blood pressure starts to rise. And then sure enough, then you start going "Raaarrr!!!" Cannons! Get back.

Emotional discourse is an index of social relations; it reveals inequalities of status and power, usually cast in gendered terms.[34] Given Jeff's and

Kevin's susceptibility to emotion and to being depicted as emotionally overwrought and out of control, perhaps the inequalities at work here involve class distinctions as well.[35] Speaking with and against educated professionals who could manage their sentiments as well as the appearance of racial interests, these whites grew increasingly frustrated. As dramatically captured by television and sound crews, this emotionality proved "racism" was at the core of their concerns. But considered in a broader frame, as a function of a complexly coded struggle over limited resources, their emotions also convey the classed contours of this contest. Diana asked Karen to tell me about the TV crew that came out to her house. Her account, worth quoting at length, sharply renders the class stakes these whites faced.

> KAREN: [big sigh] I was on Bill Bonds [a local news anchor man] with uh, Deborah McGriff. Well she's a politician, and she knows how to talk, and she just kept interrupting and she monopolized the whole thing. I didn't get to say much of anything. But at the end, Bill Bonds said he'd like to have us back again. So I said, real quick, "Well, I'd like to have more than one second to talk about all the issues," and he said yeah, about me being interrupted, and how she's a quick talker. Well, I got a call the very next morning from the station manager saying, "You alluded to some issues that you felt you didn't get to touch on." So they'd like to do a live interview. First they wanted me to come down there, and I refused. I said, "Absolutely not. You bring a crew out here." So they were going to do an interview with me, letting me say the issues. Because, none of the issues, they won't let 'em out. For the longest time they played up "Warrendale racists, don't want blacks in neighborhood." They would not let any of the issues about Carver come out at all, or about the community wanting the school, and all of the younger people moving in. So I said this. Well Frank Turner from Channel 7 says he'll come to the house, and that I can invite a couple of mothers. So I invited . . . A lot showed up, but I just invited a few mothers over. And when he walked in the door . . . I was told by the station manager that I could say the issues. They would give me a chance to speak finally. . . . Off the camera, he talked to us, and we were all pouring out our hearts about all the issues at Carver and how the poor kids got to sit in the hall. We sat there and told him everything. We all poured out our hearts. Well then he turns on the camera and the microphone and the camera and says 'I understand that there are 25 percent of the slots available to the neighborhood kids. Will you be enrolling your son in this school Mrs. Soper? and I'm like [stammer] "Yes." And then he had asked W.B. a question along the same line, about enrolling your child, and I got real pissed off and I told her don't answer it. I got real mad at him. While the cameras were rolling, I told him, "We sit here and tell you all the issues off camera. You turn the camera on and the very first thing you start about is those damned twenty-five slots." Put my hand in

front of the camera, and I had it right in front of his microphone. And I told the guy turn that damn thing off or I'm gonna break it. And I just went nuts.

To Karen's surprise, her defense of the neighborhood against media distortions was severely censured by the other women present for the interview. "I got yelled at after that interview. Not by him, not by Bill Bonds. I got yelled at by the damn ladies! I got yelled at by the ladies. Frances was all pissed off at me because I was so 'unprofessional' and I blew up. I got pissed off and said, wait a minute, I stuck up for us. If I would've answered any of his stupid ass questions again, the only thing that would've showed up on the 6:00 news was 'Mrs. Soper refuses to send white child to black school.' "

For these whites, the process of making statements on the matter of the Malcolm X Academy was an education in how racial discourses operate and are publicized. They found themselves stammering and frustrated, not only by their delimited and seemingly predetermined speaking roles but also by their lack of dexterity in making their voices sound different. The racial aspects of their statements, though, were hardly the only issue. Karen's account begins with a class-oriented perspective; in their showdown, Karen's inability to speak is contrasted with Dr. McGriff's ability with language. And there is a somewhat more subtle class component to Karen's frustration in the second televised format. When she decides to make a scene rather than have her comments delimited, Karen's neighbors are furious. The accusation of her being "unprofessional" suggests that she had ruptured a decorum of propriety that the other working-class women felt compelled to maintain in the media spotlight on their neighborhood. In the contest over the presentation of self—emotionally "pouring out" their hearts, only to have their words edited and objectified—these whites articulated contrasting sensibilities, informed as much by class distinctions as by an attention to racialness. The conflation of fluctuating racial and class interests is evident in various discursive labels—"white enclave," "racist," and "curriculum"—treated in the next sections.

"White Enclave"

If I had opened this school in a black
neighborhood, I wouldn't have heard a peep.
People really believe that housing segregation
should define the makeup of schools, even in 1992.
　　—Dr. Deborah McGriff, on the opening day of
　　the Malcolm X Academy[36]

"Warrendale is full of white people who forgot to
move out of the city when the rest of them did, or
they are too poor to move out of there, or they are
city workers or something."
—*Tandrea Black, president of the Malcolm X
Academy Local School Community
Organization, featured on flyers circulated
to draw residents to rallies at the school*

As the quote from Dr. McGriff suggests, school officials promoted the
interpretation that these whites were upset by the mere presence of blacks
in their neighborhood, an area they were supposedly trying to keep segregated. The media largely followed this line, reading the complaints of
whites in Warrendale as deriving from a desire to maintain a segregated
neighborhood—a "white enclave."[37] This impression had its basis in the
concentration of whites in this zone (80 percent of residents), which
seemed to confirm the charges that whites were policing their neighborhood out of racist motivations. "White enclave" operated as a compact
discursive objectification of white interests and desires. This characterization mobilized certain assumptions about whites in Warrendale: that they
were afraid of blacks; that blacks were an unfamiliar, physical embodiment of a threatening sense of otherness; that whites in Warrendale desired a racially homogeneous residential zone. For whites opposed to the
academy, "white enclave" undermined their ability to speak about race
and to address and assess the interests of blacks connected with the Malcolm X Academy. They had to struggle to speak apart from their residential background, which stood as a material substantiation of their implicit
interests in whiteness. Its class character—evident in the tract housing
and the residents' occupations (ranging from retired autoworkers to me-
chanics and janitors)—additionally shaped the significance of their racialness.[38] As in Corktown, this concentration compelled whites to address
the difficult matter of their identification with a certain residential zone.
When they discussed the relevance of applying the term "white enclave"
to Warrendale, what was at stake for them was the question of whether
there existed any neutral or noninterested space for them to assess the
significance of race.

Whites on both sides of the controversy were disconcerted by this objectification, for contrasting reasons, but they commonly recognized that
it drew overdetermined significance from the relative whiteness of this
zone in relation to the rest of Detroit. In challenging this representation,
whites grappled with the difficult matter of how to characterize spatial
formations racially—how to assess the significance of elements of racial
heterogeneity in a landscape that seemed increasingly susceptible to

characterization as "all white" or "all black." Against different back-grounds—the adjacent suburb of Dearborn, 98 percent white, or the city as a whole, 77 percent black—their whiteness could be alternately dif-fused or accentuated.[39] When they reflected on their relation to represen-tations of Warrendale, they grappled with what it means to be white, not as an abstract or generic matter but in this particular location, in a dis-tinctly classed predicament.

Characterizations of Warrendale as a "white enclave" underscored a more general reading by many blacks involved with this conflict that these whites were "behind the times" and literally out of place in Detroit. However explicitly or implicitly this opinion was stated, Warrendale whites took offense at the sentiment that they no longer belonged in De-troit. Whereas commentators and school officials saw a static concentra-tion of whites resisting progress, Warrendale residents countered that their community was actually changing and gradually integrating. They pointed to the northeast corner of Warrendale, where the black popula-tion had grown from 18 percent in 1980 to 38.5 percent in 1990.[40] This shift, they argued, proved not only that Warrendale was an open commu-nity but that, as whites, they were not striving to keep their neighborhood segregated. They expected that relative degree of integration would dif-fuse the significance of their spatial racialization.

Whites proudly pointed to the ease with which blacks were moving into parts of Warrendale, but they were also uncertain about the future presaged by this development. When they looked out across the South-field freeway—the neighborhood's eastern boundary—at the rest of the city, they saw it largely as an "all-black" entity. They wondered if their neighborhood would be any different from the rest of the city in ten years. Although I did not meet any white who was interested in maintaining a racially pure zone, few were confident that the area could be "success-fully" integrated, either, since this region offers such stark spatial prece-dents. When these whites discussed the relevance of "white enclave" to their neighborhood, they did so with few points of reference for zones apart from the "all-white" suburbs and the virtually "all-black" neigh-borhoods in the surrounding portions of the city.

Indeed, totalizing rhetorical labels such as "all white" or "all black" have a material basis in the demographics in Detroit and its suburbs. Forty-two of Detroit's forty-four suburbs have populations that are more than 95 percent white.[41] Historically, residential areas in Detroit have tended to go from "all white" to "all black." The interim is brief and tenuous. The George Washington Carver and Malcolm X schools are in Area B of the DPS. In this broad region, thirty-four of the forty-two schools have student populations that are more than 92 percent black; thirty of these schools are over 96 percent black, and in twenty schools, more than 98 percent of the students are black. Carver is the only school in the area with a white majority; 77 percent of its students are white.[42] "White enclave," with its connotations of a homogeneous, actively segregated whiteness, may have been misapplied in Warrendale (at least in comparison with Detroit's suburbs), but this characterization followed from the resolutely polarized racial representations of space in the metropolitan area.

White supporters of the academy were in an interesting bind when they tried to counter descriptions of Warrendale as a "white enclave." They had to evaluate both local rhetorical practices of white neighbors and their numerous points of class contrast with the actions and interest of suburban whites. Paul, a white schoolteacher in the DPS, conveys this nuanced situation.

> There are people who tend to be the more racist . . . I first heard this a couple of years ago, when they started saying that Warrendale's boundary was Tireman, the next half-mile road up. If you go north of Tireman, the majority is black, but still, y'know, two-thirds to one-third, still very mixed. And then, now, the latest round, since this Malcolm X thing, I've heard the most . . . y'know, flagrant, loud-mouth racists say Warrendale is from Warren Road south. Basically, when they say Warrendale, what they mean is the white! Polish! people! here! [pounds the table with his fist for emphasis]! And wherever they are, they call that Warrendale. And our organization [WCO] is supposed to be fighting that. Saying No! Warrendale goes from Joy Road! [pounds on the table]. That is Warrendale. Warrendale is a very racially mixed . . . only 59 percent of the children in Warrendale are white. So when you say, "Why are they putting a black school in a white neighborhood?" Only 50 . . . okay, it's a majority, 59 percent. But hardly a "white" neighborhood! Would you call Southfield a "white enclave"? NO! But they're more white than we are.

Paul's characterization of "racists" in Warrendale concludes by drawing a contrast with the suburbs, which he insists are "more white than we are." As in Corktown, Warrendale whites have a keen sense of their differential position and status in relation to suburban whites. Although the neighborhood contains a greater concentration of whites than Corktown, Paul stresses the element of heterogeneity that distinguishes this zone from the whiteness of the suburbs. To be a "white neighborhood," he asserts, you have to be more politically savvy, both to preclude any form of racial mixing and to elude the representational mode that considers class as well as racial homogeneity in designating areas as "white enclaves."

The people Paul labeled as "racists" contested Warrendale's designation as a "white enclave" in a similar fashion. People like Jeff and Joyce not only disputed the accuracy of the label, they also saw it as a function of the media's tendency to sensationalize community conflicts. They complained that media coverage intentionally focused on the portions of Warrendale that were demographically the whitest, in order to keep the issues surrounding the Academy linked to the racially charged aspects of the controversy—that is, they mimicked the signifying practices that Paul claimed he recognized among his neighbors. Wally, the WCO's president, also complained that reporters honed in on the whitest portion of Warrendale. "That is the very white segment of the community. So they portrayed the whole community . . . These people did not come around and look at the racial makeup of the total community. They just looked over there. And of course, there were a few people over there that just jumped on the bandwagon: 'We don't want these blacks coming to school here. They're gonna start breaking into our homes.' Well the kids are bused in, and they're bused out! How are they gonna start breaking in? 'Excuse me teacher, I got to go across the street and break into that house.' Sure! [heaves a disgusted sigh]" I asked him why the media just focused on that side of Warrendale. He looked at me as if I was stupid, then slowly explained by asking, "What does the media do?"

"Sensationalize?" I offered.

"Sensationalize. That's right. What does the media want? They want viewers, they want readership. And they're gonna write, or they're gonna portray on television, every aspect that they can that will sensationalize their story."

These residents did not contest the fact that Warrendale was predominantly white. In contrast to Corktown, whites in Warrendale were consistently frank about the fact of white dominance in the area. But they did attempt to short-circuit the way this depiction located the significance of their racialness as a strictly univocal interest in preserving an "all-white" area. They were upset about representations that made it "look more white than it really is." Warrendale could easily be characterized as "only" 59 percent white, as Paul chose to read it, but this was not as interesting a designation as "white enclave," which involved a discursive operation similar to the blanket assumption of "racist" motivations. Both objectifications undermine an attention to the ambivalences that residents felt about their community and the academy. Frances, a white woman opposed to the school, while admitting that "you could hear the racism" in the meeting with Dr. McGriff, qualified its connection with an interest in maintaining the neighborhood as white.

> JH: The racism that you heard at the first meeting, where do you think that was coming from?
> FRANCES: Okay. I think, number one, a lot of people have very set attitudes. Warrendale, though it's not predominantly known for that, it has always been . . . with all of the neighborhoods changing, outside of Warrendale . . . It has

always been predominantly white. I mean, people from the suburbs come here because, for buying houses, because it's so affordable. And then once the kids get beyond elementary school age they may tend to sell out and everything like that, but then younger families move in. And it's always been a great rental area [Frances is a renter]. And I think that a lot of people are just so used to . . . this is a white area. And it's one of the few white . . . bastions . . . left in Detroit, because most of the neighborhoods are very integrated. Except for, I believe there is one on the east side near Harper Woods that is a "white enclave" or whatever you want to call it. I mean, I find "enclave" to be an offensive term, but I . . . I mean, it's a legitimate term, in a sense, but it just has very negative connotations to me.

JH: Because it's too defensive about boundaries?

FRANCES: Right. Like it's an impenetrable force, which it is not. And . . . we have sat there, and people have moved in who are from Iraq, Chaldean . . . Hispanic, ahh. I mean, it's not a real integrated, integrated area, but there is nothing . . . nobody has ever tried to keep people out or anything. It's just been basically . . . I don't know, if I was a black person, whether I would feel comfortable about moving into an all-white area, because I wouldn't feel comfortable about moving into an all-black area. But, I mean, there have been people that have moved in. Like on Minock . . . on every single block there has been a black family that is living on the block. It's just not a problem per se. People just get along. I just found out that this woman I'm delivering [newspapers] to on Minock, has just taken her daughter out of St. Suzane's and is sending her to Malcolm X. This woman does not know that I am working against the school. But we get along terrifically. She is a very nice person. And if she ever finds out, I'll just tell her, it's a difference of opinion.

The bottom line in Frances's assessment of "white enclave" is whether or not whites are trying to preserve a racially segregated zone apart from blacks. In her reading of the interplay between race and space, she considers the relative whiteness of this zone to be unmotivated. In this example of the black neighbor to whom she delivers newspapers, Frances points to both the permeability of Warrendale's boundaries and the fact that whites have not been racialized in relation to black inmovers. This view suggests that the significance of white racialness in this zone only materialized when the Board of Education decided to open the Malcolm X Academy. Frances notes an ambivalence in statements like, "What about the white kids?" Joyce, in her view, articulated a racial interest that would not have emerged if the Afrocentric academy had not been placed in their neighborhood. Such statements are racialized in relation to the school, and to Frances they hardly relate to a core of values. This assumption is also evident in the way supporters of the school criticized the label "white enclave." Pointing to other parts of Detroit, as Frances did, they would see areas that looked "the same" as their neighborhood (predominantly white) but that were not being objectified as "racist white enclaves."

I asked Yvonne, one of the academy's fiercest neighborhood support-ers, "If you were going to define whiteness, how would you do that, and is Warrendale constructed as a white community in that regard?" She laughed and asked,

> Is Warrendale what we've been described as—a white enclave? Uhm . . . Yes Warrendale is a white enclave . . . But Warrendale is a white enclave not through any fault of their own, okay. Because you have the people who bought the homes when the subdivision was built. And because you have their children who grew up in a good area, a nice atmosphere, you have their children buying homes in the area. So . . . it's a white enclave only because you have generations remaining where they are. They're not moving out to the suburbs. That's the only reason why I can see that Warrendale is still a white enclave. Uhm but only for that reason. But then you have the same type of white enclaves on the east side. You have the same thing that we have here. Through the fault of a very few, that's been portrayed quite a bit in the media, without them looking at other areas of the city that are like this.
>
> JH: So do you think that if they drew comparison between border neighbor-hoods, east side and west side . . .
>
> YVONNE: They would find the same thing. They would find the same thing.

Yvonne's conviction that "they would find the same thing" points to the core frustration and confusion experienced by these whites. When they looked at other neighborhoods on the boundaries of Detroit, or when they drew comparisons with the suburbs, they saw essentially the same thing: predominantly white neighborhoods. But the whiteness of these other areas remained unnoticed and eluded objectification. The his-torical record in Detroit, in their reading, associated "white neighbor-hoods" with defensive resistance by whites to black inmovers. Here, they could point to a clear demographic trend of black inmovers who were meeting no resistance. More important, they are whites who have bucked the massive tide of "white flight." Yet, in the glare of the media coverage, their racialness was fused with the neighborhood's demographics and the "few people" who "jumped on the bandwagon." To be racially objec-tified as white could mean only that they were, at heart, "racists." In response, they attempted to articulate a neutral mode of racial sig-nificance, highlighting the critical historical difference of their relation to "white flight."

The critical matter for Yvonne (supporter) and Frances (opponent) is the distinction between intentional and unintentional articulation of community interests and boundaries, as if their community is not racially identifiable unless there is an ideological component, some conscious articulation of racial interests, desires, identities. Implicit here is also a sense that whites, in the absence of blacks or other races, are not racially constituted. In Yvonne's historical version, it is as if whites arrived here before race was an issue. Yvonne's remark about "through no fault of their own . . . ," and Frances's disclaimers about racial motivation on the part of Warrendale whites can be considered naive, if they are suggesting that white racialness bore no significance prior to this circumstance. Such an assumption ignores the privileges of whiteness that are inscribed in the material conditions of Detroit's outlying neighborhoods. But the accompanying frames of reference they draw upon indicate that more than simplistic assumptions are at work in the interpretive repertoire they employ in critiquing "white enclave." Their remarks are made from a precarious position: These whites are responding, in part, to the reductive racial reading of whites generated in the controversy over the academy; their comments also reflect varying degrees of personal experience with Detroit's charged racial history and an understanding of the policing techniques of racial boundary maintenance that white suburbanites subtly employ. Although their naiveté is debatable—certainly their consciousness of racial privilege would strike antiracist activists as meager—the terrain illuminated in their discursive efforts to articulate a position between "all-white" and "all-black" rhetorical and spatial constructs is critical to understanding how the significance of white racialness is defined by class-and place-specific dynamics.

These whites were confronted by statements by black school officials and city politicians that reductively read the significance of white racialness in absolute terms. The nuances of their position in the wake of "white flight," in particular, was rendered insignificant in comments by certain representatives of the academy, as Joyce relates:

> Well what about Tandrea Black saying about this neighborhood, that we were too stupid to get out?
> JEFF: She made the statement that "the people of Warrendale forgot to move out when the rest of them did. Or they're too poor to move or they're city workers or something." That was her!
> JH: So what were your reactions to that?
> DIANA: It ticks you off . . .
> JOYCE: Oh it pleased us immensely [laughs].

Recalling this comment immediately brought to mind another register of statements to which they were exposed for the first time.

> BONNIE: "Well even at Martin Luther King [School] that night, she got up and said, "We are the majority now," meaning the blacks. "We will do what we want to do." Basically, "it's our turn, it's our turn . . . "

DIANA: Right, "We are the majority now."

BONNIE: And we're sitting there wanting to sink in our seats. We went there to another board meeting, where there was the flag dispute. People in the audience are screaming, "Burn the flag, burn the flag." And I mean . . . I was very afraid that night. I was afraid.

JEFF: Oh yeah, I was happy to just get out of there. That was the last board meeting I went to. I got up to speak and right away, "white devil worshiper," WARRENDALE! WARRENDALE! I couldn't even finish, they shut the mike off on me.

Even whites who did not attend numerous board meetings were well aware of the comments made by black school officials that in ways, subtle or not, expressed the sense that these whites were out of place in Detroit. And it was a sentiment with which they uniformly took offense. Janice supported the academy opening in Warrendale, yet she was upset about the comments made by some blacks connected with the school. "And they kept telling us . . . we want . . . 'If we wanted to be like the suburbanites, we should move to the suburbs, or something.' Well we know where we are! This is Detroit! And if I want to live in the suburbs, I would've been there. Y'know what I'm saying? I wanted to BE HERE! I wanted to be in the neighborhood. I wanted to be in this community. I like this area."

The significance of statements asserting that these whites were out of place in Detroit also resonated with a distinct spatial background—the city's blackness. This rhetoric further underscored their uncertainties concerning the spatial transformation that was unfolding in this corner of Detroit. They wondered whether their neighborhood, as it was struck full force by the economic tsunami working outward from Detroit's inner city, would become "balanced" or go "all black." Even supporters of the academy, like Paul, were concerned that Warrendale would go "all black." Paul explained,

I feel like, now, that this block and most of this area is very mixed. People who want to live in an all-white area, when the older people die or somebody moves out, they're not even going to want to move in here. Right? And so who's going to move in here is either going to be, uhm, whites who are tolerant . . . or black families. And . . . therefore, I think you're weeding out the racists in the process. My real concern is that . . . uhm . . . it seems like . . . I guess my question is, is it possible for a community to become a truly racially! mixed! community! [raps the table for emphasis after each word]—a solid, stable, racially mixed community? Or is a racially mixed community simply a transition point, a transition phase from being all white to being all black?

JH: What's your sense?

PAUL: Well . . . If you look at Detroit as a whole, and its history, the history has gone from all white to all black. Once a neighborhood gets to be about half black, that's it, it goes all black. . . . Y'know, this isn't the '60s, this is the '90s! We've had thirty years of watching Detroit. Are we going to learn from the mistakes of other communities or not? . . . Because the older people are going to die, and blacks are going to move in. And then . . . then when blacks move in, they can be rude and nasty to them and break up the community, and make this sort of sour feeling. And then all the whites move out. And then when all of the whites move out real quick, you have all of these houses being dumped on the market at real cheap prices, and then you have landlords buying them up, and then slumlords take over . . . and there . . . okay, you have an all-black, but not a black empowered, solid community.[43] You have sort of a bitter black relation that watched all of these nasty whites run. Okay? Then that's like the rest of the city, and we've accomplished nothing.

The history that Paul observes positions Warrendale on the cusp of absolute racial orders, posing the question whether "a racially mixed community [is] simply . . . a transition phase from being all white to being all black."[44] The "all-black" result carried an array of economic connotations that were implied in the deterioration of surrounding Detroit neighborhoods. Another supporter of the academy, Mickey, drew a similar sense of the neighborhood's position in the city. Mickey worked at St. Thomas Aquinas, and helped arrange a workshop on racism that was held at the church during the height of the conflict. Her articulation was based on personal experiences with the city's "failed" neighborhoods.

I watched my neighborhood . . . My folks lived on Six Mile and Gratiot. The neighborhood deteriorated considerably, with . . . because of crime and abandoned housing, and, uh, drug houses. And where people were not open to communication, where you . . . I mean you just close your eyes to the changes happening around you and just say they're not changing . . . and by that time . . . I watched my mom sit on her bed . . . in a home that she lived in for over forty years, in a neighborhood she lived in for about sixty years . . . and cried because she had to go because there was a drug house two doors away from her, and . . . they had been . . . my dad was lying on the couch and she was on the front porch, and they had been broken into. And to this day, I feel sorry that we forced them out. I mean, we literally forced them out. My dad kept saying, "We can make a difference." When everybody is moving out . . . that you can . . . because of you, you can make a difference? You can't make a difference anymore! Now all you can do is go where you're safe and pray for the community. But we have an opportunity here, in this area of Detroit, to really make a difference. And there are enough people committed to it because we have come a long way . . . and we have the example of what can happen if you don't make that effort to get people involved in the community.

Both Mickey and Paul are concerned about the area becoming "all black." The point of staying is to maintain a balance. The "racists" would leave and they would soon have a "well-balanced" community. But if the area became "all black," it would soon be "like the rest of the city," and both Mickey and Paul were disturbed at this prospect. Whites in Warrendale, whether or not they were susceptible to being labeled "racist" for their opinions on the academy, were concerned about situations (residential or otherwise) that were "all black." They regard this concern as possessing a certain validity that made it different from "racist" sentiments. Indeed, comments about "all-black" areas were often pointedly contrasted with "racist" statements. Whites felt that "all-black" contexts provoked a change in racial attitudes among blacks, crossing a threshold that involved an inevitable racialization of themselves. Such situations certainly heightened their susceptibility to being judged in reductively racial terms.

Frances described this dynamic in the context of the west-side Detroit neighborhood where she was born and raised. She lived in her childhood neighborhood until 1982, as the area slowly deteriorated. She was pregnant when she and her husband left. They decided to leave when their neighbor's garage was burned down by a five-year-old boy, and a mentally unstable woman neighbor charged Frances with a knife. She explained, "The neighborhood started changing racially back in 1973. My dad died that year, and one of my neighbors across the street sold her house. And it was really stupid. Because, back in the '70s, people were so scared—'Oh my god, a black person is moving into the neighborhood.' And my family was like, 'Who the hell cares as long as they're good people.' Y'know, my mom and dad were like that."

After her father died, her mother decided that they would stay because "It was the best that we could do on a limited income." But, "all of a sudden, ch, ch, ch, ch—For Sale signs ALL OVER the place. I mean, it was scary. A few people wouldn't even put For Sale signs up, because they didn't want it to be known that they were leaving." They stayed while neighbors she described as "very racially prejudiced" sold their homes to black families.

> The area changed over . . . By the time I left it was probably . . . I'd say 97 percent black. In nine years, it sat there and went very fast. Because a lot of the younger people moved out . . . We had a lot of people that just moved into the neighborhood that were black, and they turned around and moved out, because it just got to be such a . . . Yeah, I babysat for an insurance executive—his daughter. They had bought a brick house. And there were so many problems on the block, with the influx of people. So then they just started renting out the houses, and they did get a lot of people in that were what I term "undesirable." And he sat there, he ended up selling his house at a loss, and moving out to Bloomfield, because he said he didn't want to live in an area where he had to worry about his children growing up. And that is one of the things, irregardless

of race or whatever, is that people are concerned about crime, and where you live, you've got to feel secure. And that is one thing, we didn't feel secure in that area.

As she continued talking, Frances highlighted the sense of physical threat they felt in the area, but did not solely equate this with the racial conditions. She did not specify the race of the woman who threatened her, or of the child that burned the garage, or of the insurance executive who moved in as whites were pouring out. Frances, did, however, note a shift in attitudes that followed the increasing concentration of blacks in the neighborhood.

> It was dangerous. I was pregnant at the time, and my husband had just gone into the military. And I came home with my new daughter, and I was . . . Basically, she was only a month old, maybe, and she was getting called "honky" already. Which is . . . Some of these children, their parents had experienced racial discrimination, and in turn, were teaching their children, "Don't wait till they sit there and they hurt you—fight back!" And that was sad, because we sat there and we had some beautiful neighbors . . . we still go back there and talk to people . . . And I realize nine years is not that short a period of time, but still it seemed to go so quickly. When we came back we had a chance to rent the house again, and it would've been a ridiculous price. But I just said, "No. I am scared. I am terrified to live in that neighborhood."
>
> JH: The racial comments, like honky, did they start up as soon as blacks started moving in?
>
> FRANCES: No. No . . . I think it was more of a case of where, number one, when you sat there and got a geographical change, or a racial change, I should say . . . It was more a case where everybody was kind of "Hi, how are you". . . Admittedly, I think some of the people were kind of apprehensive about moving into what was at that point in time a nearly all-white neighborhood. I mean, it would be like moving into our neighborhood, though we do have a black family that lives down the street from us. They have had no trouble or anything like that. But, uh . . . I guess . . . as time went by . . . And y'know, it went from 25 percent to 50 percent to 75 percent . . . some of the kids would get a little more cocky . . . and you would just see a climate change . . . and they'd take no grief off of anybody kind of attitude . . . and . . . it didn't help that some of the whites that were used to living there had an attitude against anybody that was of racial difference from them . . . and it would be kind of egged on by that.

However such conflicts developed, and whatever the initial attitudes of residents living in or moving to such neighborhoods, what is clear from stories like Frances's is that whoever remains behind has become, in the process of the neighborhood's transition, racialized in relation to that place and its particular history.[45] Race matters because of what other neighbors do, how power is wielded at the city level, and because of the effects of economic shifts, all factors that were out of their control. It did not matter to the blacks who called her daughter a "honky" that Frances did not feel like the whites who left or who contested the movement of blacks into the area. After all the conflict and hardship, she was just another white, out of place in what was becoming an "all-black" area. [46]

Whites I spoke with in Warrendale talked about conditions in Detroit by relying on a temporal bifurcation. They saw themselves and their neighborhood poised between a tumultuous past and an uncertain present. This view separates the collapsing core of the city from its fringes, and the majority-black areas from the majority-white neighborhoods. The drastic changes transforming this city within their lifetimes were obvious; they were also obviously connected to race. But it was not solely the "all-black" spatial figure that bothered them. These whites were astute about policing techniques that effectively maintained the adjacent suburbs as "all white"—a zone they had either rejected or been unable to occupy. This casually surfaced when Joyce reported, in passing, having four cars stolen in the last couple of years. Suspecting that talk about crime would be highly racialized in Warrendale, I asked her, "Well, what's your sense of where the crime is coming from? Is it from within the neighborhood, or from outside?" There was a pause here, a silence, and they looked at each other, then slipped into a caricatured joking mode.

> JOYCE: [puffed up, hands on hips—authoritative voice while Diana giggled] Well! As it is known . . . ! Once you get passed Tireman, it's all black. The area is kinda [she slips back into her regular voice] . . . the houses are rough looking, uhm . . . to be truthful there is a Detroit Public Library over there, which I don't care to go to because . . .
>
> DIANA: We go to the Dearborn Library.
>
> JOYCE: . . . it's all black, y'know. I don't want to be just the only white person there. I don't mind it being mixed. I work at the Eastern Market [on the east side of downtown]. So I don't mind. It's just, I don't want to be the only one. And I don't want to take my kids and chance it too. So I do go to Dearborn for the library.

The problem that they both have with this arrangement is the library charges fees to nonresidents. Diana said, "You have to pay $25 for a card [shifts to snotty voice] 'Because you're not from Dearborn.' "

Joyce pointed out, "Dearborn offers a lot for the kids."

Diana observed, "If you look in the *Dearborn Press & Guide*, it says that they're open to Dearborn residents only. If I went there, they wouldn't know if I was a Dearborn resident or not, y'know. But I bet if a black person went, they'd ask 'em [haughty voice] 'Do you live in Dearborn?' "

Joyce and Diana are in a complicated racial position. On one hand, they barter in stereotypes as distorted caricatures that are, at times, proven true. On the other hand, they are also cognizant of the techniques of boundary maintenance white suburbanites engage in to maintain racial zones where blacks are recognized immediately as being out of place. They live in between spaces that appear as absolute racial formations: one "all black," the other "all white." They move in between these polarized racial zones, knowledgeably aware that their racialness both opens freedom of movement and entails a certain degree of vulnerability. They are also aware that the public language for discussing this kind of movement by whites is underdeveloped or meager.

In these and other references to "all-black" situations, I gradually noticed the texture of class contrast with the contexts described in Corktown when someone talked of being the "only white." Continuing our conversation, I asked Joyce and Diana if they had encountered much racial hostility in Detroit. They answered in terms of incidents in the neighborhood: Diana had a couple of threatening encounters with black teenage males following the opening of the academy, and Joyce, who lives farther from the school, had none to report. They summed the matter up by answering in the negative. Then Joyce related,

I was in a shelter for a while. The one by the old Hudson building, in the YMCA down there. Lovely place [they both laugh]. And yes I was harassed. I was the only white one in there after a while. So, I don't know if they wanted my bus passes [laughs], I was threatened for those. I couldn't get 'em, though, 'cause they knew I had a car. So, she was threatening me for my bus passes, and . . . after a while some of them started to hate me. And, y'know, they'd rag on me about the color of my skin and stuff.

JH: What were they saying?

JOYCE: [smiles] Oh, just calling me white trash and stuff. I kept joking with them, though. I wanted to braid my hair [they both laugh, a lot]. I wanted my hair all braided. "No way man, you've got angel's hair [she does not slip into a 'black' voice]." I guess it's too fine, but they wouldn't do it. [long pause] It wasn't that bad. They got to know me, and they kinda got an attitude . . . y'know, that's when they came after me. Not "came after me," but started with the racial slurs and crap like that. But . . . I wasn't impressed. A lot of those people were on drugs or whatever, and they just got the shit knocked out of 'em. They go there for a while, and then they go back with him . . . Y'know. I was there for a transmission of life.

JH: And that went well?

JOYCE: Well I got out of there before I needed to [laughs]. I mean, it wasn't fun, way downtown. Y'know, and I'd be walking around with a bunch of the women, and the guys, 'cause you have to walk right by the guy's YMCA, and you get, "Whoa, look at the white one [laughs]!" And I'm with my kids. So I wouldn't go out anymore. I'd take my car, because it's not a nice area. I don't go down to Hart Plaza anymore.

DIANA: Not even for the fireworks [along the downtown riverfront]?

JOYCE: Last time I went down to the fireworks, I almost got beat up by a big black guy.

JH: Really?

JOYCE: Because I yelled at him, because he was leaning over four of the kids that I had with me. So that wasn't over color [laughs].

DIANA: [laughs] Just your mouth again.

JOYCE: No [laughs]. It was my children your messing with, bud. Y'know, come after me instead.

These stories particularly underscore the distinct manners in which whites in Warrendale and in Corktown are racialized. Whites in Corktown, too, could relate situations in which they were the "only white," but any racial ambiguities in these settings were squelched by overarching decorums of the political or social contexts of a night at the theater or a meeting with the mayor; the "moral" of their stories was either that race did not matter or that it was something to be effectively managed. But the class position of Warrendale whites made them prone to racialization. Whether in a shelter, a drastically changing neighborhood, or in a carnivalesque crowd on the waterfront, the "all-black" situations Warrendale whites recounted clearly signified the forms of precariousness typically experienced by the working class.[47] The added degree of vulnerability that distinguished the settings in which whites from these two neighborhoods were racially outnumbered is that Warrendale whites had children to contend with, which, even under the best of circumstances, is a cause for anxiety. Whereas few people in Corktown had children of school age, the whites in Warrendale who were engaged in opposing the academy all had children who were in the Detroit public schools.

Another prime difference in "all-black" versus "only-white" situations is that many of the residents of Warrendale had gone through the public school system themselves when it was at its most volatile stage. This was not an experience they wanted their children to repeat. When I spoke with Kevin, the first thing he explained was how he had "gone through all this before" during desegregation of the DPS (see "Franklin School"). His time at Cody High School was a blur of racial violence in which he and his friends were well outnumbered. "You want to know why somebody like me doesn't have an education, that's the cause right there. I was afraid for my life every day in that building." Like other whites I spoke with, he was upset that he had been called a racist by people who did not know him. To provide a context for his statements and attitudes, he returned to detail his experiences at Cody.

I got kicked out, and the deal with the guy that . . . uhm . . . I'm trying to think of his name. He used to own a car called Purple Passion. I want to say Paul Zeep or Zapp. [To Karen] His older brother went there so you probably know him. The kid got beat up by a bunch of black kids, and his eye was hanging out and all that. And from that point on it turned into your normal racial riot. And I basically got pulled over in a car and I had this box opener. They didn't kick me out after the first incident, but the second time I got caught, they did.

JH: So this was over a few days?

KEVIN: Yeah.

JH: So did you come out of there hating blacks?

KEVIN: Not really, no . . .

KAREN: It was hard not to . . .

KEVIN: Not really hating . . .

KAREN: Not all of them . . .

KEVIN: Not really hating the blacks, but to the point where I wouldn't put myself in a position where I would feel comfortable going into a restaurant with all black people. I mean . . . to me, as far as black people are concerned, I even had a relationship with a black woman for over a year and a half. And to me, it wasn't the race that was the issue.

For Kevin, there was a difference between worrying about being in a situation that was "all black" and being a racist. This was a distinction that some supporters of the academy also drew, but based on very different personal histories in Detroit. Reverend Nelson—then pastor at the United Brethren in Christ Church, where the WCO holds their monthly meetings—presents a complicated picture of the supporters of the school on the WCO board. At one point, he was lamenting the loss of the "good reputation" that the neighborhood had previously established. I asked him how that reputation was achieved, and he suggested the neighborhood's George Washington Carver School.

I think that Carver school really projects a good image, and that helped. Listen, word gets around where there's a good school. That may be the biggest draw. So if you've got kids, and you want to send them to a public school, and you want to send them to a good one, that's probably . . . lets say, that's not all black. 'Cause I took Joshua [his oldest son], when we first got here, I took him up to Lessinger, and we went through Lessinger with him. And when we got through, he said, "Dad, I just wouldn't be comfortable there. Everybody there was black, everybody." And I said, "Okay, I understand." And it wasn't a racist remark. It's just that he came from Virginia, and to put him into a school that size with all black kids would've been a foolish thing to do, so I said no.

Even supporters of the academy had an ominous sense about settings that were "all black." Here, the reverend's qualification for schools, which contrasts "a good one, that's probably . . . lets say, that's not all black," is naturalized as an order apart from racism. He makes the point explicitly when he notes that his son's statement of discomfort was not a "racist remark." Other whites with similar views on the academy were a bit more reflective about the racist connotations associated with "all black." Janice, though she supported the academy, admitted that her first response was one of "there goes the neighborhood." In discussing her initial reaction, she covered discursive ground worth quoting at length.

> JH: Where do you think that first reaction you mentioned comes from?
>
> JANICE: From the fact that I was brought up the other side of Telegraph in an all-white neighborhood. And was never, never, never exposed to a black person until I came to work here [at a drugstore]. And when I was in the drugstore when the place was robbed, it was a black man that put a gun to my head. So . . . I have to say that I probably feel a lot . . . and I can't even say that it has anything to do with my parents. Because I never heard my parents say one way or another about anything. I think [laughs], I think I made all of the judgments all by myself, just because of experience [laughs]. When I used to go there after school to work, just for a couple of hours, uh, I was going over to McDonald's and some girl tried to take my shoes [she states this in a tiredly appalled tone]. And the same thing. And I think that's where all of my judgments came from, 'cause it scared me half to death. I thought, "Oh wow, my new shoes!" Not that they couldn't be replaced [laughs]. So that did scare me. But other than just those two incidents . . . I don't know where it's come from. I guess . . . I don't know. I've seen so much . . . There's so much racial stuff going on around us. And . . . they . . . It seems that they're targeting the white people. . . . You can live where I live, I have no problem. You want to live on my street, I have no problem with that. Um . . . On the other hand . . . in my mind . . . I look at, I look at Joy Road. From when I went there twenty-one years ago . . . Because it was all white, and it was a nice neighborhood, and then the blacks did start moving in. And drive down there now. Why is the neighborhood so bad? Would it be that way if it was all white people? And not to sound racial or anything, but, but is that what really . . . You want us to help you, and you want us to give you this, but you're not taking care of and utilizing what we're giving you. . . . And granted there are bad places in Taylor, or Garden City, y'know, the white people did do that, too. But I've got to look at what's right here what's happened.

Unlike Glen—the only Corktown white to narrate being a victim of a crime with black perpetrator—Janice's exploration of her racialized re-action to black people involves multiple encounters and a lengthy obser-vation of the residential areas around her. But it evidences a similar ease of projecting racial judgment based on limited instances. Her effort "not to sound racial or anything" includes responses to caricatured political voices, patronizing paternalism, and fear of being racially targeted, all tangled in the local view afforded by her location in Warrendale; all, too, turning on an axis that could downplay these "racial" aspects with the comment that "white people did do that, too."

> JH: Well how do the whites that are a problem here compare to the blacks that are a problem on that side of Warrendale?
>
> JANICE: I think they're just as bad. I really think so. I think there are really good . . . Look at the black people who live in Rosedale Park, that's beautiful! And I mean, those are all black people. That's okay. But you get your scummy black, and you get your scummy white, and they want to move into our nice neigh . . . [stops] "Our nice neighborhood" [mimics her own voice, laughs]. Boy did that sound racial or what! They want to move into the nice neighborhoods because they want to live. And I don't blame them. I'd want to live in a nice place too. But take care of it! And keep it nice. That's what's going to keep the whole thing nice and keep everything going.

Janice was at her most animated when she described the influx of "renters" into the area, a category fundamentally involving class: "scummy white" people wanting move into "our nice neighborhood." The attention to intraracial class differences plays two key discursive roles here. An attention to class counters the focus on the significance of race in the transformations of residential areas in Detroit. But more profoundly, invoking class divides seems to naturalize the fundamental category of "undesirable" people, people who are *truly* and *objectively* dangerous, the "scum" of any race. "It makes you so mad, you just want to go up to people and say, [shouting] 'Why don't you take care of your stuff!? Don't you care about your neighborhood!?' And that's why I believe a lot of them are renters. Because this isn't their home they don't care, they just don't care. 'I can pick up and I can move my stuff and I can go anywhere at anytime.' Y'know, so . . . That makes it bad, it really makes it bad. And the poor people that have to live next to these slugs [laughs] . . . it's even harder."

Her contempt for renters and her frustration with their lifestyle was something that she shared with other long-term residents of Warrendale, like Wally, Yvonne, and Kevin. They read the class content of the shift in surrounding residential areas and their own neighborhood with as keen an attention as they paid to race.[48] Kevin's two daughters attend St. Peter and Paul Elementary School. They started out in kindergarten at Carver, but his wife insisted that they go to a different school with a different class composition. "My wife came back and told me, 'These people in this school are trash!' And she didn't say that they were people of the black race. She just plain out bluntly said, 'That school is full of nothing but white trash.'"

Long before the academy became an issue, whites in this neighborhood were concerned about the transformation in the area's class composition. After the issue of the Malcolm X Academy faded, the shifting class status of residents continued to concern them. Of the three Detroit neighborhoods where I worked, this was the only area in which the term "white trash" was used, and it was used with some frequency. In many regards, poor whites in Warrendale were more frustrating to residents than blacks were. The conflation of race and class in the perception of demographic shifts in Warrendale is a complex matter, particularly because residents were struggling to find a means not to give in to the play of racial stereotypes. But their self-consciousness about the significance of race was critically developed at the expense of more polarized positions relating to class distinctions.

Wally was explaining, "There's no such thing as a better home in Detroit. Not unless you get into some of the rich areas like Rosedale Park or Indian Village." He described driving around other parts of the city, first through burnt-out neighborhoods, then suddenly coming across an area of beautiful, wealthy homes populated predominantly by black people. Wally exclaimed, "And see, this is not a black and white thing. Because in those areas, it's mostly black. They're the ones who own those beautiful homes." He then recounted how quickly Warrendale was deteriorating, pointing to houses on his street that were showing signs of decay. There's a place two doors down from him. "They've got four cars in their backyard, and he's always messing around with them. Then they got two parked out on the street that don't run. And they got four more that they drive around. And these are white folks! . . . I would prefer to have black people move next door. As long as they keep up the house, I don't care what color they are. I really don't. All that matters is that we have some kind of harmony. We don't need all of this fighting and carrying on, at each others' throats." As did Paul, a white attorney in Corktown, Wally relies on the point that, "these are white folks" to efface the racial connotations of his anxiety over the changes transforming his neighborhood. I asked Wally if he thought that Warrendale's decline was connected to events in the inner city.

> Well, to a degree, yes. Ahh, I recall, I had a black man at work, on the midnight shift as a crane operator. And he lived down in the inner city, and then he moved over on Dexter. And he said, "Boy, it was real nice, until they started to build freeways." Then he said, and this is his words . . . He said, "The goddanged niggers moved out into my neighborhood, and the next thing I know we've got fires and ambulances, and police cars, and sirens going all night long. So I'm having to move again, so I can get out in a nicer neighborhood, so I don't have to put up with all that crap." But, nowadays, it seems like it's not neces-

sarily the blacks . . . We've got white trash moving into this neighborhood. We've got one family on Stahelin and Tireman, they park a vehicle right on the front lawn—they do car repair right in the garage, the place is strewn with junk.

In Wally's account, and in Frances's earlier story about the executive who left her old neighborhood when crime started to become a problem, there is the figure of the black middle class now also leaving the city as the white middle class has largely already done. It is against this flight that the figure of "white trash" comes increasingly into view, making clear that the matter of neighborhood transition is not solely, or perhaps even primarily, linked to race.[49] Kevin, describing Warrendale, said, "It's nowhere near what it used to be . . . not being race-wise either. Just being that of the type of people that are overall in the community now; the community's changed." Kevin contrasted Warrendale to Rosedale Park: "People aren't separated by race, they're separated by class. That's what happened to the cities, we've lost the middle class. Not just, not just white people left, but you lost the black middle-class people. Black and white, you lost the middle class, that's what's hurt the city." This stress on the threat posed by lower-class whites was not the only class-based means of equivocating the racialized aspects of the situation in Warrendale. Opponents of the academy were obsessed by the class status they saw embodied in the parents of children at the school. They charged the academy with being a reserve of the new black "elite" emerging in Detroit, accusing them also of cynically manipulating black intraracial class divides.

Other residents of Detroit were also upset about the academy's designation as an "empowered" school, a concept elusively defined by the Board of Education. The "empowerment" designation was a key issue in the lengthy and contentious teachers' strike that year, and it raised many criticisms from parents across the city who felt that such schools were elitist.[50] "Empowerment" was supposed to allow certain schools more discretion in spending their allocated funds. Detroiters whose children did not attend one of the few "empowered" schools, however, complained that these schools were actually receiving more funds than other schools; they charged the board with creating "a caste system, bringing new inequalities" to an overburdened educational system.[51] Members of the Workers League flocked into Warrendale to make their class-based case that "the essence of the 'schools of choice' program and the policy of local school autonomy, or 'empowered' schools, is to set up a number of elite schools which will receive a disproportionate share of public funds. . . . The sons and daughters of the well-to-do will gain access to these schools, while the vast majority of schools will be left to rot, along with the youths who attend them."[52] This attention to the classed aspects

of the controversy had varying degrees of resonance with whites in Warrendale. Residents saw many signs indicating that the academy was catering to students of a higher class than those it purported to be serving.
When residents articulated their suspicions about funding differences between the academy and Carver School, one indicator they pointed to was
the fleet of new school vans that had been given to Malcolm X. Supporters dismissed this attention as a mere "smoke screen," but these impressions did have a material basis.[53]

I tried, unsuccessfully, to find out the economic background of the parents who sent their children to the Malcolm X Academy.[54] Apparently the
DPS keeps no such statistics on individual schools. But it is useful to compare the poverty index ratings (a figure based, in part, on the number of
students on welfare in a given school, and the number of free lunches the
school distributes) for the Malcolm X Academy, George Washington
Carver, and Owens Elementary School in Briggs. The poverty index was
actually lower at Malcolm X (45.65) than it was at Carver (46.6), and
both were well below that of Owens Elementary (77.9) in Briggs.[55]
Whites who opposed the academy harbored a class-based suspicion that
the academy really was not geared for "high-risk," poor, inner-city black
children at all, that this was just useful rhetoric. Instead, they argued,
the school was catering to an elite core of children from politically well-
connected families in Detroit.[56]

Frances, for example, referred to the cars parked at the academy to
convey her sense of a game of class hypocrisy being played out through
the academy.

> FRANCES: I went over there a few times, and I have never seen so many Mer-
> cedes Benzes in our little neighborhood in my whole life! I counted five of them.
> And Bonnie [the mother of the only white boy at Malcolm X] is sitting there,
> and whispering to me, "You don't know how much these parents make; double
> what you and I make." I said, "Money be damned! Then let them send their
> kids to a private school." . . . They say that they are helping uplift the children
> that need the esteem. These children have far more self-esteem than my children
> probably do because their parents are so militant about . . . They're good in a
> lot of ways; they're sitting there, protecting their young, they want them to
> learn and everything . . . But what about those children whose parents don't
> have the skills within themselves because they're not all there, for whatever
> reason. Those kids are still at risk, and walking the street and they're going to
> end up six feet under, or in jail, whatever. This is what bothers me: They say it
> is such a helping program, for the elite, for the rich, for wealthy, yes it is. For
> those who are the downtrodden and the poor, the single parent, forget it.

It would be a mistake to read her class animosity as only masking
racism, just as it would be misguided to assert that the true basis of her

concern is really just class. The two registers are hopelessly conflated, but they are, too, read simultaneously and with some dexterity by these whites. The transformations facing this neighborhood are complex; the residents' efforts to assess them, although perhaps lacking sophistication, do strive to represent the multiplicity of their concerns, which media representations of the conflict simplified.

Their frustration over both racial and class divides is driven by an emotional intensity that stems from the fact that what is essentially at stake here is their children. Just as Frances respects even the "separatists" for their ability to defend their children's interests, Karen argues that her "jealous" view toward these same parents stems from an emotional core deeper than race prejudice. What stands out about whites in Warrendale is their sense of vulnerability. They are threatened by the classed actions of those both above and below them on the ladder of social status and economic stability. In addition to the vans, the smaller class sizes, and the superior classroom equipment, Karen seethed about how such local institutions as the University of Michigan at Dearborn found it important to support the racially disadvantaged over those who were disadvantaged by class.

> KAREN: That college has been there for as long as I can remember, and not one damn professor ever came to teach any of our kids. But now they've got all of this time to teach these kids. And if I sound jealous, that's just too bad, because my kid deserves just as good as anybody else's kid. Especially when it's in my community, four doors from my house. My kids deserve more than some other kid being bussed in. I live here, I pay taxes here. I pay $1,300 a year.

Karen knew the reasons justifying the need for the Afrocentric academies, and she recognized that on a national or citywide scale, young black males were severely "at risk." But it was an argument that she felt was more easily supported by someone whose children were not competing for the same limited funds in a public school system that was badly overburdened and underfinanced.[57]

"Racist"

"Racist" was applied to any white who opposed either the opening of the Malcolm X Academy in the old Leslie Elementary building or who raised contentious questions about the school's curriculum. The significance of race was so overdetermined in this spectacle that any white in Warrendale seemed susceptible to being marked by the epithet; whites contested "white enclave" exactly because it implied that *all* residents of this zone were racist.[58] Indeed, the "racist" opponents of the academy countercharged that its white supporters were solely motivated by a fear of being labeled "racists" themselves. What proved most frustrating for whites opposing the academy was that an attention to race was largely read as "racist." There seemed to be no neutral language, short of saying nothing at all, through which racial differences and interests could be framed and discussed. The younger whites, brought into the WCO for the first time because of the Malcolm X controversy, were appalled to find debate about the issue curtailed in meetings. Unable to exert control over their statements in the media, they also encountered constraints against speaking about race in their own community group. In contrast to Corktown, where the community was represented by a board of similar-minded people who were able to discuss touchy matters involving race, meetings of the WCO were just another site of conflicting class and generational divides.

An intraracial contest ensued, similar in some respects to the exchanges of "gentrifier" in Corktown—the term was almost exclusively applied to whites, and among whites who were concerned to limit their connection to the category—with one notable difference. The discursive dynamics were thoroughly skewed by the role of the media and the intense scrutiny by people in the city at large. Swift assessments of whether a person was a "racist" were based on comments made in public and recorded by the media. Statements about the academy circulated widely as concretized chunks of sentiment and attitude that served as a repertoire of examples of what counted as racism. This gave greater fixity to "racist" than to the objectification "gentrifier." In part, media images reified identities susceptible to absolute judgments; but also, because people who engaged in this issue were strictly polarized as either for or against the school, there was an emphatic evaluative register for assessing whether someone was a racist.

The class distinctions mobilized in designating certain whites as "racist" are not as sharply evident as in the case of "gentrifier," which clearly conflated white racialness with economic advantage. "Racist" was singularly fixed upon those perceived to be defending a working-class neighborhood against black incursions; the ruptures of an idealized middle-class decorum—a measured calmness or rational detachment ("civility") in matters of public debate—were evident in the loud, emotionally charged protests against the school. But the intraracial work of "racist" was not primarily oriented toward inscribing or enforcing class distinctions. Rather, it was used to delimit which whites would be marked or unmarked in relation to race in this conflict. When whites countered public invocations of "racism" or their designation as "racists," they did so by challenging the terms' policing of what forms of *race-talk* were permissible.[59]

For opponents of the academy a central question in the drama was whether or not their motives were racial. They struggled with reporters, station managers, and parents at the school to distinguish their concerns and frustrations from base racial motivations. They tried to avoid "sounding racial," but at the same time, they did not feel that they were hiding racist impulses. Whites who supported the academy refused to see a distinction, and repeatedly insisted that claims of being "not racist" were merely "smoke screens" over true, core values. In this contest, as in many such public conflicts over limited civic resources, there was no more sophisticated set of terms for evaluating nuances of these racial matters than the caustic, charged designation of "racist." The term inscribed an interesting demarcation in terms of the significance of white racialness: "Racists" were viewed as having only racial motivation, whereas the racialness of whites who either eluded or hurled the epithet went unexamined and remained relatively unmarked. As the previous section showed, whites on either side of this demarcation actually had a great deal in common. Notably, they mobilized the same interpretive repertoire in assessing charges of racism and deployed a common topography of the self by which statements or emotional outbursts were to be judged as "racist" or not. [60] They all looked either to a person's social context or their "heart" for factors that might qualify or disprove this determination.

The media coverage of the controversy ratified the conviction that "racism" was evidenced in succinct, often fragmentary, statements. Reporters rendered the comments of residents as self-evident objects in a limited economy of examples. When whites like Karen talked about their representations, they inevitably invoked what reporters (either willfully or negligently) missed or discarded—the lengthy commentaries or extended narratives produced in response to questions about the academy. There was an abiding belief among opponents of the academy that an understanding of their social contexts would undermine charges of racism. The nuances of past and present relations with blacks, their manifest ability to be around blacks and not ostensibly treat them as an embodiment of cultural or ontological difference, proved to themselves that they were not "racists." Karen appealed to this register to counter the charges that she was a racist: "I was raised seven houses from the Herman Gardens Apartments [a low-income housing project built in the 1940s] which has been black since the '60s. My next-door neighbor was black. The guy across the street was black. I went to Herman Elementary [which was over 75 percent black]! I have been with blacks since I was four years old. So I don't need anybody coming in that don't know me, telling me that I'm racist and I'm complaining because . . . or I'm afraid of little black children being four doors from my house." She made this comment in response to a quote attributed to her in an article published before the

community meeting with Dr. McGriff.[61] Karen insisted that she was mis-
quoted in a *Free Press* report that had her saying, "I don't know enough
about black people to know whether they would accept a little white
kid." Karen insisted to me that she had specified "*these* black people . . .
when I say that, I mean the people who are for Malcolm X. I don't mean
'blacks,' I mean whoever is for Malcolm X." Her enduring concern, after
all, was with the Afrocentric curriculum at the academy and the intentions of its promoters. She recognized an ideological distinction between
proponents of Afrocentric approaches to education and blacks in general,
a distinction that was easily lost in the crossfire of rhetorical absolutes
drawn in black and white.

Opponents also felt that considering a person's "heart" was the only
sure way of judging whether they were "racist." This insistence neatly
reversed the journalists' and school officials' mode of reading emotionality—for them, excess signaled a purity of intent. The emotions evident
when someone's "heart" was involved were read by local whites as either
emphatic evidence or a mitigating factor in designations of "racist."
Kevin appealed to this register when he countered his marking by this
objectification. "That's probably why I was the one picked to go on the
first TV show, because I was the one standing out there, yelling and doing
all of the talking, and everybody else would talk, but when it came time
for them to talk to a producer of the show, or a TV camera, people
weren't saying . . . they were trying to say it too nice. And my opinion
was . . . I'm not running for political office. Somebody isn't going to like
what I say no matter how nice I say it. So too bad. Maybe it's because my
heart was involved in it. This is a community I've been involved in all of
my life."

Kevin's sense that other whites "were trying to say it too nice" references the perception that a prevailing decorum determined how racial
matters could be articulated and addressed. In breaking this decorum,
"yelling and doing all the talking," he is drawn into the media production
of emotional statements, demonstrating unalloyed "racism." Rupturing
this formal etiquette was hardly an intentional matter, since his "heart
was involved." As with Karen and her neighbors—"pouring out" their
hearts to the TV crew—white opponents' emotionality stemmed from
frustrations over the implicit class and racial designations that outsiders
saw as obvious.[62] For most observers this emotionality signified only
racism, but opponents contextualized outbursts either as products of
media manipulations (as in the last section) or as signifying a broader set
of concerns over their children's place in the city's changing institutions.

Interestingly, school supporters willingly allowed both "heart" and a
broad sense of social context as mitigating factors in judging "racists";
but they refused to grant these specifically to people like Kevin, Karen,

and Jeff. Although allowances could be made for unsophisticated ethnic whites, some whites still had to be subject to categorical judgments. Yvonne, explaining how some of the long-time Polish residents held opinions that were now "out of fashion," offered a qualification for certain statements that might be construed as "racist" by casual observers.

> We have people who . . . this is the ideas that they grew up. This is the ideas they tried to . . . that they taught their children, but as their children got older they saw that it was different. And yeah, you're going to hear comments of "I'm glad I don't have blacks living next door to me." But if a black family moved in, there would be acceptance there. They want to believe that they wouldn't like it, but overall, there is a general feeling of acceptance. But the media wouldn't print any of that. All they printed was the blatantly racist comments. And anything that was either neutral or good, they wouldn't even print it, or they printed such a small excerpt of it that it wasn't even worth it. They turned everything around to the way they wanted the story to be heard.

She went on to deploy a distinction between interior physical locations of racism as in either the heart or the head. The topography of the self that Yvonne deploys is mobile enough to read class distinctions between whites in her neighborhood and those in the suburbs. She suggested that in one-on-one situations in Warrendale, there would be acceptance for blacks, "where in Dearborn, it would not be—plain and simple. I mean the opportunity would never be presented there. In Dearborn, you have people . . . I guess the best way to put it is that in Dearborn . . . You've got white people in Dearborn who deep down in their hearts believe that they are upper! middle! class! and they! are! better! [bangs the table for emphasis on each word]. In Warrendale, you have people who think they are, but they don't have it in their hearts, because deep down inside, if it came down to, 'could I accept . . . a person of a different race living next door to me?' yes they could. In Dearborn, that would never become a factor because that would not ever be allowed. On one hand you have people who believe they are, and on the other hand you have people who think they are, but have more heart to them."

Paul, too, suggested that class differences were key in understanding whether or not comments or sentiments were truly racial. He also contrasted older, predominantly Polish residents with suburban whites.

> I compare it to Royal Oak, the little more upscale, more upper-middle-class [areas], like Farmington. I think that there is more of a class difference. And the first difference I'd say, is that I think that, the people in this neighborhood, I actually, uh . . . I don't know how to word this, but, I almost have more respect for their racism. Not that I respect racism at all. But because they do live in the city, they do have face-to-face contact all the time. And a lot of people who will

say racist things, will have black friends! And they'll always say, "Well not Joe," or "Not so-and-so." But all blacks are bad, except for the ones that I know. It's always that kind of, y'know, . . . or, a lot of their racism, they'll tell . . . it will come from experiences that they've had. Even though they mis-interpreted those experiences, and turned it into a racial thing. They HAVE maybe been robbed, or, y'know, had bad experiences with black people. Then they just fell into the trap of simplifying that along racial lines, y'know. But at least they come from somewhere. Where I find, ah . . . like a good friend who was brought up in Birmingham who never saw a black person until he was out of high school. You can actually live that sheltered. And so many of those people, you get out so far from reality, and their racism is based completely on media. It's completely a mental conjecture that has no connection with reality or experience or anything. And what bothers me more about that racism is, it is often so couched in liberal intellectual language; they'll always . . . they're always so good at sounding not racist.

He went on to talk about his political experiences in Ann Arbor, how the white students there were so enthusiastic about challenging the univer-sity's investments in South Africa or forming solidarity politics with Cen-tral American groups, yet they ignored or remained oblivious to the urban crisis in Detroit. "And here's Detroit, fifty miles away with an in-fant mortality rate that's higher than Haiti's. And no one ever talked about that."

In this lengthy evaluation, Paul elaborated on how the appearance of racism can be deceptive or at least involve a disjuncture from a deeper reality or potential that lies latent within seemingly racist whites in the neighborhood. He allowed this for these whites because of their context. But the basis for such an allowance on his part seems to be a denial of contextualizing possibilities to opponents of the academy in Warrendale, whose statements and actions he read in an absolute register. Paul re-mained convinced that their efforts at trying to not sound racist were merely "smoke screens." In particular, he charged that "Jeff and com-pany try to get whites to follow their racist agenda by cloaking it in some-thing that at least looks not racist, the religion issue or something."

The "religion issue" was a serious matter for "Jeff and company"—many whites in this heavily Catholic neighborhood detected religious symbolism in the academy's curriculum and asserted that such symbols had been barred by the state for use in public schools (see the next sec-tion).[63] But it was hard for a secular-oriented white like Paul to under-stand this, especially since he assumed that any white opposing the academy must be a "racist." Paul's and Yvonne's discriminating uses of "racist" involve ethnicity and class, just as in Corktown, but with a con-trasting orientation. They juxtaposed the surface appearances of whites in Warrendale with those of higher-class status in the suburbs, stressing that the impression of racism in their neighborhood, while easier to objectify for the media since it resonates with images of blue-collar racism, is deceptive. Suburban whites manage appearances in such a way that they never have to express the racist interests that have informed their racially exclusive zones. But if exceptions were to be made for some of the clearly classed whites of Warrendale, then others had to be regarded with no ambiguity concerning their "racism."[64] Mediated statements allowed Yvonne and Paul to make absolute judgments about "racist" supporters of the academy. Not surprisingly, "racists" evaluated their objectified comments—again, relying upon the same repertoire of mitigating factors—and found ambiguity where other whites recognized only unequivocal expressions of racism.

Opponents of the school recognized a range of valences in racial statements; comments like "what about the white kids?" were treated as the products of certain "heated" contexts—their contents, hence, ambivalent. On the one hand, no derogatory sentiment is implied or intended; on the other, there is an explicit assertion of white racial interests. At the core of this statement, opponents heard an emotional concern voiced about neighborhood children. Whites like Frances tried to contextualize their emotion to counter the charge of racism. As Frances was trying to convey why the initial informational meeting got so out of hand, she contrasted the emotional anger of residents with racist rage. I asked her how she distinguished these.

> I think a lot of it was, like at that first meeting. Joyce stood up, and it wasn't a racist statement, but it could be construed as such. It was after they had said "Well we need this for OUR children, this and that." And then Joyce stood up and said, "What about the white children?" And I mean, that could be taken like a racist remark, but it's like, it wasn't racist in the sense that, "Hey, don't play race against race. Our kids should all grow up together." I mean . . . this is where you're getting a more separatist society, because of these people. But, that's the thing, you can take that both ways. If I were a black, I would probably take that as a racist statement. But I had a black person sitting next to me during the whole thing, and it turned out she was a reporter.

She told me that this reporter did not seem to take offense at Joyce's statement, though other blacks in the audience reacted angrily. To Frances, this just proved that the matter of racism was less clear-cut than many people involved wanted to believe. Although she acknowledged that Joyce's statement was racially interested, Frances felt that the rhetorical context, in which speakers relied upon a racial idiom, demonstrated that the expression was not racist in nature. But taken out of context and flashed across the next day's newspapers, the statement seemed obviously racist. Joyce, like Kevin and others, were specifying race in relation to whites in certain ways that echoed the race-specific language of the Afrocentrists they countered; they assumed, though, that racism was not unambiguous, that it formed a continuum depending on degrees of racial interest.

Viewing "racist" as a matter of gradation placed them in an interesting posture in relation to this label. Karen, Joyce, and Frances did not categorically deny the possibility that they were to some degree racist; they were each willing, at times, to admit as much. They did not nervously elude the label the way that whites in Corktown skirted the marking "gentrifier"; nor did they discretely refer to "the r-word." What they objected to was the way the term's usage limited their ability to express broader concerns about the school and the curriculum. They did not mind the contaminating marking as much as they were frustrated by the rhetorical limits "racist" brought with it, reinscribing blacks and whites as qualitatively different orders.[65] Although, they argued emotionally that their opposition to the school was not primarily inspired by racist motivations, what upset them just as much was the tenet maintaining that blacks could not be racist. They heard this stance very strongly voiced in a workshop on racism sponsored by St. Thomas Aquinas Church during the controversy.

> DIANA: It was a workshop on "What is racism?" and how do you deal with it. And we were invited to it because we were former CPW [Concerned People of Warrendale] members.
>
> JH: So what were they asking you to do?
>
> DIANA: Just to understand why racism exists.
>
> JOYCE: In the mission statement they [St. Thomas Aquinas] came up with at the first meeting, one of the statements was "to educate ourselves on racism" so . . .
>
> JEFF: Well they were trying to tell us that since we're white, we're racist.
>
> DIANA: And black people are not racist, they're . . .
>
> JEFF: And black people CANNOT be racist!

Mickey Troutman, one of the organizers of this workshop, summed up this reasoning by noting that this definition of racism stresses the structural aspect of historical privileges and power relations that support whiteness. She explains, "My impression of racism is that only whites can be racists. I don't believe that you can have reverse racism because only people who are in power . . . it's the people who are in power. You can have prejudice, and you can have bigotry, but racism is different than both of those. Racism is a system that excludes . . . other people from that system. . . . How can the people who don't have power be racist?" Victor

Gibson, who acted as a press secretary for the Malcolm X Academy and attended some of the informational community meetings, was of a similar opinion. "Whenever a white person calls a black person a racist, it lets me know the level that they're thinking on, the level they're functioning on, because they really don't know. I might be a bigot, I can be prejudiced. But I can never be a racist . . . Because the power's not there. And without power you can only be a petty bigot at best."

In contesting the charge of "racism," these whites implicitly confronted this evaluative criterion and the way this definition of "racist" circumscribed how they could talk about race. They put as much effort into insisting that blacks, too, could be "racists" as they did in avoiding the ascription themselves. The language and the issues linked to the academy were relentlessly racial, but "racist" implied that their attention to the racial stakes in this debate was illicit and ignorant; also, that they were the only racially motivated actors. Whether or not they believed the academy's curriculum featured "racist" teachings, or was assembled by "racist" black nationalists, white opponents of the school wanted to draw attention to the way the Afrocentric curriculum was explicitly geared to foster and enhance a sense of racial identity. In their insistence that "these" blacks were "racists" whites tried to objectify the conjunction between race and power in the dynamic over opening the academy.

The matter of scale is crucially important in characterizing connections between powerful positions and racialness, and there were conflicting scales at work in this dispute. Residents' appeals for context generally stressed the personal realm of their lives in this neighborhood; black school officials saw context as a matter of citywide politics—defined by the profound demographic shift in Detroit—or in a national scale of events that placed Warrendale in the history of white resistance to black inroads in the education system, and as part of the long tradition of white supremacist oppression. Whites in Warrendale argued that blacks, indeed, did have power and were capable of using it in racially interested ways; this extended or repositioned rather than discounted the interpretive scale that black school officials relied upon. The personal scale of events stressed by Warrendale whites, required that race not be treated through categorical abstractions oriented primarily toward the past or the nation's racial formation, but through more open-ended recognition of the rapid reconfiguration of the racial power structure in 1990s Detroit.

The absolute negation of a connection between black positions and racism, these whites asserted, failed to acknowledge that "race" could be a matter of manipulation no matter what color characterized social or political positions. Although white opponents of the school were cognizant of the fact that as a demographic aggregate blacks are socially and politically disadvantaged, they could not easily contend with the way that the local, powerful position of black school officials did not provoke a more nuanced reading of this situation. As Bonnie described earlier, at school board meetings opponents encountered vocal assertion of racial claims to political dominance, such as, "It's our turn now." Diana complained about the racial speech that she had heard on the "black talk shows." "I hear callers all the time saying, 'We've got to keep the [city] council black! We've got to keep the council black.' But can you imagine the reaction if I called in and said we've got to keep the council white? 'We've got to keep it black, that's where the power is.' That's what they say." Frances described comments made at school board meetings as "an example of black supremacy" comparable to the positions expressed by white separatists that she lived around in the 1960s and 1970s. "The attitude I got from several people that I had talked to was, 'You have to understand, we tried it your way in the '50s and '60s, and everything like that, and you were brought up in a Eurocentric education. Now we are the majority, we are 75 percent of the city, and therefore you do it our way or no way.'"

Whites cited this type of statement to call attention to the ability of blacks to wield power in a racially interested and effective manner, but also to convey their experience of being racialized in relation to these powerful assertions. Their critical comparisons regarding how the "same" statement would be received differently when voiced by speakers of different races both challenged the decorum relating to public discourse on race and indexed their relative lack of political power in this situation.[66] Diana's question highlights the racial reconfiguration of the political landscape in Detroit, as well as asserting that the ability of whites to speak about the conjunction of power and interests they observed in the actions of black school officials was cut off. But, additionally, each of these women conveys a sense of experiencing simultaneously racial objectification and exclusion in relation to statements made by blacks during this controversy. "Its our turn now" and "you do it our way or no way" linked the significance of their white racialness to the passing era of white domination in Detroit; it was not clear how or whether they belonged in the new racial order in the city. Whatever their personal opinions, and quite apart from any claims they might make regarding the significance of race, these whites could not escape being racially objectified by the power discourse that they heard blacks speaking, both in terms of the curriculum itself and its justification by backers of the academy. In such objectifications, these whites felt the relevance of their personal opinions and their past experiences dissolving.

Their criticisms of the public discourse on race, however, were not solely tuned to the decorum that shaped interracial exchanges. They also challenged the selective listening habits of whites generally when the subject of "race" arises. The comments cited here were gleaned from sources—from radio talk shows to school board meetings—that many white Detroiters ignore or avoid; they could not get other whites to comprehend what they heard in these forums. Furthermore, Warrendale residents in general were frustrated with an inability on the part of the media to narrate a different story about race, one that took into account the nuances of their situation. Paul described his repeated efforts to get reporters and editors to expand their coverage of the controversy.

> The community organization joined in welcoming the academy, all of our churches, there were two large prayer vigils, and we had over one hundred white residents at each of them. [St. Thomas Aquinas and United Brethren sponsored them.] The media didn't touch those. At all. It should've been like, "LOOK! This splits the mold. This is what people need to see." And all of the community institutions, all of the community leaders have supported the academy. It's just a few people who . . . in no way represent the community, but have been making all the noise and getting all of the attention. And the media knows that. But they chose . . . they don't know how to make a story out of that.

Paul's complaint that "they don't know how to make a story out of that" was shared among supporters and opponents of the academy. Residents were cynically aware that established narrative requirements for racial conflict entailed polarized, angry voices, drawn in stark tones of black and white with no gray scale of nuanced shadows, resonances, and subtle voicings. Despite this awareness of how racial markings and comments work in media representations, "racist" whites were not interested in restraining their more heated and emotional comments, and they derided people who "were trying to say it too nice." They insisted that "race" be complex and multivalent, irreducible to absolute demarcations like "racist," which allowed everybody else to speak confidently from a space removed from racial interest.

What upset them most was dissembling on matters of race and the fear their white neighbors held of being labeled a "racist." I asked Frances if she found herself policing her comments now, to make sure that they did not "sound racial." "Not really. Not really. People know me for who I am. I have never sat there and hidden what I do, or who I am." She referred to an earlier point in our conversation when she had been talking about a black friend who lived in Warrendale. "I never said to myself, I can't say this because she's black. I talk with her one-on-one. I mean, we

all know that racism exists, and it's in both of us. But . . . I just don't sit
there examining my words . . . If I had to examine all of my words before
I spoke, I would still be waiting to talk. If . . . the way I feel about it is, if
people can't accept me for what I am doing, my actions speak louder than
my words. That's the bottom line right there." I asked her if she thought
there were people in WCO who would not talk about race for fear of
sounding racist.[67]

> Oh, I think so. I think so. If they're scared . . . if they're scared that if they say
> something it will come off as being racist, and a lot of people are more comfort-
> able saying nothing than saying something because of the situation, that it
> might be taken derogatorily. Like Yvonne . . . She has come across with some
> very derogatory remarks . . . towards us, which I found offensive . . . I was
> sitting there and I told her that I could not support welcoming the school into
> the community because we had voted against it as a group [CPW]. And she
> stood there and stated that I was a racist in front of thirty of my friends. And
> I stated, 'Number one, you don't know me. I can't support the school, and I
> have reasons for that. And if you don't feel that my reasons are valid or legiti-
> mate, that's your personal problem. I'm not going to stand here and be called
> a racist. Have a nice day,' and I walked out of Joyce's basement and quit.

But where white opponents of the academy recognized a profusion of
similarities and resemblances obscuring the starkness of racial positions
and identities, the label "racist" obliterated all of this and severed any
sense of commonality. Across this charged inscription, few perceptions
were held in common: The meeting that Frances refers to above was described quite differently by other whites who had been there; their versions convey the divide that "racist" inscribed.

When it became clear that the WCO was not going to provide a forum
for articulating their concerns about the school, Joyce and another Warrendale woman, Chris Martinez, organized a new community group,
Concerned People of Warrendale (CPW). For a few weeks, this group
provided the primary means by which opposition to the school was organized. The group lost all but a few of its members after a vote on a contentious and confusing proposal to welcome the students at Malcolm X
while still contesting the academy. This proposal was raised in response
to the negative images of whites in Warrendale that dominated the media
coverage. (The organization was later taken over by Paul and now functions as a means of countering "racists" in Warrendale).

Yvonne described the meeting of CPW on the night of the vote over
expressing support for the students. "I sat there, and I heard Karen, Joyce,
and one other person, it may have been Frances or it might've been Bonnie. But I sat there and I heard three or four women sit there, and come

straight out and say 'I do not want a nigger school in this neighborhood, and I will not stop until it is gone.' So they can sit there and say all they want that it's not a racial issue and that they're not racists. I heard it myself, I heard it myself."

Karen, Joyce, Frances, and Diana remembered the same meeting quite differently. When I asked Karen about that night, she responded to Yvonne's assertions by saying, "She's a damned liar. She's a liar and you can call her back and tell her I told her that. Tell her she can call me if she wants to talk about it. But she is a damned liar, because I did not say anything about 'nigger school' or even used the word 'nigger,' and I'm the worst one of the bunch. I'm probably the most prejudiced person in that group, but I didn't use that word. And I'm the one that's had a gun held to my head, and I'm the one whose mother was knocked down and beat up for her purse. So sure, I'm prejudiced, but I didn't say anything about 'nigger schools.' It's a black academy, and if I talked about it, I said, 'black school.' "

As we talked, she grew increasingly furious over Yvonne's version of events. Karen was convinced that Yvonne made the claim because she had already decided that Karen and the rest of the residents there were racists. "If she heard 'nigger' it's because she came to that meeting with the notion already in her head that we were just a bunch of racists. If I was comparing the two [schools] and said black and she heard 'nigger,' that's her problem, because you can call Joyce and you can call Diana or anybody else that was there, and they will tell you that not only did I not say 'nigger,' nobody else did either." Diana also insisted that the word "nigger" was never used. She explained that people were furious and demanded to know why the school "had to be for black kids," but "nobody used the word 'nigger.' " Karen said that Yvonne kept saying all the "reasons" were "smoke screens" to hide the racism, but she was opposed to the use of taxpayer funds for teaching what she considered to be a religion. "If it was a religious school, I wouldn't care. If it's a Detroit public school, then I'm going to keep bitching." She felt that Yvonne accused her of saying "nigger" because she was so vocal in her opposition to the academy. "She said that because I was a little bit more outspoken than all the rest. But I did not want that academy here! No way! I wanted it gone, out of there, get it out of there. I didn't want that school here at all."

Yvonne gave this account of the meeting:

I sat there, and I was listening. I was there mainly as an observer, not a participant, but an observer. But it got to the point where I sat there and I said, "Excuse me one moment, but I've been sitting here listening to you people, not as a Warrendale resident . . . I've been trying to keep myself totally and completely . . . y'know, just listening. And I've been sitting here with the mentality that I am just a person who doesn't really reside anywhere." And I told them, "I'm going to tell all of you right now, you sound very very very racial. And if this is going to be the mode of the organization, I'm going back to the WCO and I'm going to tell them that, no, we have no business supporting the formation of this organization, because it is based on racism." And I got told that "I am not a racist!" "That school and that curriculum is not geared for a white child!" And I was like, "What is wrong with your 'white child' learning that there were more people than Caucasians that contributed to civilization as a group?" Why should kids have to wait until they get into college to learn history a little bit differently? All they ever learn about is the white contributions to civilization. History is learning about how we got to the point where we are today. And without putting that . . . that . . . multicultural thing in there, that civilization grew because of the contributions of all of these people and all of these races, without them knowing that . . . from the onset, I think that that also doesn't help the racial situation at all. I mean, we're supposed to learn by our mistakes . . . and if our children . . . I mean, face it, our forefathers did not do everything 100 percent correctly. And if, as children, they don't learn about the mistakes that were made, if they don't learn that . . . Yeah these were all great people. They did make mistakes, but we learn from those mistakes. And we try not to do that sort of thing again. And if they don't learn that from the get go, then how are we supposed to ever hope that we are going to have a harmonious plane?"

In this dense version, Yvonne maneuvers through interesting terrain. She begins by invoking a context-free perspective as "a person who doesn't really reside anywhere." This "observer" position allows her to see the racism of her neighbors. What she hears about is the "white child"; she does not hear what they think is wrong about the curriculum. Her view, too, of the "multicultural thing" is quite amorphous compared to opponents of the academy, as will be seen in the last section. But it is her version of history that I think is most revealing of how the perceptual divide operates between "racists" and other whites in Warrendale, especially in relation to the possibility that "race relations" will ever be resolved on a "harmonious plane."

For Karen, this possibility depends upon whites and blacks being able to talk openly about race and racial interests, and to recognize that this talk is distinct from racial name-calling.[68] She explained this after I had asked her, "Given that you call yourself the worst of the bunch regarding prejudice, why do you feel it matters not to say 'nigger'?"

Because these are kids—they're just kids, and I don't have anything against them. They are not grown men beating up a woman even after they got her purse. These are just kids. It's not the fact that they're black that bothers me, it's what they're teaching the kids. They're teaching them not about equality, but about how they're better than everybody else. And they're teaching hatred for the whites. They keep telling them the whites did this to you, the whites did this to you. Look, ALL children need to learn about what happened. It was a holocaust or whatever you want to call it. As bad as you want to put it, it was . . . And there's no excuse for it, not slavery, not none of it. But there was a president who set the slaves free, and that was a long time ago. And you have to teach them that it's been a long struggle, and it's been vicious, and many hurtful things have happened, but you have the power within yourself to make things different. They shouldn't be teaching them that "The whites are still oppressing you, so don't shop at white stores, don't go to white banks, don't work with whites." And they shouldn't be teaching them that whites are the devil, or all that about melanin, and how they're not equal with everyone else, they're better than everyone, because they've got more melanin.

It is interesting to consider which woman's reflections on the past crimes of the white race are more compelling: Yvonne's acknowledgment that "our forefathers did not do everything 100 percent correctly" or Karen's sense that slavery represented a "holocaust," and that the intervening years have involved "a long struggle, and it's been vicious, and many hurtful things have happened." They were two white women living mere blocks from each other in the same neighborhood but, based on their distinct personal histories, they had very little in common in relation to white racialness. Yvonne grew up on the southwest side of Detroit in an area that is predominantly white and Hispanic; to this day there are still few blacks living in that part of the city. She did not attend the Detroit public schools in their tumultuous period. Her father was a supervisor in the post office. As a civil servant, she told me, he was positioned favorably along a critical cusp; he got his promotion before affirmative action was established. Rather than being subjected to it directly, he had to enforce the policy, which Yvonne refers to now as "a good concept gone bad." When she looked at the statements of whites like Karen, duplicity was all she recognized, even when they spoke out against the curriculum or were concerned about overcrowding at Carver or the meddling of the state with religion in the public schools.

> YVONNE: I think they were grasping at . . . at . . . some kind of smoke screen to cover up that initial racist feeling.
> JH: And where do you think that initial experience was coming from for them? Was it from experience, was it generational . . .
> YVONNE: Generational, definitely. It's like I said, it's just a generational thing. Taking a look, again, at living on the border . . . uh . . . growing up with what they've been taught by their parents, being in an ivory area and not really having any experience with black kids, and the experience they did have of

black kids was when they went to Cody High School, and again, because you have that imaginary line, ah . . . I think a lot of Cody's problems are . . . the fact that you have that racial line, you have black kids who don't understand white kids because they're not in a racially balanced, mixed area. And you've got kids from here that are not in that racially balanced area, and you constantly have that conflict. You've got black kids going to Cody High School . . . whose parents are telling them that white people feel that they're superior, because they don't know any better. And you've got white kids whose parents are telling them all black people are bad, therefore you're going to have a bad experience.

In this description, Yvonne explains her sense of how white children in Warrendale grew up. She might be on target if the child in question was a young Kevin, but she misses the complexity of Karen's different experience of racial animosity in her childhood across the Southfield freeway:

Well, for me, my problem started . . . Like I said, I went to Herman and grew up with black people and had no problem! Went to Ruddimen, still mixed, 75/25, 75 black, no problem. Then bussing started. Somehow, they scooped me up, me and two of my girlfriends [one of whom was Bonnie] and put us on a bus with all black and bussed us to Lessenger, all white. And . . . all of my friends, that had been my friends since first grade . . . now I was "whitey." 'Cause they had such an attitude going to this new school. All the whites in this school were afraid 'cause they had never been around blacks. They didn't bother me, because I grew up with them. But then, now, see, I was in it. I've seen my friends change, my black friends change. It was total aggression towards the white kids—Total!

JH: Like as soon as they got there?

KAREN: It's like "I'M SUPERIOR, I'M GONNA BEAT YOUR ASS!" and they were going after whitey. And then, my girlfriends, and people that I had known for years . . . I got lumped in with the new white people even though I'm on the bus every day with the people I grew up with. I'm now white! It's like, all of the sudden they woke up: "Karen Soper's white! Beat her ass!" But I wasn't a quiet person that was going to let you beat my ass. [Diana and Kevin laugh] So I fought right back with them. And then they left me alone. But then, when I started meeting white people, started hanging around with them, it wasn't that I didn't like the black friends any more . . . so black friends turned on me! I was now white. I was one of them, I was the enemy. And I'd seen it; it wasn't all in my head. Y'know, you don't go home, people stomping on you for being in your head.

JH: Had you thought about being white before that?

KAREN: Well, it's like I said, we just all hung around together, and it was a peaceful coexistence. . . . But somehow when we got to the white school, all at once, it mattered. I was white . . . and they didn't want to have anything to do with me after that. Everybody went their own clichés [sic] then, it wasn't groups here and groups there. It was whites here and blacks there. And that was around teenage years, when you did start changing and all that.

Yvonne's explanation for white attitudes also does not take into account situations like the one Frances was raised in, watching her neighborhood change from "all white" to "all black." Frances attended a meeting for parents at Malcolm X; one of her black neighborhood friends invited her to come. The meeting turned hostile quickly because of Frances's presence, and she felt herself thoroughly racialized by the other parents.[69] But she stressed that this experience was distinct from the way she had been racialized in her old neighborhood.

I said, "If I don't go, I am basically saying, I don't give a care, I don't have an open mind." I said, maybe I will find out something that will change our point of view . . . But I wasn't given a chance. It was basically, "You are white, you don't believe in this curriculum, therefore you are scum and you are going to hurt our children." Which is about the same as saying that uh . . . if a person doesn't believe in something that I believe, and they're black, therefore, they're scum and they're going to hurt me, and stuff like that [she verged on tears, for the second time in our conversation]. It just doesn't work like that. You can't judgmentalize people.

JH: Did you feel yourself as white as you might have in your old neighborhood?

FRANCES: I never felt as aware of my color as I did when I lived in a black neighborhood. I was very conscious of the fact that I stuck out. There would be little remarks, racial ones.

JH: Would those come from the kids, or the adults?

FRANCES: More from the kids and from the ones in their twenties, the black males. Sexual stuff, y'know.

Whether or not Karen or Frances was "racist" seems to be a simplistic question in comparison to the matter of how they were first racialized and, subsequently, how they attempted to negotiate this racial discourse. But in the heated exchange between white supporters and opponents of the school, "racists" were people who lost or were denied all context, whose mediating circumstances dissolved as their statements were objectified. Often what wiped out an attention to context was the loudness and the uncouthness with which "racists" made their opinions known. In this matter, a clear class division might not have been apparent, but classed distinctions were active in the decorums around race that these "racists" ruptured. This was a point that Joyce stressed. After asking Diana about the comments Yvonne alleged that Karen and others had made about "nigger schools," I checked with Joyce for her recollection of that

meeting. She largely conceded Yvonne's version, though Joyce disputed
her assertion that she had said "nigger." "Yes, there probably were some
racist comments made there. We lost a lot of people that meeting. People
were taking it bad and they were angry. We lost a lot of members at that
meeting because people thought that we were voting to just welcome the
school—they didn't realize we were just talking about the children."

After reflection, she recalled that Karen "most likely" said the line
about not wanting a "nigger school." I asked Joyce what her opinion was
of Yvonne's response, walking away from the group because its demands
sounded "very very very racial," and her decision to avoid dealing with
such "racist" whites. After a long pause, she said,

> I think we're all racists—everybody. It's like poor people display it more than
> others, but everybody has a bit of racism in them. Everybody. Nobody I know
> minds things being equal—that's good. But it seems like blacks don't want to
> just be equal anymore, they want to be better than everybody else. People were
> mad because of the way the black kids were getting treated as better than every-
> body else. They're getting better classrooms, better technology, better teachers
> and better materials, then here comes this black school. So people were mad
> about that, y'know, "What about the white kids?" When you're mad, you say
> a lot of things—it just comes up because you're furious that your kid's not
> getting as good as the other kids. Who you're mad at just so happens to be the
> other race, that's all.

"Racists" in Warrendale insisted that their motives, interests, and intentions were based on a contextual view of their particular position in
Detroit and in the nation's shifting political and economic orders. They
were called "racists" by whites who considered their opposition to the
academy to be motivated solely by ignorance, hatred, and fear. Of the
many ways of distinguishing these whites, one telling difference lies in
their distinct senses of the effects of "face-to-face" exchanges between
whites and blacks. Paul and Yvonne spoke in hypotheticals, confident
that the ostensible racist sentiments of older or ethnic white residents
would evaporate in face-to-face encounters, of, say, blacks moving into
the neighborhood; a future of race-neutral exchanges was waiting to be
grasped. Kevin, Karen, and other opponents reflected on their personal
experiences of interracial settings; these had always been uneven, there
had always been a disadvantaged minority, and the violent history of
such contacts in Detroit weighed against the possibility of race ever not
mattering, politically and socially. For the "racists" there was no space
apart from the politicized, historical ground, across which inevitably unequal power relations were shifting and changing rapidly; race would
continue to be a means of manipulating the city's limited resources, and
could never be treated hypothetically or simply willed away.

Curriculum

The local political aspects of this clash—the contest over uses of a neighborhood school and the citywide debate about "empowered" schools—were riven by a matter that distorted and undercut the frames of reference familiar to white residents. Long after the academy's opening made these local issues moot, the school's Afrocentric curriculum remained an elusive, haunting concern for white supporters and opponents—elusive because school officials were reticent on this question; haunting because engaging this subject led whites into a disorienting, powerful assemblage of racial imagery and narratives. Afrocentrism, a molten, formative array of assertions, claims, facts, and theories more evocative than established, confronted white residents as a bewildering perspective that challenged, threatened, and certainly racialized "whites," whether or not they contested the academy directly.[70]

The dispute over the school arose from procedural problems and a lack of communication between the Board of Education and Warrendale residents, a matter board members both acknowledged and apologized for. Yet initial questions raised by whites about the curriculum largely remained unanswered months later, leaving concerned parents to undertake their own research on what an Afrocentric curriculum entailed. Sources of information were plentiful on the broad subject of Afrocentrism: whites listening in to WDTR and WCHB heard "melanin scholars" and advocates of African-centered curriculums discuss and lecture on the connections between melanin and intelligence or cultural superiority; a handful of white opponents bought books from the Shrine of the Black Madonna that championed the black nationalists' goals of establishing a separate country for blacks in the southern United States. But the matter of what exactly was being taught at the school remained a mystery to residents.[71]

The curriculum and other aspects of the academy were never clear for me, either. Despite my repeated attempts to arrange interviews with school officials, it was not until the end of February 1994, when Victor Gibson, an employee at the academy assigned the task of dealing with the press, made time to talk with me. In our interview, he avoided specifics, stressing that the curriculum was still being developed and in an experimental stage. At the time, the "African-Centered Education" program, which the DPS planned to infuse into all of its schools, was still under development.[72] Our brief exchange was too slight a basis for me to gauge how accurately white residents' view of the Afrocentric curriculum reflected what was actually being taught at the academy. But I relate their disparate impressions and concerns here because they offer a final, critical glimpse of how white racialness matters. The curriculum provided a screen of sorts on which whites' anxieties and fascinations were projected. Discussions of the curriculum also convey a sharp contrast in the forms of engagement that characterized supporters' and opponents' reaction to the blackness of this school and its goals. For all of their stigmatization in the media and in debates in the neighborhood, the white "racists" were thoroughly immersed in the issues raised by Afrocentrism; conversely, supporters' opinions and comments on the school's curriculum revealed a troubling perspective on race.

The initial neighborhood meeting on the Malcolm X academy, led by Dr. McGriff, provided most white residents with their first glimpse of an Afrocentric worldview; they were largely disturbed and confused by her presentation. This meeting, which generated the first ugly media images of white "racists" for the city at large, also jolted many Warrendale residents with a stark recognition of how much things have changed in Detroit over the last twenty years. I asked Joyce and Bonnie what they thought of that meeting.

> JOYCE: I don't think it was all that hostile. I think that they should've expected something. They dropped a bomb on a neighborhood. Here the head lady is coming . . . we don't feel she answered our questions. What did they expect?
>
> BONNIE: What didn't go good was that she started out her speech with this thing about how they needed this Afrocentric education and how we all evolved from one human being in Africa, and she was going on and on about this, which, y'know, disturbed the people in the audience. . . .
>
> DIANA: It's time to start teaching the TRUTH!
>
> BONNIE: Well then this isn't for our children, if it all centers around black culture. So that's where that it came in, "Well I didn't come from Africa," or I can remember Karen standing up and screaming, "I came from Eve" [Joyce and Diana laugh].
>
> BONNIE: Y'know, like that, because of the way that she started out, "We're going to teach the truth [bitter voice]!"
>
> DIANA: And she also made the statement that "We are coming and there is nothing you can do to stop from us coming!"
>
> JOYCE: Meaning that all of the black children have been basically set aside . . . They're in jail, they're killing each other . . . the white people have not . . .
>
> DIANA: Because of the Eurocentric education . . .
>
> JOYCE: Right, because of the Eurocentric education that . . . [unclear] So now it's time to turn it around and basically look at the black children . . . And . . . [garbled, inarticulate rage]

The points of cognitive dissonance provoked by Dr. McGriff's presentation to this white audience were numerous. They included the continually contentious matter of teaching evolution in the schools, with an added racial subtext; the disastrous state of affairs across the city; and the precarious conditions of poor black youth, laid in their laps as the reason why this community school was going to be "set aside," reopened with its mission centered around "black culture." And this was all conveyed by an articulate, professional black woman as the voice of a power structure that really did not require or desire their opinions or input. It was, by all accounts, a shocking event for everyone present.

For residents who wanted more details about the curriculum being developed by the DPS and how it related to Afrocentric curricula in other school districts, a clear account was hard to come by from the Board of Education. Questioning the curriculum, or trying to find out more about its premises, put whites at a distinct disadvantage in relation to black school officials. Kenyatta and other board members spoke with an unmarked voice of authority on these matters, and they did not feel compelled to engage whites in Warrendale in a contest over intellectual matters. Kevin researched the Portland School's African-American Baseline Essay, a series used by the school systems in Detroit, Atlanta, and Milwaukee to develop their own Afrocentric curriculums.[73] He had not been able to find out from the Board of Education exactly how the essays were being used in Detroit. "They're not teaching it, they're 'studying it.' And when we've brought up the question of religion, that's the kind of answer we got. That's the kind of shuck and jive you get from these people that are involved in this. They feel that they don't have to answer your questions. They feel that they don't have to debate with you. 'We're not here to fight Afrocentrism. We're here to fight two-bit street racism.' That was a comment from Kwame Kenyatta."[74] In their pursuit of information on the curriculum, Kevin and the others invariably accentuated their image as "racists," which set other Warrendale whites on edge. But it was the general concerns they raised about this aspect of the academy that had the most resonance with whites who publicly supported the school.

For whites who spoke out in favor of the academy's opening, the curriculum was at best an ambivalent matter. Their amorphous understanding of the curriculum acknowledged that it filled a need or had some necessity, yet they retained anxieties about its scope and implications. Wally felt there was an appropriateness to an Afrocentric perspective in the schools, while conceding that Jeff "might have a point" in being concerned about broad implications of the curriculum. His impressions of the curriculum, though, convey only a vague understanding of what was being taught at the academy and of the philosophical, social basis for such an educational program.

> WALLY: Now I can see . . . If they have . . . If they're saying that people . . . the white people are not aware of what the continent of Africa was . . . uh . . .

that there was a lot of history there, they're right in what they're saying. Because when I went to school, we didn't talk much about Africa. Really, back then, we talked about Rome, we talked about Greece . . . and uh . . . things of that nature . . . and England. It was more of the European stuff. I'm not saying that there wasn't some talk of Africa, but it wasn't, by and large, central. The *National Geographic*, back in those years, they used to have pictures of Africa, and African women. . .and the children . . . and then they had articles and stories, and the African men. But most of that was perceived as being a lot of cannibalism and what not. And that may very well have been very true. . . . But if they're going to . . . to just tell the youngsters that there's only one place, that's Africa, then that's not fair to the children. My problem with most of the schooling today is the way they speak.

JH: How so?

WALLY: Well . . . uh . . . One, two, three, foo . . . Uh, they'll say po-lice instead of police, and uh . . . it's the infliction [sic] I mean we have, in our country, the Philadelphians, the New Yorkers, we have the Bostons . . . and we have the Southerns. But theirs is entirely different. . . . But if they would make these youngsters learn to speak properly, to add and subtract properly, and what not. These kids aren't getting that kind of education! I don't give a damn if they're getting Afrocentric, or Eurocentric, but teach them the basics. And if you want to say, yeah, there was an Africa, well, hell yes there was an Africa. There definitely was an Africa. Because Egypt is in Africa, right? And uh . . . the dark continent was, a lot of people wouldn't go out into the jungle. And I'm not sure if it was too much of worrying about getting cannibalized, and for the lions and all the other stuff in the jungle.

As with many of his fellow whites who asserted that the academy should open in Warrendale, Wally's view of the "curriculum" was terribly vague and comprehended little about the process of socialization it was designed to counter. Indeed, his perspective of Africa—derived largely from the *National Geographic* and prey to all manner of mythic imagery—and his regard for forms of Black English as an ignorant corruption of language stand more as evidence of why Afrocentric approaches have been developed for schools than a reliable account of its propositions and implementations. Aside from a concern over the "basics," and a sense that black children were not being normalized to be like standard white Americans, Wally was not too concerned about the particulars of the curriculum. Though he had been a key community figure in supporting the academy, he had learned very little about its tenets. He even suggested, "That's one of the things that Testa's been very vehement about. And in a sense, he may have a good point. Uh, again, I don't feel a youngster should be taught one thing, one side only, okay?"

Claudia (then serving as the WCO's vice president), much closer in age to Jeff, was a harsher critic of the academy than Wally. Although she supported its right to open, over the course of the first school year she grew dubious about the academy's operation. Like Wally, she allowed that Jeff and the others had valid concerns in relation to the curriculum. This recognition, though, had to transcend her initial repulsion by Jeff, who like Kevin, unnerved people because of his strident challenging of the academy. "Jeff Testa does have some good points. But at first I just wanted to have nothing to do with him. 'Cause it appeared to me that he was just being completely racist, but now I hear . . . some of the things he is saying actually make sense, like he said, 'Why should this curriculum be Afrocentric?' And if it's true that that's where Man came from, origi- nated, fine, that makes sense. But you don't just expose children to the African point of view and not teach the anything at all Anglo-Saxon. I'm sorry but a complete reverse does not . . . two wrongs don't make a right."

Unlike Wally, though, her opinions were based on experiences that she had inside Malcolm X. She told me about going to the academy, offering to tutor students, "because I wanted to see what it was like from the inside." What she encountered was a divide between blacks she perceived as being interested in effacing racial divides and those projecting a sense that racial divisions were indelible. "One woman I talked with over there, she seemed like she genuinely cared about racial harmony. She was sadly the only person I talked to that gave me that feeling. The rest seemed to have an attitude of . . . like . . . that blacks are better than whites just because of the color of their skin. I'm like, excuse me, but I thought you said that curriculum was going to be multiple cultures . . . and . . . I just sensed a real bad attitude problem with most of the people over there. They're real arrogant."

When I asked her to elaborate, she replied, "Okay, they're trying to make up for things that happened in the past by completely reversing the roles, and that's not the way to go about it. It's like, you don't solve a problem by wronging a person in exactly the same way you feel you were wronged. That does not solve the problem. Yet, that's the feeling I get when I've gone to their meetings. I've gone to two different meetings about Malcolm X with predominantly Malcolm X parents there, and that's the feeling I got . . . was ah . . . an arrogant attitude."

She was upset that they celebrated Kwanzaa, but not Christmas, Cha- nukah, or St. Valentine's days. "They just trash 'em all. They just trash 'em all. And I don't agree with that." She also charged that the academy does not celebrate Presidents' Day.

I'm sorry those men were white, but that's our country, right or wrong. That's our country. It's like the same thing when they fly the African flag but they don't fly the U.S. flag! It's great to be proud of your heritage, but you're also from this country, y'know. This country comes first now. Y'know, that's your heritage, and it's great to believe in your heritage and to continue on your culture, but you don't do that at the expense of your current country. I mean, if you hate America so much, why are you here? Y'know, if I hated America so much, and I wanted to go to Poland, fine, I could do that. But I don't want to go there, I have more freedoms here. So if it's so bad here, why are you here? That's my point of view.

JH: So there's a lot of hostility towards the U.S. as a nation?

CLAUDIA: No, it's towards whites. Towards whites and anything whites touch or anything the whites are mainly in control of. They're very anti. So the government. They're very anti with the government, history—this country's history . . .

The subject of the curriculum, while it revealed a sense of similar perspective and positioning among these whites, also made clear a broad gulf in understanding and degrees of articulateness among Warrendale whites regarding the scope of racial inequalities and the political means of their redress in the United States in the 1990s. The curriculum's fierce critics were cognizant of the general situation of blacks in this country and how their plight was addressed through programs such as those at the Malcolm X Academy. But supporters were generally not astute about the basis of this Afrocentric curriculum. Janice, an academy supporter, commented, "I see where they want to have more of the Afrocentric curriculum schools . . . um . . . What was the matter with our schools all along? This is the way our schools . . . they've always run this way. Why do they want to change them now? And if you're going to change them this way, then we're going to have to have Arabic . . . They're going to have to have their own special schools . . . And uh . . . the Polish, and the Italian [she smiles], everybody's going to want their own uh . . . separate thing, and uh . . . this . . . I don't understand why they have to have it. I don't understand the separatism business."

Reverend Nelson was a very vocal, active supporter of the academy. He had no tolerance for Jeff and other whites who opposed the school, but he also had problems with the academy's mission. When I asked him what he thought of the curriculum, he answered,

Do I agree with it? No I don't. I don't agree with Afrocentric religious sort of thing y'know. You see, I don't understand this "I'm an Afro-American" stuff. Because, what am I supposed to do, walk around saying that I'm a Swedish-American because my grandfather came from Sweden? I'm an American. I live here. I don't stress all the customs of Sweden or I don't stress all the customs of Italy, and they don't stress all the customs of Germany. I'm an American. And I don't understand that kind of thinking. And I don't buy this thing that they're lost and that they can't find their way. They're human, they live in America, let

them make their way like everybody else. . . . the curriculum is too much . . .
There's no reason for them to ah . . . have to learn Zulu and Swahili and . . .
and learn African dances and the religion of Africa and all that stuff. That's
ridiculous. That's dead ground.

These whites, who all supported the opening of the academy, had little
patience for a curriculum based on reviving or imbuing a sense of racial
heritage in these children. Reverend Nelson and Claudia were more animated in their feeling of unease in relation to the curriculum, largely because they had actually been in the school and had felt racialized by their
encounters there. Although Nelson did not detect the hostility toward
whites that Claudia reported, he was made uncomfortable by implications of the emphasis on heritage. The "black stuff" that was emphasized
at the academy disturbed him greatly, in part, because they were not striving to be "normal" like whites.[75]

> NELSON: I have a problem with the curriculum in that I don't agree with
> where it's coming from. Now, the other stuff they teach over there, I sat in on
> a science class, and they did good. But they overstressed black stuff to the
> normal stuff.
> JH: How so?
> NELSON: Because they only study black scientists, or they only study black
> politicians. They claim that all history that's been taught over the years has left
> out all the black. So they overemphasize all the black and leave out all the
> white.

The Reverend's contrast between "black stuff" and "normal stuff" is perhaps a classic example of the way in which whites equate whiteness with
normativity, as an unmarked condition from which "race" signifies difference. And it certainly resonates with Wally's primary concern that
young blacks were not learning Standard English.

On the other hand, Jeff, Joyce, Kevin, and Diana had become quite
familiar with the research and the arguments supporting the Afrocentric
curriculums. They knew the deficiencies that the academy was designed
to correct. Whereas Janice had to ask, "What was the matter with our
schools all along?" they would correctly reply, it was the Eurocentric
curriculums of "our schools." They were deft at reciting positions of various Afrocentric scholars, and quite ironic when relating the counter-
arguments to the controversial question of whether or not the curriculum
involved a form of religious teaching. Yet their efforts to understand
Afrocentric approaches were highly motivated and oppositionally based.
They got little credit from people like Mr. Gibson, who attended one of
the community meetings that Kevin had arranged to educate people
about the academy and its curriculum.

I mentioned to Mr. Gibson that I had come across a few whites who were avidly reading about Afrocentric theories, and I wondered what his impressions were of such whites. He laughed. "Y'know, I've always thought . . . that whites studying black history . . . was always cute . . . Because it never matters to them. If you do it, you do it . . . like you're saying, people doing it to do research. And they're doing their research. But I always know, they have a mindset. Even when they're reading a book, they have a mindset." He concluded succinctly: "Cute. All you can say is cute. Because there's no way you can pull that off."

These white opponents also did not get much credit from the white "experts" on education or race relations they encountered over the course of the controversy. For example, opponents were well versed in the "philosophy" of Ma-at. The Board of Education defined "the principles Ma-at (order, harmony, balance, reciprocity, truth, justice and propriety)"[76] as the basic support for the academy's curriculum; Testa preferred to emphasize that Ma-at was listed in the Egyptian Book of the Dead as a goddess representing some of these same values. But their critiques of its place in a state-funded school system were often dismissed by whites outside of the Warrendale area. The following exchange begins with Bonnie describing the Afrocentric scholars like Molefi Asante and Na'im Akbar who had been brought in as consultants by the Board of Education.

> BONNIE: We pay this guy [Asante] to come in. He's a consultant. They come in and give speeches, and they try to push their books, and their curriculum. And these books are wild. These guys are nuts. And we made him $12,000 this year . . .
>
> JEFF: Just to speak.
>
> BONNIE: Na'im Akbar! I mean . . . They're all, all of these Afrocentrists.
>
> JEFF: That was even funny. St. Thomas [Aquinas] had this meeting [the workshop on "What is Racism?"], that Joyce called me about and I came to the second or third meeting. They gave this handout . . . They were quoting Akbar, and uh . . . and they even had a section in there on melanin . . . This is our own church now!
>
> JOYCE: And after the second meeting, Jeff brought her over some stuff to read to get her better informed about what's going on with these black people. You want to talk about them . . .
>
> JEFF: She didn't really want to hear anything about it. I asked her, "What do you know about this curriculum that you're teaching us about, and the way we're reacting? Do you know what they're preaching?" "Yeah they've got Kwanzaa." "Do you know what Kwanzaa is?" "Yeah it's a holiday. I've been to . . . [He mimics her voice]." "DO you know what it is? It's being taught in the schools. Do you know the religious implications, and the political implication behind it? Do you know anything about Maulana Karenga, the man who

invented it Kwanzaa?"[77] I mean I went right down the line with her. Okay. Are you familiar with the libation ceremony in Kwanzaa that's similar to partaking of communion in the Roman Catholic Church, and they're doing this in our schools, except that the children are drinking out of what they call a Timbiko cup, with their dead ancestors. IN SCHOOL! Now that is a religious ceremony.

When I suggested that I could see the connection he was drawing, Jeff sarcastically challenged,

No. That's your Eurocentric way of thinking. That's it. We went to the fair they had for the Schools of Choice. Bonnie and some other friends, and one black person in particular, named Kevin Wilson. And they had Ed Vaughn there. And he's with this Ma-at and Hotemp School, which is a high school—it's a choice school. So I went over there, knowing a little bit about Ma-at. But I ask him, "So what is Ma-at?" He said, "Well, Ma-at is the belief . . . " "BELIEF! Do you mean RELIGION?" "Oh no no no," he said. "Not in the holistical sense. That's just your European upbringing." I said, "Well, hey, I didn't have a European upbringing. I was raised in an American-centered curriculum. I was taught that I was no better or worse, or superior or inferior due to the color of my SKIN." And he was all, "No no no, again that's what you were taught. You don't even know you were taught. . ." and here's Kevin, this guy that's with me, and his mouth is about hitting the ground. "You can't be for real now?!"

The matters of Ma-at—with its rites of passage and daily harambee [Swahili for "pulling together"] assemblies[78]—and melanin were the prime concern of opponents to the school. These two matters fused the emotional conflict over the line between "religious" and "secular" in the schools with the question of instilling a sense of racial identity in young students. On both these topics Mr. Gibson was elusive when we spoke. On the question of whether or not melanin was stressed as a basis for racial superiority he was dismissive, telling me that "our kids can't even spell melanin" and, effacing the concern, insisting that "It's just positive reinforcement. Say something good about melanin!" On the matter of "rituals" related to the "rites of passage," he offered no details, and provided only a reductionist perspective that found "rituals" in numerous mundane matters. "Rituals are 'Sit down and shut up.' That's a ritual. 'Sit down, shut up.' That's in every school across this nation."

After numerous similar such examples, I asked him specifically about the timbiko (libations) ceremony. He explained,

What they do, in the form of libations, they give thanks to . . . to the spiritual idea of understanding . . . that we're connected, that everybody is connected with a spiritual base. You can call it Jehovah, Christ, God, Buddha. There's millions of different names, you can claim them. What is wrong with saying thank you Lord? Just saying in a general, base sense, lets give thanks to what got us here. Without the religious aspect . . . without God there would be no human being. Without having the Beginning . . . , you can call them Adam and Eve or you can call them Adam and Steve if you want to . . . but without having all this to say that we're connected. If we don't remember who we are, and give thanks to the first whoever . . . we wouldn't be able to have society. Kids wouldn't respect parents, and parents wouldn't respect grandparents. So the idea of us having . . . of giving thanks to where we come from.

However the "rites of passage" at the academy are to be understood, as "spiritual" or as "routine," there was enough free play in its possible articulations and definitions that whites opposed to the school were always finding new material to support their suspicions. Mr. Gibson was frustratingly vague on the matter of the curriculum. He insisted that they largely just used BASAL readers that were illustrated with African-Americans as well as (or instead of) whites. Although he spooled through the range of Afrocentric scholars and their work, he maintained that such lofty studies were too erudite for grade-school students, and insisted that their curricular materials were quite innocuous. I asked him, finally, "How does race get taught here?" He replied,

We present it from a cultural point of view. If you don't know self you cannot know anyone else. And knowing self is first and foremost in any individual. In this country, since they have taken the legacy, or the historical cultural aspect of African Americans away from them . . . And they did it to the Spanish to a certain degree, more or less, to a certain degree. Now everybody has to speak English, everybody has to walk this way and dress in a certain way, okay. That was all right, to a degree. Now we're saying, "If our kids are going to be functional adults in this country, let's know about self." . . . We're saying, for our kids, race is most important because you must know, or have an understanding of and appreciation of self.

It was exactly this simple matter—"We teach race in the guise of knowing about self"—that so thoroughly unnerved whites who paid attention to what went on inside the academy. From this equation of "race" with self-identity a web of implications and conjectures unfolded. In our long afternoon together, Mr. Gibson insisted many times that the goal of the school was to instill a positive sense of self-identity in its students. And as the "Framework and Definition for African-Centered Education" published by the DPS in 1992 declares, "each student will have a more balanced view of 'self' and 'group identity,' and America will be better for it."[79] However melanin entered into the picture, what was disturbing for whites in Warrendale was this assertion of an interest in, and a need for, promoting a sense of group- and self-identity that ran seamlessly together with racialness.

As already mentioned, white opponents of the school synthesized their knowledge of Afrocentric tenets from a number of sources. They processed an amalgamation of fact and fiction regarding topics such as melanin, mimicking the black speakers whom they heard asserting that melanin was the basis of "their" racial superiority. Joyce and Jeff at one point asked me what I knew about melanin. I recited the version I offered students in the "Introduction to Physical Anthropology" course I had previously taught: that it was the basis of skin pigmentation, and that the endless attempts to correlate racial characteristics with populations were always illfounded. They then insisted that Bonnie tell me "the story they're teaching our kids."

BONNIE: In the Nation of Islam, they believe that so many black people were taken to an island.[80] And, with needles and things, they would draw out certain genes and lighten them. And as people started to get lighter, they would mate the lighter ones until finally they got white. And then when we became white, we were sent off into Europe, into the cold caves where we became these devil people, because we didn't walk right or talk right, or all these things, and they just kind of cast us aside. And their belief was that we were only to rule the world for so many thousands of years. And, in the melanin theory, the melanin . . . In the one article, there's a Bernard Ortiz de Mantolano . . . He found some of the curriculum of the Portland Baseline essays, they were teaching this melanin theory.[81] And one of the history pages, they taught that George Washington Carver, because of the blackness of his skin, he could just walk through the woods, and the plants would talk to him and tell him what to do with them. . . .

JEFF: Now another aspect of this melanin. Now the pineal gland, which is supposed to be located right here, where the third eye would be. In, blacks, it's soft and it produces melanin and that's what makes their skin darker. Now the more melanin you produce, the darker your skin, the more intelligent you are. So in the same way that Adolph Hitler and his Aryan-centric curriculum in the '30s would tell the blond-haired blue-eyed people that the fairer you are, or the whiter you are, the larger your brain is, thus the more intelligent you are, now they're telling them that the more melanin your pineal gland . . . and in white people, it's calcified, so it doesn't work. But you see, if you take me, I'm darker than you [he gets up and comes over to the sofa and places his swarthy, sundarkened forearm against mine]. So by their theory, I'm more intelligent. I'm the smartest person in this room.

These two versions had been synthesized from months of their involvement with the Board of Education and with Afrocentric writings, research, and polemics. In the process they had congealed an impression of what was being taught in the three Afrocentric academies, in programs that would later be infused throughout the DPS. Through their engagement with proponents of the academy's curriculum and the political figures who held sway on the Board of Education, they had moved gradually from a very local conflict to a disorienting and abstracted zone where racial discourse had unnerving powers. Whether or not they were right about the curriculum, they had become caught in an elaborate, seemingly boundless, discourse in which the most outlandish claims, through repetition, took on a certain grudging credence.[82] And this discourse had hollowed out a special relation to their place, their community, and their social or political position, which provided reiterations all around them of the power of this discourse.

It was not just the black officials and researchers who generated or manipulated this discourse. White "outsiders" were also drawn into the events and exchanges in Warrendale. The most influential of all of these, by far, was the lawyer Constance Cumby. Joyce described the change that Cumby wrought as if she gave them a speaking position and affirmed their fledgling grasp of the Afrocentric vernacular. She offered me a tape that had been made of one of Cumby's informational meetings with people in Warrendale. Joyce told me, "That one is really hard to follow. When Constance Cumby started talking, it was like wheeew—we were all lost. I mean, she was up there just talking and we couldn't catch any of it. She was on about Kwanzaa, and Ma-at, and all the rest, and if you didn't know something about it, there was no way you could follow her. She's been studying this for so long, and it's all interconnected and dependent on the next thing. She and Kevin, it was like they were carrying on a conversation. But to the rest of us, it was a different language. The meeting at the Knights of Columbus was a little better—she really slowed down. She took more time to explain things."

Constance Cumby was contacted by Kevin Malczyk when he heard her speaking on the radio show, "Law Talk." She was then hired in November of 1992 by a group of Warrendale parents to sue the DPS for violating the First Amendment by teaching religion at Malcolm X. Cumby considers herself a crusader against New Age religions, and has lectured widely over the past decade on the dangers of meditation and Aquarian conspiracies. Her book *Hidden Dangers of the Rainbow* sold over 400,000 copies.[83] She was quick to assert a connection between the New Age and the curriculum at Malcolm X because each emphasizes meditation: Students at the academy participate in daily harambee assemblies that feature "thirty minutes of meditation, self-esteem building, and history lessons."[84]

Cumby presented Warrendale residents with the thesis that proponents of the Afrocentric curriculum in the DPS had purposefully pushed to have the Malcolm X Academy located in this largely white neighborhood in order to provoke a violent response by whites that would initiate a race riot that, in turn, would be the precursor to a global race war and conflagration. Residents tired of her before a lawsuit could be filed, but much of her imagery and rhetoric remained in peoples' minds, especially her allusions to a black nationalist conspiracy at work in the DPS among advocates of an Afrocentric approach to education.

Her message that the positioning of the academy was part of a plot to instigate a racial riot touched a nerve among white residents in this west-side neighborhood. They had tensely watched the rebellion unfold in Los Angeles earlier that summer, and they waited for a similar conflict to explode in Detroit when a verdict was finally rendered in the trial for the murder of Malice Green—quite contrary to the stance of whites in Briggs. Black voices seemed to sound everywhere, calling for retribution and revenge, and threatening violence if their calls for justice went unsatisfied. Months after the controversy had cooled in Warrendale, these exchanges and rhetorics haunted whites who had been deeply involved in the dispute; but there was more at work here than the suggestive correspondences traced by Cumby. A host of forces combined to interject these whites into the odd subject position that loomed before them of "white devils," a figure they began to take seriously—began to feel fitting over their skin—as they directly experienced objectification by authoritative black speakers. White opponents were caught not simply in a powerful discourse; the concreteness of their place seemed to be dissolving through the overdetermined significance of their association with the tradition of "blue-collar racism" and white dominance in Detroit. As well, critical forms of sociality in this place were disintegrating through the effects of the media coverage and their own mobilization of intraracial distinctions—local whites grew estranged and literally unable to recognize their neighbors. The specificities that once composed their social contexts seemed to disintegrate, and the stereotyped features of their thoughts and deeds came to predominate; hence, the ambiguities that complicate racialness also dispersed, leaving in their wake a compelling image conveying the power of race disembodied and dislocated.

> JOYCE: Let me tell you about the mother cosmic ship [Diana laughs]. I lost a few nights' sleep over that one.
>
> JEFF: Oh yeah, the black cosmic mother. They talk about her on [W]DTR.
>
> JOYCE: Yeah that's what they're training these children for. And people with the melanin, are they going to go into the center or the outside?
>
> BONNIE: No, we will be drawn into the center of the earth, after all of this disastrous stuff, like floods and everything. Then all of the white people will go to the center and black people will be told where to go so the mother ship can take them away. Then we'll all be blown up when they're safely away.
>
> JOYCE: When Chris [Martinez] told me all about that, I was literally on her front room floor, rolling in laughter . . .

DIANA: Then when you came over to my house afterwards, she stood at the door, you were looking up at the sky [laughs].

JOYCE: I looked up . . .

DIANA: . . . Is it coming? Is it coming?

JOYCE: . . . and y'know, as stupid as it sounds, and as hard as I laughed when I heard it [voice suddenly drops to a whisper] it is damn scary if it's true.

BONNIE: I was having Kwame nightmares after I started reading all of those Afrocentric books.

JOYCE: I couldn't sleep for days knowing it's like . . .

JH: What do you mean, "If it's true"?

[they all talk at once]

DIANA: If the children are being taught this. They're going to be adults when our kids are adults.

Jeff launched into another comparison with Hitler, how he started changing the minds of the youth in the schools. So I asked Joyce, again, what she was thinking.

JOYCE: At the time it seemed impossible, that all of that could happen. But if that's what they're indoctrinating into the kids at that school, if that's the technology, because, allegedly, they have this ship almost ready.

DIANA: It's supposed to be here at the year 2000.

JOYCE: . . . and I mean this ship is almost done; this is going to happen within seven years. And I thought, as stupid as this sounds . . . If it were possible, it's scary as hell. Even to be living in the neighborhood I'm living in, because, the whole world would come to an end.

JH: Why?

JOYCE: Because these black people, I don't mean to sound like that . . . but . . . they've got all of this technology and they're hiding something from the white people.[85] And the white people have slipped up on it, and we're picking up their knowledge and they're threatening us . . . It just seems too outrageous to believe . . . But I've lost nights of sleep over this.

While Joyce's credulity hung in the air, Jeff and Bonnie went back to talking about the plan for a black nation in the southern states, which they claim Kwame has supported; they were trying to recall if it is supposed to have five or fifteen states. How had she come to believe this story? She had clearly stepped into a position left open for her and other "whites" in this unbounded narrative, one that countered or retold previous racial myths and stories, that "enclosed within a figure something which in itself escapes figuration."[86] The power of this figure of a black cosmic mothership has circulated in popular culture for decades; why had its invocation here so troubled Joyce?

Perhaps it is simply the strength of conspiracy theories, both at this social moment in the United States and in the long, troubled history of race relations in this country. Certainly, combined with apocalyptic elements—"the whole world would come to an end"—this kind of narrative is traditionally compelling to humans, and Detroit has long been fertile ground for such apocalyptic imagery. Then, taken with the escalating rhetoric around race in pubic discourses, the invocations of "Ice people" against "Sun people" or rappers being pilloried for calling open season on whites, how could this figure not attain a compelling air? This narrative condenses the extremes of scale and perception that were jarring in the dispute over the Malcolm X Academy: The gulf between politically polarized whites and blacks grew exponentially out of the conjuncture of a means to redress centuries of oppression with a more recent history of whites assenting to a delimited rebalancing of the racial order through reallocations of resources located in working-class communities. As amplified voices found no means to converse across this abyss, quite simply the ground for countering the power of racial language dissolved. What else could she believe?

Conclusion _____

My INTERVIEW with Pat (see "Riots and Race" and "Franklin School") was winding down; I had run out of questions and was getting ready to go. In the closing lull, she said, "I have to tell you about one incident." It was a story that she had started to tell earlier that afternoon when we were talking about her efforts to keep the Franklin School open. She had gone off on a tangent instead, but now she wanted to get back to it. It involved a school district meeting, one of many in which she and her friend "would be the only white people there."

> When there was this teachers' strike . . . And uh . . . They had a big meeting for the community about the teachers' strike. And it was at Northwestern I think, or one of the other high schools. So Martha and I went to the meeting. And I'm not sure if the community advisory boards had started at that point or not. Anyway, we went to this meeting and we were . . . This was before people got to know us. This was early on. And we're in this high school auditorium, jam packed. And there were some teachers there. And they were black teachers and they were upset because they felt the children needed to be in school. And the statement was: "The children need to be taught. And they can't afford . . . While we're out picketing, they're losing." And uh . . . "I intend to teach that black child! I intend to see that that black child is taught."
>
> Well here's my friend, goes up to the mike up front. And as I told you, she's heavy and white. And she says, in response to that male teacher saying that he was going to see to it that that black child was taught. She says, "If my child is sitting next to you, you better make sure that my child is taught also." And the whole auditorium applauded her. But I had been sitting there thinking, "Oh my god, we'll never get home" [laughs]. But see, they were all there for the same reason. They were there because of their concern for the kids. And that's what I think makes a difference, when you have a common goal. And uh . . . the goal is a good education, you can work together. If the goal is a good neighborhood, you can work together. It doesn't matter what color you are, you've got the same goal. And that's the whole key right there.

Sometime later, as I began to write up this fieldwork, this story came back to me. In it, I heard Joyce's question resonating—"What about the white kids?" At least a dozen years and several miles separate her comment from Pat's white friend, who insisted to the black male teacher, "You better make sure that my child is taught also." In the distance and proximity between these two statements lies the nuanced terrain of class and racial difference.

The juxtaposition of these two statements struck me as an appropriate way to conclude this book. The similarities and the dissonances between these two women's stories succinctly convey the variable significance of racialness in the divergent inflections their whiteness casts on each comment. The similarities (in terms of context and content) show that white racialness is commonly in question or at the root of these statements; the distinctions between these two comments (the classed nuances and the difference in locations) convey the thesis of this work: that the significance of white racialness varies by class position. The particular contours of spatial formations, with their distinct racial and class compositions, informs the discursive modes through which the significance of racialness is assessed, manipulated, and negotiated.

The similarities and distinctions between these two whites and among whites more broadly remains a perplexing, troublesome matter. I have primarily argued against the notion that whiteness can be uniformly defined and designated, rendered the object of well-intentioned analytical tinkering and, thereby, dismantled. Although I recognize the analytic value and political efficacy of designating such an historically determining, powerful ideology as "whiteness," I think that an attention to the differences between whites importantly reframes a singular focus on "race" within a critical understanding of its conflations with class and locational distinctions. Still, if it were championed as the sole "correct" view, this attention might obscure the connections between whites and the operations of power and privilege that structure this society; or worse, suggest that whites can only be studied by emphasizing their differences and distinctions, never taken together as a problematic collective. These positions are points best kept in productive tension, rather than emphatically resolved in one direction or the other.

Critical efforts to objectify whiteness have deployed this concept as a means to compel whites, first to recognize themselves as racially constituted, and second to cease using the designation "racial" only for the actions, beliefs, and experiences of peoples of color. The fundamental assumption of projects examining whiteness is that it is organized relationally, in polarized opposition to a black other. The preceding stories and analyses operate at a critical remove from these assumptions, but not with the intention of absolutely dismissing or disputing them. In emphasizing intraracial discourses that organize and prioritize class distinctions between whites, I am not suggesting that the notion of a black other is unfounded. Rather, I am arguing that such a dynamic operates with limits and according to matters of scale such that it cannot be regarded as the motivational core of whites' racial constitution. I have found whites confronting the significance of race through their positioning within marked racial categories. These situations of white Detroiters

are obviously at a vast remove from what might be posited as the normative experience and existence of whites in the United States, but they do
suggest that whites' awareness of racial operations are not only (or even
best) raised through critical accountings of ideological structures—that
is, "whiteness."

Michel Foucault, in the *Archeology of Knowledge*, summarizes the
shift in perspective he recognizes in the way historical operations are perceived: "Thus, in place of the continuous chronology of reason, which
was invariably traced back to some inaccessible origin, there have appeared scales that are sometimes very brief, distinct from one another,
irreducible to a single law, scales that bear a type of history peculiar to
each one, and which cannot be reduced to the general model of consciousness that acquires, progresses, and remembers."[1] I am suggesting a similar shift, moving from treating whiteness as a "model of consciousness"
to regarding the disparate scales of racial significance constituted by the
various social conditions of whites. In this regard, I have analyzed the
statements and narratives of whites not by seeking a core that serves as
an "authoritative interpretation of the facts"; instead, I have attempted
"the analysis of their coexistence, their succession, their mutual functioning, their reciprocal determination, and their independent or correlative
transformation."[2]

The marked identities of whites in each of these sites—"hillbilly,"
"gentrifier," "racist"—are adumbrated by a paired term—"nigger,"
"history," "Afrocentric." If you want to understand the commonalties
between these whites, you can consider the variable degrees of control
each of these pairs offered whites trying to manage or engage the significance of racialness. Or, if the differences between whites seem more intriguing, then reflect upon the lack of equivalence, first in these modes of
objectifying whites, and second in how differently the second term in each
pair either emphasizes or diffuses attention to race. Only "nigger" serves
as an obvious marker of racism, but its use was the most nuanced and
complicated of any of these terms—certainly fraught with the most power
of derrogation, but also applied in unusual ways that actively marked and
undercut an interest in whiteness. In trying to convey the nonobvious
racial significance of the other two terms—along with making evident the
ways whites in these three settings were in various ways able to elude
being racially objectified—I did not rely on "racism" as the singular measure, because I think the significance of race exceeds its explanatory register. A core racism hardly accounts for the array of possible readings of
how race matters in these zones, the anxieties of open-ended settings satu-
rated with potential racial meanings, the ambiguities spawned from the
ability of these whites to be objectified in strict racial terms.

Racism can be located alternately in an individual's psychohistory or in society and its institutions, but I see the significance of race, in addition to its historical determinants and its contemporary institutional inscriptions and maintenances, as generated in the recursive interplay of settings and the modes of articulating social notions of self and difference. This interplay is subject to constant interpretation through an array of discursive devices that are shaped by or conform to class etiquettes. Whether or not racism can be eradicated, race will remain significant because it permeates the textures of society, animating peoples' thoughts and actions; given sociality's extreme plasticity and generative possibilities, "fixed" beliefs or sentiments are only a tip of the proverbial iceberg.

"Racism" and "whiteness" emphasize deterministic structures or impulses, unconsciously and emphatically informing peoples' views of and reactions toward racial difference, but this underestimates the fact that people actively make sense out of difference using whatever signifying materials are at hand. This process is variably referred to as "making something" out of race. In this work, I have focused on racial situations, rather than deterministic constructs; the model of racial analysis that emerges from this study is one in which race is examined in situ, where peoples' situated knowledges come to the fore.[3] Part of the shift entailed by this model involves recognizing the theorizing and studying of "race" that people engage in on a regular basis in the course of their daily lives; it will take more than a vanguard of critical, antiracist theorists to undo the power of whiteness, after all, and it is important to catch glimpses of the critical work being performed "in the field" already. In attending carefully to "the field," we should recognize that peoples' understandings and experiences of race are always situated, conflated continually with the complex social contours of distinctions active in particular places.

This work has tracked a range of racial situations, whether directly observed or narrated from a recent or more distant past. In such situations, the definition or scope of meaning of "racial" is somewhat different from what may be assumed in its uses for describing institutional practices or the array of forms of discrimination or stereotyping. Situations bring to the fore the interpretive process whereby subjects make judgments and assessments of the interests, intentions, motivations, actions, and words of themselves and others. What predominates in racial situations are the places where they occur and unfold; this is not an assertion that the significance of race in these encounters is more primary, real, or authentic than in other settings (institutions and so on); a different scale of relevance pertains. Some certainties and generalizations that operate at other levels are suspended here; not that these other levels are not present—the national economy and the political process have shaped every yard and front porch in each of these sites to some degree. But the determining power of these large forces are held in abeyance or are uncertainly active and powerful. What does dominate in such situations are the interpretive repertoires that people deploy to make sense of encounters. These repertoires can certainly invoke, with varying degrees of certainty or authority, larger forces, but the strength and surety of such invocations will ultimately stand or fall depending on their resonance with local discourses and experiences.

Rather than bring great refinement to definitions of whiteness—in fact, I resist defining it at all—I treat race as an interpretive medium, riven and animated by discourses, local, national, or global in their orientation. The shape and contours of this medium, race, are formed by an array of interests with varying degrees of coherence and stability—class and gender, to name the prominent examples. Stressing the degrees of indeterminacy in these interpretive repertoires is not a suggestion that sometimes race simply does not matter, just that this evaluation is always part of an assessment of whether it matters more than anything else. Instead of drawing generalized assertions and summary judgments about race, I suggest that the economy of racial explanations and analysis needs to be reoriented toward a greater dependence on and retention of the particular situations and settings where race is at work. That is, by considering the specific circumstances of racial situations, we can counter the allegorical tendencies that render peoples' lives as abstractions, such as "white" and "black."

As noted in this book's introduction, I am not suggesting this shift in attention will miraculously dethrone these abstractions, but we can begin to dissolve their power by recognizing that it is not the figures that solely control this form of significance; the meaning of race is also generated and transformed as people think through these matters in their everyday lives. I have not marshaled the specificities of peoples' daily lives to support a series of theoretical generalizations on race, but rather to develop the reader's ear for how "race" sounds in different sites. This book may best be described as a treatise on how to listen to the interplay of race and class in place-specific discourses that shape the articulation of social positions, and how to hear the multiple inflections that these positions generate between the absolute orders of whiteness and blackness.

In the end, I want to insist upon the importance of being specific in any discussion, assessment, or theorizing of how race matters. When talking about race, in everyday life but also, most critically, as academics and cultural critics, it matters very much that we be specific. It is altogether too easy to move into generalizations about race; it is already hard enough to grasp the very particular circumstances and elements through which race continues to be culturally significant in this country. "Race" operates in multiple levels and registers, informs myriad perspectives, remains both inchoate and loudly articulated. In these manifestations, realizations, and expositions what remains surprisingly hard to accept or remember is that there is very little abstract about it in the end, on the ground, in people's lives.

Notes

Introduction

1. Toni Morrison's edited collections are obvious examples of the importance of such readings: see *Race-ing Justice, En-Gendering Power: Essays on Anita Hill, Clarence Thomas, and the Construction of Social Reality* (New York: Pantheon Books, 1992); *Birth of a Nation 'hood: Gaze, Script, and Spectacle in the O. J. Simpson Case* (New York: Pantheon Books, 1997).

2. These abstractions, after all, are not mere phantoms; they demarcate an arena in which the social order is made to cohere to the binary nature of racial thinking; they refer to a range of inscription practices that definitively shape the material conditions and experiential contours of life in the United States. This book is not an attempt to refute these sociological and political forms of addressing race; it is, instead, a glimpse of another arena in which the significance of race is characterized by its plasticity rather than its static consistency.

3. Cultural figures mold experience and narratives into comprehensible accounts in an interpretive process connecting events or persons as replications or fulfillments of anticipated social identities. See Donna Haraway, *Modest_Witness@Second_Millennium.FemaleMan©_Meets_OncoMouse™: Feminism and Technoscience* (New York: Routledge, 1997), 9–12.

4. "Ethnographic texts are inescapably allegorical, and a serious acceptance of this fact changes the ways they can be written and read." Clifford asserts that it is impossible to abandon the allegorical tendencies of ethnography, but we can at least resist the impulse to use the "salvage" mode of allegory, and thus open "ourselves to different histories." See "On Ethnographic Allegory," in *Writing Culture: The Poetics and Politics of Ethnography*, edited by James Clifford and George Marcus (Berkeley and Los Angeles: University of California Press, 1986), 98–121, esp. 99, 119

5. Media coverage of Detroit relies upon a range of allegorical images of the city. See Jerry Herron, *AfterCulture: Detroit and the Humiliation of History* (Detroit: Wayne State University Press, 1993).

6. This was a matter of citywide debate. A *Detroit Free Press* headline that read, "Racism Killed Green"—quoting an area minister—sparked a heated debate among readers, featured in full spreads on the editorial page of the November 18 and 30 editions.

7. *Detroit News*, August 26, 1983.

8. The survey was conducted by Nordhaus Research, Inc. The sample was of 400 Detroiters.

9. I do not mean to suggest that there is no value to such surveys or statistical representation of racial attitudes. I am simply arguing that they need to be read more creatively, with an attention to the discrepancies as well as the uniformities.

10. United States Bureau of the Census, "Census of Population and Housing," summary tape files 1A and 3A, 1990 (CD-ROM).

11. For a full elaboration of this assertion, see *White Trash: Race and Class in America*, edited by Matt Wray and Annalee Newitz (New York: Routledge, 1997).

12. Perhaps one of the finest demonstrations of this fundamental point is Pierre Bourdieu's *Distinctions: A Social Critique of the Judgment of Taste*, translated by Richard Nice (Cambridge: Harvard University Press, 1984). As Michael Katz notes, "Social science scholarship on the underclass generally ignores these connections. It lives off the underclass, which it places alone under a very high-powered microscope. It offers class analysis based entirely on the analysis of one class; it uses the language of class but misses or ignores its relational dimension. Indeed, it defines the underclass as outside of, beyond, not part of the class structure. Social science thereby misses a very important point: the process creating an underclass degrades all our lives." *The "Underclass" Debate: Views from History* (Princeton: Princeton University Press, 1993), 442.

13. Media coverage frequently resorts to presenting a racialized image of the "face" of any problem, even when that face seems to challenge the history of white hegemony in this country; see Roger Rouse, "Thinking through Transnationalism: Notes on the Cultural Poetics of Class Relations in the Contemporary United States," *Public Culture* 7.2 (Winter 1995): 353–402.

14. In this and other references to the issue of scale, I am drawing on arguments I have made elsewhere regarding the scaling of cultural phenomena in relation to the patterned irregularities that pertain to levels of meaning. "While whiteness may be fixed ideologically at the national level, 'on the ground' that unity quickly becomes illusory. Instead of one firm 'ground,' there is a shifting series of domains (local, regional, national, transnational) across which whiteness materializes according to distinct centers of significance, assimilating or effacing a varying array of internal differences, and projecting or excluding a host of corporal others. . . .The intervals and gaps between domains creates an irregular and unpredictable basis for the cultural reproduction of this racial category, white." "Locating White Detroit," in *Displacing Whiteness: Essays in Social and Cultural Criticism*, edited by Ruth Frankenberg (New York: Routledge, 1997), 180–213.

15. *The Truly Disadvantaged: The Inner City, the Underclass, and Public Policy* (Chicago: University of Chicago Press, 1987), 58, 62. I develop a more thorough critique and review of the concept of the urban underclass, showing how it variably encompasses "poor whites," in "Green Ghettoes and the White Underclass," *Social Research* 64.2 (1997): 339–65.

16. In the areas of Delray/Springwells (63 percent white) and Chadsey (67 percent white) the poverty rate stands at 37 percent and 38 percent, respectively. See *1990 Census Subcommunity Profiles for the City of Detroit* (Detroit: Southeast Michigan Census Council, October 1993).

17. In Detroit, 87,149 whites live in "distressed" neighborhoods, and 47,977 inhabit "severely distressed" areas. In stark contrast, New York has 77,036 whites living in "distressed" areas, with only 12,921 whites dwelling in "severely distressed" neighborhoods. The "distressed" portions of Chicago are home to 19,525 whites, and only 5,902 whites in Los Angeles live in such neighborhoods; the "severely distressed" areas in Chicago hold 5,781 whites, whereas

in Los Angeles only 3,373 whites live in such zones. See the Urban Underclass Database; New York: Social Science Research Council; John Kasarda, Principle Investigator.

18. Reynolds Farley, Charlotte Steeh, Tara Jackson, Maria Krysan, and Keith Reeves, "Continued Racial Residential Segregation in Detroit: "Chocolate City, Vanilla Suburbs Revisited," *Journal of Housing Research* 4.1 (1993): 1–38. Moreover, as Joe Darden states, "The overall index of dissimilarity between African Americans and whites of all occupational, educational, and income levels in metropolitan Detroit in 1990 was 87.0 percent, an increase of 1.2 percentage points from the level in 1980." "African American Residential Segregation: An Examination of Race and Class in Metropolitan Detroit," in *Residential Apartheid: The American Legacy*, edited by Robert D. Bullard, J. Eugene Grigsby III, and Charles Lee, CAAS Urban Policy Series, vol. 2, 82–94 (Berkeley: Regents of the University of California, 1994); quote on p. 90. See also Joe Darden, Richard Hill, June Thomas, and Richard Thomas, *Detroit: Race and Uneven Development* (Philadelphia: Temple University Press, 1987).

19. Douglas Massey and Nancy Denton, *American Apartheid: Segregation and the Making of the Underclass* (Cambridge: Harvard University Press, 1993). Alhough infant mortality rates have been declining in Michigan, in 1996 black infants were still dying at a rate nearly three times that of white infants. "The state's improvement came mostly among white children, whose rate fell from 6.2 to 6. The mortality rate for black children increased from 17.3 to 17.5." "Mixed Infant-Death Record," *Chicago Tribune*, October 2, 1997, sec.1, p.3.

20. The "promise" of the suburbs was, of course, massively subsidized by the federal government through infrastructure developments (freeways, sewer systems, etc.) and supports for home financing that massively benefited whites. See George Lipsitz, "The Possessive Investment in Whiteness, Racialized Social Democracy and the 'White' Problem in American Studies," *American Quarterly* 47.3 (1995): 369–87.

21. *City on the Edge: The Transformation of Miami* (Berkeley and Los Angeles: University of California Press, 1993), pp. 8, 16; Setha Low, "The Anthropology of Cities: Imagining and Theorizing the City," *Annual Review of Anthropology* 25 (1996): 383–409.

22. Figures are from the Bureau of the Census "Census of Population and Housing (1990) and the "Briggs Community Survey" conducted by Gerald Luedtke and Associates, October 17, 1991.

23. *A Social Analysis of Corktown and Hubbard-Richard* by Michail Curro, Ghaith Fariz, David Grinell, Marty Newingham, and Alexandra Smith (Ann Arbor: University of Michigan, 1990).

24. Statistics compiled and reported by the *Detroit Free Press* (*DFP*), "Warrendale," August 5, 1992.

25. As often happens now, the story of the residents' "racism" was conveyed through a form of temporal othering or distancing, similar to that described by Johannes Fabian in *Time and the Other: How Anthropology Makes Its Objects* (New York: Columbia University Press, 1983). Allusions to the desegregation of the Little Rock school system in the 1950s were constant; commentators, though,

missed what is undeniably current about such protests and disruptions, particularly in Detroit, where the coloring of power relations has been reversed from those that held sway in the South in the 1950s.

26. "A Taste of 'the Other': Intellectual Complicity in Racializing Practices," *Current Anthropology* 35.4 (1994): 333–48. I draw my use of objectification from Dominguez, *People as Subject, People as Object: Selfhood and Peoplehood in Contemporary Israel* (Madison: University of Wisconsin Press, 1989).

27. An example of this tendency is Robert Smith's *Racism in the Post-Civil Rights Era: Now You See It, Now You Don't* (Albany: State University of New York Press, 1995), with its chapters neatly delineated: "Individual Racism in the Post-Civil Rights Era" and "Institutional Racism in the Post-Civil Rights Era."

28. This development is reviewed by Virginia Dominguez, "Invoking Culture: The Messy Side of 'Cultural Politics,'" *South Atlantic Quarterly*, 91.1: (Winter, 1992): 19–42. Also see Faye Harrison, "The Persistent Power of 'Race' in the Cultural and Political Economy of Racism," *Annual Review of Anthropology* 24: (1995): 47–74; *Race*, edited by Roger Sanjek and Steven Gregory (New Brunswick, N.J.: Rutgers University Press, 1994); Eric Wolfe, "Perilous Ideas: Race, Culture, People," *Current Anthropology*, 35.1 (February 1994): 1–12; Verena Stolcke, "Talking Culture: New Boundaries, New Rhetorics of Exclusion," *Current Anthropology*, 36.1 (February 1995): 1–24; David Theo Goldberg, *Racist Culture: Philosophy and the Politics of Meaning* (Oxford: Blackwell, 1993).

29. Daniel Segal, "'Race' and 'Colour' in Pre-Independence Trinidad and Tobago," in *Trinidad Ethnicity, edited by Kevin Yelvington* (Knoxville: University of Tennessee Press, 1998), 81–115.

30. This claim derives from a great number of studies on the spatial dynamics of racial identity, in addition to my work in Detroit. See Helan Page and R. Brooke Thomas, "White Public Space and the Construction of White Privilege in U.S. Health Care: Fresh Concepts and a New Model of Analysis," *Medical Anthropology Quarterly* 8.1 (March 1994): 109–16; Roger Hewitt, *White Talk Black Talk: Inter-racial Friendship and Communication amongst Adolescents* (Cambridge: Cambridge University Press, 1986); Steven Gregory, "Race, Rubbish, and Resistance: Empowering Difference in Community Politics," *Cultural Anthropology* 8.1 (1993): 24–48; Mark Allan Hughes, "Misspeaking Truth to Power: A Geographical Perspective on the Underclass Fallacy," *Economic Geography* 65.3 (1989): 187–207; Peter Wade, *Blackness and Race Mixture: The Dynamics of Racial Identity in Colombia* (Baltimore: Johns Hopkins University Press, 1993); Kenneth Jackson, "The Spatial Dimensions of Social Control: Race, Ethnicity, and Government Housing Policy in the United States, 1918–1968," in *Modern Industrial Cities: History, Policy, and Survival*, edited by Bruce Stave, Beverly Hills: Sage Publications, (1982), 79–128; Peter Jackson, *Maps of Meaning: An Introduction to Cultural Geography* (London: Unwin Hyman, 1989); Joel Streicker, "Remaking Race, Class, and Region in a Tourist Town," *Identities* 3.4 (1997): 523–55. Peter Wade observes "how region has become a powerful language of cultural and racial differentiation and how the country's racial order and its images of emerging nationhood are intimately bound up with a geography of culture. I look at space as a landscape of meaning, a 'moral topography,' exploring it as a metaphor for race and culture, but I also look at it as a means

through which social relations constitute themselves in a concrete form." He further emphasizes that "social relations that involve racial identities operate through regional structures, and in this sense race relations are regional relations. Spatial structures can be seen as the outcome of and the medium for social relations that have a discourse of race" (*Blackness and Race Mixture*, 43, 54).

31. Michael Taussig, *Shamanism, Colonialism, and the Wild Man: A Study in Terror and Healing* (Chicago: University of Chicago Press, 1987), 179.

32. I draw my notion of cultural poetics primarily from Kathleen Stewart, *A Space on the Side of the Road: Cultural Poetics in an "Other" America* (Princeton: Princeton University Press, 1996), and José Limón, *Dancing with the Devil: Society and Cultural Poetics in Mexican-American South Texas* (Madison: University of Wisconsin Press, 1994).

33. My attention to situations draws upon Donna Haraway's discussions in "Situated Knowledges: The Science Question in Feminism and the Privilege of Partial Perspective," 183–202 in her *Simians, Cyborgs, and Women: The Reinvention of Nature* (New York: Routledge, 1991).

34. In the city's mayoral election of 1994, the idea that race could be "interjected," even in a contest that primarily paired two African-American candidates, was frequently expressed. In particular, see "McPhail Warns of Influence of Suburbs," *DFP*, June 25, 1993, 1A+.

35. By attending to the discursive construction of racial identities, their localized dynamics and textures become more apparent. As anthropologist Greg Urban notes, "The discourse-centered approach to culture is founded on a single proposition: that culture is localized in concrete, publicly accessible signs, the most important of which are actually occurring instances of discourse. While seemingly innocuous, that proposition opens up alternatives to the view of culture as an abstract system of meaning through which reality is apprehended and social order established." *A Discourse-Centered Approach to Culture: Native South American Myths and Rituals* (Austin: University of Texas Press, 1991), 1. The range of uses of "discourse" to analyze race are demonstrated by E. San Juan Jr., *Racial Formations/Critical Transformations: Articulations of Power in Ethnic and Racial Studies in the United States* (Atlantic Highlands, N.J.: Humanities Press, 1992); Margaret Wetherell and Jonathan Potter, *Mapping the Language of Racism: Discourse and the Legitimation of Exploitation* (New York: Columbia University Press, 1992).

36. There is an increasing attention to ambiguity and ambivalence (among others, see David Theo Goldberg, *Racial Subjects: Writing on Race in America* [New York: Routledge, 1997]), but it has always been a hallmark of ethnography, in contrast to other modes of producing social knowledge. See Donald Levine, *The Flight from Ambiguity: Essays in Social and Cultural Theory* (Chicago: University of Chicago Press, 1985).

37. Wetherell and Potter use this term because "it suggests that there is an available choreography of interpretive moves—like the moves of an ice dancer, say—from which particular ones can be selected in a way that fits most effectively in the context. This emphasizes both the flexibility of ordinary language use and the way that interpretive resources are organized together in developed ways." I additionally see these repertoires as generated by spatial formations, in often

rough, disjointed correspondence with national political discourses and positions. Wetherell and Potter, *Mapping the Language of Racism*, 90, 92.

38. Michael Omi and Howard Winant review this position in *Racial Formation in the United States: From the 1960s to the 1980s* (New York: Routledge, 1986). Karen Brodkin Sacks provides insightful critical elaborations of the reductivist invocation of "class" that often arises in hackneyed forms of this debate. "Towards a Unified Theory of Class, Race, and Gender," *American Ethnologist* 16.3 (1989): 534–50.

39. In developing this attention to class, I stress what Peter Wade describes as the processual aspects of these labels. He asserts that "racial categories are processual in two ways: First, as a result of the changing perceptions of the nature/culture divide that they themselves mediate; second, as a result of the interplay of both claims to and ascriptions of identity, usually made in the context of unequal power relations." The latter aspect is the most relevant to my study, since I see marked categories like "hillbilly," "gentrifier," and "racist" being heatedly exchanged between whites. As Wade notes, people "constitute themselves intersubjectively in a welter of claims and attributions of identities, made, of course, in the context of differentials of power and wealth which may separate 'black' from 'black' as well as from 'mestizo' or 'white'. These differentials structure such claims and ascriptions . . . and claims and ascriptions structure differentials of power and wealth, helping to reproduce them, although they also have power to change them." *Blackness and Race Mixture*, 4, 336.

40. See Eleanor Wolf and Charles N. Lebeaux, *Trial and Error: The Detroit School Segregation Case* (Detroit: Wayne State University Press, 1981); Ronald Formisano, *Boston against Busing: Race, Class, and Ethnicity in the 1960s and 1970s* (Chapel Hill: University of North Carolina Press, 1991); J. Brian Sheehan, *The Boston School Integration Dispute: Social Change and Legal Maneuvers* (New York: Columbia University Press, 1984). An excellent ethnographic view of these conflicts is in Jonathan Rieder, *Canarsie: The Jews and Italians of Brooklyn against Liberalism* (Cambridge: Harvard University Press, 1985).

41. See "Schools: The Fairness Zone," in Benjamin DeMott's *The Imperial Middle: Why Americans Can't Think Straight about Class* (New York: William Morrow, 1990).

42. This is made distinctly clear in contrast with situations like that in Canarsie Brooklyn, where ethnic whites linked black children in the schools to violations of neighborhood boundaries tied to racial identity. In Briggs, there is no basis for such a defensive, territorial perception by whites; daily life here is similar to that described by Roger Hewitt in his study of two interracial neighborhoods in London. "Furthermore, the 'cultural space' associated with the district could not be perceived by young whites as transected by conflicting interests that demanded defensive actions, because black culture, and specifically black youth culture, was by now incontrovertibly woven into the local social fabric." *White Talk Black Talk*, 79.

43. Another critical term I use—etiquette—is resonant but freighted with a complicated usage in relation to race. The core of my interest lies in how etiquettes establish class boundries and in the revealing structural insights that result from their ruputure through rudeness; indeed, I suspect that many of the instances

that whites publicly regard as forms of racism are simultaneously transgressions of class etiquettes. As Michael Herzfeld relates: "Such retorts are hardly polite. But what, afer all, is etiquette but a set of labels (French *etiquettes*), taxonomic devices, grounded in the same history of manners that represents itself as the apogee of high culture." Etiquette is a formalized means—striving to be naturalized, as well—for sorting out who belongs and who is out of place. Michael Herzfeld, "Productive Discomfort: Anthropological Fieldwork and the Dislocation of Etiquette," in *Field Work: Sites in Literary and Cultural Studies*, edited by Majorie Garber, Rebecca Walkowitz and Paul B. Franklin (New York: Routledge, 1996), 47–48. In this and other references to "belonging," I am drawing on Constance Perin's analysis of this key symbolic term in American culture. *Belonging in America: Reading between the Lines* (Madison: University of Wisconsin Press, 1988).

44. Ruth Frankenberg, *White Women, Race Matters: The Social Construction of Whiteness* (Minneapolis: University of Minnesota Press, 1993); David Roediger, *The Wages of Whiteness: Race and the Making of the American Working Class* (New York: Verso, 1990); bell hooks, "Representing Whiteness in the Black Imagination," in *Cultural Studies*, edited by Lawrence Grossberg, Cary Nelson, and Paula Treichler (New York: Routledge, 1992), 338–46.

45. Since there are over seventy books published around this topic, it is impossible to summarize them in a single footnote. Please see the superb collection of reviews of some of the central works in "The White Issue," *Minnesota Review*, 47 (1996), guest editor Mike Hill. Other reviews are: Jennifer Brody, "Reading Race and Gender: When White Women Matter," *American Quarterly* 48.1 (1996): 153–59; Shelly Fishkin, "Interrogating 'Whiteness,' Complicating 'Blackness': Remapping American Culture," *American Quarterly* 47.3 (September 1995): 428–66; and Cheryl Hyde, "The Meaning of Whiteness," *Qualitative Sociology* 18.1 (1995): 87–95.

46. The signs of black dominance in Detroit are pervasive and mundane, running from the statue of Joe Louis's fist—confronting commuters as they exit the Lodge freeway into downtown—or radio station WJLB's emblematic billboards with the powerful black forearm busting through the background, to the fact that checkout lanes in grocery stores across the city carry more than a dozen magazines marketed almost solely to black audiences. The trends of black consumerism are a frequent subject of local media scrutiny: See "Shopping for Black Dollars," *DN*, August 23, 1992, D1+; "The Trend Is African," *DN*, September 10, 1993, D1+.

47. "Marked" and "unmarked," in my usage, are not reified positions. They are relational, as Frankenberg, too, stresses, but more important, they are also shifting and unstable. To talk about race in Detroit is to effect what Linda Waugh refers to as a "reversal," such that blackness is the assumed or unmarked category and whiteness is marked. The key point—often neglected by theorists of whiteness—is that all of this is relational; you cannot just refer to a category as generically marked or unmarked. White racialness can be marked in one domain and unmarked in another. As Waugh asserts, "Markedness relations are understood as being relevant given particular contexts." Linda Waugh, "Marked and Unmarked: A Choice between Unequals in Semiotic Structure," *Semiotica* 38. 3–4

(1982): 299–318, quote on 310; see also David Schneider, who first applied these designations in delineating the construction of kinship in American culture in *American Kinship: A Cultural Account*, second edition (Chicago: University of Chicago Press, 1980).

48. Howard Winant, *Racial Conditions: Race, Theory, Comparisons* (Minneapolis: University of Minnesota Press, 1994), 59. White identity is undergoing a range of transformations, which are examined by Richard Alba in *Ethnic Identity: The Transformation of White America* (New Haven: Yale University Press, 1990) and Stanley Lieberson in "Unhyphenated Whites in the United States," *Ethnic and Racial Studies* 8 (1985): 159–80.

49. "In its wake, North Americans have witnessed state and policy reforms (such as affirmative action), demographic changes (influenced in large part by the 'liberalization' of immigration policy), and dramatic shifts in sociocultural understandings of race and racism." The legacy of racism and the ongoing benefits whites derive from its historical and current operations are increasingly objectified in public and political discourses. "As a result," Winant argues, "white identities have been displaced and refigured: They are now contradictory, as well as confused and anxiety-ridden, to an unprecedented extent." Howard Winant, "From behind Blue Eyes: Whiteness and Contemporary U.S. Racial Politics," in *Off White: Readings on Race, Power, and Society*, edited by Michelle Fine, Lois Weis, Linda C. Powell, and L. Mun Wong (New York: Routledge, 1997), 41.

50. I use the term "racialized" to convey a situation in which the racial aspect of an individual's identity and social position are sharply objectified. Whites' identities have "always" borne a racial component, but they are unevenly confronted with that aspect of their constitution. Whites have also generally avoided being confronted by the distinctive reduction of their perceptions and concerns to a racial reading. In my usage of this term, I try to convey both the occulted aspects of white racialness and the still-common shock whites experience when they are racially objectified in public debates or interpersonal exchanges. My definition of "racialized" is partly drawn from David Theo Goldberg's reflections on this term, particularly in his insistence that "race is a discursive object of racialized discourse that differs from racism." *Racist Culture*, 42.

51. As the contributors to *Off White* (the "last book" on whiteness) express, "We worry that in our desire to create spaces to speak intellectually and empirically about whiteness, we may have reified whiteness as a fixed category of experience and identity; that we have allowed it to be treated as a monolith, in the singular, as an 'essential something.' We despair that a terrifying academic flight toward something called white studies could eclipse the important work being done across the range of race, postcolonialism, ethnicity, and 'people of color'; that research funds could shift categories; that understanding whiteness could surface as the new intellectual fetish, leaving questions of power, privilege, and race/ethnic political minorities behind as an intellectual 'fad' of the past." *Off White*, xi–xii.

52. David Roediger argues strongly against such an approach: "To make its fullest possible contribution to the growth of a new society, activism that draws on ideas regarding the social construction of race must focus its political energies on exposing, demystifying and demeaning the popular ideology of whiteness,

rather than on calling into question the concept of race generally." *Towards the Abolition of Whiteness: Essays on Race, Politics, and Working-Class History* (London: Verso, 1993), 12.

53. A cursory sketch of those who have made this case include: Bettye Collier-Thomas and James Turner, "Race, Class and Color: The African American Discourse on Identity," *Journal of American Ethnic History* 14.1 (1994): 5–31; Faye Harrison, "Introduction: An African Diaspora Perspective for Urban Anthropology," *Urban Anthropology*, 17. 2–3) (1998): 111–40, and "The Persistent Power of 'Race' "; Manning Marable and Leith Mullings, "The Divided Mind of Black America: Race, Ideology and Politics in the Post Civil Rights Era," *Race & Class*, 36.1 (1994): 61–72; Livio Sansone, "The Making of Black Culture: The New Subculture of Lower-Class Young Black Males of Surinamese Origin in Amsterdam," *Critique of Anthropology* 14.2 (1994): 173–98; Steven Gregory, "The Changing Significance of Race and Class in an African-American Community," *American Ethnologist* 19.2 (May 1992): 255–74; Vera Green, "The Confrontation of Diversity within the Black Community," *Human Organization* 29.4 (1970): 267–72.

54. There are limits to the cultural construction of whiteness model, as Howard Winant notes. "Despite their explicit adherence to a 'social construction' model of race . . . theorists of the new abolitionist project do not take that insight as seriously as they should. They employ it chiefly to argue against biologistic conceptions of race, which is fine; but they fail to consider the complexities and rootedenss of social construction, or as I would term it, racial formation. Is the social construction of whiteness so flimsy that it can be repudiated by a mere act of political will?" Winant, "From behind Blue Eyes," 4.

55. On the conflation of racial and class identities, see Brackette Williams, *Stains on My Name, War in My Veins: Guyana and the Politics of Cultural Struggle* (Durham, N.C: Duke University Press, 1991) As Robert Blauner asserted almost thirty years ago, "Race affects class formation and class influences racial dynamics in ways that have not been adequately investigated." This is still the case, *Racial Oppression in America* (Berkeley and Los Angeles: University of California Press, 1972).

56. Key here is Waugh's observation that "the marked term necessarily conveys a more narrowly specified and delimited conceptual item than the unmarked." This allows a more vague sense of whiteness to operate. "The fact that the marked term is more narrowly specified than the unmarked leads to the various effects of markedness noted by many investigators." In this case, these terms embody the marked condition in "the asymmetrical and hierarchical relationship between two poles of any opposition." "The dynamic dialectic between unmarked and marked terms, then, entails the dichotomy of general meaning versus more narrowly specified, contextually conditioned meaning as well." "Marked and Unmarked," 299, 301–2, 304.

57. "Hillbillies" are an odd, but not unheard of, anthropological object. Anna Tsing invokes the figure in her account of the Meratus: "marginal 'hillbillies' are disturbing to the urban consciousness in quite a different way: They confuse boundaries of 'us' and 'them,' and they muddle universalizing standards of propriety, deference, and power." *In the Realm of the Diamond Queen: Marginality*

in an Out-of-the-Way Place (Princeton: Princeton University Press, 1993), 7. Also, see Phillipe Bourgois's account of Puerto Rican "Jíbaros" ("a term that could be translated in English as 'hillbillies' ") straddling urban and rural contexts amid the contradictions of rapidly changing political and economic contexts. *In Search of Respect: Selling Crack in El Barrio* (Cambridge: Cambridge University Press, 1995), 50ff. As for the intraracial dynamic informing the significance of hillbillies, Carolyn Martin Shaw describes a similar dynamic in late nineteenth-century Kenya, where poor whites fractured articulations of white solidarity. "An upwardly mobile middle class, rather than all colonialists and most definitely not the aristocrats, was most concerned with white prestige, and it was this group that felt most threatened by Africans and by poor whites. They wanted a clear distinction between themselves and blacks that was thwarted by poor whites." *Colonial Inscriptions: Race, Sex, and Class in Kenya* (Minneapolis: University of Minnesota Press, 1995), 6–9.

58. I take as a guiding principle in this study Floya Anthias's assertion that "the construct of race has to be analytically separated from racism although they are clearly related." "Race and Class Revisited—Conceptualizing Race and Racism," *Sociological Review* 38.1 (1990): 19–43. Since I track ascriptions and exchanges of the term "racist," I have not relied upon racism as the primary analytical focus in making sense of peoples' comments. Although Etienne Balibar's delineation of new forms of racism are relevant here, my emphasis falls on the way the class predicaments of whites in Detroit suggest rethinking the way anthropologists consider race generally. Balibar, "Is There a 'Neo-Racism'?" in *Race, Nation, Class: Ambiguous Identities*, edited by Etienne Balibar and Immanuel Wallerstein (London: Verso Books, 1991), 17–28.

59. For an interesting account of how "racist" often operates as a classed epithet in U.S. public discourse, see Jim Goad, *Redneck Manifesto* (New York: Simon & Schuster, 1997).

60. Michael Hanagan, in an introduction to "New Perspectives on Class Formation: Culture, Reproduction, and Agency," in a special edition of *Social Science History* 18.1 (1994): 77–94, asserts: "Proletarian identity does not come included as a standard accessory in the crates that bring the machine technologies to the factory floor; it has to be constructed using local materials drawn from the larger context of social life in which factory and machines are located" (78).

61. Micro and macro models race like the play of yin and yang; both pose requisite but distinct views. My stress on microanalysis is not to refute accounts of race that deal in social aggregates; rather I want to counter the distortions that arise when macro concepts are applied to the give-and-take of daily life. See Philomena Essed, *Understanding Everyday Racism: An Interdisciplinary Theory* (Newbury Park, CA.: Sage Publications, 1991); John Gulick, "The Essence of Urban Anthropology: Integration of Micro and Macro Research Perspectives," *Urban Anthropology* 13 (Summer/Fall, 1984): 295–306.

62. My work follows in the developed tradition of inner-city ethnography. In addition to works cited below, I draw upon the example of Elijah Anderson, *Streetwise: Race, Class, and Change in an Urban Community* (Chicago: University of Chicago Press, 1990); Terry Williams, *Crackhouse: Notes from the End of the Line* (Reading, MA: Addison-Wesley, 1992); Jay McLeod, *Ain't No*

Makin' It: Leveled Aspirations in a Low-Income Neighborhood (Boulder: West-view, 1987).

63. Douglas Foley, *Learning Capitalist Culture: Deep in the Heart of Tejas* (Philadelphia: University of Pennsylvania Press, 1991); Shirley Brice Heath, *Ways with Words: Language, Life, and Work in Communities and Classrooms* (Cambridge: Cambridge University Press, 1983).

64. My use of ethnographic discourse analysis is also informed by Carolyn Martin Shaw, *Colonial Inscriptions*, and Faye Ginsburg, *Contested Lives: The Abortion Debate in an American Community* (Berkeley and Los Angeles: University of California Press, 1989).

65. John Frow, *Cultural Studies and Cultural Value* (Oxford: Clarendon Press, 1995), 111.

66. Halle rejects "investigations of the class structure based primarily on the open-ended question, 'What does the phrase 'social class' mean to you?'"; he also dismisses the "class identification question with fixed responses, the second main way of investigating class consciousness." Both of these, he argues, are hopelessly flawed, masquerading as "neutral" approaches when they are each freighted value assumptions, imposing static categories of class identity rather than actually glimpsing the fluid forms in which people parse classed terms of meaning. *America's Working Man: Work, Home, and Politics among Blue-Collar Property Owners* (Chicago: University of Chicago Press, 1984), 202–4, 229–30. Pierre Bourdieu makes a similar critique of sociological approaches to class in *Distinctions*.

Chapter 1
History of the 'Hood

1. Figures are from Stuart Walker, *Changes in Population—1940–30 and in Dwelling Units—1940–1938 by Detroit Census Tracts*, Report No. 160 (Detroit: Detroit Bureau of Governmental Research, July 1941). Also, *Population (1930 Census) and Other Social Data for Detroit by Census Tracts*, Report No. 143 (Detroit: Detroit Bureau of Governmental Research, March 1937). I use the term 'hood because there is no proper name for this area. A small community group that formed and dissolved in the space of five years (1989–1994) chose the name "Briggs" from the name of an engine manufacturer who once owned the nearby field where the Detroit Tigers play baseball; it is somewhat anachronistic to invoke this name while conveying this neighborhood's history. But I also use 'hood to engage aspects of the myth making associated with the inner city. Like Steven Gregory, I aim to "deconstruct the arsenal of images, tropes and narratives" that reify a figure of imposing otherness in the inner city. Rather than demonstrate the emptiness of the trope, though, I proceed by accentuating the unruly discrepancies within the mythic site. See *Black Corona: Race and the Politics of Place in an Urban Community* (Princeton: Princeton University Press, 1998), 251.

2. Census tract 5,215, which comprises almost exactly the Briggs neighborhood in the 1990 census, makes an approximate but not exact match with tracts 35–39, which covered the area from 1930 to 1950. Since the tract also includes a

predominantly black apartment complex adjacent to Briggs—though interestingly separated from it by a cyclone fence—there is, overall, a larger percentage of African Americans in this area than would otherwise be the case.

3. I draw here on interviews I conducted with fourteen residents over the age of sixty—eight whites and six blacks. I combine their stories with material drawn from a range of the archival sources listed in the notes below.

4. Ze'ev Chafets offers a collection of such perspectives in *Devil's Night and Other True Tales of Detroit* (New York: Vintage, 1990).

5. By 1930 there were 79,274 white southerners living in Detroit. Elmer Aker, *Southern Whites in Detroit* (1936; reprint Ann Arbor: University Microfilms 1977). They arrived in Detroit with an equally large migration of southern blacks: between 1920 and 1930 79,228 blacks moved to Detroit. During the 1930s, auto companies in Detroit sent "their labor agents to recruit hillbillies from Kentucky, Tennessee, Louisiana, and Alabama. These hillbillies are for the most part impoverished whites, 'white trash' or a little better from the rural regions. . . .They have had no close contacts with modern industry or with labor unionism—this, of course, is their best qualification." Louis Adamic, "The Hillbillies Come to Detroit," *The Nation* 140.3,632 (February 13, 1936): 177–78. Also see Erdman Doane Beynon, "The Southern White Laborer Migrates to Michigan," *American Sociological Review* 3 (June 1938): 333–43. The literature on the migration of southern whites and blacks is quite broad. To contextualize the migration to Detroit, I have relied on the following works: Cleo Boyd, "Detroit Southern Whites and the Store-Front Churches," report for the Department of Research and Church Planning, Detroit Council of Churches, in Detroit Urban League Papers, Michigan Historical Collections, box 44, folder A8–25, Bentley Library, University of Michigan; Robert Coles, *The South Goes North, vol. 3* of *Children of Crisis* (Boston: Little, Brown, 1970); Neil Fligstein, *Going North: Migration of Blacks and Whites from the South, 1900–1950* (New York: Academic Press, 1981; James S. Brown and George A. Hillery, Jr., "The Great Migration, 1940–1960," in *The Southern Appalachian Region: A Survey*, edited by Thomas R. Ford (Lexington: University of Kentucky Press, 1962), 54–84; Pete Daniel, "Going among Strangers: Southern Reactions to World War II," *Journal of American History* 77.3 (December 1990): 886–911; *The Great Migration in Historical Perspective: New Dimensions of Race, Class, and Gender*, edited by Joe William Trotter, Jr. (Bloomington: Indiana University Press, 1991); Nicholas Lemann, *The Promised Land: The Great Black Migration and How It Changed America* (New York: Vintage, 1991); Jacqueline Jones, *The Dispossessed: America's Underclass from the Civil War to the Present* (New York: Basic Books, 1992).

6. The Great Migration has justifiably received a great deal of attention by historians, but it is important to keep in mind, especially considering the compartmentalization of "racial subjects" by academics and politicians, that during this period when America's inner cities were beginning to take shape, migrants were moving from a range of geographic locations. As Stanley Greenberg notes, "The poor neighborhoods of America's inner cities are a result of three great population movements. One originated in the Atlantic Coastal Plain, the Black Belt and Delta regions of the South, a second in the rich, bituminous coal fields of the

Cumberland Plateau, and the third in the populous elevated plains of central Mexico." *Politics and Poverty: Modernization and Response in Five Poor Neighborhoods* (New York: John Wiley & Sons, 1973), 15.

7. Grand Boulevard stood as the ring of containment for the "poverty-stricken Negroes . . . [and] the lower-class whites plowed aside by urban renewal and freeway construction. . . . The shift of the lower-class white population was directly northward along the west side of Woodward Avenue. The Negroes, who had been moving northward in parallel along the east side of Woodward, crossed over and shifted west. By the end of the 1950s, one fourth of all housing within the Boulevard area stood vacant." Robert Conot, *American Odyssey: A History of a Great City* (Detroit: Wayne State University Press, 1986), 436, 481–83. As early as 1935, a plan was being developed that envisioned "an ultimate rehabilitation of the entire boulevard area which has suffered depreciation and deterioration in excess of general depression effects on real estate. Such rehabilitation would depend largely on private initiative but would be encouraged and stimulated by transformation of areas in advanced states of decay into low-rent housing projects soundly constructed and well managed." *The Second Annual Report of the Detroit Housing Commission* (Detroit, 1935), 27. Financial constraints made this project infeasible. In a monthly report of the City Plan Commission (April 1961), planners refer to "the Boulevard Area" as the "the Inner City." Box 8, Developing Urban Detroit Area Research Project, ALUA. Also see United Community Services of Metropolitan Detroit files, and David Allan Levine, *Internal Combustion: The Races in Detroit, 1915–1926*, Contributions in Afro-American and African Studies No. 24 (Westport, CT: Greenwood Press, 1976). Joel Garreau suggests that Grand Boulevard, as an intersection of an early beltway with a hub-and-spoke lateral road (Woodward), marks the spot that the new "Edge City was probably born." *Edge City: Life on the New Frontier* (New York: Anchor Books, 1991), 110.

8. On the interracial speech commonalties in Detroit in the period, see Werner Landdecker, "Class Boundaries," *American Sociological Review*, 25 (1960): 868–77, and reports from the 1966 Detroit Dialect Study in Roger Shuy, *Linguistic Correlates of Social Stratification in Detroit Speech* (Washington, D.C.: U.S. Department of Health, Education, and Welfare, Office of Education,1967), and *A Study of Social Dialects in Detroit* (Washington, D.C.: U.S. Department of Health, Education, and Welfare, Office of Education, Bureau of Research, April 25 1968); Walter Wolfram, *A Sociolinguistic Study of Detroit Negro Speech* (Washington, D.C.: Center for Applied Linguistics, 1969). Shuy notes in his 1968 study, which featured such social identifiers as "Detroit Inner City Southern White In-migrant," that "One good reason for postulating speech communities which are not exclusively racial is that at least one white informant in the present sample, and several of the negro informants, exhibit language behavior which would tend to identify them as members of the group which is made up predominantly of persons of the other race" (53).

9. The contours and contents of a lived, daily sense of whiteness are difficult to reconstruct with accuracy for this period, and certainly warrant further analysis. The structures of privilege and power were clearly in place, but how was whiteness experienced and imagined on the ground in Detroit's crowded port-of-

entry neighborhoods? The crucial time frame in question (1900–1940) stands as a significant gap between historical studies of whiteness, which concentrate on the nineteenth century, and investigations of its contemporary operations. In addition, the urban Midwest, with its large concentration of German and Slavic immigrants—Germans greatly outnumbered native-born American whites in Detroit through the 1890s—featured dynamics of ethnic and class identity formation different from those that pertained in the eastern seaboard cities that have grounded much of the historical attention to whiteness. See Olivier Zunz, *The Changing Face of Inequality: Urbanization, Industrial Development, and Immigrants in Detroit, 1880–1920* (Chicago: University of Chicago Press, 1982). The muddled heterogeneity of Detroit's pre–World War II white population also speaks against any simple, confident sketch of its characteristics. As Conot further describes the Grand Boulevard area, "[A]mong whites, migrants from the South and from foreign countries were almost equally divided, 28 percent from the South and 20 percent from overseas. Many of the foreign-born were long-time residents who had bought homes and settled in the inner city, and lacked the income to move out." Conot, *American Oddysey*, 482.

10. In this labeling, "hillbilly" can be compared with "guinea" and "hunky" or "honky." The key difference is that "hillbilly" designates a regional rather than an ethnic distinction. See James R. Barrett and David Roediger, "How White People Became White," in *Critical White Studies: Looking behind the Mirror*, edited by Richard Delgado and Jean Stefancic (Philadelphia: Temple University Press, 1997).

11. Burton Bledstein, in *The Culture of Professionalism: The Middle Class and the Development of Higher Education in America* (New York: Norton, 1976), 26–39, details the way regional differences between whites in the United States were used to articulate stark class divisions between these two white groups during the early 1800s.

12. Aker, *Southern Whites in Detroit*, 6. This image of listlessness, with all its connotations of depleted gene pools and degraded intellect, remained remarkably consistent in descriptions of southern whites in the urban Midwest. Thirty years later, George Henderson wrote: "Unlike lower-income Negro students who, when angered, will become verbally or physically aggressive, the southern white students tend to withdraw and become passive. 'They are like vegetables. They just sit there and stare . . . ,' a puzzled teacher frowned." "Poor Southern Whites: A Neglected Urban Problem," *Journal of Secondary Education*, 41.3 (March 1966): 111–15.

13. Aker noted with bemusement that "hillbilly" was used rather indiscriminately by northern whites, who ignored the critical intraracial distinction that the term involved in the South. In the South, "hillbillies" were instead called "mountaineers" or "highlanders" and generally considered to be a "better class" of southerners than the "white trash lowlander." "The lowlander, if we may so denominate them, are much more likely to be lazy, shiftless, untrustworthy, slovenly, and devoid of self-respect." *Southern Whites in Detroit*, 5–6. Aker stressed that there were few "highlanders" in Detroit. Lewis Killian complained that "hillbilly" is still used derogatorily to designate "working-class, white, southern migrants" in the Midwest. See *White Southerners* (Amherst: University of Massachusetts Press, 1985), 97–119.

14. The *Michigan Chronicle*, the newspaper of Detroit's black community, almost gleefully reported the appearance of advertisements for rental properties insisting that "No Southerners" need apply. The article, "Detroit Landlords Refuse to Rent to Southerners" (May 1, 1943) announced that "Discrimination Finally Catches up with Dixie Whites."

15. Vincent Crapanzano demonstrates this point in his ethnography of South Africa. See *Waiting: The Whites of South Africa* (New York: Random House, 1985), 25–39. Arnold Hirsch, relating racial conflicts in Chicago during this same time frame, also stresses the role of intraracial dynamics: "Conflicts of interest were thus reinforced by conflicts of class and culture, which animated and emphasized intrawhite differences." *Making of the Second Ghetto: Race and Housing in Chicago, 1940–1960* (Cambridge: Cambridge University Press, 1983), 173. Also see Carolyn Martin Shaw's discussion of the fracturing of white solidarity in colonial Kenya: *Colonial Inscriptions: Race, Sex, and Class in Kenya* (Minneapolis: University of Minnesota Press, 1995), 6–9, 186–89.

16. Evelyn Stewart had a four-part series on "Southern Whites" in the *Detroit Free Press* (August 26–30, 1957); the lead article was "Why Detroit Has a 'DP' [Displaced Persons] Problem: City Fails to Help Southern Whites." A year later, *The Wage Earner* (see "Detroit 'Chills' Southern Whites," November 1958) opined that "Detroit should stop saying in effect, 'We know everybody on the block—except, of course, the hillbillies.'"

17. See Thomas J. Sugrue, *The Origins of the Urban Crisis: Race and Inequality in Postwar Detroit* (Princeton: Princeton University Press, 1996); also Joe T. Darden, Richard Hill, June Thomas, and Richard Thomas, *Detroit: Race and Uneven Development* (Philadelphia: Temple University Press, 1987).

18. Arthur Kornhauser, *Detroit as People See It: A Survey of Attitudes in an Industrial City* (Detroit: Wayne State University Press, 1952), 46–48.

19. U.S. Department of Commerce, "Characteristics of the Population, Labor Force, Families, and Housing, Detroit—Willow Run Congested Production Area: June 1944," Series CA-3, no.9. Record group 212, NA.

20. The 1940s did feature the second largest surge in black migration to Detroit, with black population growing by 151,387. But it seems that the brunt of this migration occurred in the latter half of the decade. The period that stands out in residents' reflections on the neighborhood's decline are specifically the war years, when Southern whites poured into the area.

21. The contours of this contempt generally followed long-standing stereotypes of rural folk held by urban dwellers, but additionally drew on racial dynamics. This "class" line was examined in a study directed by Forrester B. Washington for the Detroit Mayor's Interracial Committee, *The Negro in Detroit* (Detroit: Detroit Bureau of Governmental Research, 1926). This study asserted that "the type of Negro drawn to Detroit is, in general, of the rural, uneducated farmhand or unskilled laborer groups" (section II, p. 16). The study asserted that "[W]hile there are no distinct class lines among the Negroes in Detroit, today, a line of demarcation is sometimes drawn between the 'Old-Detroiters' and the 'New-Detroiters.' . . . But with the growth in numbers of the Negro population caused by the influx of the rural southerners and with the consequent results that came out of this unadjusted class's attempt to adapt itself, a changed attitude on the part of the whites caused a change in the status of the Old Detroiters. The Old

Detroiters recognized this and resented it, and this caused a tendency towards the establishing of a class line. The New Detroiter, in his turn, resented the attitude of the Old Detroiter. Unaccustomed to the northern mores he had come with the expectations of receiving a friendly welcome, and he was disappointed to find what to him was 'a cold world' " (section II, pp. 19–20). George E. Haynes, in the *Negro Newcomers in Detroit* (1918; reprint New York: Arno Press and New York Times, 1969), also noted the regional differences and resentments that animated this "class line." As Elizabeth Anne Martin relates, "[S]ignificantly, the existing Black community of Detroit worried as much as whites did about the influx of 'uncivilized' migrants. . . . They feared that the influx of rural migrants would cause whites to see all Blacks as dirty, loud, and disrespectful." *Detroit and the Great Migration, 1916–1929*, University of Michigan, Bentley Historical Library Bulletin No. 40 (Ann Arbor, January 1993), 5.

Detroit was not the only city in which such an intraracial class line formed. Elizabeth Pleck, in *Black Migration and Poverty: Boston 1865–1900* (New York: Academic Press, 1979), examined a similar dynamic in the cities on the east coast (see chapter 3, "Southern Migrant"). Nor was this phenomenon entirely a product of migration to urban areas. Benjamin Wilson, in *The Rural Black Heritage between Chicago and Detroit: 1850–1929* (Kalamazoo: New Issues Press, 1985), detailed the emergence of "a caste system" that distinguished recently arrived southern blacks from blacks with longer tenure in rural Michigan. "For the new emigrees, integration with the dominant oldtimers was virtually impossible, because they had developed barriers that purposely hindered the upward mobility of the Southern transplants" (88). See also St. Clair Drake and Horace Cayton, *Black Metropolis: A Study of Negro Life in a Northern City* (Chicago: University of Chicago Press, [1945] 1993), 73–76, and Joe Trotter, *Black Milwaukee: The Making of an Industrial Proletariat, 1915–1945* (Urbana: University of Illinois Press, 1985), 109–10, 127–33. Anti-migrant sentiments, with their attention both to the "rude," "backwards" habits of transplanted southerners and to the shifting instability of the color line, seem to be more than a simple extension of the intraracial class distinctions that have long operated among urban African Amercians; see W.E.B. DuBois, *The Philadelphia Negro: A Social Study* (1988; reprint Philadelphia: University of Pennsylvania Press, 1996). Like the intraracial resentment expressed by whites toward southern white migrants, they appear to mark a new means for assessing the significance of race.

22. This case is made in detail by Levine in chapter 3 of *Internal Combustion*.

23. See David M. Katzman, *Before the Ghetto: Black Detroit in the Nineteenth Century* (Urbana: University of Illinois Press, 1975), and Richard W. Thomas, *Life for Us Is What We Make It: Building Black Community in Detroit, 1915–1945* (Bloomington: Indiana University Press, 1992).

24. White Appalachian migration to Detroit continued strongly through the 1950s, the migrants pouring in from Kentucky, Tennessee, and West Virginia. Only Chicago, Washington, and Atlanta received more migrants than Detroit between 1955 and 1960. During the 1960s, the migration to metropolitan areas declined somewhat, but by then Detroit was the third most common destination of the migrants. See Richard Anderson, Commission on Community Relations, City of Detroit, "Detroit Population Mobility, as Reflected by School Census

Data: 1949 to 1959," March 23, 1960, Urban Assimilation Committee, box 11, ALUA. Also Clyde B. McCoy and James S. Brown, "Appalachian Migration to Midwestern Cities," in William W. Philliber and Clyde B. McCoy, eds., *The Invisible Minority: Urban Appalachians* (Lexington: University Press of Kentucky, 1981), 35–78.

25. Lewis Killian tracked the negative reception of southern whites in Chicago: "The Adjustment of Southern White Migrants to Northern Urban Norms," *Social Forces* 32 (October 1953): 66–69. Also see Hal Bruno, "Chicago's Hillbilly Ghetto," *Reporter* 30 (June 4, 1964): 28–31, and James Maxwell, "Down from the Hills and into the Slums," *Reporter* 15 (Dec 13, 1956): 27–29. Maxwell's essay begins with a white woman's long, furious complaint about "those people." Then he notes, "The woman in this instance was not a New Yorker denouncing Puerto Ricans or a San Franciscan belaboring Mexicans. She was, in fact, a resident of Indianapolis, and the subject of her diatribe was an ethnic group usually considered to be the most favored in American society—white Anglo-Saxon Protestants. Her term for them was 'hillbilly' " (27).

26. Albert Votaw, "The Hillbillies Invade Chicago," *Harper's* 216 (February 1958): 63–67.

27. The process by which "white trash" migrated north is fascinating but also, as of yet, little understood. Established whites availed themselves of the term to stress intraracial class distinctions as they negotiated the colorline, as the following quote cited in *Black Metropolis* illustrates: "I'd rather have good Negro neighbors than some of the white trash that's coming in as the Negroes come. But I feel lost in this neighborhood now." Drake and Cayton suggest that this white man conveys "the feeling (and it seemed to be a fact) that the area was deteriorating irrespective of the influx of Negroes—i.e., in terms of new, undesirable white residents, and of the physical appearance of the community" (*Black Metropolis*, 189). But it seems that blacks made the most active uses of the term to convey contempt for lower-class whites—particularly members of interracial couples—living in black ghettos. Drake and Cayton referred to this as "a reciprocal and defensive 'racial prejudice' on the part of the Negroes" (180, 144–54).

28. Votaw, "The Hillbillies Invade Chicago," 63.

29. The sociological model of "assimilation" predominated in academic studies of the problem of "hillbillies." It extends from Grace Leybourne, "Urban Adjustments of Migrants from the Southern Appalachian Plateaus," *Social Forces* 16 (December 1937): 238–46, to Killian's "The Adjustment of Southern White Migrants to Northern Urban Norms." See Denny Stavros, "The Assimilation of Southern White Factory Workers in Detroit," Master's Thesis, Wayne State University, Department of Sociology and Anthropology, 1956. The United Community Services (UCS) of Metropolitan Detroit established the Urban Adjustment Committee to develop means of helping disoriented inmigrants from Appalachia who were arriving in Detroit's "inner city." This committee was disbanded in December 1963. A staff report had recommended disbanding the committee, noting "[t]he apparently obsolete concepts of 'inner city' and 'urban adjustment' upon which service has been based. . . . Vast population changes in recent years have dispersed many so-called problem families and the 'inner city' is now *only one* area in need of service rather than *the one*" (emphasis in original). The report

pointed out that UCS must recognize "Detroit as a problem area itself and not merely as a city that has within it well-delimited problem populations." UCS memo, December 9, 1963, "Community Affairs," box 11, folder 13, ALUA. But as Ellen Stekert observed, "hillbillies" remained an unassimilated population in Detroit. "Focus for Conflict: Southern Mountain Medical Beliefs in Detroit," *Journal of American Folklore* 83 (April-June 1970): 115–56. Other studies on the problem of assimilation for white Appalachian migrants to the urban Midwest include Gerald Hyland and Richard Peet, "Appalachian Migrants in Northern Cities," *Antipode* 35 (March 1973): 34–41; E. Russell Porter, "When Cultures Meet—Mountain and Urban," *Nursing Outlook* 11 (June 1963): 418–20; and George Henderson, "Poor Southern Whites: A Neglected Urban Problem," *Journal of Secondary Education* 41 (March 1966): 111–15.

30. The concepts of both "assimilation" and "mainstream white culture" provide signposts rather than clear, well-bounded sociological or historical objects. The dynamics of assimilation and the contours or content of whiteness in this period are subjects of unresolved debates and ongoing research agendas. As Russell Kazal points out, historians grappling with the manifold versions of assimilation in American culture—whether emphasizing the processes that affected multitudes of ethnicities (each in complex interraction with others as well as with 'mainstream' whites), the formation of a more unified working class out of an ethnically divided work force (including formal "Americanization" programs), or the development of a shared identity among European ethnics as "whites" (asserting white skin privilege)—have recognized that "the concept of an unchanging, monolithic, Anglo-American cultural core is dead." "Revisiting Assimilation: The Rise, Fall, and Reappraisal of a Concept in American Ethnic History," *American Historical Review* 100 (April 1995): 437–71. In its place—in accounts of the privileges and meanings assigned to whiteness and the variable processes of homogenization and upward mobility people engaged in to achieve this self-identification—we need to draw upon the dynamics that pertain in the place-specific contexts in which contests over racial and class belonging are fought out. Perhaps such nebulous, spectral signposts were highly influential in the cramped settings of urban neighborhoods shifting slowly in their class composition. To this day, white Appalachian migrants remain an "unmeltable" subgroup that warrants study as an ethnic group. See Chapter 2, n. 33. Also, see Jonathan Tilove, "Stereotypes Hem in a Neighborhood: Poor White People are Scorned, Forgotten," October 27, 1994, *DFP*, 2A+.

31. I develop an analysis of rhetorical identities in "Unpopular Culture: The Case of 'White Trash,'" *Cultural Studies* 11. 2 (1997): 316–43. Also see Susan Harding, "Representing Fundamentalism: The Problem of the Repugnant Cultural Other," *Social Research* 58.2 (1991): 373–94.

32. A thorough account of this popularization of the "hillbilly" stereotype is provided by James Branscome, "Annihilating the Hillbilly: The Appalachians' Struggle with America's Institutions," in *Colonialism in Modern America: The Appalachian Case*, edited by Helen Matthews, Linda Johnson, and Donald Askins (Boone, N.C.: Appalachian Consortium Press, 1978), 201–27. Allen Batteau in *The Invention of Appalachia* (Tucson: University of Arizona Press, 1990) details the developed historical tradition in which images of poor, mountain-

dwelling whites have ratified variously inflected images of otherness for "America." Also see J. W. Williamson, *Hillbillyland: What the Movies Did to the Mountains and What the Mounatins Did to the Movies* (Chapel Hill: University of North Carolina Press, 1995).

33. The color line is an odd and difficult object to describe since it involves both intangible, muddled perceptions and emphatic material constructs; usually it is clearest when transgressed. In Detroit, as in Chicago, cultural differences between segregation and color consciousness in the South and in the North confused the line. "A great deal of what the South would call 'social intermingling' takes place in Midwest Metropolis without exciting apprehension or antagonism. In fact, lack of color-consciousness is the rule in most of the day-by-day contacts between Negroes and whites. Members of the two groups treat each other as individuals and react in terms of occupational roles, individual personality traits, or socio-economic and cultural attributes rather than in terms of race. Chicago Negroes and whites are thrown together in large numbers in work situations where maintaining a rigid color line would not only be a nuisance, but would sometimes be economically unprofitable" (Drake and Cayton, *Black Metropolis*, 117, 130–54). The specter of interracial marriage or residential integration, though, drove frenzied whites to make the color line again emphatic. What is interesting in the situations related in this chapter and in *Black Metropolis* are whites' abilities to alternate between detachment and fury in relation to ruptures of the color line. "Isolated examples of full social equality do not seem to threaten the general pattern of segregation, and so long as they do not involve a given person's friends and relatives they do not necessarily disturb him. . . . That some Negroes and whites associate as intimate friends, or even court and marry, can be viewed with a certain amount of detachment so long as the incidents remain remote" (118–19). Proximity and a shift in scale continue to be crucial factors in white perceptions of race. As Drake and Cayton noted in relation to the remarks cited earlier about "white trash": "Most of the white people did not object to the presence of a few Negroes, but they were very much afraid that they, as individual white families, would become completely isolated in a Negro area" (189). Class, of course, is a key factor and is always susceptible to manipulation by "propagandists" and "speculators": "The problem of how to react toward Negroes confronts the average white person in a piecemeal, disjointed fashion" (274); Drake and Cayton found that "racial doctrines are not taught in any systematic fashion in Midwest Metropolis, nor do they form an integrated ideological framework" (269). And, in stark contrast with the South, "a tradition of native-American white supremacy is absent" (758). But there is a fierce "power of economic interest in holding the color line tight" (272). "[I]t seems likely that there are hundreds of people in Midwest Metropolis who have very little strong race-consciousness and no particular aversion to social relations with Negroes of a similar socio-economic status. Social pressure, however, effectively keeps them in line" (274). Drake and Cayton did not see "economics" reductively, and stressed that it "alone cannot account for the persistence of the color line. One of the most powerful factors implementing it is the concern for the preservation and enhancement of social status" (273). This broader definition of class returns us to the critical role the middle class plays in defining race relations: "And the whole problem is

complicated by middle-class emphasis upon maintaining a relatively high social status" (275).

34. See Levine, *Internal Combustion*.

35. Dominic Capeci Jr., *Race Relations in Wartime Detroit: The Sojourner Truth Housing Controversy of 1942* (Philadelphia: Temple University Press, 1984); Bette Smith Jenkins, "Sojourner Truth Housing Riots," in *Detroit Perspectives: Crossroads and Turning Points*, edited by Wilma Wood Henrickson (Detroit: Wayne State University Press, 1991), 408–17.

36. Sugrue, *Origins of the Urban Crisis*, 234.

37. *The Second Annual Report of the Detroit Housing Commission* (Detroit, 1935). Also, Bette Smith Jenkins notes in her study, "The Racial Policies of the Detroit Housing Commission and Their Administration," Masters Thesis, Wayne State University, Detroit, 1950, "There are several streets which have been housing Negro families since 1928 or earlier. The writer has personally verified this by walking through the site daily . . . from 1928–1931" (43).

38. Figures from *Population (1930 Census) and Other Social Data for Detroit*.

39. Bill was the only black man I spoke with who had lived in the Briggs area in the early 1940s. I found his account of the lack of animosity toward blacks in the area supported by another black man, James Lane, who rented a room on Cochrane in 1940. His biography was recorded in the neighborhood's community newsletter, "Neighborhood Voice" in the summer of 1988. I located two other such biographies of blacks in this neighborhood. One woman, Fannie Jackson, who moved into the area in 1949, recalled a great deal of harassment from older whites; another woman, Sarah Parker, who moved in only a year later, in 1950, had no such troubles. Drake and Cayton suggest that such disparate experiences were not uncommon: "The experiences of individual Negroes during this filtering-in process depended on many factors, including the social-class and ethnic composition of the area, as well as the class and skin color of the Negro. When only a few Negroes were involved, and they were of equivalent social status to the whites, or when whites were of lower class position than the colored people, initial hostility usually gave way to tolerance or even friendliness. But when large numbers of Negroes followed, anatagonisms were aroused and eventually the white population would move away. Old settlers frequently refer to the relative ease with which they made adjustments, once they filtered into some types of white neighborhoods." *Black Metropolis*, 176–77.

40. When I told the brothers that I had heard that the first blacks to move into the area had been received viciously by whites, they did not know of any such incidents and asked who I had spoken with. When I named the two people who told me stories of racial harassment, John pointed out that they both lived across 12th Street, an area they were less familiar with as children. Patrick added, "I don't know about over there. It was mostly Maltese in there."

41. "Homeowners' and neighborhood groups shared a common bond of whiteness and Americanness—a bond that they asserted forcefully at public meetings and in correspondence with public officials. They referred to the 'white race,' and spoke of 'we the white people.' Some called for the creation of a 'National Association for the Advancement of White People,' and others drew from the

'unqualified support of every white family, loyal to white ideas.'" Sugrue, *Origins of the Urban Crisis*, 212.

42. Realtors' expertise at manipulating white racial anxiety, driving them to sell their homes cheaply, was quite widespread in the United States. See W. Edward Orser, *Blockbusting in Baltimore: The Edmondson Village Story* (Lexington: University of Kentucky Press, 1994).

43. Sugrue, in analyzing the "intricate dynamics of personal and group interaction" in their "interplay with structural forces" that decimated Detroit, asserts that "the word 'racism' oversimplifies what was a complicated and multifaceted reality." The way "blackness and whiteness assumed a spatial definition" in the city—and the way that spatial organization collapsed—is an outcome of "the convergence of the disparate forces of deindustrialization, racial transformation, and political and ideological conformity," played out in the "the choices made and not made by various institutions, groups and individuals." This list includes corporate executives and managers, labor leaders and rank-and-file members, federal and local politicians and policy makers (industrial, transportation, housing, etc.), real estate agents, individual home buyers and sellers, and members of numerous community organizations. *Origins of the Urban Crisis*, 8–12.

44. As throughout this book, I use the term "investment" with the range of connotations detailed by George Lipsitz in "The Possessive Investment in Whiteness: Racialized Social Democracy and the 'White' Problem in American Studies," *American Quarterly* 47.3 (1995): 250.

45. See Sam Bass Warner, *The Urban Wilderness: A History of the American City* (Berkeley and Los Angeles: University of California Press, 1995).

46. This quote is taken from a form letter sent by the POA to real estate brokers in the area. The letter was dated December 5, 1945. Memorandum H, 3–4, Detroit Commission on Community Relations files, box 3, folder "Demonstrations, 9/1/45–9/1/46," ALUA.

47. From "Summary of Demonstrations Protesting Negro Occupancy of Houses," Detroit Mayor's Interracial Committee, n.d., box 3, folder "Demonstrations," ALUA (cited hereafter as "Summary of Demonstrations," DMIC), 2.

48. Ibid.

49. Ibid., 3.

50. Letter from POA, Memorandum H, 3–4.

51. Of the five census tracts in Briggs, three counted as "Invasion" tracts by 1950 (this designation denotes an increase in the nonwhite population and a decrease in the white population): "less than 250 non-whites in initial year [1940] and over 250 in terminal year of the decade." By 1960 the remaining two tracts also became "Invasion" tracts, and the three other tracts became "Succession" areas, which also involves the demographic dynamic of an increase in the white population accompanied by a decrease in the nonwhite population, starting, however, from a size of more than 250 residents. See Karl E. Taeuber and Alma F. Taeuber, *Negroes in Cities: Residential Segregation and Neighborhood Change* (Chicago: Aldine, 1965).

52. The *Michigan Chronicle*, Detroit's black weekly newspaper, covered some of these incidents. The editors expressed perplexity over why recent black

inmovers provoked such protests, when blacks had been living in the area for some time. As their first report noted, "There has been at least one colored family in the neighborhood since 1901." They also pointed to black families living on blocks adjacent to the home on Vermont that was first vandalized." White Mob Destroys Negro Home," *Michigan Chronicle*, September 8, 1945, 1.

53. Author's calculation based on the *Census of Population and Housing Tracts, 1940 Census Tract Statistics for Detroit, Michigan and Adjacent Area* (Washington, D.C.: U.S. Government Printing Office, 1943).

54. Cited from a pamphlet, "Comparison of Public Carrier Racial Incidents with Monthly Passanger Loads," (Detroit: Detroit Street Railway, 1946) in Detroit Commission on Community Relations Files, box 3, folder "Demonstrations, 9/1/45–9/1/46, ALUA. In contrast to the 14th Street lines, the Jefferson line reported twenty-two racial incidents over the same period, and the Crosstown line recorded eighteen incidents. The 14th Street line's ridership varied from approximately 760,000 to 875,000 for the coach line and 543,000 to 625,000 for the streetcar line. Descriptions of the types of violent incidents occuring on other DSR lines are included in Dominic Capeci Jr., and Martha Wilkerson, *Layered Violence: The Detroit Rioters of 1943* (Jackson: University Press of Mississippi, 1991).

55. "Report of Incident. Thomas H. Kleene, 18 October, 1945," Memorandum F, Detroit Commission on Community Relations files, box 3, folder "Demonstrations, 9/1/45–9/1/46," ALUA.

56. It is important to see how intraracial matters of belonging are negotiated through class distinctions. Again, Drake and Cayton make a related observation: "The native-born, middle-class, white population is the group that sets the standards by which various people are designated as desirable or undesirable. The attitudes of this middle-class group are probably decisive in restricting Negroes and other groups to special areas of the city. These attitudes become translated into economic terms, and though the kinds of people the white middle class desires as neighbors do not affect property values adversely, their dislike and fear of other groups is reflected by a decline in the sales values of residential property when such people begin to penetrate a neighborhood." *Black Metropolis*, 174.

57. "Memorandum C," "Summary of Demonstrations," DMIC, 2.

58. "Memorandum L," "Summary of Demonstrations," DMIC, 1.

59. Ibid., 2, emphasis added. The *Michigan Chronicle* reported this exchange, additionally noting, "Mrs. Nelson said that she suspected that something was wrong because, 'Mrs. Valentine appeared to contradict herself from time to time.'" "Omega Nelsons Told Whites to Burn House again," August 10, 1946, 1.

60. David Wellman argues that this form of displacement is also evident in the assumptions informing the theoretical models and empirical studies of prejudice by sociologists, who primarily study this subject by objectifying "the poorly educated; the aged; those living in rural areas; poor minorities; dogmatic religious groups; those of low socioeconomic status; social isolates; people raised in authoritarian families. If Archie Bunker is fiction, sociological theories about prejudice have helped create him." *Portraits of White Racism* (Cambridge: Cambridge University Press, 1977), 9.

61. Detroiters were more than willing to believe that "racism" was a germ carried north by white Southerners. Their decades of violent, tenacious defense of "all-white" neighborhoods should easily refute this notion; however, it continues to be a myth of convenience relied upon by scholars who are hesitant to delve more deeply into the complicated routes of formations of racial identity and difference. An example of the enduring strength of this assumption is Jacqueline Jones, *The Dispossessed*.

62. "Homeownership was as much an identity as a financial investment. Many of Detroit's homeowners were descendants of immigrants from eastern and southern Europe, for whom a house and property provided the very definition of a family. They placed enormous value on the household as the repository of family values and the center of community life. In addition, for immigrants and their children, homeownership was proof of success, evidence that they had truly become Americans. A well-kept property became tangible evidence of hard work, savings, and prudent investment, the sign of upward mobility and middle-class status." Sugrue, *Origins of the Urban Crisis*, 213.

63. "Regional" provides too brief a summary of Laura's account; her attention to "North" and South" as collective orders is also inflected by class distinctions and perhaps other contrasts of communal identity. Rather than regard Laura's account as idiosyncratic, it is worth recognizing that, however extremely polarized such conflicts may appear, riots are often events in which participants and spectators internally identify discrepant loyalties from an elaborate web of possibilities that are neither predetermined nor unconsciously ordained. See Beth Roy, *Some Trouble with Cows: Making Sense of Social Conflict* (Berkeley and Los Angeles: University of California Press, 1994), 160–61, 187–88.

64. Ibid.; Ted Swedenberg, *Memories of Revolt: The 1936–1939 Rebellion and the Palestinian National Past* (Minneapolis: University of Minnesota Press, 1995).

65. A basic finding of my historical research is that the transformation of racial and class orders in Detroit began much earlier than the "white flight" narrative suggests. Thomas Sugrue, in *Origins of the Urban Crisis*, makes this case in compelling fashion.

66. Capeci, *Race Relations in Wartime Detroit*, 44–46; Detroit Department of Health, "Population and Certain Rates by Census Areas, Detroit, 1943," n.d., Detroit Commission on Community Relations, box 17, folder 15, ALUA.

67. The "white slum" seamlessly melded the areas now known as Briggs and Corktown. The racial composition of this area was attractive to city planners looking for sites to clear for new public housing in the 1940s. Such projects involved a stipulation that new housing could not change the former area's racial composition; thus, if new housing for whites was to be established, a white "slum" needed to be demolished. *The Sixth Annual Report of the Detroit Housing Commission* (Detroit, 1939). When the project—the Jeffries Homes—was finally undertaken, the Detroit Housing Commission still sought to maintain its "white" racial designation, thinking that the Homes would stand as a racial bulwark against the concentration of blacks in the inner city. But the preponderance of black applicants over white applicants made this unfeasible. See Jenkins, "The Racial Policies of the Detroit Housing Commission and Their Administration."

68. These practices are detailed in Douglas Massey and Nancy Denton, *American Apartheid: Segregation and the Making of the Underclass* (Cambridge: Harvard University Press, 1993).

69. In analyzing this interplay, I drew upon the works of Edward Soja, *Postmodern Geographies: The Reassertion of Space in Critical Social Theory* (London: Verso, 1989); Roger Sanjek, "Urban Anthropology in the 1980s: A World View," in *Annual Review of Anthropology* 19 (1990): 151–86; Setha Low, "Spatializing Culture: The Social Production and Social Construction of Public Space in Costa Rica," *American Ethnologist* 23.4 (1996), 861–79. David Harvey, *The Condition of Postmodernity* (Oxford: Blackwell, 1990); and Allen Feldman, *Formations of Violence: The Narrative of the Body and Political Terror in Northern Ireland* (Chicago: University of Chicago Press, 1991).

70. Feldman's study of sectarian riots in Belfast offers an interesting contrast that might clarify the unique position of inner-city whites. He relates how geographers have tracked "a repetitive pattern of territorial extension and mixing of Catholics and Protestants. Elements of both groups move outward from segregated ethnic enclaves, mix, and subsequently reaggregate along more rigid sectarian divisions in periods of crisis and over conflict. Permeating surface events and class formations, this spatial cycle constitutes a structural mechanism for the reproduction of ethnicity." *Formations of Violence*, 26. Arguably, contours of this pattern are reflected in metropolitan Detroit, where whiteness and blackness reaggregated in materially and politically distinct formations. In this comparison, it becomes more apparent that the significance of race for whites who were not "properly" respatialized would be more unstable.

The differences between sectarian and racial formations are, of course, stark but the commonalities are suggestive, especially when considered in relation to their shared grounding in the dynamics of urban cultures. Belfast and Detroit have significant points of correspondence; residents of both places conduct their daily lives in "the wasteland of industrial culture," which underscores the relevance of Feldman's findings to my own work. Ibid., 5. Furthermore, the social identifiers of sectarian belonging are similar to racial markings in that they are both indelible and ambiguous. As Begoña Aretxaga observed in her study of Belfast, "In the absence of physical marks of ethnicity, territory and a myriad of other signs become crucial diacritics of identity." *Shattering Silence: Women, Nationalism, and Political Subjectivity in Northern Ireland* (Princeton: Princeton University Press, 1997), 33. On other connections between the two cities, also see William Neill, Diana Fitzimons, and Brendan Murtagh, *Reimaging the Pariah City: Urban Development in Belfast and Detroit* (Aldershot: Avebury, 1995).

71. Author's calculations based on *Census of Population and Housing Tracts, 1950 and 1960 Census Tract Statistics* . . . (Washington, D.C.: U.S. Government Printing Office. 1953 and 1962).

72. The racial backdrop of the raid was clear: white policemen attempted to arrest black patrons. The role that race played in the amplification of this event across the city, through several days of looting, is not as easily rendered. Sidney Fine challenges the application of a simple racial reading to this event by pointing to the diverse motives of arrestees: "Blacks and some whites looted for a variety of reasons, some because they were needy, some because they were greedy, some

to vent their grievances against a particular merchant, some because they were 'gangsters and hoodlums,' and many because the opportunity presented itself with modest if any risk since the police at the outset looked the other way if they were present at all. Middle-class Blacks caught up in the disorder stole goods that they later ashamedly returned—more than thirty thousand items ended up in police hands, some of this returned voluntarily after the riot. When asked why some people looted, 54 percent of a community sample of Detroit Blacks gave as their first answer 'saw others doing it or saw [a] chance to get things' or acted as they did because of 'opportunity, lack of sanctions.' Only 9 percent gave 'revenge' against merchants or the characteristics of the business looted as their initial response. Despite what we can safely assume would have been a tendency to attribute their actions to other than selfish reasons, even slightly less than half of the arrestees claimed that looting and firebombing were directed at stores that had mistreated them." Sidney Fine, "Chance and History: Some Aspects of the Detroit Riot of 1967," *Michigan Quarterly Review* 25.2 (1986): 403–23, quote on 405.

73. Capeci and Wilkerson, *Layered Violence*, 155.

74. Wanita is "backtalking" the "white-flight" version of events in the city, which she considers to be a too-simple, racial rendition of events that created an "inner city" in Detroit. This may be usefully considered as a form of "negative" racial consciousness, adapting Gramsci's notion of "negative class consciousness. Ted Swedenburg, in tracking memories of a revolt that ran counter to its hegemonic representations, provides the following definition: "Negative consciousness involved the reversal of dominant views, not the articulation of a positive lower-class program. It represented a form of consciousness, moreover, that was circumscribed by regionalism and that often overlapped or combined in rather inconsistent ways with religious, kinship-based, or nationalist discourses." *Memories of Revolt*, 114.

75. In the first twenty-four hours, Detroit police tried to mollify the crowds by being extremely restrained in the use of force or in making arrests. Many residents hence reported a sense of a free-for-all on the first day of the riot.

76. Howard's reflections resonate with a comment from a black man whose family was one of the first to move into an all-white neighborhood in the 1940s. "My playmates were all white. I used to go to their parties and they would come to mine; but after I was old enough to go into high school, that was where the trouble started." Drake and Cayton, *Black Metropolis*, 177. Drake and Cayton attribute this shift in experience with "adolescence"; I think a more important factor is that at this level of schooling, students are drawn from all over the city, strangers to each other, and "race" becomes an abstract matter rather than one of individual relationships; see Karen Soper, in the section "Racist" in Chapter 4.

77. Although looting was not extensive in Briggs, there were many buildings burned and damaged by fire. For maps of the concentration of riot activities, see Hubert G. Locke, *The Detroit Riot of 1967* (Detroit: Wayne State University Press, 1969).

78. Capeci and Wilkerson, *Layered Violence*, 31.

79. Ibid., 61–62.

80. Arnold Hirsch relates an excellent example of this dynamic in Chicago conflicts over the residential color line in the same era. "Nothing would have

shocked Hyde Parkers more than the assertion that they were part of a generalized 'white' effort to control the process of racial succession. The imputation of a brotherhood with the ethnic, working-class rock throwers would have been more than they could bear. Yet, there was such a consensus. . . . There was certainly wide divergence in the means deemed acceptable to manage succession, but the Hyde Park proclivity for sending building inspectors rather than debris into the homes of new black residents stemmed from the same fears that called forth crowds elsewhere. . . . Although the rhetoric of integration was in sharp contrast to the virulent racist diatribes that were offered in some quarters, the justifications given for actions taken reveal the differences among the various white groups to be more in the vehemence of language and the sophistication of the resistance than in fundamental assumptions." Hirsch, *Making of the Second Ghetto*, 171–72.

81. Kathleen Stewart, "Backtalking the Wilderness: 'Appalachian' En-genderings," in *Uncertain Terms: Negotiating Gender in American Culture*, edited by Faye Ginsburg and Anna Tsing (Boston: Beacon Press, 1990), 43–56. Substituting "race" for "gender" in the following assertion by Stewart suggests a keen insight about the discursive construction of identity in this zone: "Gender 'identities' are not left as inert 'internalized' essences but constantly questioned and their meanings set in motion when people insist on 'speaking for themselves'" (50).

82. Sidney Fine explains one basis for this reading: "Although the rioters spared some establishments with 'soul brother' signs, stores were looted, generally speaking, whether white-owned or black-owned, whether they treated their customers well or poorly. It is a myth that looting was selectively aimed at hated white merchants alone." "Chance and History," 406.

83. (Ann Arbor: University of Michigan Press, 1989), 351–52.

84. "The motive of whites in joining the riot remain obscure. Some of them, no doubt, shared the resentment of black rioters, but others, judging from their responses to questions about the disturbance, were probably seeking nothing more than personal gain. Whatever the reason for their participation, white rioters appear to have been guilty of a disproportionate number of the major crimes committed during the riot." Ibid., 341–42.

85. Capeci and Wilkerson, *Layered Violence*, 163–65.

86. Detroit's version of "Chinatown" was adjacent to Corktown.

87. In Leonard Gordon, *A City in Racial Crisis: The Case of Detroit Pre- and Post- the 1967 Riot* (Dubuque, IA: Wm. C. Brown, 1971), 120–42.

88. See Wilbur C. Rich, *Coleman Young and Detroit Politics: From Social Activist to Power Broker* (Detroit: Wayne State University Press, 1989).

89. Franklin School was established in 1866 to relieve overcrowding of westside children "who were being housed in an unhealthy basement of the Cass Elementary School and several rented quarters on Grand River and Michigan Avenues." When the old building was razed in 1899, a new "larger, modern, brick building" was built and opened in its place in 1900. Additions were made until 1922, when the school's capacity was doubled. Franklin's enrollment seems to have peaked at 2,172 in 1961, a number slightly smaller than the current population of the entire neighborhood. Board of Education of the City of Detroit, *Histories of the Public Schools of Detroit*, vol. 2 (1967), 434–35. The section of this

volume on Franklin School reports an enrollment figure of 2,172 "at the present time," although by 1964 and 1965 enrollment hovered around 1,400. Since the volume includes updates on Owen School from 1961, I suggest this as a reasonable date for the cited figures.

90. Coleman Young offers this observation of how whites experienced this situation: "White people not only have lost control of Detroit, but find it, as a rule, racially foreign and consequently frightening, and identify with it in those terms." *Hard Stuff: The Autobiography of Coleman Young* (New York: Viking, 1994), 204.

91. William Julius Wilson argues that the significant increase in the poverty concentration in inner-city neighborhoods is primarily related to the outmigration of black middle-class and working-class families. *The Truly Disadvantaged: The Inner City, The Underclass and Public Policy* (Chicago: University of Chicago Press, 1987), 50–62.

92. It is difficult to gauge the class character of black residents in this area based on census data alone. Only two tracts featured sufficient concentrations of black residents (over 400) to be separately tallied in the 1970 census. Interestingly, the median value of homes was highest in these two tracts (among the five that encompassed the area presently known as Briggs) and, in one, black homeowners outnumbered white homeowners. Occupationally, blacks in these tracts included a number of professionals and craftsmen or foremen, but the largest portion were machine operators. At the same time, the black poverty rate was extremely high in this area, around 30 percent—much higher than it was for blacks in the city at large. Clearly a class bifurcation characterized black residents.

93. Conot, *American Odyssey*, 613–14, 437–38.

94. These terms, "invasion" and "breach," are standard in any analysis of early racial integration of residential areas; here, I am merely transposing them into a class register linked to this demographic dynamic.

95. Conot, *American Odyssey*, 437.

96. I draw my theoretical inflection of "threshold" partially from Foucault's *Archeology of Knowledge and the Discourse on Language* (New York: Pantheon, 1972); he lists it as one of the "concepts that enables us to conceive of discontinuity," enabling the analyst to "detect the incidence of interruptions" occurring within an apparent social unity (4–5). Rather than deriving from an objective condition, thresholds reflect the tenuous and contingent matter of how interpretations of slights, comments, and challenges are regarded as alternately personal or collective matters. The connotations embedded in a range of encounters shift as these judgments are made. A similar sense of threshold is expressed below by Betty Hogan: "When you get more than 50 percent black, that's it, the whites move out." The threshold she uses here is hardly absolute, but it indicates the way whites shift from viewing black neighbors as individuals to seeing them as vulnerable or threatening collectives.

97. Eleanor Paperno Wolf and Charles N. Lebeaux, in *Change and Renewal in an Urban Community: Five Case Studies of Detroit* (New York: Praeger, 1969), provide a range of views of neighborhoods in Detroit as they contended with shifts in their racial composition.

98. "Total Action Against Poverty," City of Detroit, Community Action Program 6–1B, p. 1–4, in Wayne State University Library, Detroit.

99. This point is illustrated by enrollment at Franklin. Between 1965 and 1966, the number of white students dropped from 960 to 868, a 10 percent drop that was matched by that among black students, who declined from 355 to 319 in the same period. When the school opened in the fall of 1967, following the riot, there were only three fewer white students attending Franklin. The number of black students, though, declined to 254, a drop of 21 percent from the previous year. By 1969, the number of black students plummeted to 182. Clearly, the white families who were leaving this zone did so for reasons other than the increased presence of blacks in the area. Figures are taken from the *Racial-Ethnic Distribution of Students in the Detroit Public Schools* (Detroit Public Schools) for the years 1965–1969.

100. Dorothy Day was born in Brooklyn in 1897. The *Catholic Worker* was both a newspaper and an ideal: "a dream for a new social order, concern for the poor, voluntary poverty, pacifism, love for the land, all based on a strong belief in the church, in its intellectual, liturgical, sacramental, and mystical dimensions." Genevieve Casey, *Father Clem Kern, Conscience of Detroit* (Detroit: Marygrove College, 1989), 107. Louis Murphy, whose daughter was elected to the Detroit City Council in 1993, established the St. Francis House of Hospitality in Corktown, drawing his inspiration from the work of Dorothy Day. For a more complete account of Day's work see William Miller, *All is Grace: The Spirituality of Dorothy Day* (Garden City, NY: Doubleday, 1987).

101. School community agents were one aspect of an ambitious program, the National Great Cities School Improvement Project, an innovation of Dr. Samuel Brownell, superintendent of schools in Detroit, and superintendents from fourteen other cities. The project was a response to worsening conditions in the inner cities of urban areas across the United States. See Conot, *American Odyssey*, 435–40.

102. In 1964 Owen School, on 15th Street, had 488 black students and 210 white students; Franklin had 932 white students, 356 black students. Franklin continued to have a clear majority of white students until the school closed. "Racial Distribution of Students and Contract Personnel in the Detroit Public Schools," n.d., Detroit Public Schools Community Relation Division Collection, box 16, folder 2, ALUA.

103. All but one of these students were black. When Franklin Elementary (K–5) closed, it had a total of 313 students, 49 percent of whom were white. Owen Elementary had 276 students (80 percent were black). *Detroit School Statistics*, compiled by Detroit Public Schools, Administrative Research and Evaluation Department, Office of Research, Planning and Evalution, Detroit: Detroit Public Schools, vol. 60, pt. 1 (1981) and vol. 59, pt. 1 (1979).

104. There are two excellent works that track the racial politics and rhetoric in Detroit as the city shifted from one racial majority to another: Joel D. Aberbach and Jack L. Walker, *Race in the City: Political Trust and Public Policy in the New Urban System* (Boston: Little, Brown, 1973), and Peter K. Eisinger, *The Politics of Displacement: Racial and Ethnic Transition in Three American Cities* (New York: Academic Press, 1980). J. David Greenstone and Paul E. Peter-

son, *Race and Authority in Urban Politics: Community Politics and the War on Poverty* (Chicago: University of Chicago Press, 1973), place Detroit in a comparative context with other cities in the United States as they examine the racialization of community politics in a slightly earlier period. Briggs was one of several neighborhoods targeted in the Model Cities program for receiving funds for the Department of Housing and Urban Development. Federal politicians charged with disbursing these funds were troubled, though, by the black dominance of the community power structures. As a *Wall Street Journal* article observed, even though the area's population "is divided equally between white and Negroes, the Negroes clearly hold the upper hand in organization. Only one white is on the 16-member committee of residents formed to conduct the coming election [for the Citizens Governing Board]." The article noted that the area's whites—"largely migrants form the Appalachian hill country, and those of Polish extraction who have not fled the inner city for the suburbs"—were both poor and too "'timid' about participating in community affairs." One observer noted, "They're growing Negro leaders while the poor whites go down, down, down." An area minister related an instance in which he tried to mobilize these Appalachian migrants to seek greater representation in the Model Cities program: "The minister did manage to round up about 50 of his whites to attend a December meeting designed to stimulate citizen interest in the coming election. But failure came quickly—at the hands of the Negro women [who held 12 of the 16 seats]. 'The haranguing and shouting were too much for my people,' Mr. Redmond recalls. 'They're not used to such meanness. Never again will I get them to go.'" Monroe Karmin, "Model City Muddle: Whites Shunted aside while Negroes Argue over Detroit Program," *Wall Street Journal*, February 20, 1968, 1+.

105. Some readers may suspect that Betty's perspective derives primarily from racist sentiment. I could not make that determination based on the two interviews I conducted with her. Such a determination would, in any case, overlook the discourses that inform her thinking and the political contexts she participated in or observed.

106. This period is described in great detail by Conot, *American Odyessey*; Eleanor Paperno Wolf, *Trial and Error: The Detroit School Segregation Case* (Detroit: Wayne State University Press, 1981); Jeffery Mirel, *The Rise and Fall of an Urban School System* (Ann Arbor: University of Michigan Press, 1993). Wilbur C. Rich provides a comparative perspective in *Black Mayors and School Politics: The Failure of Reform in Detroit, Gary, and Newark* (New York: Garland, 1996).

107. Mirel, *The Rise and Fall of an Urban School System*, 308.

108. Ibid., 310, 356–57.

109. Ibid., 331, 333.

110. Ibid., 342–43. The stakes this time, however, were somewhat different. Detroiters argued, correctly, that desegregation would accelerate white flight, and thus ruin the city.

111. See Mirel on the precarious state of records for the Detroit School Broad, ibid., 412–13.

112. Since he spoke with me candidly, I decided it best to use a pseudonym.

Chapter 2
"A Hundred Shades of White"

1. When I first returned to Briggs, in June of 1994, Jerry and his family had been tossed out by Frank. Jerry has been badly injured in a typically bizarre fashion: drunk, he jumped on the hood of their Gremlin as Jessie Rae was driving away, after refusing to take him to the bar—after his second heart attack, she had tried to get him to stop drinking. He tumbled off the hood and onto the street, where his skull cracked open. While he was in the hospital, Frank evicted them. The next year when I returned, both the yellow and gray houses had been burned to the ground—some suspected Jerry did this—and only the red brick house remained.

2. I am suggesting that whites and blacks developed a distinctive style of socializing based on locality. This type of development has long been recognized among "inner-city" dwellers, as Gerald Suttles notes: "On the basis of stochastic processes alone, one might expect that a distinct locality would become a common arena within which people arrive at a fairly standard code for deciphering and evaluating one another's behavior. All models of social behavior which emphasize frequency, convenience, and continuity of interaction generally imply that relatively separate local groupings provide the occasion for cultural patterns to become standardized and differentiated from those of other local groupings." *The Social Order of the Slum: Ethnicity and Territory in the Inner City* (Chicago: University of Chicago Press, 1968), 6. See also his *The Social Construction of Communities* (Chicago: University of Chicago Press, 1972).

3. *The Signifying Monkey: A Theory of African-American Literary Criticism* (New York: Oxford University Press, 1988), 45. My use of signification mobilizes its ethnographic uses as well as its mode of usage in literary criticism, which are summarized well by Kathleen Stewart, who suggests that "signification is taken as a social praxis always already in-filled with social conflicts and cultural poetics and politics. The social order is itself mediated by forms and so subject to doubt and room for maneuver." *A Place by the Side of the Road: Cultural Poetics and an "Other" America* (Princeton: Princeton University Press, 1996), 189.

4. Gates, *The Signifying Monkey*, 49.

5. Gates develops this contrast alternately in specific terms—defining standard English as "conventions established, at least officially, by middle-class white people (ibid., 47)—and sweeping, poetic gestures, such as "the language of blackness" (66). However, he allows that we can "think of American discourse as both the opposition between and the ironic identity of the movement, the very vertigo, that we encounter in a mental shift between the two terms [signification as "white," signification as "black"] (50).

6. Ibid., 82.

7. As Constance Perin relates, "The natural ambiguity of neighbor [or of race/whiteness] arises from the variety of concepts its meanings can draw on"; as well, by the always-changing situations to which "neighbor" applies. "Strangers" entering the field of personal relationship provoke a shift in the social topography, "and we may lose our bearings. . . . For it is not the stranger per se that is unsettling, *but the necessity it signals of realigning* what is already in that field:

the possibility that the concept organizing a settled system will have to apply in untried ways, leaving us unsure how to act and what to expect from others." *Belonging in America: Reading between the Lines* (Madison: University of Wisconsin Press, 1988), 28–29. In relation to this form of indeterminacy, T. O. Beidelman—as part of an analysis of etiquette that I draw upon below—stresses that it opens "up" continued negotiations as to which tones and meanings will be stressed at various encounters, and what they will mean." *Moral Imagination in Kaguru Modes of Thought* (Washington, D.C.: Smithsonian Institution, 1993), 65.

8. Discussions of the significance of race in the United States are generally developed through national perspectives, with scant attention paid to the regional variations in how people articulate their understandings of racial meanings. Peter Wade offers a powerful example of the importance of paying attention to shifting geographical scales; in Colombia, he argues, "Race is often spoken of in a locative voice." He tracks "how region has become a powerful language of cultural and racial differentiation and how the country's racial order and its images of emerging nationhood are intimately bound up with a geography of culture. I look at space as a landscape of meaning, a 'moral topography,' exploring it as a metaphor for race and culture, but I also look at it as a means through which social relations constitute themselves in a concrete form." See *Blackness and Race Mixture: The Dynamics of Racial Identity in Colombia* (Baltimore: Johns Hopkins University Press, 1993), 54, 43.

9. This insight derives fundamentally from the work of Mary Douglas but also draws on Constance Perin's application of this mode of analysis to American culture. *Belonging in America*, 11–15.

10. Bonnie Urciuoli and Signithia Fordham—in very different contexts, but each attending to the construction of racial identities through the projection of ascribed categories—stress that the designation "acting white" is keenly tied to class mobility and displays of sophistication with language or status symbols. See Bonnie Urciuoli, *Exposing Prejudice: Puerto Rican Experiences of Language, Race, and Class* (Boulder, CO: Westview, 1996), and Signithia Fordham, *Blacked Out: Dilemmas of Race, Identity, and Success at Capital High* (Chicago: University of Chicago Press, 1996). In regard to the situation in Detroit, Carolyn Martin Shaw's observations about the construction of whiteness in Kenya are quite relevant: "White prestige was built on middle-class morality and discipline, and on the maintenance of distinct boundaries between the colonizer and the colonized. This boundary was transgressed by poor and uneducated whites." *Colonial Inscriptions; Race, Sex, and Class in Kenya* (Minneapolis: University of Minnesota Press, 1995), 8.

11. Several of the few interracial couples in the area involved "hillbilly" women and black men. I examine this and other kinship patterns in Briggs in "Locating White Detroit," in *Displacing Whiteness: Essays in Social and Cultural Criticism*, edited by Ruth Frankenberg (Durham, NC: Duke University Press, 1997), 180–213.

12. As Virginia Dominguez explains, such labels are elusive because "the identities they name are both affirmed and contextualized in each instance of usage, . . . [which] means that there is never a single isolable meaning of a label. Changes

in context can, and do, reorder priorities that then trigger reordering of distinctive features." See *White by Definition: Social Classification in Creole Louisiana* (New Brunswick, NJ: Rutgers University Press, 1986), 11.

13. "Conflation" is a term used in many venues to convey the various combinations of "race" and "class" as components of social identities and structures; in particular see Brackette Williams, "A Class Act: Anthropology and the Race to Nation across Ethnic Terrain," *Annual Review of Anthropology* 18 (1989): 401–44, and *Stains on My Name, War in My Veins: Guyana and the Politics of Cultural Struggle* (Durham, NC: Duke University Press, 1991). This term is useful to short-circuit debates over how to prioritize one or the other, since one is rarely seen without the other; both are always simultaneously active and evident in social settings in the United States.

14. These "hillbillies" did not evidence forms of a possessive investment in whiteness, either because their class position precluded such investment or because they were individually disinterested in such forms of self-identification. See George Lipsitz, "The Possessive Investment in Whiteness: Racialized Social Democracy and the 'White' Problem in American Studies," *American Quarterly* 47.3 (1995): 369–87.

15. Nor did I ever hear blacks in this area make intraracial use of "Bamas," a term, like "hillbilly," that links regional (southern) identity with a lower-class status. "Bama" is much more actively used in a place like Washington, D.C., where black class distinctions are more elaborate. See Harry S. Jaffe and Tom Sherwood, *Dream City: Race, Power, and the Decline of Washington, D.C.* (New York: Simon & Schuster, 1994).

16. See Bill's reference to "hillbillies and whites," p. 38.

17. His version of how things have changed, and how fights are more deadly now, is an oft-recounted inner-city narrative. See Elijah Anderson, *Streetwise: Race, Class, and Change in an Urban Community* (Chicago: University of Chicago Press, 1990).

18. Jerry got by in a variety of ways, while he was waiting for his disability claim—for an array of ailments—to be processed; these included scavenging scrap metal, car repairs, and working as a "bouncer" in a local grocery store.

19. Residents, white and black, almost exclusively used the generic term "people" as a kinship term. "Jerry's people," or "my people" marked specific family networks and connections rather than referring to racial or even regional collectives.

20. I collected numerous such stories from "hillbillies" in area bars during a 1985 student-faculty fieldwork project. See Steve Austin, et al., *Down Home up North: Appalachian Images of Migration and Place in the Hills and in Detroit,* Student Faculty Research Community Report no. 12 (Ann Arbor: University of Michigan, 1985).

21. See D. K. Wilgus, "Country Western Music and the Urban Hillbilly," *Journal of American Folklore* 83: 328 (April-June 1970): 157–84.

22. As with much of the social texture of Detroit, the culture of the local bars changed irrevocably during the war years. The oldest residents with whom I spoke recalled numerous corner bars whose patrons were almost entirely male, most of whom were linked in a common ethnic heritage. Blacks, "hillbillies," and

women were broadly barred from the drinking establishments. Several of the older female residents recalled being able only to look in through the open door at the men assembled, standing elbow to elbow along the crowded length of the bar, each with a foot propped on the brass rail running along the floor. In Armand's bar, O'Leary's earlier incarnation, women were allowed in only if accompanied by men. These couples were restricted to a back room, and the men were required to stay with the woman they had brought to the bar. Some of the same women who were once denied entrance to the bar have now been regulars for many years.

The greatest change in the culture of the corner bars in this area is that they are all owned by women. The first women who residents reported owning bars bought them in the sixties. The three women who own the remaining bars are of a later generation that bought drinking establishment in the 1970s. Two of the bars are owned by white women, and one by an Hispanic woman. Although there were once a couple of black-owned bars, they went the way of the majority of pubs in this area, and remain just a memory for residents.

23. D. K. Wilgus points to Detroit as one of the key sites where the synthetic identity of the "urban hillbilly" was fashioned, largely through the mixing of black and white rural music; "Country Western Music and the Urban Hillbilly." James Cobb documents the city's mythic status in this country western music, "From Rocky Top to Detroit City," in *You Wrote My Life: Lyrical Themes in Country Music*, edited by Melton McLaurin and Richard Peterson (Philadelphia: Gordon and Breach, 1992), 63–79.

24. Such blind pigs are numerous in Detroit. Over 500 illegal drinking establishments were raided in 1992, and police ticketed some 24,000 people. L. A. Johnson, "Bars Say Not Enough Being Done to Stop Illegal Clubs," *DFP*, December 29, 1992, 3A+.

25. The best example of this dexterity is located in the strip of kitsch shops in Pigeon Forge, Tennessee, home to Dollywood and gateway to the Great Smoky Mountains. Reams of "hillbilly" paraphernalia line the aisles, pitched mainly to the preponderance of southern tourists most familiar with the imagery.

26. Orin replied to my query, "Well, Big Jerry's got a place. He's in that yellow house on Sycamore, that big yellow house, you can't miss it. But I ain't never seen nothing but hillbillies down there." I asked for more explicit directions, like a house number, but he patiently explained to me again about the color of the house and the alley and just ask for Big Jerry. "It's just a bunch of hillbillies up there. Least that's all I ever seen over there."

27. "Hillbillies" are a spoiled identity in the sense that they bear "features" that are incongruous with whiteness as a normative condition; importantly, it's an ascription that delineates an anxious relationship with whites who at least strive to match class standards of white decorum. This clearly follows Goffman's claim that at stake in any stigma is a set of relationships: "The normal and the stigmatized are not persons but rather perspectives." Also, "hillbillies" correspond to the "high concentration of tribally stigmatized persons" he located within the "urban milieux"; "they will neither have a capacity for collective action, nor a stable and embracing pattern of mutual interaction." See Erving Goffman, *Stigma: Notes on the Management of Spoiled Identity* (New York:

Touchstone, [1963] 1986, 138, 23. See also Gaylene Becker and Regina Arnold, "Stigma as a Social and Cultural Construct," in *The Dilemma of Difference: A Multidisciplinary View of Stigma* (New York: Plenum Press, 1986), 39–57.

28. Douglas Foley deftly interjects critical ideas concerning class cultures and speech communities into Goffman's analysis of alienated communicative labor. Foley uses this theoretical melding to distinguish a distinctive working-class style of speech, one that "retain[s] a more traditionalistic organizational character" governed by "normative emphasis on various forms of social reciprocity or social obligation." Although distinctly classed, the speech of "hillbillies" did not seem clearly more or less alienated than that of the working-class or middle-class speech communities that Foley delineates. But his approach is suggestive in calling attention to the "class cultural codes of speech," which are always relational. See "Does the Working Class Have a Culture in the Anthropological Sense?" *Cultural Anthropology* 4.2 (1989): 137–62.

29. As Bonnie Urciuoli stresses, "All of this is a tricky balancing act. Markedness by its very nature is segmentary. Being unmarked in one group ('typically Puerto Rican' among Puerto Ricans) may mean being marked in a larger group ('Americans'). If one unmarks oneself, one risks being seen as 'acting white' and therefore marked among Puerto Ricans. There is no simple or general solution, only a constant, painful, and risky struggle in which people are hurt all the time. Social meaning is not determinate, and the indeterminacy can be painful when one is caught between such opposed categories as 'educating oneself' and 'acting white,' that is, when 'one person's individual achievement in the eyes of authority becomes betrayal for the others.'" *Exposing Prejudice*, 151. An observation from Perin pertains to the dynamics of this predicament: "The intertextuality of symbols keeps denigration, distrust, and stigma emotionally available, for all daily signs of lesser social respect are perpetual reminders that some meanings and the people who represent them (or are made hostage to them) are constituted and eccentric to some middle ground." *Belonging in America*, 230.

30. "The Irony of Stereotypes: Toward an Anthropology of Ethnicity," *Cultural Anthropology* 2.3 (1987): 347–68; quote on 360.

31. This invocation of "hillbilly" follows a dynamic described by Judith Butler, whereby "one who is excluded from the universal, and yet belongs to it nevertheless, speaks from a split situation of being at once authorized and deauthorized. . . . That speaking is not a simple assimilation to an existing norm, for that norm is predicated on the exclusion of one who speaks, and whose speech calls into question the foundation of the universal itself. Speaking and exposing the alterity within the norm (the alterity without which the norm would not 'know itself') exposes the failure of the norm to effect the universal reach for which it stands, exposes what we might underscore as the promising ambivalence of the norm." *Excitable Speech: A Political of the Performative* (New York: Routledge, 1997), 91.

32. Chock, "The Irony of Stereotypes," 350.

33. Key works in this field of study are: Phillip Obermiller, "Appalachians as an Urban Ethnic Group: Romanticism, Renaissance, or Revolution?" *Appalachian Journal* 5.1 (1977): 145–52; William Philliber, *Appalachian Migrants in Urban America: Cultural Conflict or Ethnic Group Formation?* (New York:

Praeger, 1981); William Philliber and Clyde McCoy, eds., *The Invisible Minority: Urban Appalachians* (Lexington: University of Kentucky Press, 1981); Michael Maloney, "A Decade in Review: The Development of the Ethnic Model in Urban Appalachian Studies," in *Too Few Tomorrows: Urban Appalachians in the 1980s*, edited by Phillip Obermiller and William Philliber (Boone, NC: Appalachian Consortium Press, 1987); Kathryn Borman and Phillip Obermiller, eds., *From Mountain to Metropolis: Appalachian Migrants in American Cities* (Westport, CT: Bergin and Garvey Press, 1994); Michael Maloney, "The Question of Urban Appalachian Culture: A Research Note," in *Down Home, Downtown: Urban Appalachians Today*, edited by Phillip Obermiller (Dubuque: Kendall/Hunt, 1996). While arguing that urban Appalachians feature many of the criteria that constitute an ethnic identity, these researchers also make the case that their experiences as migrants in midwestern urban areas provoke a reevaluation of what constitutes ethnicity.

34. Austin, et al., *Down Home Up North.*

35. Philliber, *Appalachian Migrants in Urban America*, 120.

36. See Clyde McCoy and Virginia Watkins, "Stereotypes of Appalachian Migrants," in William Philliber and Clyde McCoy, eds., *The Invisible Minority: Urban Appalachians* (Lexington: University of Kentucky Press, 1981), 20–34.

37. See Yvette Alex-Assensoh's study of concentrated poverty areas in Columbus, Ohio, where "whites and African Americans exhibit statistically indistinguishable and substantively similar levels of such behaviors." "Myths about Race and the Underclass: Concentrated Poverty and 'Underclass' Behaviors," *Urban Affairs Review* 31.1 (1995): 3–19.

38. See Michael Herzfeld, "On the Ethnography of 'Prejudice' in an Exclusive Community," *Ethnic Groups* 2.4 (1980): 293–305.

39. Frank tried several times to get Rebecca and me to move into one of his "better" rentals, and in attempting to persuade us smeared Jerry's "hillbilly"ness repeatedly.

40. See Urciuoli, *Exposing Prejudice*, on the classed codings of ethnic identities.

41. See Phyllis Chock, "The Landscape of Enchantment: Redaction in a Theory of Ethnicity," *Cultural Anthropology* 4.2 (1989): 163–81, and Urciuoli, *Exposing Prejudice.*

42. Stewart, *A Place by the Side of the Road*, 188; Stewart makes the following point in relation to means for conceptualizing and spatializing racial difference in the coal camps of West Virginia: "It is not as if *ideals* were like fixed norms set in a heaven of ideas above the daily poetics of agency, encounter, and conflict in the camps. Rather, they emerge in a social semiotics as signs to be deployed and read, and they themselves become the subjects of talk. Deployed in a contest of claim and counterclaim, they give rise to a social imaginary that grows dense with the tensions of a cultural real" (184).

43. The precinct in which Briggs was located—an area "of smoky industry, open fields and decaying houses"—had the highest homicide rate in the city during the period I conducted this study. This mystified city officials, who pointed to the generally low incidence of other forms of violent crime in this precinct. This discrepancy, however, reflects the unruly complexity of social life in this area,

resisting easy characterization as absolutely "safe" or "dangerous." Jim Schaefer, "Deadliest Precinct is near Stadium," *DFP*, September 10, 1993, 8A.

44. Sally Merry comments on the cultural construction of danger in poor, interracial urban settings, suggesting that "dangerous experiences include far more than crime. Insults, mockery, racial slurs, harassment, and flirtatious sexual comments that assault a person's sense of order, propriety, and self-respect awaken feelings of danger even when they contain no threat of physical violence." *Urban Danger: Life in a Neighborhood of Strangers* (Philadelphia: Temple University Press, 1981), 143.

45. In a manner very similar to the setting Merry describes, residents did not use broad racial terms to characterize crimes because they usually knew individual perpetrators, often for years: "Blacks and whites, significantly similar in culture and life style, feel relatively little animosity and suspicion towards one another." Ibid., 144–45.

46. In this fieldwork project, I was greatly influenced by Roger Hewitt's study of two racially mixed neighborhoods in London, examining the way adolescents negotiated interracial friendship in settings where ideological circuits of racism were alternately short-circuited or boosted, according to an array of influences informing these localities. I found the shifting modes of attention to race operating in Briggs quite similar to the dynamics he describes: "Transacted as these youngsters' lives were by differing and sometimes contradictory ideological strands and by contradictory social practices, it was inevitable that different aspects should have been brought to the fore by different interactive situations. The combination of these contradictory elements and practices differed from person to person, and even within individuals from time to time. The notion of fixed, one-dimensional 'attitudes,' by which degrees of racism might be measured, would be quite unhelpful in attempting to understand adolescent race relations in this context." See *White Talk Black Talk: Inter-Racial Friendship and Communication amongst Adolescents* (Cambridge: Cambridge University Press, 1986), 82–83.

As far as my claim that they recursively tested their social contexts, using various ascriptions—often in contests of claim and counterclaim—to sound out the significance of race, I am drawing upon a consistent strand in current theoretical approaches to cultural constructions of race. Peter Wade, in analyzing the relation between racial structures and the political economy, envisages "a recursive relation in which larger structures of race, class, and power are in one sense themselves the outcomes of the repetition and interconnectedness of individual actions, but are also the medium for those actions, being the generative context in which choice, interest, and perception arise. . . . It is not just a matter of race or of choice about race: The recursive relations between racial patterns and racial choices are structured, principally by economic factors, and some choices are more likely than others under certain conjunctures of circumstances." *Blackness and Race Mixture: The Dynamics of Racial Identity in Colombia* (Baltimore: Johns Hopkins University Press, 1993), 43. See also Sugrue, *The Origins of the Urban Crisis* (Princeton: Princeton University Press, 1996), 11.

47. See Wade, *Blackness and Race Mixture*; Urciuoli, *Exposing Prejudice*; Fordham, *Blacked Out*.

48. Again, this situation warrants a comparison with the dynamics described by Merry: "White patterns of social interaction, family organization, conflict management, and economics are similar to those of the blacks. Aggressiveness is admired, and people who are tough, able to defend themselves, and clever in talking themselves out of tight situations are respected. Differences of opinion are often expressed in loud voices." *Urban Danger*, 147.

49. See Mari Matsuda, Charles R. Lawrence III, Richard Delgado, and Kimberle Williams Crenshaw, *Words That Wound: Critical Race Theory, Assaultive Speech, and the First Amendment* (Boulder, CO: Westview Press, 1993). Also see Henry Louis Gates, Jr., Anthony P. Griffin, Donald E. Lively, Robert C. Post, William B. Rubenstein, and Nadine Strossen, *Speaking of Race, Speaking of Sex: Hate Speech, Civil Rights, and Civil Liberties* (New York: New York University Press, 1994).

50. Butler, *Excitable Speech*, 100.

51. Ibid., 49, 78.

52. Ibid., 13.

53. Ibid., 100.

54. This strikes me as different from a status as "honorary black," since it is effected in a mode of compiled differences that undercut the certainty of Donnie's superficial whiteness. See Philippe Bourgois, *In Search of Respect: Selling Crack in El Barrio* (Cambridge: Cambridge University Press, 1995), 41–44; and Hewitt, *White Talk Black Talk*, 175–76.

55. The stress I lay on the local forms of racial significance reflects the power of place to disrupt abstract social ideals. Or, as Suttles expressed it: "The most obvious reasons for centering in on locality groups is that their members cannot simply ignore one another. People who routinely occupy the same place must either develop a moral order that includes all those present or fall into conflict." *The Social Order of the Slum*, 7. An observation by Perin is also suggestively insightful here: "Sharing territory confers consubstantiality; that is, in sharing common ground, people believe themselves to share common substance, analogous to Blood." *Belonging in America*, 50.

56. Ruth Frankenberg analyzes similar comments by whites, in which an array of colors is deployed in addition to black and white to suggest that they do not see race. *White Women, Race Matters* (Minneapolis: University of Minnesota Press, 1993), 142–57. She regards such instances as a form of white "race evasion." But in this case—as in others I analyze in "Locating White Detroit"—Billy Lee's usage of "nigger" unavoidably foregrounds race. He certainly does not claim that he cannot "see it," but he does assert that such a usage effectively disrupts abstract distinctions between whites and blacks. He is not avoiding or evading race, but opening a rather perverse discussion of how it matters. I revisit this issue in the last chapter of the book.

57. This claim seems to bear a folkloric status, which I am unsure how best to analyze. James Baldwin raises this in *The Fire Next Time* when he discusses how whites "need the nigger." He construes the term as representing aspects of the human condition that exists in all peoples and races. Andrew Hacker echoes Baldwin's comment, asserting that "Needless to say, white people—paragons of civilization—cannot allow that 'niggerness' is part of their being. . . . By creating such

a creature, whites are able to say that because only members of the black race carry the taint, it follows that none of its attributes will be found in white people." In this regard, what is notable about white uses of the term in this part of Detroit is that they so often use "nigger" to label other whites, especially family members. Some expressed the type of rationale that Tom (see below) and Billy Lee articulate, asserting a biracial valence to the term, while others left the logic of their usage implicit. But what I found commonly articulated is the perception that as whites they, too, were racialized or "colored," in all the manifold resonances of that term: either as the forgotten population of the inner city, or as the socially scorned and castigated members of an odd minority, "hillbillies." See Andrew Hacker, *Two Nations: Black and White, Separate, Hostile, Unequal* (New York: Charles Scribner's Sons, 1992), 61. I found this passage from Hacker analyzed in Pamela Perry's excellent study, "Beginning to See the White: A Comparative Ethnography in Two High Schools of the Racial Consciousness and Identities of White Youth," Ph.D. dissertation, University of California, Berkeley, 1998, 246.

58. "Color, for anyone who uses it, or is used by it, is a most complex, calculated, and dangerous phenomenon." James Baldwin, "Color," in *The Price of the Ticket: Collected Nonfiction, 1948–1985* (New York: St. Martin's, 1985), 319–20; 322.

59. As Bonnie Urciuoli observes, "Racialized people are typified as human matter out of place: dirty, dangerous, unwilling, or unable to do their bit for the nation-state." *Exposing Prejudice*, 15. I think this characterization easily applies to "hillbillies" in Briggs.

60. In an exchange between two white youths, Hewitt analyzes the way one's use of "nigger" undercuts the assumption of racial solidarity held by the other; this account—one of the only developed analyses of uses of "nigger" between whites—is particularly relevant to uses of the term by "hillbillies" in Briggs, *White Talk Black Talk*, 227–37. Certainly such usage would offend the middle-class mores of whites and blacks, and I am not drawing out their usage to suggest a "political" practice or usage for whites generally. These whites were not attempting to fashion political responses to the complications of their daily lives. Indeed, using "nigger" this way conveys the extremely local nature of racial significance, both in the distinctiveness in this style and in the cautions we should observe concerning extrapolations from or condemnations of this situation. Notably, they did not make use of the term "wigger," which was all the rage in the city's suburbs at the time. It refers to whites who listen to rap music and buy the latest gangsta-style clothing. See "'Wiggers': White Teens Identify with Black Hip-Hoppers," *DFP*, April 25, 1993, 1A; "Wiggers See Style as a Way into Another Culture," *DFP*, June 21, 1993, ID.

61. Wade's description of the complex connotations of "negro" in Colombia is apropos: "To call someone a black to his or her face is not always taken as a sign of disrespect: Its meaning is highly context dependent, which is not to say arbitrary. Indeed, in its various uses there is a central reference to inequality. For example, negro can be used as a friendly term of address to people easily classifiable as 'black.' The friendliness, however, draws its power precisely from the contravention of a more basic meaning: Intimacy is implied by the ability to use a potentially derogatory term without derogation. The same goes from the term

negre or negrita, used as a sign of intimacy or endearment from men to women."
Blackness and Race Mixture, 260.

62. I found that she was born in a fairly well-off middle-class family when she asked me to give her a ride uptown to her mother's house. Gale had just heard that her daughter, whom her mother was raising, had broken her leg in a baseball game. In the half hour it took to get to her mother's, Gale explained how she and her parents became estranged over her drug use and her friends. I waited in the car while she went inside; her daughter was gone, and she was back out in about ten minutes with some cash, and asked me to stop at the liquor store on the way back home.

63. Jerry's usage of epithets was too varied to be easily characterized as reflecting a certain view of race. Through our morning coffee routine, for instance, I found out that Bill and Jerry were one-time drinking buddies; Bill also helped Jerry out of a bind when his daughter, Jean, ran away from home when she was sixteen. Bill deployed the resources of the community watch group to find her. Jerry's stint of dealing cocaine, however, disrupted their friendship. Bill suggested that I ask Jerry about him: "I'll bet he calls me a black motherfucker." Jerry laughed when I asked him about Bill, recalling their good times, but he only referred to Bill as "that motherfucker," not bringing any racial markings to bear. When I related this to Bill, he told me, "Anybody he likes, he cusses. He's always, 'Fuck you motherfucker,' if he likes you."

64. I take the term "minstrelization" from Goffman, *Stigma*, 110, "whereby the stigmatized person ingratiatingly acts out before normals the full dance of bad qualities imputed to his kind, thereby consolidating a life situation into a clownish role."

65. Richard Bauman and Charles Briggs, "Poetics and Performance as Critical Perspectives on Language and Social Life," *Annual Review of Anthropology* 19 (1990): 59–88, quotes on 60–61, 70.

66. If "acting black" is an accurate characterization of Jerry's actions, then it needs to be distinguished from perhaps corresponding behaviors in more commercial realms. (See n. 60, on "wiggers").

67. Jerry is not representative of whites in this regard; no single white is, of course. Many whites completely eschewed the use of "nigger" and avoided whites who did use it. In one instance, I was talking with Mr. Howell and another white man on the street. A white resident approached and made about a comment about "the niggers." Mr. Howell and his companion abruptly turned their backs to the man and continued with their conversation, ignoring him altogether. This is one of many forms whites used to discourage the use of "nigger."

68. The complicated operation of "nigger talk" is briefly documented in Goffman's *Stigma*, 29.

69. Ethnographic studies of urban poverty have consistently documented the association of masculinity with "street culture." Although this generally holds true in Briggs as well, I am cautious here about overdrawing the gendering of racialness in this zone. The distinctions between white men's and white women's approaches to race are not easily generalized and were always displayed in dense correlations with other registers of sociality. What I find useful, then, is Anna Tsing's treatment of the mutual embeddedness of gender, race, and class by taking

"gender" as points of divergent positionings within a site and national system. Rather than attempting to abstract out homogenized "typical" perspectives held by either women or men, or using gender to designate communities of interest, Tsing situates women and men in particular, usually asymmetrical, contexts. See *In the Realm of the Diamond Queen* (Princeton: Princeton University Press, 1993), 8–9, 220–25.

70. I draw the notion of "hard words" from Annette B. Weiner, "From Words to Objects to Magic: 'Hard Words' and the Boundaries of Social Interaction," in *Dangerous Words: Language and Politics in the Pacific* edited by Donald Brenneis and Fred Myers (New York: New York University Press, 1984), 161–91.

71. Perhaps the matter of ambiguity here is more nuanced than I realize. As Perin notes, "So do we play upon ambiguities, yet ambiguities also play upon us. In personal life, we're apt to talk them out; in work life, we map them out; but in social life, we're more apt to act them out, mutely coping with uncertainties and confusions, contradictions and ironies that inevitably escape our nets of meaning. . . . [A]mbiguities can bring on painful, disappointing encounters with social paradoxes and unreliable understandings." *Belonging in America*, 4. Roger Hewitt also makes an observation that is relevant here: "At the same time, the possibility of ambiguous attitudes over these matters was philosophically accepted by both black and white informants. It seemed to be taken for granted that, in same-race interactions, general antipathy to the out-group might from time to time be expressed." *White Talk Black Talk*, 82.

72. He had been scammed by two black men near Tiger Stadium, who sold him a box he thought contained a VCR—it was empty, except for some bricks. In his lengthy narration of this embarrassing, humbling incident in which he lost a lot of money, I was surprised that he only used "black" to describe the men—and he noted their race several times—but never "nigger." Telling the story, he repeatedly stressed how impressed he was that they manipulated his "greed" so thoroughly, without racializing his frustration at being scammed.

73. I want to be careful to distinguish my analysis of the forms of ambivalence active in Briggs from a similar approach critiqued by Wetherell and Potter. They challenge the assertions of J. McConahay and I. Katz regarding the "ambivalent class" of whites, who experience emotional conflict over seemingly prejudiced sentiments because they have moderately negative feelings toward blacks but also value political equality. Margaret Wetherell and Jonathan Potter, *Mapping the Language of Racism* (New York: Columbia University Press, 1992), 195. As Wetherell and Potter argue, this "type of approach thus locates conflict and ambivalence, along with the conundrums and dilemmas characterizing contemporary racism, within the emotional and cognitive apparatus of the individual" (197). Instead, I find it a function of place, of the nexus of discursive orders, interpretive repertoires, and the variable stabilization of the spatialization of racial identity and difference. This ambivalence does not derive primarily from individuals' experiences of dissonance between political values or explanations and personal feelings or experience; rather, it arises from their recognition that the significance of race shifts contextually and that they have not fashioned modes of decorum that limit or allow for degrees of control over how, as whites, their racialness matters.

74. Roger Hewitt stresses this same point in relation to his subjects; *White Talk Black Talk*, 82–83.

75. See David Theo Goldberg's critique of how social scientists, in the process of generating "racial knowledge," inevitably engage in "perpetuating presuppositions and concepts that have been fundamental to the history of racist expression." He further asserts that "empirical research in these disciplines continues to presuppose the existence of races and racial differentiation, if not of 'racial attitudes,' whether conceived as natural or social." "The Social Formation of Racist Discourse," in *The Anatomy of Racism*, edited by David Theo Goldberg (Minneapolis: University of Minnesota Press, 1990), 295–329; quote on 312.

76. There are many difficulties in drawing effective theoretical links between legal arguments for regulating hate speech and the kind of racial rhetorics at work in this zone. Primarily, the willingness by Mari Matsuda to claim the national public sphere as the proper frame of reference for such regulations runs exactly counter to the type of attention to the specifics of racial discourses that I am trying to develop here. And certain assumptions of these theorists are not sustainable in this setting; for instance, Richard Delgado's assertion that, "The intentionality of racial insults is obvious: What other purposes could the insult serve?" or his conviction that racial epithets "serve to keep their victim compliant"—there are few surer ways that whites can risk their safety than by using "nigger" inappropriately in Briggs. See Matsuda et al. *Words that Wound: Critical Race Theory, Assaultive Speech, and the First Amendment* (Boulder, CO: Westview, 1993), 94.

77. Butler asks, "Even if hate speech works to constitute a subject through discursive means, is that constitution necessarily final and effective?" After all, "such structures suffer destructuration through being reiterated, repeated, and rearticulated. Might the speech act of hate speech be understood as less efficacious, more prone to innovation and subversion, if we were to take into account the temporal life of the 'structure' it is said to enunciate?" The temporal transformations of structures of racial significance in Detroit are an excellent case in point. Also: "Is there a repetition that might disjoin the speech act from its supporting conventions such that its repetition confounds rather than consolidates its injurious efficacy?" Each of these repetitions of "nigger" offers instances for consideration. Butler, *Excitable Speech*, 19–20.

78. The concept of "racial etiquette" is certainly freighted with uneasy connotations; perhaps, like "race," it endures both because the weight of its previous invocations are so galling even while its relevance to various novel circumstance is hard to dismiss. Elijah Anderson, in *Streetwise*, revisits Bertram Doyle's study of racial etiquette to understand the social interactions that whites and blacks provisionally fashion in negotiating racial matters. In Doyle's worldview, etiquette is the basis of social control and a means for maintaining races within proper, hierarchized space. The scenes of social disorder and chaos that Doyle insisted would ensue should etiquette "fail" are a commonplace of social life in Briggs. But, as in Anderson's Northton, etiquette reemerges in the ruins, not as a coherent formulation (legalistic and materially inscribed) but rather as a posture that aims toward a decorum-bound disposition that *might* pertain, in the subjunctive "as if" mode that Stewart describes. *The Etiquette of Race Relations in the South: A Study in Social Control* (Chicago: University of Chicago Press, 1937).

79. There were also a couple of outlying areas that were so designated: The adjacent suburb of Hazel Park was called "Hazeltucky" by "hillbillies," as was Ypsilanti: "Ypsitucky."

80. In addition to previous citations, I rely heavily on T. O. Beidelman's discussion of etiquette among the Kaguru. "The word *etiquette* derives from a term for label, for the attributes we stick upon others, and hope they stick upon ourselves. Yet this sounds misleadingly limiting, for etiquette also has roots in terms for embroider, as in stitch, and, true enough, it provides means not merely for labeling but for a wealth of elaboration and shading, depending upon the protagonists' means and training. Above all, as [Norbert] Elias well appreciates, etiquette creates culture through bodily discipline, through modulation and repression of our appetites." *Moral Imagination in Kaguru Modes of Thought*, 61.

81. The relationship between Willie and Jerry was strained many times, and they came close to physical fights. In this regard, I think Jerry would have enjoyed Willie "getting his."

82. This emerging, tension-filled difference came to a head in a rent dispute between David and Jerry. When Jerry pounded on David's door, demanding the money he still owed, David fired off two rounds from his pistol through the door past Jerry's head. Jerry then knocked the door down, and demanded that David "go ahead" and shoot him, but David ran out the back of the house instead.

83. "Faggot" performed a range of derogatory functions. In this case, it was a way to "feminize" David's refusal to play with the family and with blacks. The men considered it unmacho of him to refuse to play with blacks. They did not express a sense of concern over his being a "racist." Rather, as men in this volatile zone, part of their role was to engage in situations no matter how conflicted or unpleasant. More than seeing racist sentiment, they read him as being "afraid" for no reason, a much worse failing in this situation. But in David's case, the application of "faggot" resonated with very classed uses made of the word. Several times when I had been riding with Sam up to the large grocery store near Wayne State University, upon seeing white male "student types," he would use "faggot" to describe them. The men in this family and in this zone made frequent references to "butt-fucking" each other, or to "cock-sucking" in general. These remarks were ambiguously related to homosexuality. They stemmed, largely, from their experiences in prison or jail (or the experiences of their friends). These expressions were always animated and playful in the sense that I never saw them taken "seriously" as cause for a physical fight. They formed, instead, another dialect in which these men articulated their dominant or submissive relations to each other.

José Limón criticizes analysts who find "aggression and its generative conditions, inadequacy and inferiority, are directly expressed through anal references and the theme of male sexual violation in this humor. I would not deny the existence of these values and meanings. . . . I would, however argue that such references might be multivocal symbols possessing several meanings and not reducible to a single one that fits with a preconceived psychoanalytic scheme." *Dancing with the Devil: Society and Cultural Poetics in Mexican-American South Texas* (Madison: University of Wisconsin Press, 1994), 131.

Chapter 3
Eluding the R-Word

1. See Robert Conot's *American Odyssey: A History of a Great American City* (Detroit: Wayne State University Press, 1996), 416–24, for a description of both the urban renewal project and the "inner-city syndrome" affecting residents of Briggs and Corktown that this renewal project was intended to eradicate.

2. *A Social Analysis of Corktown and Hubbard-Richard*, by Michail Curro, Ghaith Fariz, David Grinell, Marty Newingham, and Alexandra Smith (Ann Arbor: University of Michigan, 1990); available in the CCDC files. Corktown is fairly well contained by block group 3 of census tract 5214. In this block group there are 654 whites and 444 blacks. However, 364 (82 percent) of these blacks live on only two boundary blocks at opposite ends of Corktown. United States Bureau of the Census, "Census of Population and Housing," Summary Tape Files 1A, 1B, and 3A, 1990 (CD-ROM).

3. The programs operated by Casa Maria include a Multi-Ethnic Health Care Network, an after school program, and Youth Social Adjustment events. They receive funding from the Michigan Department of Social Services, United Way of Southeastern Michigan, Neighborhood Builders Alliance, and Wayne County Office of Health and Community Services.

4. Neither of these white men is indigenous to the area. They, too, are part of the recent arrival of whites, but their positions in their respective churches gives them a somewhat different perspective from that shared by the other recently arrived whites.

5. I am grateful to Russell Kohler for giving me a copy of an historical account of the neighborhood's earlier years, recorded in "Remarks of Mr. John A. Russell on the Occasion of the 75th Anniversary of the Cornerstone Laying of the Church of the Most Holy Trinity, Detroit; At the Celebration Thereof in the Auditorium of Cass Technical High School, November 9, 1930."

6. The history of the Mexican migration and the Mexicans' construction of community in Detroit is narrated in several accounts; see Eduard Adam Skendzel, *Detroit's Pioneer Mexicans: A Historical Study of the Mexican Colony in Detroit* (Grand Rapids: Littleshield Press, 1980); Dennis Valdes, *El Pueblo Mexicano en Detroit y Michigan: A Social History* (Detroit: Wayne State University, College of Education, 1982); and Zaragosa Vargas, *Proletarians of the North: A History of Mexican Industrial Workers in Detroit and the Midwest, 1917–1933* (Berkeley and Los Angeles: University of California Press, 1993).

7. This woman, Betsy, neatly represents a critical issue of how gender matters in relation to gentrification. D. Rose argues that many women may be drawn to gentrifying inner-city zones either because they can afford such housing for the first time or they cannot afford anything else. Betsy is one of many "marginal gentrifiers," whose limited economic circumstances complicate an analysis of how class figures in this process. As Rose asserts, we must not assume that all gentrifiers have the same class position. In this regard, as Liz Bondi additionally notes, classes are always in the process of constitution, just as are genders and sexualities. D. Rose, "Rethinking Gentrification: Beyond the Uneven

Development of Marxist Urban Theory," *Environment and Planning D: Society and Space* 2.1 (1984): 47–74; Liz Bondi, "Gender Divisions and Gentrification: A Critique," *Transactions of the Institute of British Geographers* 16.1 (1991): 190–98.

8. I asked this question, initially, in an effort to get a sense of the neighborhood's demographics. But when I found that the concentration of whites here was much greater than people estimated, I continued to ask the question systematically. In concentrating my interviews on CCDC board members, I could assume that they were well informed about the neighborhood's demographics.

9. Members of the CCDC had an extensive knowledge of the neighborhood. Phil, like others, reeled off statistics on real estate values, survey data on Corktown, and participation rates in social programs in the area with ease. I obtained the demographic data on Corktown from the CCDC office, and the study that reported these percentages was familiar to people whom I interviewed. Although it may seem presumptuous to assume that they would be precise about such an issue, I do not think that it is unwarranted to read their distinct underestimations of the whites in this zone as significant.

10. The Maltese were initially read as "nonwhites," at least in Detroit. A Detroit Housing Commission survey of the area in 1940 gave the following breakdown: "The families are predominantly American born Whites. 83.5 percent are White and were born in this country. 13.9 percent are foreign born Whites; 1½ percent are colored and 1.1 percent are Maltese or Orientals." *Second Annual Report of the Detroit Housing Commission* (1940), 29. In this regard, Maltese are clearly not marked as "White."

11. In this and a following comment about eluding invocations of the "r-word" (racist), Glen effects a rhetorical stance similar to that described by Wetherell and Potter. They suggest that "it is most helpful to view the speaker as caught in a dilemma of stake or interest. Such a dilemma is present when performing any potentially offensive, problematic or sensitive action which could be reacted to as interested, biased, or motivated. The dilemma . . . is managed by constructing evaluations as part of the world, as a bad thing which is simply being described, rather than an expression of personal negative attitudes to this group. The discourse is organized in various ways to avoid a prejudiced or racist identity . . . at one and the same time it attempts to establish the factuality of the version and it attempts to display the criticism as not blindly prejudiced but based on understanding." That is, as "just a fact." Margaret Wetherell and Jonathan Potter, *Mapping the Language of Racism* (New York: Columbia University Press, 1992), 97.

12. There are many similarities between the forms of etiquette devised by whites in Corktown and those described by Elijah Anderson in *Streetwise: Race, Class, and Change in an Urban Community* (Chicago: University of Chicago Press, 1990). But rather than being regarded in strictly racial terms in Corktown, residents' objectification of this disparate collective responds broadly to what Brackette Williams described as their "movement across social grid and public spaces [that] disrupts the specificity of the ideological juxtapositions we have consciously and unconsciously produced." "The Public I/Eye: Conducting Fieldwork

to Do Homework on Homelessness and Begging in Two U.S. Cities." *Current Anthropology* 36.1 (February 1995): 25–39; quote on 35.

13. Earlier in the conversation, when Peter mentioned that the neighborhood was "becoming more middle class," I asked if there were any class tensions in the area. He answered no, generally, and added that one difference that was emerging was that "people like us . . . yuppies, whatever [laughs], our kids are younger." As a class identity, the term "yuppies" is notoriously general but irresistable in its rhetorical charge. "Coined apparently in 1983 to refer to those young, upwardly mobile professionals of the baby-boom generation, the term 'yuppie' has already achieved a wide currency; few words have had such an impressive debut in the language." Neil Smith, *The New Urban Frontier: Gentrification and the Revanchist City* (London: Routledge, 1996), 92. See also William Roseberry, "The Rise of Yuppie Coffees and the Reimagination of Class in the United States," *American Anthropologist*, 98.4 (1996): 762–75.

14. The dexterity they evidence at managing racial discourse is not simply a function of their whiteness. Black professionals are also adept at this, as Adolph Reed, Jr., observes. As "black people have increasingly assumed administrative control of the institutions of urban governance," a substratum of these professionals "now constitute a relatively autonomous interest configuration within black politics. This dimension of incorporation short-circuits critiques of those agencies' operation crafted within the racially inflected language most familiar to black insurgency." "Demobilization in the New Black Political Regime: Ideological Capitulation and Radical Failure in the Postsegregation Era," *The Bubbling Cauldron: Race, Ethnicity, and the Urban Crisis*, edited by Michael Peter Smith and Joe R. Feagin (Minneapolis: University of Minnesota Press, 1995), 182–208.

15. The scholarly literature on gentrification is booming, but I initially relied upon the following sources: Kathryn Nelson, *Gentrification and Distressed Cities* (Madison: University of Wisconsin Press, 1988); Bruce London, and John Palen, *Gentrification, Displacement and Neighborhood Revitalization* (Albany: State University of New York Press, 1984); Sylvia Sensiper, "The Geographic Imaginary: An Anthropological Investigation of Gentrification," Ph.D. disseration, University of California, Los Angeles, 1994; Neil Smith and Peter Williams, *Gentrification of the City* (Boston: Allen and Unwin, 1986); Brett Williams, *Upscaling Downtown: Stalled Gentrification in Washington, D.C.* (Ithaca, NY: Cornell University Press, 1988); Sharon Zukin, "Gentrification: Culture and Capital in the Urban Core," *Annual Review of Sociology*, 13 (1988): 129–47, and *Landscapes of Power: From Detroit to Disney World* (Berkeley and Los Angeles: University of California Press, 1991).

16. As with other aspects of this study, scale has a critical effect on how gentrification is perceived and interpreted. Neil Smith stresses this point, as well. "The causes and effects of gentrification are also complex in terms of scale. While the process is clearly evident at the neighborhood scale it also represents an integral dimension of global restructuring." *The New Urban Frontier*, 51.

17. A key issue is what type of explanatory framework is best invoked in characterizing gentrification. Theorists are divided "between those stressing culture

and individual choice, consumption and consumer demand on the one side and others emphasizing the importance of capital, class and the impetus of shifts in the structure of social production." Ibid., 40–41. This debate turns on questions of whether new forms of urbanity (the "postmodernist city") and class identity have emerged. The subject remains contested and difficult to resolve because, although its structural components resemble traditional modes of analyzing class, spatial practices are preeminent. Sharon Zukin succinctly states this shift in perspective, noting that gentrification develops "from a *place-defining* into a *market-defining* process." *Landscapes of Power*, 215.

18. See Gary Bridge, "Gentrification, Class, and Residence: A Reappraisal," *Environment and Planning D: Society and Space*, 12 (1994): 31–51; and "The Space for Class? On Class Analysis in the Study of Gentrification," *Transactions of the Institute of British Geographers*, NS 20.2 (1995), 236–47.

19. Smith, *The New Urban Frontier*, 32. See especially chapter 2, "Is Gentrification a Dirty Word?"

20. Using census data for quantifying "gentrification" is problematic, both because the social construction of neighborhoods often does not conform to the abstraction of census tracts—in the case of Corktown, acts of boundary maintenance by whites countervail against the logic of "block groups" and tracts—and what constitutes relevant data is still unclear. Daniel Hammel and Elvin Wyly, "A Model for Identifying Gentrified Areas with Census Data," *Urban Geography* 17.3 (1996): 248–68. For further reflections on what counts as "evidence" in debates over gentrification, see Loretta Lees, "Rethinking Gentrification: Beyond the Positions of Economics or Culture," *Progress in Human Geography* 18.2 (1994): 137–50; Eric Clark, "On Gaps in Gentrification Theory," *Housing Studies*, 7.1 (1991): 16–26; and Lawrence Knopp, "Some Theoretical Implications of Gay Involvement in an Urban Land Market," *Political Geography Quarterly* 9.4 (1990): 337–52.

21. These figures are drawn from a comparison of the 1980 and 1990 census tracts that most closely approximate the contours of Briggs and Corktown; it is somewhat inexact since Corktown's tract includes a poorer area to the west. The median value for homes in the block group more or less containing Corktown is $27,200.

22. Although this process was easily disregarded by residents when I conducted my fieldwork, the rise in home values has become increasingly obvious, anecdotally and in terms of the shift in bank lending practices. Local reporting on Corktown focuses both upon stories such as the couple selling the Queen Anne-style house they bought in 1985 for $12,000, asking $125,000 for it now, and the shift in bankers' lending practices. See "Restored with Rewards," *DFP*, June 15, 1997, 1J, and "Corktown Comeback," *DFP*, June 4, 1996, 1D.

23. According to Curro et al., "Corktown's proportion of homeownership jumped 36% over a twenty-year period [1970–1990]." *A Social Analysis of Corktown and Hubbard-Richard*, 25.

24. U.S. Bureau of the Census, "Census of Population and Housing," Summary Tape Files 1A, 1B, and 3A for block groups, 1990 (CD-ROM).

25. Laurie Medina examines a similar contest over class identity, in which the

contours of a collectivity are drawn by small citrus growers in Belize, in relation to shifting official discourses on national interests. She stresses that "the heterogeneity of class experiences reveals class unity as problematic." A similar situation pertains in Corktown, suggesting "the contingent and contested nature of class unity." Farmers measure national "discourses against their own material practices as they negotiate collective class identities and interests" in a manner similar to the interpretive process in which whites are engaged with the discourse on "gentrification." As in Belize, discrepancies of scale render this discourse into "contradictory frameworks" for interpreting class belonging and difference. Although Medina sees these farmers as variably threading competing discourses together to negotiate a collective identity, I think whites in Corktown use "gentrifier" to project a collective identity, marked by racial interests, that they are trying to elude. "Development Policies and Identity Politics: Class and Collectivity in Belize," *American Ethnologist* 24.1 (1997): 148–69; see especially 149–50.

26. For a similar analysis of racial linkages as the basis for a relational disavowal of class identity, see Edward Lipuma and Sarah Meltzoff, "The Crosscurrents of Ethnicity and Class in the Construction of Public Policy," *American Ethnologist* 24.1 (1997): 114–31.

27. It is important to note that in most places where the term is used, "gentrification" involves a great deal of ambiguity. This is partly due to the term's career as a key element in publicity efforts on the part of real estate agents and city planners to change perceptions of inner-city properties. Kathryn Nelson suggests that these publicity uses, along with a preponderance of city-specific case studies and the conflicting matters of scale and scope that "gentrifying" neighborhoods present, lead to the fundamental lack of consensus among researchers as to what constitutes gentrification. "In sum, many actors—city officials, developers, homebuyers, real estate investors and sellers, and city residents—wished to influence public perceptions about the extent of gentrification. Unfortunately, almost all had reasons for overstating its extent and possibilities, and for seeking publicity to influence public opinions and public decisions about zoning, redevelopment, and controls on condominium conversions. These efforts and motivations increased public recognition of gentrification but made assessments difficult. Such a variety of concerns will continue to draw attention to ongoing urban changes, maintaining the need for accurate current evaluation." *Gentrification and Distressed Cities*, 16.

28. However, M. Smith and N. LeFaivre have demonstrated that, counter to such assumptions, persons displaced by gentrification are predominantly white. See "A Class Analysis of Gentrification," in London and Palen, *Gentrification, Displacement and Neighborhood Revitalization*, 43–63.

29. Philip Kasinitz reports a similar dynamic in the Boerum Hill area of Brooklyn. In an organized protest of gentrification, "[m]ost of the protesters belonged to a group of young whites that included commune dwellers who had banded together some years before." See "The Gentrification of 'Boerum Hill': Neighborhood Change and Conflicts over Definitions," *Qualitative Sociology* 11.3 (1998): 163–82.

30. My argument is that this assertion overlooks the other social fields in

which Americans strive to establish a sense of normativity. Since analysts have examined whiteness in fairly homogeneous class contexts, this has not been apparent. In places like Detroit, it is obvious. Essentially, I am suggesting that analysts develop means for recognizing in racial matters aspects of other social dynamics as more important than belonging.

31. As early as the 1930s, the Detroit Housing Commission had been interested in designating portions of Corktown and Briggs as slums, in order to effect their removal, thereby clearing land for more profitable uses. Their efforts met with disparate frustrations, however, ranging from the heterogeneity of the material structures to the resistance of residents. As Robert Mowitz and Deil Wright observe, "Foremost among the difficulties in the choice of Corktown as a redevelopment site was the refusal of some residents to consider it a slum. These residents considered the statistics gathered by the Plan Commission staff purporting to prove the existence of slum conditions irrelevant, inaccurate or both. . . . Moreover, Corktown was not composed of the indifferent, unorganized, depressed masses commonly associated with slum sites." Housing in Corktown ranged from crammed rowhouse apartments to grand Victorian single-family dwellings. Residents were rallied to counter city planners' designs by Ethel Claes, who organized homeowners (only 7 percent of all residents) to protest at City Hall. They were aided in their protest by the fact that "the scientific criteria for making a determination that an area was or was not a slum were lacking." The end result was that the section of Corktown which included the greatest concentration of homeowners was spared, and the areas of densest multifamily dwellings were demolished. "The Urban Renewal of Corktown: A Neighborhood Challenges the Bulldozers," in Mowitz and Wright, *Profile of a Metropolis: A Case Book* (Detroit: Wayne State University Press, 1962), 81–139; quotes on 110, 135. Also see Robert Conot's *American Odyssey*, 416–18, 421.

32. Lynn Bachelor and Bryan Jones provide a history and critique of the Community Development Block Grant program in "Managed Participation: Detroit's Neighborhood Opportunity Fund," *The Journal of Applied Behavioral Science* 17.4 (1981): 518–36.

33. But much like other whites "returning" to inner-city neighborhoods, Mike was also drawn by "ethnicity." As he explains it, "My dad always . . . He's from Irish-Canadian farm stock, big families and stuff like that. And he's a professional Irishman, and he always valued ethnicity. And I couldn't find anything outside of other ethnic groups that even vaguely reminded me of the world he tried to describe to me." He got a dose of such sociality hanging around with "Lithuanian DPs [displaced persons] in Chicago and Cleveland. And they have whole cultural networks of large families and cultural institutions. I got a real flavor of ethnic uh . . . living when I was about eighteen or nineteen years old . . . And I thought, 'this is really wonderful . . . warm, close, a nice way to live. And so I had kind of an interest in ethnic groups from that experience. And when I came to Corktown, I sort of found it again, with the Maltese. And to some extent, Mexican families are like that. So I kind of idealized ahh community." Mike was not the only one. Desire for "ethnicity" animates many white "gentrifiers." Sharon Zukin, noting the links between the flourishing of ethnic restaurants and the process of gentrification, asserts, "Gentrifiers are either former urban residents who seek to re-

capture an old ethnicity, aspirants towards a higher level of cultural consumption, or small-scale investors in housing development." *Landscapes of Power*, 207.

34. Such land contracts were common in Corktown. "When houses were cheap in 'Corktown' and mortgages were impossible to get, neighbors sold to the neighbors' kids and took payment on land contract. But now, realtors are following the money into 'Corktown.'" "Restored with Rewards," *DFP*, June 15, 1997, 1J.

35. In 1930, more than 4,000 people lived in the area that today houses just over 1,000 residents. Stuart Walker, *Changes in Population, 1940–1930*, Report no. 160 (Detroit: Detroit Bureau of Governmental Research, July 1941).

36. Skendzel, *Detroit's Pioneer Mexicans*.

37. This comment is linked to a broad mode for articulating anxiety about the content of urban social ties, a mode in which dogs and their behavior provide a charged symbolic medium. See Constance Perin, *Belonging in America: Reading between the Lines* (Madison: University of Wisconsin Press, 1988).

38. Several whites assumed this to be the case, but from what I was able to learn, although some voiced reluctance initially, the Maltese generally supported the historical designation.

39. As Medina, too, emphasizes: "It is also clear that the collective identities that emerged from the contests described above were grounded as much in material practices as they were ordered and constituted discursively." "Development Policies and Identity Politics," 163.

40. This comment was a barely veiled reference to the director of the Casa Maria program.

41. As Michael Jager has noted, much of the ambiguity involved with "gentrification" stems from a gradual erosion of earning differential between members of the working class and the lower middle class. Such an erosion plays out in a heightened aestheticization of Victorian-style homes. "The creation of Victoriana possessed the merit of rendering immediately perceptible both those strategies for social differentiation and distinction. Housing rehabilitation strategies, together with other key consumption activities in the inner areas, had to be both clearly visible and relatively ostentatious; hence they are conspicuously represented. With a decline in real differences between levels of blue-collar and white-collar wages during the 1970s, ... status differentials had to be all the more forcefully marked than before." Michael Jager, "Class Definition and the Aesthetics of Gentrification: Victoriana in Melbourne," in *Gentrification in the City*, edited by N. Smith and P. Williams (Boston: Allen and Unwin, 1986), 78–91.

42. Lipuma and Meltzoff find "individuality" playing a key role in the effacement of racial and class identity by white retirees in Florida. See "The Crosscurrents of Ethnicity and Class."

43. When describing how he had been demonized as a "gentrifier" for organizing a development project that would renovate the Porter Street Apartments building, opening up some units at "market rate," Herb pointedly told me: "See, I consider myself working-class poor. That's basically, if you look at my income, it's there." Since he did not give his actual income, this would be a difficult statement to evaluate objectively. But the interesting point here is that he positions himself carefully between the "gentry" and the advocates for the "poor."

44. Michael Jager argues that "[t]he restoration of Victorian housing attempts the appropriation of a very recent history and hence the authenticity of its symbols as much as its economic profitability is in the beginning precarious. It succeeds only to the extent that it can distance itself from the immediate past—that of working-class industrial 'slums.' This is achieved externally by esthetic-cultural conferrals, and internally by remodeling. The effacing of an industrial past and a working-class presence, the whitewashing of a former social stain, was achieved through extensive remodeling. The return to historical purity and authenticity (of the 'high' Victorian era) is realized by stripping away external additions, by sandblasting, by internal gutting. The restoration of an anterior history was virtually the only manner in which the recent stigma of the inner area could be removed or redefined. It is in the fundamental drive to dislodge, and symbolically obliterate, the former working-class past that the estheticization of Victoriana took off." "Class Definition and the Aesthetics of Gentrification," 83.

45. See Robert Verry and Laura Henley, "Creation Myths and Zoning Boards: Local Uses of Historic Preservation," in *The Politics of Culture*, edited by Brett Williams (Washington, D.C.: Smithsonian Institution Press, 1991), 75–107.

46. Figures from U.S. Bureau of the Census, "Census of the Population," 1950 (CD-ROM).

47. Mowitz and Wright, *Profile of a Metropolis*, 133.

48. My Maltese landlords owned property in both Briggs and Corktown, reflecting the endurance of ties between these now distinct neighborhoods that were once one entity.

49. The powerful phrase "white privilege," while insightful, obscures many ambiguous aspects of the social significance of white racialness. In this setting, for instance, the term is relevant in many regards; notably, as Peggy McIntosh or Alice McIntyre would no doubt have noticed, they never talked about their advantages, which were certainly numerous in contrast to the whites in Briggs. But as Stephanie Wildman and Adrienne Davis assert, the primary power of the privileged is that they "define the societal norm. . . . The characteristics and attributes of those who are privileged group members are described as societal norms—as the way things are and as what is normal in society." "Making Systems of Privilege Visible," in *Critical White Studies: Looking behind the Mirror*, edited by Richard Delgado and Jean Stefancic (Philadelphia: Temple University Press, 1997), 314–19, especially 315–16. Although their interactions with mediations of pop culture or national politics may reassure these whites of their normative status, their heated exchanges over ascriptions of "gentrifier" illustrate their inability to establish an unmarked, normative space locally. Certainly, charged name-calling practice was keyed to evidence of privilege, but it always revealed social rifts and distinctions, rather than ratifying an unproblematic sense of normality. See Peggy McIntosh, "White Privilege and Male Privilege: A Personal Account of Coming to See Correspondences through Work in Women's Studies," in *Race, Class, and Gender: An Anthology*, edited by Margaret Anderson and Patricia Hill Collins (Belmont, CA: Wadsworth, 1992), 70–81; and Alice McIntyre, *Making Meaning of Whiteness: Exploring Racial Identity with White Teachers* (Albany: State University of New York Press, 1997).

Chapter 4
Between "All Black" and "All White"

1. "Malcolm X Academy's New Beginning," *Metro Times*, February 3–9, 1993. Parents at all three academies protested the federal ruling requiring girls to be admitted by refusing to enroll their daughters. In the fall of 1993, only 76 of Malcolm X's 490 students were female.

2. The Malcolm X Academy was originally housed in the Detroit Public School's Woodward school. The program was largely the innovation of Woodward's principal, Clifford Watson, who originated it as a series of Saturday classes and after-school enrichment programs. Later, he convinced the University of Michigan-Dearborn to adopt the school in a sponsorship that included tutoring and field trips. These activities were further expanded through sponsorships by Michigan State University and the Henry Ford Museum and Greenfield Village.

3. Quoted in Sara Mosle's "Separatist but Equal? Afrocentric Schools Get a Mixed Report," *American Prospect* 15 (Fall 1993): 74–82. Also see Clifford Watson and Geneva Smitherman, "Educational Equity and Detroit's Male Academy," in *Equity and Excellence: The University of Massachusetts School of Education Journal* 25. 2–4 (Winter, 1992): 90–91.

4. "Malcolm X Academy Has New Home," *WP&G*, July 16, 1992.

5. "Neighbors Wary about Malcolm X School Move," *DFP*, July 30, 1992; "Malcolm X: Residents Deserve Answers; Academy Deserves Chance," *DFP*, July 31, 1992.

6. Susan Watson, in her weekly column in the *Free Press*, wrote to the graffitist(s), "You, my misguided soul, are the living embodiment of the American nightmare. Your actions stereotype your community; your cowardly deeds are the kindling that fuels the flames between different groups of human beings." "Lesson in Bigotry Painted on Academy Walls," *DFP*, August 5, 1992. Later in the week, the *Free Press* editorialized the incident as "a critical test of Detroit's unity in the face of separatist hostility—a test the city cannot afford to fail." *DFP*, August 6, 1992. The *Detroit News*, however, opined: "The backlash surprised district officials, but it shouldn't have. The uproar is a reminder that when schools stress race and nationality, as opposed to universal education, it is a recipe for social tension." *DN*, August 7, 1992.

7. At least a dozen of the residents that I interviewed said that the swastikas on the building predated the announcement of the buildings' reopening, and two who lived near the school claimed to have seen the local kids who spray-painted them.

8. It is very difficult to convey the media coverage of this conflict. The televised reports were highly sensational, and regularly stressed the reading of Warrendale whites as racist, but this was not true of all coverage. What I have relied upon here is largely the print media coverage, which tended to offer a "balance" of views and opinions on the protests against the academy. The more outraged and emphatic voices, which were featured on radio talk shows and in "person-on-the-street" televised clips, are missing from this account.

9. "Swirl of Controversy," *WP&G*, August 13, 1992.

10. "Detroit Schools Face $4 Million Aid Lost," *DN*, October 28, 1992; "Swirl of Controversy," *WP&G*, August 13, 1992.

11. "McGriff Addresses Hostile Warrendale Meeting," *WP&G*, August 6, 1992. The *Free Press* cited a 1991–92 report that Carver's capacity was 728 students ("They Had 'No Say' in School Change," August 5, 1992), but its enrollment that fall was 898 students. "Fall 1993 Distribution of Students by Race and Sex," Student Information Systems, Division of Information Services, DPS (November 1993).

12. "Reaction to New Academy is Understandable," *WP&G*, July 23, 1992; "Group Wants Answers from School Board," *WP&G*, August 20, 1992. As these headlines suggest, the *Warrendale Press and Guide* had a sympathetic view of opponents of the academy. Due to the overcrowding, the Carver School had already begun requiring that sixth grade students attend the nearby Ruddiman Junior High School. School officials acknowledged that class sizes were very large, ranging around 32–33 students, though not exceeding the maximum allowed for the various grades (34 students in K–3, 35 for grades 4–7). But some parents insisted that there were 36 or more students in their children's classes. Also, residents who voted at the school in the last election noted that some classroom activities were being carried out in hallways.

13. "McGriff: 'We Must Apologize,'" *WP&G*, August 6, 1992. "X Marks the Spot," *DN*, August 28, 1992.

14. Susan Watson, "Old Hatred Doesn't Fit Detroit," *DFP*, September 30, 1992. From the beginning, comparisons were drawn with both Little Rock and other civil rights battles. One headline asked, "Is this the '50s or the '90s?" *WP&G*, August 6, 1992.

15. The vacated school building was immediately occupied by the Mae C. Jemison Academy, another school of choice that draws students from across the city. The student body is 99 percent black, but neither students nor staff (nor the academy in general) have encountered hostility or protests from white residents, according to Shelia Jenkins, the academy's principal.

16. The use of the critical terms "marked" and "unmarked" becomes quite tenuous in this ethnographic setting. I invoke them here to try to convey a consistent mode of attention to how racial identities and their connotations are conventionalized, and the way that positions of power and authority are maintained by remaining "unmarked." It is obviously a questionable characterization of the Afrocentric academy to claim that it is "unmarked": it is, after all, marked as "Afrocentric." Yet, given the conventionalized order of black political control in Detroit, this usage does reflect very local discursive operations and assumptions.

17. "X Marks the Spot," *DN*, August 28, 1992.

18. Although there was an initial effort to present more nuanced, reasoned voices ("Malcolm X Academy Draws White Neighborhood Support," *DN*, August 14, 1992), this was not the predominant mode of coverage.

19. Edward Lipuma and Sarah Meltzoff examine how this type of figuring of class conflict played out through the development and contests over land-use patterns in southern Florida, specifically how the crosscurrents of ethnicity and class delineate their design and implementation. The important connection that I see

here is that Warrendale whites were enveloped in a discursive predicament in which only their class conditioning was marked; this was accentuated by their racialness. Lipuma and Meltzoff describe retirees who owned second homes: "Their style of dress (often casual but tailored clothes of natural fibers), their assured delivery and choice of words, their posture, and the respect they expect to command all indicate that they are comfortable, confident, and poised. . . . In this way, the class interests of second-home owners/retirees combine with their ideology to generate practices that are both more restrained and more nuanced than the unbridled pursuit of class-based interests, and, because they are restrained and nuanced, mask those interests." Conversely: "If second-home owners/retirees fit 'naturally' into the hearing process, fishermen could not be more ill-adapted. They lack the rhetorical style, accent, posture, and other indexes that would mark their words and views as important. The hearings . . . are geared to those with a college education. . . . Fishermen experience shame and frustration at the meetings because of their relative lack of linguistic and educational capital." "The Crosscurrents of Ethnicity and Class in the Construction of Public Policy," *American Ethnologist* 24.1 (1997), 114–31; quotes from 125–26.

20. See David Wellman, *Portraits of White Racism* (Cambridge: Cambridge University Press, 1977).

21. The most consistent aspect of this controversy that linked it to other conflicts over schools was that the class dimension, while fundamental, received little attention in the media. This dimension was particularly prevalent in the Boston disputes, as Brian Sheehan observed: "A coalition of blacks and young white professionals who favor reforms often seem to be aligned with financial and real estate interests against the social and economic displacement experienced by lower-income whites in the creation of New Boston." *The Boston School Integration Dispute: Social Change and Legal Maneuvers* (New York: Columbia University Press, 1984), 2. See also Ronald Formisano, *Boston against Busing: Race, Class, and Ethnicity in the 1960s and 1970s* (Chapel Hill: University of North Carolina Press, 1991); Eleanor Wolf, *Trial and Error: The Detroit School Segregation Case* (Detroit: Wayne State University Press, 1981); Jonathan Rieder, *Canarsie: The Jews and Italians of Brooklyn against Liberalism* (Cambridge: Harvard University Press, 1985).

22. During one WCO meeting in the late spring, when the windows in the church were open wide, I noticed that there seemed to be more residents out on the street and working or playing in their yards than there were inside. Those outside seemed blissfully oblivious to the whole conflict.

23. The hosts of two shows, M'zee Nabowe's "Word Up" on WDTR and Tahira Ahmed's "African World View" on both WDTR and WCHB—who were featured speakers in a panel discussion on "The Importance of Black Talk Radio," sponsored by the Malcolm X Center in January, 1993—stressed that what makes these shows "black" is that they present the views of "Africans in America." Also see "Talking Issues in Detroit, City Tunes into Black Radio," *DFP*, February 15, 1993.

24. Kenyatta further stirred Warrendale whites with his assertion that white Catholic priests were not qualified to run an all-male academy (Loyola) designed for inner-city youths. He stated, "My concern is whether we as a people should

allow white men—whether they are priests or pimps—to be the educational guardians over our black boys." "Blacks Urged to Boycott New Jesuit School," *DN*, March 3, 1993.

25. Kevin asked, "How can a board member say that he can level a community?" and Karen commented, "If I was to get on the phone and say something like . . . that I have the power in my house to level the school, I'd have a SWAT team here, and helicopters overhead. The FBI would be here, the phone would be tapped, I would be followed, because I made a comment like that. But he gets on the radio and says that he can level the community and that he's going to send out his 'army,' his men, right."

26. These statistics were compiled and reported by the *Detroit Free Press*, "Warrendale" August 5, 1992.

27. Both of these women worked full time at raising their children, although Joyce additionally had a part-time job at a farmer's market downtown.

28. This perceptual formula that extreme emotion equals racism is widespread. Alice McIntyre provides an example of this in her analysis of "white talk," declaring certain whites' "strong, affective responses" to be "tools for resisting critique." She is frustrated by the way their "feelings of powerlessness, fear, and defensiveness shielded many of the participants from challenging the polemical nature of race talk." *Making Meaning of Whiteness: Exploring Racial Identity with White Teachers* (Albany: State University of New York Press, 1997), 77. I hope that the example of whites in Warrendale, who also grow frustrated over their inability to disrupt "the polemical nature of race talk," conveys the possibility that strong emotion is not merely a means designed to counter the insights of those engaged in antiracist work.

29. Jeff ran a lawn-mowing service and Kevin managed an auto parts store.

30. "Talk Show Canceled," *WP&G*, September 3, 1992.

31. Warrendale, like the pre-World War II subdivisions that David Halle studies, is "typical of areas that outsiders often think of as 'working-class neighborhoods.' But those who live there are less certain. . . . [F]ew stress occupational segregation as a defining characteristc of these areas, and they rarely refer to them as 'working class' or 'working men's' districts." *America's Working Man: Work, Home, and Politics among Blue-Collar Property Owners* (Chicago: University of Chicago Press, 1984), 10.

32. The release stated that the "Warrendale community, as a whole, has been misrepresented by the media, and those outside of our community may be receiving a false and possibly damaging impression of our community. The purpose of this statement is to reverse the false impression and retain the good reputation of Warrendale."

33. "An Unwanted Assault by Outsiders," in *Northwest Detroiter*, January 15, 1993.

34. Catherine A. Lutz, "Engendered Emotion: Gender, Power, and the Rhetoric of Emotional Control in American Discourse," in *Language and the Politics of Emotion*, edited by Catherine A. Lutz and Lila Abu-Lughod (Cambridge: Cambridge University Press, 1990), 69–91.

35. Alice McIntyre also stresses the correspondance of intense emotions and racism. *Making Meaning of Whiteness*, 77–80.

36. "All Quiet at Malcolm X Academy," *WP&G*, October 22, 1992.

37. The label "white enclave" was applied by both television and print journalists in characterizing Warrendale, but it seemed that its use was not as extensive as the attention the term attracted among whites seems to suggest. This label struck residents as misapplied in Warrendale partly because there was only ambiguous evidence of what Sidney Plotkin refers to as "enclave consciousness": the assumption of social homogeneity was being steadily undermined; also, the political conflict was often articulated as a contest over the terms of belonging in the city at large, rather than as simply an effort to preserve local resources from outsiders. Most notably, this was not a contest over integration or desegregation; rather, it was a clash that revealed the drastic disjuncture between assumptions held by black city and school officials, in a system where 88 percent of the students are black, and whites in a neighborhood precariously perched between the city's crumbling core and the wealthy white suburbs. "Enclave Consciousness and Neighborhood Activism," in *Dilemmas of Activism, Class, Community, and the Politics of Local Mobilization*, edited by Joseph M. Kling and Prudence S. Posner (Philadelphia: Temple University Press, 1990), 218–39.

38. The class identity of Warrendale is a tricky matter to assess, especially since my view of it is strictly grounded in what Halle identifies as the second image of working-class life, in the home and neighborhood, away from work. "This image of their position in the class structure increases the range of persons with whom workers consider they have common interests. . . . According to this second image, the class structure has a sizable middle range that displays some fluidity, permits individual movement, and takes no account of a person's occupation." This explains why the class distinctions and characters mobilized in these accounts are both blurred and fluid: "This reflects the reality of men's residential, leisure, and family situation, where such differences in some ways *are* blurred." *America's Working Man*, 229. It also accounts for the way their primary attention to class distinctions in relation to whiteness are keyed toward the status and relative advantage of suburban whites.

As Halle also notes, the prevailing sociological approaches to class have their greatest distorting effect on neighborhoods such as Warrendale, where "the two images of the class structure are hopelessly jumbled in the term working class, making it impossible to interpret. That is why working class is not a usable research category in the United States (unless carefully defined to respondents)." Ibid., 230.

39. Reynolds Farley, Charlotte Steeh, Tara Jackson, Maria Krysan, and Keith Reeves, "Continued Racial Residential Segregation in Detroit: 'Chocolate City, Vanilla Suburbs' Revisited," *Journal of Housing Research* 4.1 (1993): 1–38.

40. U.S. Bureau of the Census, "Census of Population and Housing Characteristics, 1990 (CD-ROM).

41. This figure is drawn from Joe T. Darden, Richard Hill, June Thomas, and Richard Thomas, *Detroit: Race and Uneven Development* (Philadelphia: Temple University Press, 1987), 102–3.

42. Statistics taken from "Fall 1993 Distribution of Students by Race and Sex."

43. In the summer of 1995, Warrendale was the target of a blockbusting campaign by realtors who blanketed the area with flyers reading, "TAKE THE MONEY AND RUN!" White residents made a public issue out of the fact that they considered such tactics as a form of harassment. Sheryl James, "Soliciting Riles Warrendale Home Owners, Call Cash Offers Blockbusting," *DFP*, June 26, 1995, 1A+.

44. As Eleanor Wolf and Charles Lebeaux observed long ago, "Like other metropolitan areas in the United States that have large proportions of Negroes, the middle-class neighborhoods of Detroit, after being opened to Negro occupancy, have tended to become all or predominantly Negro, rather than maintaining their biracial character." *Change and Renewal in an Urban Community: Five Case Studies of Detroit* (New York: Frederick Praeger, 1969), 1.

45. Wolf and Lebeaux suggest that individual racial sentiments have uncertain effects on the overall process of racial transformation. "The speed of racial transition in a neighborhood does not vary with the degree of individual prejudice, the moving order of households shows no consistent relationship over time to prejudice, and cities have become more racially segregated even while opinions about integrated housing become increasingly tolerant." Ibid., 10.

46. Frances's account echoes the complex racial dynamics that pertained in neighborhoods throughout Detroit. Wolf and Lebeaux observe distinct rhythms in how these demographic shifts unfold but, in this regard, they also document the distinctly racialized predicaments of the whites who remain behind after the bulk of their racial peers have moved. Ibid, 45–49.

47. Joyce was one of several area whites who related similar tales about the crowds for the downtown fireworks.

48. As Halle notes, "renters" are an intense concern for whites on the cusp between the working and middle classes. They are viewed with deep "suspicion. They are seen as contributing less than their fair share to property taxes while benefiting from the services these taxes finance. They are seen as potentially unruly. And there is also a fear that renters will include large numbers of blacks and Hispanics." *America's Working Man*, 226. Interestingly, in Warrendale, the category "renter" is frequently occupied by whites. Also see Perin on the ambiguities embodied by renters in American culture. *Belonging in America: Reading between the Lines* (Madison: University of Wisconsin Press, 1988), 65–67, 74–75.

49. St. Clair Drake and Horace Cayton, *Black Metropolis: A Study of Negro Life in a Northern City* (Chicago: University of Chicago Press, [1945] 1993), 41–56.

50. "Day 12 in Detroit: Empowerment Deal Collapses," *DN*, September 11, 1992, 4B.

51. "Detroit's Science Academy Sparks Questions of Equity," *DFP*, February 7, 1994, 1A+. This academy was prey to charges similar to those the Malcolm X program faced, without the racial subtext: "Critics say the academy is successful because it is an elite school for hand-picked, middle-class children, including 43 who transfrerred from private schools."

52. Quote from "Malcolm X Academy and the Schools Crisis—The Class Issues," a tract circulated in Warrendale by D'Artagnan Collier, Workers League candidate for the fourteenth Congressional District seat. This tract was saved by

several residents. The Workers League was a socialist party that opposed "attempts by the ruling class and its political servants to promote racial antagonism in the working class."

53. Extravagances criticized in a school district audit included providing parents with beepers and cellular phones, "Malcolm X Prides Itself on High Marks in an Uneasy Year," *DFP*, July 19, 1993, 1A.

54. Representatives of the Board of Education's Public Information Office were hesitant to provide any information to me about the Malcolm X Academy. One source acknowledged that the academy was, indeed, "an elite school," but he refused to do so "for attribution."

55. These numbers, from spring 1994, were provided by Dr. Hodge in the Board of Education's Office of Research, Evaluation, and Testing.

56. They seemed to have formulated this contention independently, though it was a case made by other parties involved in the controversy. The plaintiffs (including the National Organization for Women Legal Defense and Education Fund and the American Civil Liberties Union) in the suit against the Board of Education (Garrett v. Board of Education, 1991) relied on a similar position to contest the academy's all-male designation. In part, "the plaintiffs contended that the academies' policy improperly used gender as a proxy for "at-risk" status, by classifying all boys as at risk. The court recognized that other, nondiscriminatory, factors could more effectively target the goal of helping "at-risk" children. Since academy students were to be selected from three groups of students, ranging from "most at risk" to "least at risk," the academies were already designed to serve a mix of children, not strictly those "most at risk." The plantiffs additionally argued that the academies would reach few of those children deemed "most at risk" because the academies required parental consent and involvement as a prerequisite for application: "Because parental involvement and concern is a key indicator of school success, this requirement will effectively 'select out' many of those students who, because parents are not involved in their education, are most at risk." This passage is taken from Lisa Hsiao, " 'Separate but Equal' Revisited: The Detroit Male Academies Case (Miliken v. Bradley, 94 S. Ct. 3112 (1974)," *Annual Survey of American Law* 1992 (April 1993), 85–115.

The Workers League gave a similar spin to their arguments specifically against the Malcolm X Academy: "The contention of the school authorities that black-oriented academies such as Malcolm X are designed to give the masses of black youth the chance for a decent education is a fraud. To a large extent the black nationalist rhetoric is being used as a smoke screen for a policy that discriminates on a *class* basis against the masses of black working class families, in favor of a thin privileged layer of upper-middle-class blacks. . . . The politics of racial exclusiveness and separatism reflect the interests of a very definite and reactionary social layer." This passage is taken from the pamphlet, "Malcolm X and the Schools Crisis—The Class Issue."

57. Among the more striking comparative statistics from a study by the Council on Great City Schools is that city wide only 15.5 percent of students entering the first grade had full-day kindergarten and just 11 percent of graduates enrolled in four-year colleges (national averages are 53 percent and 41.8 percent, respectively). "Detroit Gets Less for Its Money, Report Says," *DN*, September 22, 1992.

58. Any discussion of charges of "racist" would be remiss without acknowledging its certain status as an epithet with distinct classed inscriptions. As Ronald Formisano relates, "the epithet 'racist' springs easily to the lips of middle-class persons who live in suburbs or college towns, or who if they live in urban retreats possess the resources enabling them to avoid sending their children to schools that are populated with the poor, working class, or black." *Boston against Busing*, xiv.

59. Virginia Dominguez, "Invoking Racism in the Public Sphere: Two Takes on National Self-Criticism," *Identities* 1.4 (1995), 325–46.

60. I draw this phrase from Arjun Appadurai, "Topographies of the Self: Praise and Emotion in Hindu India," in *Language and the Politics of Emotion*, edited by Catherine A. Lutz and Lila Abu-Lughod (Cambridge: Cambridge University Press, 1990), 92–112.

61. "Neighbors Wary about Malcolm X School Move," *DFP*, July 30, 1992.

62. White supporters or journalists rarely elaborated criteria for designating "racists," offering scant discursive elaboration in a manner similar to that described by Virginia Dominguez in accusations of "racism" between Jews and non-Jews: "Accusers assume the transparency—the referential clarity—of racism. Those implicated by the accusation typically regarded it as political name-calling—too vague to have semantic-referential value, too emotionally charged not to serve as a 'call to arms' more than a valid description/interpretation. 'Racism' is offered as an accusation, and taken as one." "Invoking Racism in the Public Sphere," 333.

63. Religious symbolism was also a key issue in the debates over the Afrocentric academies in Milwaukee.

64. There were many moments over the course of this project when I was struck by the similarities between these various local racial rhetorics and the discourse of witchcraft in the Bocage of France, as described by Jeanne Favret-Saada. The link is in the notion of being "caught" by a language riven by ambiguities and animated by power, with no neutral positions. This connection is strongest in the case of Warrendale, where charges of "racist" mimicked in many fashions the accusation of witchcraft, with its demonizing and ostracizing stigmas. Among the efforts of many white residents to contain the overdetermined impression of "racism" vitalizing their neighbors, Yvonne and Paul responded in a way that I think is common in such situations: They designated certain whites emphatically as "racist," almost as scapegoats, so that the polluting possibility would be contained from implicating all whites in the neighborhood. The parallel with the way Bocage peasants responded to media agents searching out spectacular stories about "backwards" people believing in witchcraft is quite strong: "Held up in this way to public scorn and derision, the 'credulous' peasantry of the Bocage is bound to refuse to recognize itself in the distorting mirror presented to it, and to deflect the image in some other direction. For example, by pointing to the *few* mad or stupid people who are really credulous [racist?]: It is not the peasant who is credulous, but the fool or the madman, in other words those outside social categories. . . . In each case, a few individuals are sacrificed and branded as idiots or madmen so as to preserve the reputation of everyone else, and to establish the

widest possible gap between them." *Deadly Words: Witchcraft in the Bocage* (Cambridge: Cambridge University Press, 1980), 35–36.

65. They certainly were not adverse to being superficially stigmatized by the label, as Jeff conveyed: "If they want to call me a racist because I say it's separatist, or they want to call me a bigot because I say, 'Well doesn't anyone else see what is going on? They're re-segregating our children,' and putting the facts out there, let 'em. If that's what they want to label me, if that's what it means to say these things, fine. Then I'm a racist bigot. But by my definition, a racist bigot is someone who looks at somebody's skin color and deals with him accordingly. I don't do that."

66. To these whites, the stakes of racial representation were clear: Blacks were expected to say one thing, and whites another; the two groups were not supposed to share speaking roles. One incident that I heard about several times involved Brandon Landers, a black man with two children in the DPS and cofounder of Save American Fundamentals in Education, a group that put out a newsletter on the problems that they saw in the Afrocentric curriculum. Brandon was one of the speakers at an informational meeting at which Constance Cumby was introduced to Warrendale residents as the attorney who had agreed to sue the DPS over violations of the First Amendment (detailed below). Several television crews were at the meeting, and carefully recorded the white speakers who preceded and followed Brandon. But when he spoke, the television lights dimmed and the camera men rested. Several people shouted questions at the crews: "Why aren't you guys filming him?" The answer, they told me, was that Brandon did not fit the speaking positions of the narrative line used to make sense of this conflict. As Diana explained it, "They didn't get him because he's black. They were out there looking for racists. They're more photogenic, they make the ratings go up."

67. Several whites had made this complaint. In particular, Kevin said, "For the people of the community who want to just say they support the school in the community, I feel it's all based on the fact that they don't want to start this racial . . . tension, this racial war. They're trying to say 'Let 'em be. Let 'em be.' Don't say nothing, 'cause if you do they're going to call you a racist. And I mean, that was the whole opinion in the beginning."

68. Karen charges, implicitly, that Yvonne succumbs to the conflation of their willingness to speak about their interests in racial terms and the signifying elements of "racism"—hence she encounters a caricature shouting "nigger," where they are "just" "sounding very very very racial." Again, Favret-Saada's analysis of witchcraft comes to bear: She suggests that a similar perceptual divide exists between those who are "caught" and those who are incredulous about spells and witches; they quite literally cannot speak to each other because their discursive positions are mutually exclusive.

69. Frances's friend later withdrew her third-grade son from the academy, asserting that "only a handful of parent leaders made all the school's decisions," that "school assemblies encouraged students to distrust whites," and that she had been "ostracized for inviting a white woman to a LSCO [Local School Community Organization] meeting." "Malcolm X Prides Itself on High Marks in an Uneasy Year," *DFP*, July 19, 1993, 1A.

70. This subject is as elusive to define as the other discursive categories treated in this work—a mix of intellectual, political, and cultural strands and endeavors. When residents sought out information about Afrocentrism, they encountered developing networks of both proponents and critics. In addition to the sources cited below, my own understanding of this subject is informed by the following works: Molefi Asante, *The Afrocentric Ideal* (Philadelphia: Temple University Press, 1987); Gerald Early, "Understanding Afrocentrism." *Civilization*, 2.4 (July–August 1995): 31–40; Lathardus Goggins, II, *African-Centered Rites of Passage and Education* (Chicago: African American Images, 1996); Brenda Thompson, *African-Centered Interdisciplinary Multi-Level Hands-on Science* (Washington, D.C.: Roots Activity Learning Center, 1994); Jualynne Dodson, *An Afrocentric Educational Manual* (Knoxville: University of Tennessee School of Social Work, Office of Continuing Education, 1983); Kwame Agyei Akoto, *Nation Building: Theory and Practice in Afrikan Centered Education* (Washington, D.C.: Pan Afrikan World Institute, 1992).

71. Although many observers insisted that concerns about the curriculum were merely a "smoke screen," the *Detroit News* opined that "the curriculum is a legitimate issue. School officials insist that the school teaches about many cultures. Why, then, call it an 'African-centered' school? Why did one Malcolm X teacher last year say that 'sharing and caring,' two universal values, are a 'very Afrocentric idea'? It's little wonder that many parents in the area are angry that Leslie school was closed in the first place, are dubious about reopening it as a Malcolm X Academy." *DN*, August 7, 1992.

72. The African-Centered/Multicultural Education Infusion Implementation Plan was approved by the Board of Education on April 7, 1992.

73. "Schools Stumble on an Afrocentric Science Essay," in *Science* 262 (November 1993): 1,121–22. "Called baseline essays because they provide a historical foundation for teachers, the documents explore science, the arts, music, social studies, and language arts from an African and African-American perspective."

74. Kenyatta made this comment on the Sally Jessy Raphael Show, September 14, 1992. He characterized Kevin and others' view of the curriculum as embodying "straight-out ignorance."

75. Ruth Frankenberg analyzes how this equation of white identity with "the normal stuff" works to maintain whiteness as a dominant ideology. *White Women, Race Matters: The Social Construction of Whiteness* (Minneapolis: University of Minnesota Press, 1993).

76. Quote taken from "The Framework and Definition for African-Centered Education," Detroit Public Schools, revised edition (March 1992), 3.

77. Maulana Karenga, *Kwanzaa: Origin, Concepts, Practice* (Los Angeles: Kawaida Publications, 1977); *Kawaida Theory: An Introductory Outline* (Los Angeles: Kawaida Publications, 1980).

78. "The Framework and Definition," 4.

79. Ibid., 2.

80. They considered the connection with the Nation of Islam sealed when parents at the academy invited Louis Farrakhan to be a keynote speaker at a scholarship fundraiser, which netted nearly $10,000.

81. Bernard Ortiz de Monellano has tracked the way melanin is posited in Afrocentric projects as the basis for superior intelligence, spirituality, and athleticism among blacks. See "Melanin, Afrocentricity, and Pseudoscience," in *Yearbook of Physical Anthropology* 36 (1993), 33–58; "Avoiding Egyptocentric Pseudoscience," *Chronicle of Higher Education* 38.29 (March 25, 1992), B1–B2; "Magic Melanin: Spreading Scientific Illiteracy among Minorities—Part II," in *Skeptical Inquirer* 16.2 (1992), 162–66.

82. As noted above, I take this notion of being "caught" in a discourse from Favret-Saada's study of witchcraft in the Bocage of France. In Ruth Frankenberg's study, she makes repeated use of "caught" in relation to how white speakers are immersed in the three whiteness discourses she analyzes, though she does not offer it as an abstract, theoretical term.

83. "Warrendale Warrior," *DFP*, November 22, 1992. Cumby spoke before probably the largest meeting of Warrendale residents ever, at the Monsignor Hunt Knights of Columbus Hall in Dearborn. Her accusations that the academy's curriculum was "racist propaganda" and involved "teaching a religion and a religion that is hostile to the predominant religion of this culture at public expense," prompted a response from school board president Frank Hayden that, unequivocally, none of the Detroit public schools taught religion. *DFP*, "150 Attend Malcolm X Academy Protest," October 23, 1992; *DN*, "School Board: Religion Not Being Taught at Malcolm X," October 26, 1992.

84. "The Framework and Definition," 11.

85. This impression seemed to have been formed from a range of sources, including an article Joyce showed me about Detroit's Focus: HOPE group developing a Center for Advanced Technology, featuring "$75 million worth of classrooms, offices, and the world's most sophisticated machine tools." According to the project's organizer, Rev. William Cunningham, "We're going to take black people to the top of the mountain. Not just to experience a dream, but so they can get there before everybody else." "Techno-Project Leaps toward Training for the Global Markets," *DFP*, December 17, 1992, 10A. Also the Davis Aerospace Technical High School developed a special program for students of Malcolm X.

86. Favret-Saada, *Deadly Words*, 74. See also chapters 4 ("Someone Must Be Credulous") and 5 ("Tempted by the Impossible").

Conclusion

1. *The Archeology of Knowledge and the Discourse on Language* (New York: Pantheon, 1982), 8.

2. Ibid., 29.

3. Kamala Visweswaran suggests "situational knowledges" as an extension of Donna Haraway's insistence upon "situated knowledges." The difference lies in regarding the "knowledges produced both in and for a specific context" by our subjects, in addition to the epistemological assessment of how our positioning affects the production of social knowledege. *Fictions of Feminist Ethnography* (Minneapolis: University of Minnesota Press, 1994).

Index

Aberbach, Joel D., 312n.104

Afrocentric curriculum, 75, 209, 211, 213, 220, 245, 247, 263, 344nn.70 and 71, 345n.83; conspiracy theory and, 274–75, 277; criticisms of, 267–70, 273–74, 343n.66, 344n.71; explained to whites, 264–65, 271–72; melanin theory of, 263, 270, 271, 273, 345n.81; as religious teaching, 250, 257, 268, 269, 270–72, 274, 345n.83

Akbar, Na'im, 270, 344n70.

Aker, Elmer, 28, 296n.5, 298nn.12 and 13

Alba, Richard, 292n.48

Alex-Assensoh, Yvette, 319n.36

Alternatives for Girls, 147

American Civil Liberties Union, 209

Anderson, Elijah, 294n.62, 325n.78, 328n.12

Anthias, Floya, 294n.58

Aretxaga, Begona, 308n.70

Aryan Nation, 222

Asante, Molefi, 270, 344n.70

assimilation, 34, 89–90, 103, 301n.29, 302n.30

Bachelor, Lynn, 332n.32

"backtalk," 61–62, 111, 201–2, 309n.74, 310n.81

Baldwin, James, 116, 321n.57, 322n.58

Balibar, Etienne, 294n.58

"Bamas," 316n.15

Barbara, 129, 132, 134

Barry, 119–20

bars, 48, 95–96, 316n.22, 317n.24. *See also* O'Leary's bar

Batteau, Allen, 302n.32

Bauman, Richard, 323n.65

Beaupre, Shirley, 176–78, 179, 199–200

Becker, Gaylene, 318n.27

Becky, 137–38, 140–44

Beidelman, T. O., 315n.7, 326n.80

Betty, 64–65, 201–3, 313n.105

Bill (in Briggs), 55–57, 61, 114–15, 304n.39, 323n.63

Bill (in Corktown), 198

Billy Lee, 110–11, 116, 129, 131–34, 135, 321n.56

Black, Tandrea, 214, 215, 225, 231

black English, 266

Black Metropolis, 300n.21, 301n.27, 303–304n.33, 304n.39, 306n.56, 309n.76, 340n.49

Black Slate, 163–64

blacks, 27, 337n.23; in Briggs, 37–44, 305n.52; in Corktown, 156–58, 196, 197–98, 205; dominance of, in Detroit, 69–70, 74–77, 253–54, 287n.25, 291n.46; middle-class, 33, 70, 311n.91; movement into white neighborhoods by, 37–44, 52, 309n.76; as professionals, 220, 223–24, 243–44, 311n.92, 329n.14; racializing whites, 123; in relation to Hillbillies, 31, 32, 33–34, 127; violence toward, 30, 40–41, 46–47; in Warrendale, 217, 226. *See also* Detroiters, native black

Blauner, Robert, 293n.55

Bledstein, Burton, 298n.11

Board of Education of the Detroit Public Schools, 72, 209, 210–12, 216, 231–32, 243, 263, 265, 270, 274, 341n.56

Bondi, Liz, 327n.7

Bonds, Bill, 223–24

Bonnie, 219, 231–32, 270, 273, 275–76

Bourdieu, Pierre, 286n.12, 295n.66

Bourgeois, Phillipe, 294n.57, 321n.54

Branscome, James, 302n.32

Bridge, Gary, 330n.18

Briggs, 69, 295n.1, 307n.67, 313n.104; arrival of hillbillies in, 18, 24, 26–30, 49; blacks in, 37–44, 305n.52; demise of, 79–80; demographics of, 24, 52, 70, 311n.92; deterioration of housing in, 29–30, 46, 79; movement of blacks to, 37–43, 52, 304n.39; riot of 1943 in, 55; riot of 1967 in, 55–69; settlement of, 11, 24, 26–28; violence in, 108, 164–65, 319n.43. *See also* Cochrane Street

Bruno, Hal, 301n.25

Butler, Judith, 112–13, 318n.31, 325n.77